CIMA

Paper C05

Fundamentals of Ethics, Corporate Governance and Business Law

Study Text

CIMA Certificate in Business Accounting

Published by: Kaplan Publishing UK

Unit 2 The Business Centre, Molly Millars Lane, Wokingham, Berkshire RG41 2QZ

Acknowledgements

The CIMA Publishing trade mark is reproduced with kind permission of CIMA.

British Library Cataloguing in Publication Data

A catalogue record for this book is available from the British Library.

ISBN: 978-1-78415-285-7

Printed and bound in Great Britain.

Chartered Institute of
Management Accountants

This book comes with free EN-gage online resources so that you can study anytime, anywhere. This free online resource is not sold separately and is included in the price of the book.

How to access your on-line resources

You can access additional online resources associated with this CIMA Official book via the EN-gage website at: **www.EN-gage.co.uk.**

Existing users

If you are an **existing EN-gage user**, simply log-in to your account, click on the 'add a book' link at the top of your homepage and enter the ISBN of this book and the unique pass key number contained above.

New users

If you are a new EN-gage user then you first need to register at: **www.EN-gage.co.uk.** Once registered, Kaplan Publishing will send you an email containing a link to activate your account - please check your junk mail if you do not receive this or contact us using the phone number or email address printed on the back cover of this book. Click on the link to activate your account. To unlock your additional resources, click on the 'add a book' link at the top of your home page. You will then need to enter the ISBN of this book (found on page ii) and the unique pass key number contained in the scratch panel below:

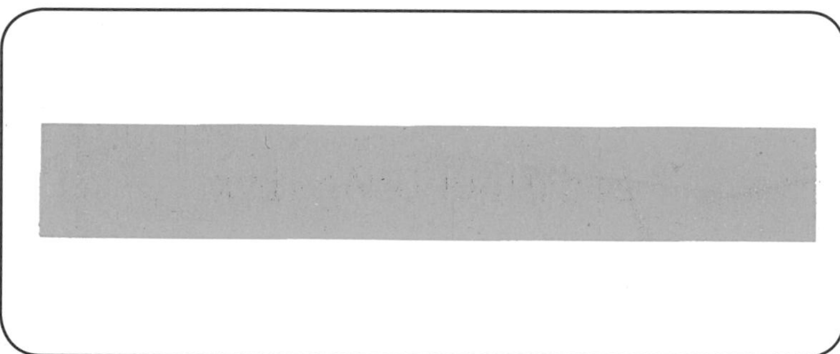

Then click 'finished' or 'add another book'.
Please allow 24 hours from the time you submit your book details for the content to appear in the My Learning and Testing area of your account.

Your code and information

This code can only be used once for the registration of one book online. This registration will expire when this edition of the book is no longer current - please see the back cover of this book for the expiry date.

Existing users

If you are an **existing EN-gage user**, simply log-in to your account. click on the 'add a book' link at the top of your homepag ... ok and the unique pass key

Contents

chapter

Intro

Paper Introduction

How to Use the Materials

These Official CIMA learning materials brought to you by Kaplan Publishing have been carefully designed to make your learning experience as easy as possible and to give you the best chances of success in your Fundamentals of Ethics, Corporate Governance and Business Law.

The product range contains a number of features to help you in the study process. They include:

- a detailed explanation of all syllabus areas
- extensive 'practical' materials
- generous question practice, together with full solutions
- a computer based assessments preparation section, complete with computer based assessments standard questions and solutions.

This Study Text has been designed with the needs of home study and distance learning candidates in mind. Such students require very full coverage of the syllabus topics, and also the facility to undertake extensive question practice. However, the Study Text is also ideal for fully taught courses.

The main body of the text is divided into a number of chapters, each of which is organised on the following pattern:

- *Detailed learning outcomes.* This is expected after your studies of the chapter are complete. You should assimilate these before beginning detailed work on the chapter, so that you can appreciate where your studies are leading.
- *Step-by-step topic coverage*. This is the heart of each chapter, containing detailed explanatory text supported where appropriate by worked examples and exercises. You should work carefully through this section, ensuring that you understand the material being explained and can tackle the examples and exercises successfully. Remember that in many cases knowledge is cumulative: if you fail to digest earlier material thoroughly, you may struggle to understand later chapters.
- *Activities*. Some chapters are illustrated by more practical elements, such as comments and questions designed to stimulate discussion.

- *Question practice.* The test of how well you have learned the material is your ability to tackle exam standard questions. Make a serious attempt at producing your own answers, but at this stage do not be too concerned about attempting the questions in computer based assessments conditions. In particular, it is more important to absorb the material thoroughly by completing a full solution than to observe the time limits that would apply in the actual computer based assessments.
- *Solutions.* Avoid the temptation merely to 'audit' the solutions provided. It is an illusion to think that this provides the same benefits as you would gain from a serious attempt of your own. However, if you are struggling to get started on a question you should read the introductory guidance provided at the beginning of the solution, where provided, and then make your own attempt before referring back to the full solution.

Having worked through the chapters you are ready to begin your final preparations for the computer based assessments. The final section of this Study Text provides you with the guidance you need. It includes the following features:

- A brief guide to revision technique.
- A note on the format of the computer based assessments. You should know what to expect when you tackle the real computer based assessments and in particular the number of questions to attempt.
- Guidance on how to tackle the computer-based assessments itself.
- Revision questions. These are of computer based assessments standard and should be tackled in computer-based assessments conditions, especially as regards the time allocation.
- Solutions to the revision questions.
- Two mock computer based assessments.

You should plan to attempt the mock tests just before the date of the real computer based assessments. By this stage your revision should be complete and you should be able to attempt the mock computer based assessments within the time constraints of the real computer based assessments.

If you work conscientiously through this Official CIMA Study Text according to the guidelines above you will be giving yourself an excellent chance of success in your computer based assessments. Good luck with your studies!

Quality and accuracy are of the utmost importance to us so if you spot an error in any of our products, please send an email to mykaplanreporting@kaplan.com with full details.

Our Quality Co-ordinator will work with our technical team to verify the error and take action to ensure it is corrected in future editions.

Icon Explanations

Definition – these sections explain important areas of knowledge which must be understood and reproduced in an exam environment.

Key Point – identifies topics which are key to success and are often examined.

Supplementary reading – identifies a more detailed explanation of key terms, these sections will help to provide a deeper understanding of core areas. Reference to this text is vital when self studying.

Test your understanding – following key points and definitions are exercises which give the opportunity to assess the understanding of these core areas.

Illustration – to help develop an understanding of particular topics. The illustrative examples are useful in preparing for the Test your understanding exercises.

Study technique

Passing exams is partly a matter of intellectual ability, but however accomplished you are in that respect you can improve your chances significantly by the use of appropriate study and revision techniques. In this section we briefly outline some tips for effective study during the earlier stages of your approach to the exam. Later in the text we mention some techniques that you will find useful at the revision stage.

Planning

To begin with, formal planning is essential to get the best return from the time you spend studying. Estimate how much time in total you are going to need for each subject you are studying for the Certificate in Business Accounting. Remember that you need to allow time for revision as well as for initial study of the material.

You may find it helpful to read "Pass First Time!" second edition by David R. Harris ISBN: 9781856177986. This book will help you develop proven study and examination techniques. Chapter by chapter it covers the building blocks of successful learning and examination techniques. This is the ultimate guide to passing your CIMA exams, written by a past CIMA examiner and shows you how to earn all the marks you deserve, and explains how to avoid the most common pitfalls.

You may also find "The E Word: Kaplan's Guide to Passing Exams" by Stuart Pedley-Smith ISBN: 978-0-85732-205-0 helpful. Stuart Pedley-Smith is a senior lecturer at Kaplan Financial and a qualified accountant specialising in financial management. His natural curiosity and wider interests have led him to look beyond the technical content of financial management to the processes and journey that we call education. He has become fascinated by the whole process of learning and the exam skills and techniques that contribute towards success in the classroom. This book is for anyone who has to sit an exam and wants to give themselves a better chance of passing. It is easy to read, written in a common sense style and full of anecdotes, facts, and practical tips. It also contains synopses of interviews with people involved in the learning and examining process.

With your study material before you, decide which chapters you are going to study in each week, and which weeks you will devote to revision and final question practice.

Prepare a written schedule summarising the above and stick to it!

It is essential to know your syllabus. As your studies progress you will become more familiar with how long it takes to cover topics in sufficient depth. Your timetable may need to be adapted to allocate enough time for the whole syllabus.

Students are advised to refer to the notice of examinable legislation published regularly in CIMA's magazine (Financial Management), the students e-newsletter (Velocity) and on the CIMA website, to ensure they are up-to-date.

Students may also find the following websites useful for providing additional sources of information:

- www.ft.com
- www.iclr.co.uk
- www.legislation.gov.uk
- www.parliament.co.uk
- www.lawrights.co.uk
- www.lawsociety.org.uk
- www.mondaq.com

The amount of space allocated to a topic in the Study Text is not a very good guide as to how long it will take you. For example, the material relating to 'Ethical Conflict' and 'Corporate Governance' both account for 10 per cent of the syllabus, but there may be more pages in one because there are more illustrations or examples, which take up more space. It is essential to know your syllabus. As your course progresses you will become more familiar with how long it takes to cover topics in sufficient depth. Your timetable may need to be adapted to allocate enough time for the whole syllabus.

Tips for effective studying

(1) Aim to find a quiet and undisturbed location for your study, and plan as far as possible to use the same period of time each day. Getting into a routine helps to avoid wasting time. Make sure that you have all the materials you need before you begin so as to minimise interruptions.

(2) Store all your materials in one place, so that you do not waste time searching for items around the house. If you have to pack everything away after each study period, keep them in a box, or even a suitcase, which will not be disturbed until the next time.

(3) Limit distractions. To make the most effective use of your study periods you should be able to apply total concentration, so turn off the TV, set your phones to message mode, and put up your 'do not disturb' sign.

(4) Your timetable will tell you which topic to study. However, before diving in and becoming engrossed in the finer points, make sure you have an overall picture of all the areas that need to be covered by the end of that session. After an hour, allow yourself a short break and move away from your books. With experience, you will learn to assess the pace you need to work at. You should also allow enough time to read relevant articles from newspapers and journals, which will supplement your knowledge and demonstrate a wider perspective.

(5) Work carefully through a chapter, making notes as you go. When you have covered a suitable amount of material, vary the pattern by attempting a practice question. Preparing an answer plan is a good habit to get into, while you are both studying and revising, and also in the examination room. It helps to impose a structure on your solutions, and avoids rambling. When you have finished your attempt, make notes of any mistakes you made, or any areas that you failed to cover or covered more briefly.

(6) Make notes as you study, and discover the techniques that work best for you. Your notes may be in the form of lists, bullet points, diagrams, summaries, 'mind maps', or the written word, but remember that you will need to refer back to them at a later date, so they must be intelligible. If you are on a taught course, make sure you highlight any issues you would like to follow up with your lecturer.

(7) Organise your notes. Make sure that all your notes, calculations etc can be effectively filed and easily retrieved later.

Computer based assessments

CIMA uses objective test questions in the computer based assessments. The most common types are:

- Multiple choice, where you have to choose the correct answer from a list of four possible answers. This could either be numbers or text.
- Multiple choice with more choices and answers, for example, choosing two correct answers from a list of eight possible answers. This could either be numbers or text.
- Single numeric entry, where you give your numeric answer, for example, profit is £10,000.
- Multiple entry, where you give several numeric answers.
- True/false questions, where you state whether a statement is true or false.
- Matching pairs of text, for example, matching a technical term with the correct definition.
- Other types could be matching text with graphs and labelling graphs/diagrams.

In every chapter of this Study Text we have introduced these types of questions, but obviously we have had to label answers A, B, C etc rather than using click boxes. For convenience we have retained quite a lot of questions where an initial scenario leads to a number of sub-questions. There will be questions of this type in the CBA but they will rarely have more than three sub-questions.

Guidance re CIMA online calculator

As part of the CIMA Certificate level computer based assessment software, candidates are now provided with a calculator. This calculator is onscreen and is available for the duration of the assessment. The calculator is available in each of the five Certificate level assessments and is accessed by clicking the calculator button in the top left hand corner of the screen at any time during the assessment.

All candidates must complete a 15 minute tutorial before the assessment begins and will have the opportunity to familiarise themselves with the calculator and practice using it.

Candidates may practise using the calculator by downloading and installing the practice exam at http://www.vue.com/athena/ The calculator can be accessed from the fourth sample question (of 12).

Please note that the practice exam and tutorial provided by Pearson VUE at http://www.vue.com/athena/ is not specific to CIMA and includes the full range of question types the Pearson VUE software supports, some of which CIMA does not currently use.

Fundamentals of Ethics, Corporate Governance and Business Law Syllabus

The computer based assessments for Fundamentals of Ethics, Corporate Governance and Business Law syllabus is a two hour assessment comprising 75 compulsory questions, with one or more parts. Single part questions are generally worth 1–2 marks each, but two and three part questions may be worth 4 or 6 marks. There will be no choice and all questions should be attempted.

Additional CBA resources, including sample assessment questions are available online at www.cimaglobal.com/cba2011

Structure of subjects and learning outcomes

Each subject within the syllabus is divided into a number of broad syllabus topics. The topics contain one or more lead learning outcomes, related component learning outcomes and indicative knowledge content.

A learning outcome has two main purposes:

(a) To define the skill or ability that a well prepared candidate should be able to exhibit in the examination

(b) To demonstrate the approach likely to be taken in examination questions

The learning outcomes are part of a hierarchy of learning objectives. The verbs used at the beginning of each learning outcome relate to a specific learning objective e.g.

Calculate the break-even point, profit target, margin of safety and profit/volume ratio for a single product or service.

The verb **'calculate'** indicates a level three learning objective. The following table lists the learning objectives and the verbs that appear in the syllabus learning outcomes and examination questions.

Certificate level verbs

CIMA VERB HIERARCHY

CIMA place great importance on the choice of verbs in exam question requirements. It is thus critical that you answer the question according to the definition of the verb used.

In Certificate level exams you will meet verbs from levels 1, 2, and 3. These are as follows:

Level 1: KNOWLEDGE

What you are expected to know.

VERBS USED	DEFINITION
List	Make a list of.
State	Express, fully or clearly, the details of/facts of.
Define	Give the exact meaning of.

Level 2: COMPREHENSION

What you are expected to understand.

VERBS USED	DEFINITION
Describe	Communicate the key features of.
Distinguish	Highlight the differences between.
Explain	Make clear or intelligible/state the meaning or purpose of.
Identify	Recognise, establish or select after consideration.
Illustrate	Use an example to describe or explain something.

Level 3: APPLICATION

How you are expected to apply your knowledge.

VERBS USED	DEFINITION
Apply	Put to practical use.
Calculate	Ascertain or reckon mathematically.
Demonstrate	Prove with certainty or exhibit by practical means.
Prepare	Make or get ready for use.
Reconcile	Make or prove consistent/compatible.
Solve	Find an answer to.
Tabulate	Arrange in a table.

PAPER C05
FUNDAMENTALS OF ETHICS, CORPORATE GOVERNANCE AND BUSINESS LAW

Syllabus overview

The learning outcomes in this paper reflect the legal framework for business and provide the underpinning for commercial activity. It includes the areas of contract law, employment law, financing, administration and management of companies. The globalisation of business is recognised by the inclusion of alternative legal systems, as well as the English legal system. Judicial precedent is included in relation to professional negligence.

Wherever business is conducted, the highest professional standards must be demonstrated for the benefit of all stakeholders. With this in mind, the place of ethics and ethical conflict is considered, as well as the role of corporate governance and its increasing impact in the management of organisations.

Syllabus structure

The syllabus comprises the following topics and study weightings:

A	Ethics and business	15%
B	Ethical conflict	10%
C	Corporate governance	10%
D	Comparison of English law with alternative legal systems	10%
E	The law of contract	20%
F	The law of employment	10%
G	Company administration and finance	25%

Assessment strategy

There will be a two hour computer based assessment, comprising 75 compulsory questions, each with one or more parts.

A variety of objective test question styles and types will be used within the assessment.

C05 – A. ETHICS AND BUSINESS (15%)

Learning outcomes On completion of their studies students should be able to:			Indicative syllabus content
Lead	**Component**	**Level**	
1. demonstrate an understanding of the importance of ethics to business generally and to the professional accountant. [6]	(a) apply the values and attitudes that provide professional accountants with a commitment to act in the public interest and with social responsibility; [6]	3	• The importance of ethics. [6] • Values and attitudes for professional accountants. • Legal frameworks, regulations and standards for business. [6] • The role of national 'Professional Oversight Boards for Accountancy' and 'Auditing Practices Boards'. [6] • The role of international accounting bodies e.g. IFAC. [6] • The nature of ethics and its relevance to business and the accountancy profession. [6] • Rules based and framework approaches to ethics. • The 'Seven Principles of Public Life' – selflessness, integrity, objectivity, accountability, openness, honesty and leadership. [6]
	(b) explain the need for a framework of laws, regulations and standards in business and their application; [6]	2	
	(c) explain the nature of ethics and its application to business and the accountancy profession; [6]	2	
	(d) distinguish between detailed rules-based and framework approaches to ethics. [6]	2	
2. explain the need for CIMA members to adopt the highest standards of ethical behaviour. [6]	(a) explain the need for continual personal improvement and life-long learning; [6]	2	• Personal development and lifelong learning. [6] • The personal qualities of reliability, responsibility, timeliness, courtesy and respect. [6] • The ethical principles of integrity and objectivity. [6] • Professional competence, due care and confidentiality. [6] • Disclosure required by law. [6] • The concepts of independence, scepticism, accountability and social responsibility. [6] • The CIMA and IFAC 'Code of Ethics for Professional Accountants'. [6]
	(b) explain the need to develop the virtues of reliability, responsibility, timeliness, courtesy and respect; [6]	2	
	(c) explain the ethical principles of integrity, objectivity, professional competence, due care and confidentiality; [6]	2	
	(d) identify concepts of independence, scepticism, accountability and social responsibility; [6]	2	
	(e) explain the reasons why CIMA and IFAC each have a 'Code of Ethics for Professional Accountants'. [6]	2	

C05 – B. ETHICAL CONFLICT (10%)

Learning outcomes On completion of their studies students should be able to:			Indicative syllabus content
Lead	**Component**	**Level**	
1. explain the various means of regulating ethical behaviour. [7]	(a) explain the relationship between ethics, governance, the law and social responsibility; [7] (b) describe the consequences of unethical behaviour to the individual, the profession and society. [7]	2 2	• The relationship between ethics and the law. [7] • The distinction between ethical codes and contracts. [7] • Corporate governance and social responsibility. • Unethical behaviour. [7] • The consequences of unethical behaviour. [7]
2. explain how ethical dilemmas and conflicts of interest arise and may be resolved. [7]	(a) identify situations where ethical dilemmas and conflicts of interest occur; [7] (b) explain how ethical dilemmas and conflicts of interest can be resolved. [7]	2 2	• The nature of ethical dilemmas. [7] • Conflicts of interest and how they arise. [7] • Ethical conflict resolution. [7] • The CIMA Code of Ethics for Professional Accountants – 'Fundamental Principles'. [7]

C05 – C. CORPORATE GOVERNANCE (10%)

Learning outcomes On completion of their studies students should be able to:			**Indicative syllabus content**
Lead	**Component**	**Level**	
1. explain the development of corporate governance to meet public concern in relation to the management of companies. [8]	(a) define corporate governance; [8] (b) explain the interaction of corporate governance with business ethics and company law; [8] (c) describe the history of corporate governance internationally; [8] (d) distinguish between detailed rules-based and principles based approaches to governance. [8]	1 2 2 2	• The role and key objectives of corporate governance. [8] • The interaction of corporate governance, ethics and the law. [8] • The development of corporate governance internationally e.g. in the UK, Europe, South Africa and the USA. [8] • Rules and principles based approaches to governance. [8]
2. explain the impact of corporate governance on the directors and management structure of public limited companies and how this benefits stakeholders. [8]	(a) explain the effects of corporate governance on directors' powers and duties; [8] (b) describe different board structures, the role of the board and corporate social responsibility; [8] (c) describe the types of policies and procedures that constitute 'best practice'; [8] (d) explain the regulatory governance framework for companies and benefits to stakeholders. [8]	2 2 2 2	• The impact of corporate governance on directors' powers and duties. [8] • Types of board structures, the role of the board and corporate social responsibility (CSR). [8] • The role of the board in establishing corporate governance standards. [8] • Corporate governance codes e.g. The UK Corporate Governance Code. [8] • Policies and procedures for 'best practice' companies. [8] • The regulatory governance framework for companies. [8] • Stakeholder benefits. [8]

C05 – D. COMPARISON OF ENGLISH LAW WITH ALTERNATIVE LEGAL SYSTEMS (10%)

Learning outcomes On completion of their studies students should be able to:			Indicative syllabus content
Lead	**Component**	**Level**	
1. explain the essential elements of the English legal system and the tort of negligence. [1]	(a) explain the manner in which behaviour within society is regulated by the civil and the criminal law; [1] (b) explain the sources of English law; [1] (c) illustrate the operation of the doctrine of precedent by reference to the essential elements of the tort of negligence and its application to professional advisers; [1]	2 2 2	• The purpose of civil and criminal law. [1] • The sources of English law: custom, case law, statute, European law and other sources. [1] • The distinction between the common law and equity. [1] • The system of judicial precedent. [1] • The essential elements of the tort of negligence, including duty, breach and damage/loss/injury and the liability of professionals in respect of negligent advice. [1]
2. describe the essential elements of alternative legal systems [1]	(a) describe the characteristics of the legal systems found in other countries; [1] (b) describe elements of Shari'ah law; [1] (c) describe the role of international regulations. [1]	2 2 2	• Alternative legal systems, including codified (civil law) systems. [1] • The general characteristics of the legal systems of France, Germany, Poland, Italy, Denmark, Greece and Cyprus. [1] • The general characteristics of the legal systems of the USA, Malaysia, China and Sri Lanka. [1] • Elements of Shari'ah Law including sources of Shari'ah law and the Five Pillars of Islam. [1] • The benefits of international regulations for commerce and professional practice through the work of key bodies e.g. IFAC, ISO, FEE. [1]

C05 – E. THE LAW OF CONTRACT (20%)

Learning outcomes On completion of their studies students should be able to:			**Indicative syllabus content**
Lead	**Component**	**Level**	
1. explain how the law determines the point at which a contract is formed and the legal status of contractual terms. [2]	(a) identify the essential elements of a valid simple contract and situations where the law requires the contract to be in a particular form; [2] (b) explain how the law determines whether negotiating parties have reached agreement and the role of consideration in making that agreement enforceable; [2] (c) explain when the parties will be regarded as intending the agreement to be legally binding and how an agreement may be avoided because of misrepresentations; [2] (d) explain how the terms of a contract are established and their status determined; [2] (e) describe the effect of terms implied into contracts by sale of goods and supply of goods and services legislation; [2] (f) describe how the law controls the use of excluding, limiting and unfair terms. [2]	2 2 2 2 2 2	• The essential elements of a valid simple contract. [2] • The legal status of statements made by negotiating parties. Offers and acceptances and the application of the rules to standard form contracts using modern forms of communication. [2] • The principles for establishing that the parties intend their agreement to have contractual force and how a contract is affected by a misrepresentation. [2] • Incorporation of express and implied terms, conditions and warranties [2] • The main provisions of the Sale of Goods Act 1979 and the Supply of Goods and Services Act 1982. [2] • Excluding and limiting terms; the Unfair Contract Terms Act 1977 and the Unfair Terms in Consumer Contracts Regulations. [2]
2. explain when the law regards a contract as discharged and the remedies available for breach and non-performance. [2]	(a) describe the factors which cause a contract to be discharged; [2] (b) explain how the law of frustration provides an excuse for non-performance of the contract; [2] (c) explain the remedies which are available for serious and minor breaches of contract. [2]	2 2 2	• Discharge of a contract by performance, agreement and breach. [2] • The law relating to frustration. [2] • The law relating to damages. [2] • The remedies of specific performance, injunction, rescission, and requiring a contract party to pay the agreed price. [2]

C05 – F. THE LAW OF EMPLOYMENT (10%)

Learning outcomes On completion of their studies students should be able to:			**Indicative syllabus content**
Lead	**Component**	**Level**	
1. explain the essential elements of an employment contract and the remedies available following termination of the contract. [3]	(a) explain the differences between employees and independent contractors; [3] (b) explain how the contents of a contract of employment are established; [3] (c) explain the distinction between unfair and wrongful dismissal. [3]	2 2 2	• The tests used to distinguish an employee from an independent contractor. [3] • The express and implied terms of a contract of employment. [3] • The rights and duties of employers and employees. • Notice and dismissal. [3] • Unfair and wrongful dismissal. [3]
2. explain the impact of health and safety law on employers and employees. [3]	(a) explain how employers and employees are affected by health and safety legislation; [3] (b) describe the consequences of a failure to comply with health and safety legislation. [3]	2 2	• The main rules relating to health and safety at work, sanctions on employers for non-compliance, and remedies for employees. [3] • Social security compensation. [3] • Civil liability for occupational injuries. [3]

C05 – G. COMPANY ADMINISTRATION AND FINANCE (25%)

Learning outcomes On completion of their studies students should be able to:			Indicative syllabus content
Lead	**Component**	**Level**	
1. explain the nature, legal status and administration of business organisations. [4]	(a) describe the essential characteristics of the different forms of business organisations and the implications of corporate personality; [4] (b) explain the differences between public and private companies and establishing a company by registration or purchasing 'off the shelf'; [4] (c) explain the purpose and legal status of the articles of association; [4] (d) explain the ability of a company to contract; [4] (e) explain the main advantages and disadvantages of carrying on business through the medium of a company limited by shares; [4] (f) explain the use and procedure of board meetings and general meetings of shareholders; [4] (g) explain the voting rights of directors and shareholders; [4] (h) identify the various types of shareholder resolutions. [4]	2 2 2 2 2 2 2 2	• The essential characteristics of sole traderships/practitionerships, partnerships, companies limited by shares and corporate personality. [4] • 'Lifting the corporate veil' both at common law and by statute. [4] • The distinction between public and private companies. [4] • Company registration and the advantages of purchasing a company 'off the shelf'. [4] • The purpose and contents of the articles of association. [4] • Corporate capacity to contract. [4] • The advantages and disadvantages of the company limited by shares. [4] • Board meetings: when used and the procedure at the meeting. [4] • General Meetings of shareholders: when used and the procedure at the meeting. [4] • The voting rights of directors and shareholders. [4] • Ordinary, special and written resolutions and their uses. [4]
2. explain the law relating to the financing and management of companies limited by shares. [5]	(a) explain the nature of different types of shares, the procedure for their issue and acceptable forms of payment; [5] (b) explain the maintenance of capital principle and the reduction of share capital; [5] (c) explain the ability of a company to take secured and unsecured loans, the different types of security and the registration procedure; [5] (d) explain the procedure for the appointment, retirement, disqualification and removal of directors; [5] (e) explain the powers and duties of directors when in office; [5]	2 2 2 2 2	• The rights attaching to different types of shares. [5] • The procedures for issuing shares. [5] • The issue of shares for an improper purpose. [5] • Payment for shares. [5] • The maintenance of capital principle: the purposes for which shares may be issued, redeemed or, purchased and the provision of financial assistance for the purchase of the company's own shares. [5] • The reduction of capital. [5] • The ability of a company to borrow money and the procedure to be followed. [5] • Unsecured loans, and the nature and effect of fixed and floating charges. [5]

Learning outcomes On completion of their studies students should be able to:			Indicative syllabus content
Lead	Component	Level	
	(f) explain the rules dealing with the possible imposition of personal liability upon the directors of insolvent companies; [5]	2	• The appointment, retirement and removal of directors and their powers and duties during office. [5] • Fraudulent and wrongful trading, preferences and transactions at an under-value. [5]
	(g) explain the rights of majority and minority shareholders; [5]	2	• The rights of majority and minority shareholders. [5]
	(h) explain the division of powers between the board of a company and the shareholders; [5]	2	• The division of powers between the board and the shareholders. [5]
	(i) explain the qualifications, powers and duties of the company secretary. [5]	2	• The qualifications, powers and duties of the company secretary. [5]

chapter

1

Comparison of English Law with Alternative Legal Systems

Chapter learning objectives

After completing this chapter you should be able to:

- explain the manner in which behaviour within society is regulated by civil and the criminal law
- explain the sources of English law
- illustrate the operation of the doctrine of precedent by reference to the essential elements of the tort of negligence and its application to professional advisers
- describe the characteristics of the legal systems found in other countries
- describe the elements of Sharia law
- describe the role of international regulations.

1 Law: criminal and civil

Law is necessary in every society, to enable the harmonious co-existence of its members. As the population expands, as people live more closely together in towns and cities, and as technology becomes more powerful, law has to become more detailed and explicit. In all modern societies, legal rules fall into two fundamental categories:

(1) criminal

(2) civil.

Criminal law	Civil law
Criminal law relates to conduct of which the State disapproves and which it seeks to control. It is a form of public law.	Civil law is a form of private law and involves the relationship between individual citizens.
Purpose – the enforcement of particular forms of behaviour by the State, which acts to ensure compliance.	**Purpose** – to settle disputes between individuals and to provide remedies.
In criminal law the case is brought by the **State**, in the name of the Crown. A criminal case will be reported as Regina v ..., where Regina is the Latin for 'queen'.	In civil law the case is brought by the **claimant**, who is seeking a remedy. The case will be referred to by the names of the parties involved in the dispute, such as Brown v Smith.
Standard of proof – guilt must be shown **beyond reasonable doubt** (higher standard of proof).	**Standard of proof** – liability must be shown on the **balance of probabilities** (lower standard of proof).
Burden of proof is on the prosecution.	**Burden of proof** is on the claimant.
Object – to regulate society by the threat of punishment.	**Object** – usually financial compensation to put the claimant in the position he would have been in had the wrong not occurred.
If found guilty, the criminal court will sentence the accused and it may fine him or impose a period of imprisonment. If innocent the accused will be acquitted.	The civil court will order the defendant to pay damages or it may order some other remedy, e.g. specific performance or injunction.

The main English civil courts

The following diagram shows the main civil courts. The term 'first instance' refers to the court in which the case is first heard. Appeals are heard in a different court. The arrows show the way a case will progress through the court system.

Supreme Court (previously House of Lords)
Five Lord Justices of Supreme Court hear appeals from Court of Appeal and exceptionally from High Court

Court of Appeal (civil division)
Three Lord Justices of Appeal hear appeals from the High Court and County courts

County court	High Court of Justice
First instance civil claims in contract, tort, landlord and tenant, probate and insolvency. One district judge hears small claims. The hearing is informal and no costs are awarded. One circuit judge hears most fast-track, and some multitrack, cases.	One High Court judge in first instance. Queen's Bench Division (QBD) hears first instance cases of contract and tort. Chancery Division (ChD) deals with land law, trusts, company law, partnership law, insolvency, etc. It hears appeals from County courts on probate and insolvency. Family Division hears matrimonial cases.

Magistrates' court
Jurisdiction is mainly criminal (see section on criminal courts) but does have civil jurisdiction in family matters such as contact orders, adoption, and maintenance. There are also powers of recovery of council tax arrears and charges for water, gas and electricity.

Prior to October 2009, the Supreme Court was formerly known as the House of Lords.

The main English criminal courts

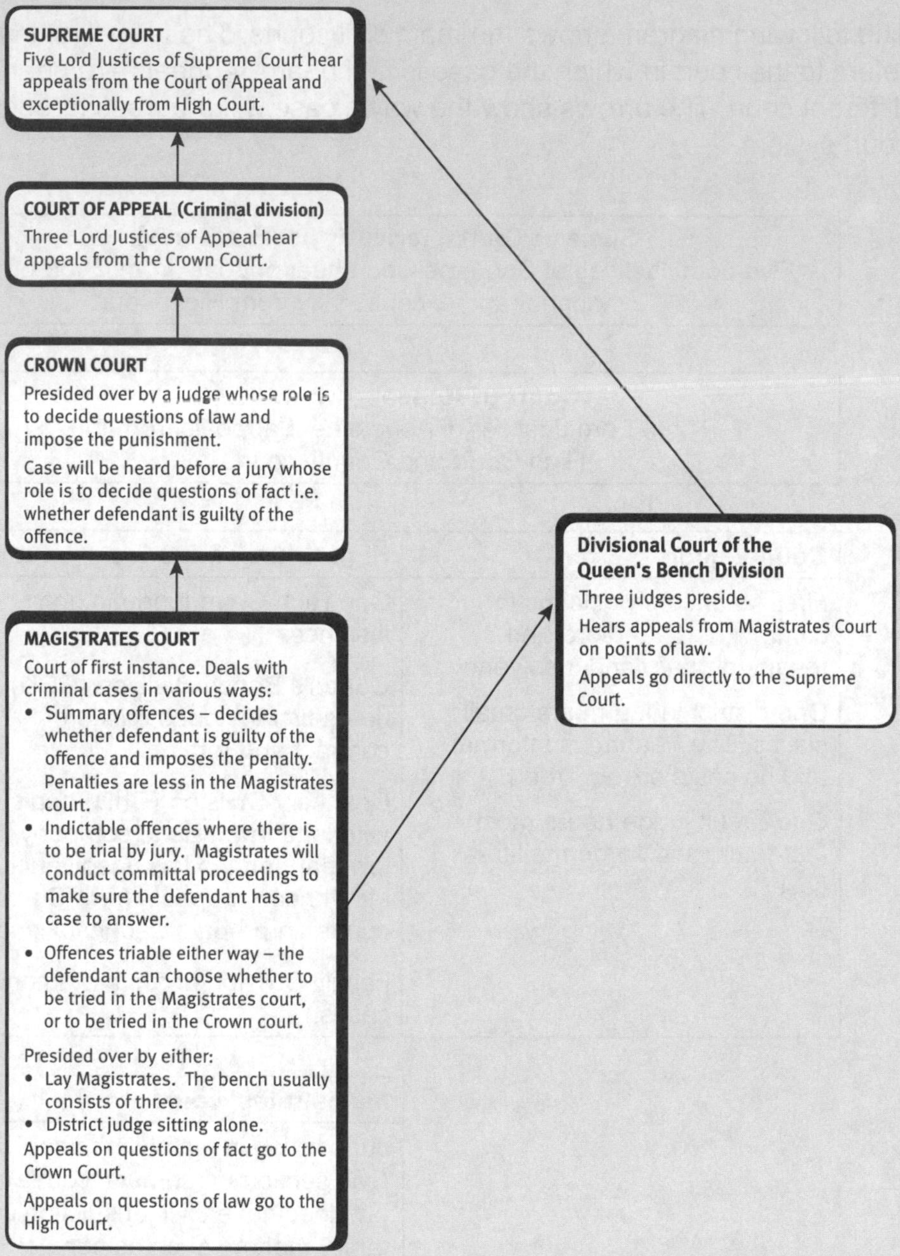

SUPREME COURT
Five Lord Justices of Supreme Court hear appeals from the Court of Appeal and exceptionally from High Court.

COURT OF APPEAL (Criminal division)
Three Lord Justices of Appeal hear appeals from the Crown Court.

CROWN COURT
Presided over by a judge whose role is to decide questions of law and impose the punishment.

Case will be heard before a jury whose role is to decide questions of fact i.e. whether defendant is guilty of the offence.

MAGISTRATES COURT
Court of first instance. Deals with criminal cases in various ways:

- Summary offences – decides whether defendant is guilty of the offence and imposes the penalty. Penalties are less in the Magistrates court.
- Indictable offences where there is to be trial by jury. Magistrates will conduct committal proceedings to make sure the defendant has a case to answer.
- Offences triable either way – the defendant can choose whether to be tried in the Magistrates court, or to be tried in the Crown court.

Presided over by either:

- Lay Magistrates. The bench usually consists of three.
- District judge sitting alone.

Appeals on questions of fact go to the Crown Court.

Appeals on questions of law go to the High Court.

Divisional Court of the Queen's Bench Division
Three judges preside.

Hears appeals from Magistrates Court on points of law.

Appeals go directly to the Supreme Court.

2 The sources of English law

Overview

European Community law takes precedence over all other sources.

Legislation takes precedence over case law.

Equity prevails over common law.

The sources of English law are:

- custom/common law
- equity
- legislation
- European law
- other sources.

Custom/common law

Custom was an important source of law historically, but is of less practical importance today.

Prior to the Norman Conquest in 1066, there was no single body of law applicable to the whole country. After 1066, the Normans attempted to rule the country through the application of local customs. Over time, customs considered capable of general application were absorbed and made common to all areas of the country so that there was one law common to all the country; hence the term, the common law.

The common law today is made up of past cases, or legal precedent, which are recorded in law reports. It is still of considerable importance, and develops from case to case in order to reflect the changing times. In order to ensure certainty, the legal principles which are pronounced by the higher courts are binding on the lower courts under the doctrine of judicial precedent (covered in more detail later in this chapter).

Supplementary reading

The organic common law

The common law is an organic and dynamic body of rules. It has grown and evolved over centuries. It continues to grow and to adapt to social change. In a case in 1954 (about child custody and illegitimacy), Lord Denning refuted the idea that the law could not adapt and modernise itself.

'What is the argument on the other side? Only this, that no case has been found in which it has been done before. That argument does not appeal to me in the least. If we never do anything which has not been done before, we shall never get anywhere. The law will stand still whilst the rest of the world goes on: and that will be bad for both.' Denning LJ, Packer v Packer [1954] P 15 at 22.

Equity

Again historically, the common law was incomplete, for example the main remedy available was restricted to monetary compensation.

Equity was developed by the Court of Chancery to fill in gaps in the common law, for example by the development of non-monetary remedies such as injunctions and orders of specific performance. An injunction is prohibitory whereas a specific performance order imposes an obligation to act. Both of these types of equitable remedy are used in the area of contract law, and can assist to ensure that requirements under the contract are satisfied.

Equitable remedies are discretionary and, in the event of a conflict between equity and the common law, equity prevails.

Legislation

Legislation falls into two categories:

- Acts of Parliament
- delegated legislation.

Acts of Parliament

Legislation is the formal enactment of rules by a body having the constitutional right and power to do so. In the United Kingdom, the only body with this inherent power is the UK Parliament. Its legislation takes the form of Acts of Parliament, also known as statutes.

The process of passing an Act can be a long one. It must pass through long proceedings in both the House of Commons and the House of Lords, and then receive the Royal Assent. The normal procedure followed requires:

(1) a green paper – outline proposal

(2) a white paper – more detailed content.

It is usually the House of Commons that considers the 'Bill' (proposed law) initially. If approved in the House of Commons, the Bill will pass to the House of Lords, where a similar procedure is followed. This procedure involves:

(1) first reading – only the title is read out

(2) second reading – a vote is taken

(3) committee stage – detailed consideration of the Bill

(4) report stage – the committee report back to the House

(5) third reading – final vote.

Exceptions to this procedure exist, for example, the introduction of the Finance Acts on an annual basis don't follow this long drawn out process.

Many Acts contain a section delaying direct effect for a short time to give those affected time to adapt.

Doctrine of sovereignty of Parliament

The courts cannot generally question the validity of an Act of Parliament. They must obey and apply the words of the statute, because Parliament has 'legislative sovereignty'.

Once enacted and in force, a statute remains law unless and until it is repealed or amended by another Act of Parliament. If the government dislikes an earlier Act, the full parliamentary procedure must be used in order to change or repeal the Act into a new one. This can always be done, however, because an Act cannot make itself unrepealable.

In one exceptional respect, the courts can challenge the validity of a provision in an Act. If a provision in a UK Act contravenes EU law, the UK court can suspend the operation of the provision.

Delegated legislation

For many reasons, Parliament has delegated some of its legislative powers to other bodies. Usually, Parliament passes an 'enabling' Act setting out the policy involved and the objectives it wishes to achieve. The Act then delegates the task of filling in the details to some other body.

Such a delegation of powers saves Parliament time which can then be devoted to more far-ranging and important issues. Also, expertise and specialist local knowledge can be used. Rules enacted under such powers are called delegated legislation, and the following are examples:

- The Parliaments of Scotland and Wales have been given some legislative powers on matters that affect their own regions.
- In the United Kingdom, the government cannot make law without the authority of Parliament. However, Parliament has delegated wide powers to government ministers within their own departments. Many rules are too detailed and technical to undergo the full Parliamentary process, and they may need to be changed too frequently. The detailed rules on motor vehicle construction and use are a good example. Therefore, individual ministers and their civil service departments are given the task of making rules within the guidelines set out in the enabling Acts. These regulations are usually in the form of **statutory instruments**.

- Local authorities have been given wide powers to make **bye-laws** within their own boundaries. Certain public bodies likewise have this power e.g. the London Underground.
- The Crown and Privy Council have the power to introduce delegated legislation in times of emergency in the form of **orders in council**. Such orders can be introduced quickly. Of further significance, is that this allows law creation, where circumstances demand that measures be introduced, but at a time when Parliament is not sitting.

Supplementary reading

Many controls exist to prevent abuse of delegated powers. Parliament itself exercises the main supervision, and it can always take away delegated powers by a new Act. A Scrutiny Committee exists to oversee delegated legislation introduced. However, the volume of delegated legislation introduced annually, and the fact that it can be introduced speedily and revoked quickly, makes thorough consideration of content impossible.

The courts also have supervisory powers over delegated legislation (unlike over statutes). If a delegated body exceeds or abuses its powers, the courts can hold that the regulations, by-laws, and so on are **ultra vires** (outside of the powers given) and therefore void.

Judicial interpretation of legislation

After Parliament has created law through legislation, it is then the role of the judiciary to interpret and apply this law. A number of rules and aids exist that can be used by the judiciary to assist them in this task.

The rules are:

- The Literal rule
- The Golden rule
- The Mischief rule
- The Purposive rule
- The Rules of language.

The aids to interpretation fall into two categories:

- The internal aids
- The external aids.

The Literal rule

Where words in a statute have only one possible meaning then that ordinary dictionary meaning must be applied even though it may result in an absurd outcome. Where an error is found in legislation, it is for Parliament to introduce new law to rectify the error.

Fisher v Bell (1960)

Facts: The court had to consider the meaning of the wording 'offer for sale'. It was an offence to 'offer for sale' offensive weapons. A shopkeeper had flick-knives with price tags attached on display in his shop window.

Held: The court applied the fundamental principles of contract law in a literal fashion, accepting that the display of flick-knives was an invitation to treat. It was the customer who made an offer to buy. In consequence, the shopkeeper was found not to be acting illegally. The aim of Parliament, however, had been to prevent sales of offensive weapons.

The Golden rule

Where words in a statute have more than one meaning the judiciary can apply the meaning that avoids an absurd consequence.

Re Sigsworth (1935)

Facts: A man murdered his mother and being the only heir, on the literal interpretation of legislation was entitled to inherit her estate.

Held: The court interpreted the wording of the content of the Administration of Estates Act 1925, applying the golden rule, in order to prevent the murderer from benefiting from his crime.

The Mischief rule

Where legislation is introduced to remedy a defect or 'mischief' in the law, then the judiciary should interpret the legislation to achieve this objective. The rule has origins in **Heydon's Case (1584)** in which judges were guided to consider:

- Relevant law prior to the legislation
- The mischief that the existing law failed to address
- The intended remedy for the mischief that Parliament sought to introduce.

Gorris v Scott (1874)

Facts: The court had to interpret the wording of the Contagious Diseases (Animals) Act 1869. The relevant content of the Act required animals being transported by ship to be in pens. The aim of this was to prevent the spread of contagious diseases. On the case facts, animals on board ship were not housed in pens and some were washed overboard.

Held: The claim against the defendant failed as the basis for the claim varied from the 'mischief' that Parliament was looking to address with that particular Act.

The Purposive rule

In more recent times, the Purposive approach has become recognised. Here the judiciary are guided to look at the purpose for the introduction of the legislation and reach decisions on that basis. This approach can be seen as a development on from, and being closely associated with, the mischief rule.

The Rules of Language

The Rules of Language offer assistance to judges through

(1) **Eiusdem generis** – where general words follow particular words in a statute, the meaning of the general words should be taken from the meaning of the particular words.

In **Powell v Kempton Racecourse Co. (1899)** the court had to consider where it was unlawful for betting to take place. The relevant legislation provided that betting was illegal in any 'house, office, room or other place'. The problem related to the wording of 'or other place'. The court decided that the wording related to any enclosed place. This being based on the meaning to be attributed to the particular words in the term.

(2) **Expressio unius exclusion alterius** – where a statute seeks to establish a list of what is covered by its provisions, then anything not expressly included in that list, is specifically excluded.

(3) **Noscitur a sociis** – where the meaning to be attributed to a word can be determined from other words around it, i.e. looking at the context in which the word is used.

(4) **In pari material** – where courts can look at previous legislation dealing with the same subject matter to discover the appropriate interpretation.

Internal/intrinsic aids

These are found within the statute itself and include:

- The long title
- The preamble identifying the intentions and objectives of the legislation
- The interpretation section
- Headings
- Marginal notes.

External/extrinsic aids

These are found outside the statute and include:

- Dictionaries
- Hansard, which are printed transcripts of parliamentary debates, provide information of what was said in Parliament when the
- Bill was being considered
- The Interpretation Act 1978
- The judiciary are also assisted by a number of presumptions. These include:
  - An Act will not bind the Crown
  - The Act will apply to the whole of the UK Legislation. It may, however, only apply to an identified area within the UK
  - The Act will not have retrospective effect
  - An Act is not intended to deprive a person of their liberty.

European Union law

In 1972, the United Kingdom joined the European Community (EC), now called the European Union (EU). Accession meant that the United Kingdom agreed to conform with existing and future EC law, and the United Kingdom complied by passing the European Communities Act 1972. There are several sources of EU law:

- **The Treaties**. They are the primary source: the Treaties of Paris and Rome that created the first EU bodies, and all subsequent Treaties. The provisions (e.g. on competition) are directly applicable and basically have legislative effect. They automatically become law in the member states, with no need for further legislation.
- **Regulations**. The regulations by the Commission and Council are similarly directly applicable, with no need for further legislation.

- **Directives**. The directives by the Commission and Council are generally addressed to the member states, and require that the states take action within an identified time period to change their own law so as to comply. In the United Kingdom, this may be done by ministerial regulations. Sometimes, a full Act of Parliament is used.
- **Decisions**. These are addressed to individuals or companies, or to member states, and are directly binding on those to whom they are addressed. They have no effect on anyone else, however, unlike legislation. The Commission has power to give decisions on various issues.
- **Recommendations**. These are self-explanatory; they have no formal legal effect, but have considerable persuasive force.
- **The European Court of Justice**. It gives decisions and rulings in disputes involving EU law, and its decisions are binding on the parties themselves in the United Kingdom. They also form precedents and are influential in building up EU law.

It should be borne in mind that the United Kingdom plays an active role in proposing, creating and drafting EU law.

Supplementary reading

Other sources

It may be that there is no English precedent to apply to a case being decided by the court. In that event, the barristers arguing the case may seek to rely on a precedent decided by a court in another common law jurisdiction, such as Australia, Canada, Singapore and other Commonwealth countries. Although cases decided in foreign courts are not binding upon English judges, the court may be persuaded to follow the case on the ground that it is an accurate reflection of English law. Again, in the absence of an English precedent, the court may be persuaded that the hypothesis of a textbook writer accurately states how the law should be applied. Such an event is rare, however, and lawyers will resort to other sources of law only in the absence of the above sources.

3 Judicial precedent and the tort of negligence

A tort is a civil wrong. Action is brought by the victim of wrongful conduct (the 'claimant') against the wrongdoer (the 'defendant'). For most torts, particularly the tort of negligence, the main remedy sought is damages, or monetary compensation.

Negligence is the most important of all torts and occurs when one person causes harm to another by failing to take the care that is legally required. It gives some excellent examples of the doctrine of judicial precedent in operation.

A tort must be distinguished from a breach of contract. A contract is a voluntary agreement. The parties may agree upon a number of stringent obligations which each party promises to observe. In the event of default, the claimant will be entitled to sue for breach of contract (see Chapter 2). In the tort of negligence, however, obligations are not accepted by voluntary agreement but are imposed upon the persons concerned by the state.

Judicial precedent

The system, adopted by the judges, of following the decisions in previous cases is called the doctrine of judicial precedent.

- Some precedents are **binding** (meaning they **must** be followed in later cases).
- Others are merely **persuasive** (meaning that a judge in a later case **may** choose to follow it but he is not bound to do so).

There are three factors to be considered in deciding whether a precedent is binding or persuasive:

- the hierarchy of the courts
- ratio decidendi and obiter dicta
- the material facts of the case.

The hierarchy of the courts

As a general rule, the precedents of higher courts bind lower courts, but not vice versa.

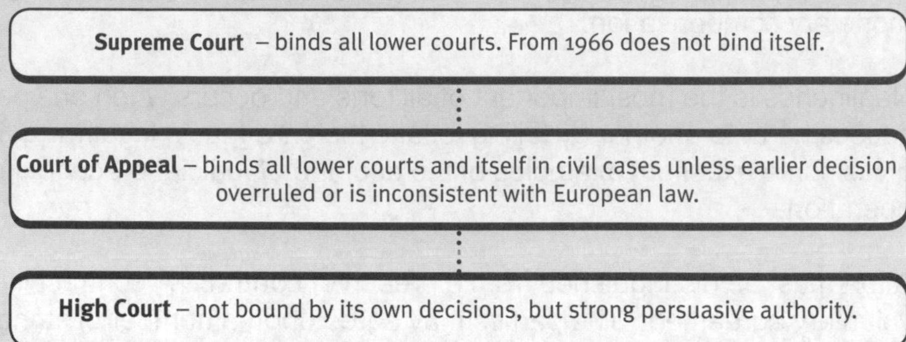

Ratio decidendi and obiter dicta

The ratio decidendi is the legal reason for the decision. It is capable of forming the binding precedent. It is a statement of law which is carried down to later decisions.

Obiter dicta are statements which are not part of the ratio, they are other statements made by the judges such as hypothetical situations or wide legal principles. They are persuasive rather than binding. This means that the judge can take the statement into account (and usually will) when reaching his decision, but he does not have to follow it.

Facts of the case

In order for a precedent to be binding on a judge in a later case, the material facts of the two cases must be the same. If they are significantly different, the precedent will be persuasive rather than binding.

When is a precedent not binding?

A precedent is not binding where it:

- has been overruled by a higher court.
- has been overruled by statute.
- was made without proper care (per incuriam).
- can be distinguished from the earlier case, i.e. the material facts differ.

The tort of negligence

Torts of negligence were recognised in many separate and individual situations in the nineteenth and early-twentieth centuries, but the leading case which tried to pull these separate strands together into principles which could apply in all situations was the House of Lords' decision in **Donoghue v Stevenson.**

Donoghue v Stevenson (1932)

Facts: The claimant, Mrs Donoghue, went into a café with a friend, who bought a bottle of ginger beer and gave it to Mrs Donoghue. The ginger beer was in an opaque bottle which had been sealed by the manufacturer. Mrs D drank half of the contents. When she poured the other half, it was found to contain what appeared to be the remains of a decomposed snail. Mrs D suffered shock and stomach pains.

Mrs D did not buy the bottle, otherwise she could have sued the café for breach of contract, and recovered full damages even though the café was not at fault. Instead, she had to claim that Stevenson, the manufacturer of the drink, was liable to her for negligence.

Held: The House of Lords held that a manufacturer of goods owed a duty of care not only to the buyer, but also to anyone else who should reasonably be foreseen as likely to suffer physical injury from defects in them. The duty was to take reasonable care.

As a wider guideline for the future, Lord Atkin also suggested his famous 'neighbour' principle.

The Neighbour Principle

One must take reasonable care to avoid acts or omissions which can reasonably be foreseen and would be likely to injure another party. A neighbour is a person, or people, who are so closely and directly affected by actions that one ought reasonably to have them in contemplation as being so affected.

In other words, everyone must take reasonable care not to cause foreseeable harm to foreseeable or potential victims.

Lord Atkin's statement was much wider than required for the actual case, and could be regarded as only an **obiter dicta**. Nevertheless, it had enormous influence in future cases.

Lord Macmillan, another judge in the case, set out the essential features of the tort. It applies where 'there is a **duty of care** and where **failure in that duty** has caused **damage**' to the claimant. These, then, are the three essential elements.

1 Duty to take care

A duty of care is essentially an individual's responsibility to have the foresight that your actions are likely to affect someone. (In other words, the so-called 'neighbour test' set out in **Donoghue v Stevenson**.)

The duty of care was extended in many cases after **Donoghue v Stevenson**. One example is **Home Office v Dorset Yacht Co Ltd (1970)**, where some 'Borstal' boys (youngsters who had been convicted of a crime) were working on an island under Home Office supervision. Some boys escaped and damaged the claimant's yacht. The House of Lords said that the Home Office could be liable for negligence.

Nevertheless, it was always made clear in later cases that there are limits to the neighbour rule.

- First, there must be sufficient proximity between the person who was careless and the person suffering harm. The duty cannot be owed over a limitless physical area, or to a limitless number of people.

Bourhill v Young (1942)

Facts: A motorcyclist was killed in a road accident for which he was responsible. A pregnant woman who got off a tram near the scene of the accident claimed that when she got to the scene of the accident, she saw blood on the road and as a result suffered shock. This put her into premature labour which resulted in the loss of her baby. She subsequently brought a claim in relation to nervous shock and the resulting loss.

Held: Her claim for damage failed because she was too far from the accident and not within the foreseeable range of harm. She was not present at the scene of the accident and she arrived after the accident occurred.

Supplementary reading

Further case law examples are:

In **Alcock v Chief Constable of South Yorkshire Police (1991),** one of a number cases arising from the Sheffield football disaster where many spectators were killed, an action was brought by relatives of the victim, who saw the tragedy from a distance or on live television. They all suffered nervous shock, and sued the police for negligence. These actions failed.

In **Sutradhar v Natural Environment Research Council (2004)**, the claimant, along with numerous other persons, had been poisoned as a result of drinking contaminated water. It was alleged that a duty of care was owed to the claimant by the party who had carried out a water survey and produced a report on findings. It was decided that there was insufficient proximity between the claimant and defendant and so no realistic prospect of establishing that a duty of care was owed.

In **London Borough of Islington v. University College London NHS Trust (2004)**, a local authority failed in its claim to recover the costs of providing care to a person who suffered a stroke as a result of receiving negligent medical advice from the defendant. It was decided that no duty of care was owed, as first the loss suffered by the claimant was not reasonably foreseeable, secondly there was not sufficient proximity between the claimant local authority and the defendant. Further, the loss suffered was due to compliance with a statutory obligation.

- Second, there may be public policy grounds for refusing to apply the neighbour principle. For example, the rule might cause absurdity or otherwise be grossly undesirable.

Mulcahy v Ministry of Defence (1996)

Facts: The defendant responsible for the army and therefore its soldiers, employed a gun commander during the Gulf War. The claimant, an artilleryman, sustained damage to his hearing when a howitzer was fired accidentally.

Held: A serviceman owes no duty of care to his fellow servicemen in battle conditions, since as a matter of common sense and public policy it would not be fair, just and reasonable to impose such a duty. For the same reason the Ministry of Defence as the claimant's employer does not have a duty to provide a safe system of work in those circumstances.

2 Breach of duty

The victim only has a valid claim for damages if the person who owes the duty is shown to have broken it. The standard required is that of the reasonable person.

Higher duties in the law of tort are placed on those who are in a position of responsibility. Similarly, the more serious the consequences are likely to be, the more care is expected. Greater care is expected towards especially vulnerable victims, such as children. Conversely, a lower duty of care is expected from children.

It may, of course, sometimes be difficult to discover why and how an accident occurred. Since it is for the claimant to prove that his injury or loss was due to the defendant's breach of duty, this can defeat his claim. Exceptionally, therefore, the courts may reverse the normal burden of proof, and call upon the defendant to prove that he has not been careless. This is contrary to the normal rules of evidence, and it will only be done where:

- the harm would not normally happen if proper care were taken
- there is no other explanation for what has occurred – the phrase res ipsa loquitur (the thing speaks for itself) – is often used. This serves to highlight the belief that the breach does not have to be proved. The very existence of the damage caused by the defendant is seen by the claimant as establishing that the defendant must have been in breach of duty
- the defendant was in control of the situation, and the victim was not.

Scott v London and St Katherine Docks (1865)

Facts: The claimant was hit by six bags of sugar which fell from the defendant's warehouse. The claimant could not say why the bags had fallen.

Held: The court ruled that the facts spoke for themselves and it was up to the defendant to prove that he was not negligent.

3 Damage caused by negligence

The claimant cannot recover damages for negligence unless he has suffered damage or injury. This can include some or any of the following:

- Personal injury claims, particularly from accidents on the road or at work, constitute a large proportion of all negligence claims – to such an extent that potential wrongdoers are required by statute to insure against possible liability, so as to ensure that victims will get any damages awarded. Personal injury can include illness from nervous shock if this is clearly caused by the defendant's negligence.
- Damage to property can be recovered (a wrecked car for instance).
- Financial loss directly connected with personal injury or to property is recoverable (loss of earnings, repair costs for instance).
- Purely financial loss is only recoverable in exceptional situations, such as for professional liability to an identified person to whom responsibility was undertaken (covered later on in this chapter). Otherwise, purely economic loss is unlikely to count.

The harm must also have been clearly caused by the negligence, and only damage which should have been reasonably foreseen at the time of the negligence will be included.

Boardman v Sanderson (1964)

Facts: A driver negligently backed his car from a garage, and injured a young boy. The father, who was known to be nearby, heard a scream and ran to the scene. He claimed damages for his nervous shock.

Held: The claimant was entitled to damages. The harm was not too remote, because he was a relative of the main victim and was known to be in the close vicinity.

Contributory negligence

The defence of contributory negligence arises if the claimant was partly the author of his own misfortune, so that the accident was partly caused by the claimant himself. In these circumstances, the courts have a discretion to reduce the damages awarded by any percentage which they consider appropriate.

Sayers v Harlow Urban District Council (1958)

Facts: The claimant having paid to use a public toilet found herself trapped inside a cubicle which had a defective lock. She tried to climb out, allowing her weight to rest on the toilet roll holder, which rotated. She fell and was injured.

Held: The injuries she suffered were a natural and probable consequence of the defendant's negligence, but that the damages would be reduced by 25% since the claimant had been careless in depending for support on the toilet roll holder.

Negligence and professional advisers

Despite an initial reluctance, the courts have extended the 'neighbour' principle to negligent advice and to purely financial loss. This has had a profound effect on situations arising when a professional person's advice is relied upon by a non-client.

The **Donoghue v Stevenson** principle was extended dramatically in the case of **Hedley Byrne v Heller and Partners**.

Hedley Byrne v Heller and Partners (1963)

Facts: The claimants (Hedley Byrne) were advertising agents, who had contracted to place advertisements for their client's (Easipower) products. As this involved giving Easipower credit, they asked the defendants, who were Easipower's bankers, for a reference as to the creditworthiness of Easipower.

Heller gave favourable references (but stipulated that the information was given without responsibility on their part). Relying on this information, the claimants extended credit to Easipower and lost over £17,000 when the latter, soon after, went into liquidation. The claimants sued Easipower's bankers for negligence.

Held: The defendants' disclaimer was adequate to exclude the assumption by them of the legal duty of care. However, in the absence of the disclaimer, the circumstances would have given rise to a duty of care in spite of the absence of a contractual or fiduciary relationship. Thus, but for the disclaimer, the bank was liable on its misleading statement.

Note: Nowadays the validity of the disclaimer could be challenged under the Unfair Contract Terms Act 1977 (UCTA 1977).

The effect of Hedley Byrne

The above case created a new duty situation by recognising liability for negligent misstatement causing economic loss in circumstances where there exists a special relationship between the parties.

A special relationship exists where a professional person advises a known person who relies on the statement for a known purpose.

Smith v Eric S Bush (1989)

Facts: A surveyor was engaged by a building society to value a house. The surveyor knew that the society would show his valuation to a specific potential buyer, who would rely on it. The valuation was negligent, and the buyer lost money.

Held: A special relationship existed, and the surveyor was liable for the purely financial loss caused to the buyer.

The concept of special relationship was redefined in the following leading case:

Caparo Industries plc v Dickman and others (1990)

Facts: Caparo owned shares in F plc and, after receiving the audited accounts, which showed a profit for the year, it purchased more shares in F plc and then made a successful takeover bid for F plc. After the takeover Caparo sued the auditors alleging that the accounts were misleading in that they showed a profit when in fact there has been a loss. Caparo said the auditors owed a duty of care to investors and potential investors as they should have been aware that a press release saying that profits would fall significantly had made F plc vulnerable to a takeover bid and that bidders might relay on the accounts.

Held: The court set out three criteria which had to be fulfilled in order to give rise to a duty of care:

(1) The standard test of foreseeability applied.

(2) The concept of proximity limits the duty to circumstances where the statement would be communicated to the claimant either as an individual or a member of an identifiable group in respect of transactions of a particular kind and that the claimant would rely on the statement. It is therefore necessary to look at the purpose for which the statement is made, the statement maker's knowledge of the person relying on the statement and the type of transaction in which it is used. In this case the purpose of the company accounts was to enable the shareholders to question the performance of the board, and not to enable them to judge whether to purchase more shares in the company.

(3) Whether it is just and equitable that a duty of care should be imposed so that imposing it would not be contrary to public policy. When the court applied these criteria to the Caparo case they found that auditors of a public company owe no duty of care to the public at large who rely on accounts when purchasing shares in a company nor was any duty owed to individual shareholders who purchase additional shares.

Caparo Industries v Dickman was itself distinguished by the High Court in the later case of **ADT Ltd v Binder Hamlyn**.

ADT Ltd v Binder Hamlyn (1995)

Facts: ADT was bidding to take over a company whose accounts were audited by Binder Hamlyn. At a 'serious' business meeting with ADT, the auditors expressly said, without any disclaimer, that the 'target' company's accounts were accurate. The auditors made this statement specifically to ADT, knowing that ADT would rely on it without further enquiry. The accounts were not in fact reliable, and ADT suffered loss.

Held: These facts were much more like the cases prior to Caparo and, indeed, similar to the facts of Hedley Byrne itself but without any disclaimer. The auditors were therefore held liable.

The case of **ADT Ltd v Binder Hamlyn** put pressure on the government at the time to prompt a rethink in partnership law and to allow partners to limit their liability by incorporating into a Limited Liability Partnership (see Chapter 4).

Supplementary reading

The potential extent of auditor liability for negligence can be reduced under the provisions of the Companies Act 2006. Section 534 introduces a 'liability limitation agreement'. This is an agreement between a company and its auditors under which the amount of liability owed by the auditor is limited '. . . in respect of any negligence, default, breach of duty or breach of trust, occurring in the course of the audit of accounts, . . .' Section 537 provides that the agreement will not be effective in limiting auditor liability beyond that which '. . . is fair and reasonable in all the circumstances . . .' This legislation comes at a time when negligence actions against large audit firms, have reduced significantly. Reforms in accounting and auditing standards are included in the reasons put forward for this reduction.

4 International legal systems

European Union and Member States

Whilst the UK and other states that are members of the European Union retain their domestic law, as we have seen, sources of European Law influence the law applicable within the domestic law of each member state.

The European Union now has a membership of twenty eight independent states. Most recently, Croatia joined the European Union on 1 July 2013.

The Institutions of the European Union are:

- The European Parliament
- The Council of Ministers (The Council) also known as the Council of the European Union
- The European Commission
- The Court of Justice of the European Communities (The Court).

Supplementary reading: EU Institutions

The Commission is the executive arm of the European Union, initiating and implementing EU legislations and decisions. The Commission is independent and Commissioners do not represent the interests of their respective Member States. However, the Commission is guided by broad guidelines and general political priorities agreed by the European Council. The Commission comprises a number of departmental Directorates-General (DGs), each responsible for one or more specific areas of policy-making.

Council of Ministers ('The Council') is the main legislative and decision-taking arm of the European Union, acting on the basis of proposals initiated by the Commission. The Council consists of a representative minister from each of the Member States. The membership is not fixed but is formulated according to the issue. For example, transport ministers will attend on transport issues, finance ministers on finance issues, and so on. The General Affairs Council ensures consistency and coordination in the work of different Council configurations. The Council is served by a permanent body of national representative known as COREPER (Comitedes représentants pérmanents).

European Parliament (EP) exercises a supervisory role over EU institutions. Importantly, since the Maastricht Treaty, it has had an increasing role in the passage of legislation under the ordinary legislative procedure. Essentially, this procedure requires the Council to consult and reach agreement with the EP over its legislative proposals, with the EP holding an ultimate right of veto. The continuing expansion of the use of the ordinary legislative procedure under recent treaties reflects the importance of the EP's democratic mandate. The EP also has important powers over the Commission, such as the ability to pass a 'motion of censure' which, if carried, obliges the Commission to resign and no budget can be adopted without its approval. The EP consists of directly elected Members of the European Parliament (MEPs) serving five year terms. The number of MEPs from each Member State reflects its population size and there are broad political groupings.

European Council is not, as such, an institution but is the name given to the twice-yearly meetings (or summits) of the heads of state or government and the President of the Commission. Foreign ministers are also entitled to attend. These meetings decide the overall strategies and policies for the European Union. The Council usually expresses itself by way of Conclusions, Resolutions or Declarations, though these have no status in law. The European Council would be formally made an institution under the draft Constitution.

European Court of Justice (ECJ) is the judicial arm of the European Union; it is the final arbiter on all questions of EU law and operates on the principle of the supremacy of EU law over national law. The court comprises judges from Member States. The ECJ adjudicates upon failures of Member States to fulfil treaty obligations or to implement community law and to decide the compatibility of national legislation. It also adjudicates upon 'failures to act' by EU institutions, as well as the legality of legal instruments adopted or actions taken by them. Where questions of EU law interpretation arise before a national court, a 'preliminary ruling' may be sought from the ECJ in order to resolve the issue.

The European Union and Domestic Legal Systems

A significant number of the European Union states have a codified system of law. In other words, a collection of comprehensive laws which can be found in constitutions, legislation, rules and regulations. The Code de Napoleon (1804) introduced in France provides an early example. Statutes which contain, in a systematic and comprehensive way, all case law and existing legislation on a particular area or aspect of law are described as codifying statutes. Although in England much law is contained in legislation, we do not have a codified system.

States of the European Union predominantly adopt civil law systems. However, origins of law sometimes differ significantly and countries invariably have some unique features in their legal systems. Austria and Greece have Roman Law influence, whilst Finland has a legal system based on Swedish law and Belgium has a system showing clear application of English constitutional theory.

Supplementary reading

The French Legal System

History often has a significant effect on the legal system that develops in a country and France is a clear example of this, with the former monarchy, demands of the people and outside influences all playing a part in the development and formulation of its legal system. In 1804, the Code Civile was created. This was a law made for the people and to be accessible by them. Today, France's law is in the main created by the legislative body and so codified. Tort law is not codified, but is created by the judiciary.

The judicial system is in two parts: private law or law of the people, including Criminal Law (the judicial order), and public law or the law applicable to government, branches of government, as well as private citizens (the administrative order).

The court structure is very similar to that in England. In the judicial order, there is a trial court level where matters are dealt with at first instance. This level is made up of six sections which distinguish between specialised jurisdictions, for example commerce, labour law and social security and the ordinary jurisdiction and criminal jurisdiction. Above the trial level is the appeal level. The appeal courts include chambers which specialise and deal with commercial, social, criminal and civil matters, for example. The courts of appeal effectively hear the whole case again and consider both issues of fact and law. A similar court structure is found at the highest level or supreme court level. If the supreme court disagrees with the decision of the lower court, the matter is sent back for the lower court to consider amending its decision. The decision of the supreme court will ultimately prevail.

Under French Law, everyone is entitled to legal representation. The advocates will make a verbal plea before the court but it is the judge who will carry out questioning in the court room. Both adversarial and inquisitorial principles apply. In English Law, an adversarial approach is taken. A further interesting distinction between French and English Law is found in the fact that in France individuals are appointed judges at the beginning of their legal careers. In England, appointment to the Judiciary will follow on from a successful career as a lawyer.

The German Legal System

Germany is a democratic and social federal state. A Constitution gives authority for the creation of legislation.

As in France, codified law established by Parliament exists. This codified law acknowledges that everyone is equal before the law. Customary law based on long-term practice must be followed by the judiciary also. Further, ordinances or statutory instruments exist. These can be likened to delegated legislation under English Law with the right to create an ordinance given under codified law, just as in England an Enabling Act or Parent Act would give such power. Also, 'statutes' can be created by public corporations. Under these statutes, the corporation can create laws to regulate its own affairs. Again, authority to create such law must be found in the constitution.

Whilst the codified law has to be interpreted through the judgments of the courts, such judgments only bind the parties to the relevant action. The decisions do not constitute a precedent and thereby law. In reality, though, the lower courts will respect decisions of higher courts to prevent the obvious consequence: if they didn't so act, this should result in matters to be taken to appeal.

The Polish Legal System

Poland is a democratic republic and has a Constitution which is the supreme law of the land. A legal system is based on the continental legal system (codified civil law). The parliament, made up of the lower house 'the Sejm' and the upper house 'Senate', has the power of creating legislation. Further sources of law are regulations, which, as in Germany, require specific authorisation under statute by bodies permitted under the Constitution. Ratified international agreements provide a further source of law as do local laws created by authorised bodies within limits prescribed.

The court structure is made up of the supreme court, that is, the highest court of appeal; also provincial courts and district courts. Both courts have jurisdiction to hear civil and criminal law matters. A higher administrative court which sits in ten distinct centres deals with public sector matters of administration.

The Italian Legal System

Italy is a democratic republic. The republic is made up of the state which has state law, as well as municipalities, provinces, metropolitan cities and regions which are autonomous and have their own statutes. Creation of legislation must be in accordance with that provided in the Constitution. Furthermore, it is limited by constraints imposed under EU law and existing international obligations. It has a parliament made up of two chambers: a House of Representatives (630 representatives), and the Senate (315 senators). The chambers act jointly in the creation of legislation. The parliamentary process for the creation of legislation is similar to that of England, with a Bill being introduced and considered by committee and both chambers. The representatives are elected on a national basis, whereas the senators are in the main elected on a regional basis.

Delegated legislation can be created by government, but clear criteria on the subject area and the time allowed for its creation must be determined by the parliament.

Jurisdiction of the courts is broken down into specific areas. These are civil and criminal law, accounting, taxation, military and administrative. A hierarchy of courts exists which deals with the civil and criminal law matters.

The Legal System of Denmark

Denmark provides a good example of a legal system that has its roots in history with the fundamental principles being traced back to the Middle Ages. Provincial laws originally existed which were integrated into a unified system in 1683. Outside influences, particularly German jurisprudence and the cooperation between the Nordic countries, have contributed to the development of the legal system. Denmark does not have a civil code. Civil law is found in established practices and legislation. Danish law can be classified into:

(1) **Public Law**
(This includes constitutional and administrative law, international law and criminal law.)

(2) **Civil Law**
(This area regulates the interests of individuals and legal persons, for example companies.)

The classification can be likened to what we find in English Law, even though these classifications are open to different interpretation.

The sources of law are:

A **The Constitutional Act:** This regulates the relationships between the organs of state. It also determines the requirements for the creation of legislation. This process, as with the classification of law, which can be compared with the English procedure, involves approval within Parliament and finally Royal Assent.

B **Acts of Parliament**

C **Case Law:** The courts do create law through decision-making where no legislation exists. However, compared to countries that have Anglo-Saxon origins, the court's role as law maker is somewhat limited.

D **Custom:** Legislation can be introduced to override a custom. Also, the courts can refuse to recognise a custom on the basis that it is unreasonable.

Denmark and International Law. The Danish government has the power to commit the country to international agreements. A Treaty will be created to incorporate the agreement into Danish Law. In some instances, it is necessary to hold a referendum before agreement to an international agreement of major significance can be approved.

Denmark and the European Union. As with all other member states, European Treaties and regulations are automatically binding, and directives must be implemented and become incorporated within the law.

A hierarchy of courts exists with the most senior being the Supreme Court. Below is the High Court, and the lowest courts are the city courts. Denmark does differ from France, Spain and Germany in not having a constitutional court or administrative court.

The Legal System of Greece

Greece was established as a presidential parliamentary republic in 1975. The Greek law is influenced by various sources including nineteenth-century continental codifications, French and Roman traditions. Its Constitution is the supreme law.

The main sources of law are:

A **Legislation:** All legislation must be published and comes into force 10 days after publication.

B **Codes:** These include:

- a civil code
- a code of civil procedure
- a code of criminal procedure
- a code of law tribune (this contains statute law).

C **Case Law**

The Legal System of Cyprus

Historical events have brought about significant changes in the politics and legal system of the country. In 1925, Cyprus became a Crown colony, and 10 years later, English common law was established in the legal system. In 1959, Cyprus became an independent republic and a Constitution was introduced which remains the supreme law.

The extent to which non-compliance with the Constitution is found following the withdrawal of the Turkish Cypriots has resulted in a doctrine of necessity being applicable and the law under the Constitution being qualified. The situation is somewhat problematic, however, following the invasion by Turkey and the northern part of the island being recognised by Turkey as the Turkish Republic of Northern Cyprus. The Republic of Cyprus joined the European Union in 2004.

The sources of law repeat to a notable extent that found in other countries, as might be expected with certain additions. These sources include:

- The Constitution
- Legislation
- Common Law
- Muslim Law
- Ecclesiastical Greek Orthodox Law
- European Union Law
- International Treaties.

Legal systems around the world

Historic events have shaped the development of legal systems in many countries. English, Roman and French laws have provided the basis for the development of legal systems to a significant extent.

Australia, Bangladesh, Canada, Egypt, Hong Kong, India, Malaysia, New Zealand and Nigeria are examples of countries that have a legal system based on English Law. Many smaller countries also have systems based on English Common Law. It would be inappropriate to try to classify the dominant influences on the establishing of legal systems around the world.

Whilst, in some instances, a common basis for legal development can be found due to the historical influence of a country in a specific part of the world, often, the features that contributed to the establishing of a legal system are complex and unique. Chile has a legal system that derives from Spanish Law, but has also been influenced by French and Austrian Laws. Egypt, whilst having a legal system based on English Common Law, has also been influenced by Islamic Law and Napoleonic codes.

The shaping of, and the content of, legal systems around the world invariably differ greatly. Equally, common features can be identified, sometimes in relation to the present sources of law, court hierarchy and classification of law.

Supplementary reading

The Malaysian Legal System

The legal system is based on English Common Law. As is so often found around the world, law primarily has its origins in the legislation or decisions of the courts. Federal and state legislatures have legislative power. The federal government has authority over the administration of justice. However, Islamic and other traditional laws apply to Muslims and other indigenous people. The court structure and hierarchy is similar to that found in England. The court structure consists of:

(1) **Subordinate Courts**
(Magistrates Courts and Sessions Courts)

(2) **Superior Courts**
(Two High Courts with the same jurisdiction and status. First, for the states of Sabah and Sarawak, the second, for Peninsular Malaysia.)

(3) **A Court of Appeal**
(The Federal Court has the highest judicial authority and is the final court of appeal.)

A Special Court was formed in 1993 to deal with any offences committed by the monarchical heads of the states. Malaysia has a constitutional monarch, a 'paramount ruler' who would also appear before this court.

The Legal System of the United States of America

Again, we find the government and the judiciary effective in establishing law with a broadly similar internal structure of government and courts. However, some significant differences lie within this broad structure.

The United States has a national government with each state having its own government. Both national and state governments have the separate branches of the executive, legislative and judicial. The United States has a federal system and where any conflict between state and federal legislation is found, the federal legislation will apply.

It is the Constitution of the United States which is recognised as the 'supreme law of the land'. It is this Constitution which guarantees rights and freedoms of all citizens of the United States. The Constitution prevails over all other laws and regulations. Interpretation of the Constitution is a role of the federal courts.

International Treaties under the Constitution which are made by the United States are also regarded as 'supreme laws' of the land.

Federal Statutes are likewise regarded as 'supreme laws'. Federal legislation is introduced by the United States' Congress. The process of creating legislation starts with a Bill which is then considered by committee. The two chambers of Congress will also consider the Bill. In many respects the procedure follows that of the United Kingdom, without of course ultimately Royal Assent being provided. If such Statutes and Treaties conflict, the more recent or more specific will normally prevail.

What can be likened to delegated legislation in the United Kingdom can be found in the United States. Executive Orders and Agency Rules can be created by administrative bodies so long as the authority is given under statute by Congress.

Law is developed in the United States through the Common Law. All states except Louisiana have a common law system, with decisions of the courts establishing precedents. Decisions of the United States' Supreme Court and the majority of states' appellate courts are reported, again very much in line with the role and process of precedent in England.

The Legal System of China

The law of China developed in the past through the teachings of Confucius which highlighted social control and social order. Whilst codified law was seen as inadequate to address the range of human activity, laws did evolve to regulate the behaviour of the people. Early in the legal development, a criminal code was established as were statutes dealing with areas of civil law. The early belief that law was secondary to self-discipline and morality was heavily criticised. Attitudes and opinions regarding the traditional Chinese legal system have varied. Some thought it backward and barbaric. Recent research, however, likens the eighteenth-century legal system to European legal systems of the same period.

In identifying the Chinese legal system of today, 1979 can be seen as a point in time when notable progress began. Since then, in excess of 300 laws have been introduced along with the development of a system for administering justice. Mediation committees are used to address legal issues and deal with disputes. There are in excess of 800,000 such committees in rural and urban areas and these have dealt with over 90 percent of civil disputes in the People's Republic of China and minor criminal matters at no cost to the litigants. Many of the judges have had no legal training.

Law has been created piecemeal with specific areas of activity and dealings often serving as the basis for new law. An approach has often been adopted whereby new laws go through a trial period and then a redrafting takes place. There was opposition to simply adopting that found within an already existing legal system. An adverse consequence of this piecemeal development of law has been the discovery of contradictions and notable omissions.

With significant progress made since 1979 in the establishing of the legal system, law reform became a government priority in the 1990s. Criminal law, procedures applicable with criminal law administration, and also human rights have been areas where significant reforms have been made.

Hong Kong and Macau, on transferring sovereignty to China, did not change their legal systems. They continue to adopt the English Common Law and Portuguese legal systems, respectively.

The Legal system of Sri Lanka

Sri Lanka become independent in 1948 and is now a commonwealth of nations. The Sri Lankan Parliament is the law-making body. Parliament is made up of 168 members who are elected by the public. Within Parliament is a cabinet made up of 49 ministers which is led by the prime minister.

Originally, British Laws were applied. These were replaced by a Penal Code which was seen as based on existing Indian Law. This Penal Code is retained today with amendments. As is commonly found in jurisdictions around the world, a hierarchy of courts exists. Minor matters will be dealt with in the lowest courts, for example criminal matters are dealt in the Magistrates Court. Above this court is the High Court, then the Court of Appeal, with the final appellate jurisdiction being exercised by the Supreme court.

Sharia Law (Islamic Law)

Sharia has been connected to the idea of 'spiritual law' and a system of 'divine law'. Social, economic and political issues as well as religious rituals are covered by Sharia. Some laws within Sharia are treated as divinely ordained and can never be altered. Other laws within Sharia are created by lawyers and judges. Law-makers are seen as establishing what is a human approximation of that which is seen as divine. Through the application of Sharia law, the allowing of people to live in harmony and the maintaining of a just society is sought.

Primary sources of Sharia law are:

(1) The Qur'an

(2) The Sunnah (the Way) recognising that approved by directions of the Prophet Muhammad

(3) For some Muslims, the unanimity of the disciples of Muhammad on certain issues.

A secondary source of Sharia law is found where no rules exist, by reasoning, possibly through analogy, and thereby law is applied to new situations. Beyond this, a further secondary source is found through consensus of the people or community, and where the public interest is seen to be served.

Today, Sharia relates also to practices which have their origins in custom, and most of the law has been codified.

In Muslim societies, the interpretation and implementation of Sharia law differs significantly. Seen as a significant cause of this is colonialisation. The relevance of Sharia law has been questioned. Today, some of the countries with the largest Muslim populations have only a few Sharia law provisions in the area of family law, and beyond this, have mainly secular constitutions and laws. These countries include Pakistan, Indonesia and Bangladesh.

A system made up of secular courts and religious courts is found in most North African and Middle East countries.

It is believed that Sharia law must provide fully for a person's spiritual and physical well-being. On this basis, it must be comprehensive.

Five categories of action are identified. The Five Pillars of Islam. These are:

(1) the shahadah (creed)

(2) the salat (daily prayers)

(3) sawm (fasting during Ramadan)

(4) zakah (almsgiving)

(5) hajj (pilgrimage to Mecca).

Sharia law can be seen as divided principally into two parts.

(1) The first relates to religion and worship. This includes prayers, pilgrimage to Mecca and fasting.

(2) The second part includes court process and the judiciary. This includes the admissibility of forms of evidence and rules relating to witnesses.

Areas that have been distinctly identified within Sharia law are:

A Family law matters.
(Within this area, marriage, divorce and child care are included. Also, the laws of inheritance and endowments.)

B Financial/commercial transactions.

C Peace and warfare.

D Penal punishments.

E Obligations related to food and drinks.

Supplementary reading

Features of Sharia law are noteworthy acknowledging that interpretations can vary. These include:

Freedom of speech

Examples of a denial of freedom of speech can be found. On strict interpretation, criticism of the Prophet Muhammad is not allowed. Individual countries also provide examples of limitations to this freedom. One example is Egypt where public authorities tried to annul the marriage of a professor without his consent. The basis of this attempted annulment of marriage was because his reading of the Qur'an was condemned as being against the acknowledged orthodox interpretation.

Muslim apostates

Apostasy is likened to the crime of treason in Muslim theology. Conversion of Muslims to another religion is one some interpret as forbidden. The consequences of a person converting to another religion depends notably on the country in which they live. If a person lives in a Western country or indeed in a significant number of Muslim countries, they will suffer no penalty or no significant penalty.

Dietary laws

Obligations exist in relation to the eating of meat. Stringent dietary requirements and a need for animals to be killed in the name of God apply on a strict interpretation. Also, the eating of pork is prohibited.

The role of women

Restrictions can be found in relation to the right to work, becoming a cleric or religious scholar, and marriage. Again, bearing in mind differing interpretations and attitudes we can see numerous examples of where any such limitations are minimal or do not exist. The non-Sharia Muslim countries of Turkey, Bangladesh and Pakistan provide good examples of where women have held the position of head of government or head of state. The post of head of Pakistan's Central Bank has been held by a woman. Also, the Pakistan army appointed a woman to the position of General and in so doing, made her the first woman in the world to hold such a position.

International legal relations

Whilst countries have their own domestic laws and legal systems, international law has developed which relates to the dealings between nations.

Public international law relates to the dealings of states between each other and the subjects and citizens of the states.

Private international law relates to issues involving private individuals where the relevant situation relates to more than one state.

Public and private international law can overlap. International law requires the recognition and acceptance by the relevant states. The primary sources of international law are customs and convention laws.

Where a number of states follow practices and procedures consistently out of a recognised obligation, customary international law will emerge. International law can then be found in the formal recognition and adoption of such common practices. The Vienna Convention on the Law of Treaties is an example of codifying, and so formalising, customary law. International agreements can take whatever form the participating parties wish to. Such agreements establish law binding on the parties to such agreements.

Just as individual countries or states can be parties to international agreements dealing with, for example, rights of the individual and standards of justice, so organisations can develop agreements that are binding on an international scale.

Commercial dealings and professional practice can justify the need for cooperation within particular fields, and areas of activity can demand collective agreements on an international scale. Numerous international bodies have been formed which serve to address the need for uniformity in the practices, procedures and demands of particular professional practices as well as the regulation of dealings.

Through international cooperation and agreement on collective regulations regarding terminology, standards, procedures and technical demands, application can be simplified. Where countries harmonise applicable regulations, and so eliminate the differences that would otherwise be found in the various countries' domestic laws, fairness in obligations and rights are achieved.

Supplementary reading

The Chartered Institute of Management Accountants is a body active in promoting the international dimension.

The following is an extract from online CIMA material:

'CIMA is a member of the International Federation of Accountants (IFAC), which is the global organisation for the accountancy profession. The aim of IFAC's Professional Accountants in Business (PAIB) Committee is to evolve the global development and exchange of knowledge and best practice. PAIB also build public awareness of the value of professional accountants. Bill Connell, Chairman of CIMA's Technical Committee, chairs the PAIB, and Charles Tilley, CIMA's Chief Executive is a member of the chief IFAC Board.

'CIMA is also a member of the European Federation of Accountants (FEE), which gives us an influence on the developments of the European Commission, the European Financial Reporting Advisory Group and other key bodies at the European Union. CIMA has quarterly meetings with the UK Department for Business, Innovation and Skills, formerly known as the Department of Trade and Industry. We are currently promoting the public affairs content of our research and development more heavily, and we will continue to increase our contact with ministers and MPs to raise the profile of our work as a membership body.'

International legal regulations applicable within areas of professional activity serve to remove barriers for individuals wishing to move from one country to another and work using their expertise. Recognition of qualifications not only in the field of accounting but also in the field of law, medicine and engineering assist the individuals and countries in achieving progress and high standards comparable around the world. Such regulations are also necessary to aid commercial activity. Many companies trade on a global scale and are aided by the uniformity in rights and obligations that emerge through the establishing of regulations applicable within particular fields of activity.

Supplementary reading: Chapter summary

At the end of this chapter, students should make sure that they are familiar with the following material:

- the differences between civil law and criminal law
- the sources of English Law – in particular:
  - judicial precedent
  - legislation
  - European Union law
- the hierarchy and jurisdiction of courts should be noted (this relates to study of judicial precedent and its application)
- elements of the tort of negligence and how judicial precedent applies to this area. Negligence can often be the subject of examination questions. The tort of negligence in relation to professional advisers is of particular importance
- the legal systems of other countries including (codified) civil law systems, noting the elements and distinguishing features
- Sharia law
- International legal regulations.

5 Test your understanding questions

Test your understanding 1

Which one of the following identifies civil proceedings?

A A prosecution for murder

B An action by a claimant for £1 million damages for fraudulent misrepresentation

C Proceedings where the accused is tried for the offence of applying a false trade description to goods

D A prosecution by HMRC for non-payment of tax

Test your understanding 2

Which one of the following statements is correct?

A The aim of the criminal law is to regulate behaviour within society by the threat of punishment

B The aim of the criminal law is to punish offenders

C The aim of the criminal law is to provide a means whereby injured persons may obtain compensation

D The aim of the criminal law is to ensure that the will of the majority is imposed on the minority

Test your understanding 3

Which of the following statements is correct?

(i) In the event of a conflict between equity and the common law, the common law prevails.

(ii) An Act of Parliament can overrule any common law or equitable rule.

A (i) only

B (ii) only

C Neither (i) nor (ii)

D Both (i) and (ii)

Test your understanding 4

All criminal cases commence in:

A the County Court

B the Crown Court

C the Court of Appeal

D the Magistrates Court

Test your understanding 5

Which of the following is not a division of the High Court?

A The Chancery Division

B The Family Division

C The Queen's Bench Division

D The Supreme Division

Test your understanding 6

Which of the following most closely expresses the ratio decidendi of Donoghue v Stevenson?

A A manufacturer of drinks must not deliberately put a snail in the bottle

B Everyone must be nice to his neighbours

C A claimant who only suffers financial loss cannot recover damages for negligence

D A manufacturer owes a duty of care to those who he should reasonably foresee might be physically injured by his products

Test your understanding 7

In Caparo Industries plc v Dickman (1991) (which was a Supreme Court decision), previous Supreme Court decisions constituting precedents were not followed. The relevant facts of the previous cases involved the making of inaccurate statements to one identified party by a defendant who knew that the statements would be relied upon.

What means were used in Caparo v Dickman to avoid following the existing Supreme Court precedents?

A Distinguishing

B Reversing

C Overruling

D Disapproving

Test your understanding 8

Which court will deal with an appeal from the Magistrates Court on a question of law?

A Crown Court

B High Court

C Court of Appeal

D Supreme Court

Test your understanding 9

What does the 'literal rule' of statutory interpretation mean?

A Words should be given their ordinary meaning

B The meaning of the words can be gathered from their context

C Words should be given the meaning which is likely to give effect to the purpose or reform which the statute intended

D Words should be given their ordinary grammatical meaning unless the meaning is manifestly absurd

Test your understanding 10

Which one of the following is delegated legislation?

(i) a statutory instrument.

(ii) a civil service memorandum.

(iii) a County Court judgment.

(iv) the Finance Act.

(v) the motor vehicles (Construction and Use) Regulations made under the Road Traffic Acts.

(vi) the articles of association of a company.

A (i) (ii) and (iv)

B (i) and (iii)

C (i) and (v)

D (ii) and (vi)

Test your understanding 11

A passenger in a car is injured in an accident caused by the negligence of the driver of another vehicle. The passenger was not wearing a seatbelt.

What effect would this have on any claim which he might have against the other driver for negligence?

A No effect because the other driver did not know that the passenger was not wearing his seatbelt

B It defeats his claim; he is the sole author of his own misfortune

C His own driver must bear the loss, because he did not insist that the passenger should wear a seatbelt

D The court will have power to reduce the passenger's damages against the other driver by such amount as the court thinks fit

Test your understanding 12

Which one of the following does not provide codified law?

A A Constitution

B Regulations

C Case Law

D Legislation

Test your understanding 13

Which one of the following areas of law is not codified in France?

A Contract Law

B Employment Law

C Company Law

D Tort

Test your understanding 14

Which one of the following countries has a legal system based on English Common Law, Islamic Law and Napoleonic codes?

A Nigeria

B Egypt

C Pakistan

D Greece

Test your understanding 15

Which one of the following institutions of the European Union proposes new legislation that is to apply to its member states?

A The European Commission

B The European Parliament

C The Court of Justice of the European Communities

D The Council of the European Union

Test your understanding 16

(a) The most superior domestic court is the . . . . . . (2 words) **(1 mark)** The . . . . . . (2 words) **(1 mark)** is a court made up of three divisions, the Queen's Bench, Family and Chancery divisions. The . . . . . . (3 words) **(1 mark)** is a court which has a civil division and criminal division.

(3 marks)

(b) Complete the following:

. . . . . . (1 word) **(2 marks)** is the supreme source of English law. However, if its provisions should contradict law of the . . . . . . (2 words) **(2 marks)** the latter will prevail.

(4 marks)

(Total: 7 marks)

Test your understanding 17

(a) In order to succeed in an action for negligence it is necessary to establish a . . . . (3 words) **(1 mark)** owed, secondly a . . . . (3 words) **(1 mark)** and finally . . . . . . (1 word) **(1 mark)**

(3 marks)

(b) Complete the following:

In the tort of negligence, the principle of . . . . . . (3 words) **(2 marks)** means that 'the thing speaks for itself'. Where this principle applies, the . . . . . . (3 words) **(1 mark)** is shifted on to the . . . . . . (1 word) **(1 mark)** who must show that he or she was not negligent in order to avoid liability.

(4 marks)

(c) Complete the following:

Under the doctrine of judicial precedent, the . . . . . . (2 words) **(2 marks)** of the case is binding upon lower courts whereas the . . . . . . (2 words) **(2 marks)** is not binding and is said to be of persuasive authority only.

(4 marks)

(Total: 11 marks)

Test your understanding 18

(a) When judges are interpreting legislation, application of the . . . . . . (1 word) **(1 mark)** rule can result in an absurd outcome. By using the . . . . . . (1 word) **(1 mark)** rule an absurd outcome can be avoided.

(2 marks)

(b) The Rules of Language include *eiusdem generis* under which judges can identify the meaning of . . . . . . (1 word) **(1 mark)** words in a statute from the meaning of . . . . . . (1 word) **(1 mark)** words found.

(2 marks)

(c) When interpreting legislation, the judiciary can rely on certain presumptions. These include the presumptions that . . . . . . (2 words) **(1 mark)** will not be bound by the relevant legislation and that the legislation will not have . . . . . . (2 words) **(1 mark)**

(2 marks)

(Total: 6 marks)

Test your understanding answers

Test your understanding 1

B

The prosecution for murder is plainly criminal (A). The terms used in (C) make it plain that this is criminal ('accused', 'tried', 'offence'). Similarly, in (C), the term 'prosecution' makes it plain that this is criminal. In (B), the terms used ('action', 'claimant', 'damages') make it clear that these are the civil proceedings.

Test your understanding 2

A

(B) is incorrect as the punishment of offenders is a feature of criminal law, but not the sole aim. Compensation identified in (C) is a remedy in civil actions. Further, the majority will being imposed on the minority is not an aim of the criminal law.

Test your understanding 3

B

In the event of a conflict equity will prevail. Therefore (A) and (D) are incorrect. Common Law or an equitable rule can be overruled by an Act of Parliament. Therefore (C) cannot be correct.

Test your understanding 4

D

(A) is incorrect as the County Court deals with civil actions. Criminal actions are heard in the Crown Court. However criminal actions do not commence in this court, therefore (B) is incorrect. The Court of Appeal hears matters on appeal from lower courts, so (C) cannot be correct.

Test your understanding 5

D

The other three are divisions of the High Court.

Test your understanding 6

D

(A) is much narrower than the ratio decidendi of Donoghue v Stevenson. The case is not limited to decomposed snails, or to drinks or to bottles. Moreover, the facts are different; for example, it was never suggested that the manufacturer deliberately placed a snail in the bottle. (B) is very different from the ratio decidendi of Donoghue v Stevenson. (C) has very little to do with Donoghue v Stevenson; it became an important issue in some later cases, but even in these the statement is not wholly accurate.

Test your understanding 7

A

This was not an appeal from any of the other decisions; it was an entirely separate case. Therefore, the earlier decisions were not 'reversed' (B). 'Disapproving' an earlier decision is a mere expression of opinion by the present court, *in obiter dicta*; it is not a valid reason to disregard a precedent (D). The earlier cases were not 'overruled' (C) (even if they could be); indeed, the House of Lords, in the Caparo case, did not suggest that the earlier decisions were wrong, only that the material facts were different from those before the court now.

Test your understanding 8

B

An appeal on a question of fact will go to the Crown Court.

Test your understanding 9

A

Under the literal rule words are given their ordinary dictionary meaning.

Test your understanding 10

C

Memoranda are not legislation, neither are county court judgments which are judicial decisions. The Finance Act is primary legislation and articles of association are the internal regulations of a limited company agreed by the shareholders. It follows that the correct solution is (C).

Test your understanding 11

D

(A) is of no effect, because the other driver still owed a duty of care to the passenger. (B) does not alter the fact that the passenger's injury is partly caused by the other driver. (C) is irrelevant to any claim by the passenger against the other driver. (D) is an example of probable contributory negligence.

Test your understanding 12

C

Codified law is found in a comprehensive collection of documents. A Constitution, legislation and regulation can all provide or contribute towards codified law. Case law decisions provide an interpretation of stated law and show the application of law, usually with a hierarchy of courts recognised that is relevant in the application of precedent. Case law is therefore an exception.

Test your understanding 13

D

Much of French Law is codified but one area that provides a notable exception is Tort.

Test your understanding 14

B

Nigeria and Pakistan have legal systems based on English Common Law with an influence of Islamic Law, but the Napoleonic codes have not contributed to the development of these systems. (A) and (C) are therefore not the correct answers. Greece has a legal system based principally on codified Roman Law, so (D) is not the correct answer. It is Egypt that has been influenced by English and Islamic laws as well as the Napoleonic codes, so (B) is the correct answer.

Test your understanding 15

A

The European Parliament and the Council of the European Union are bodies that pass new laws which are proposed by the European Commission. (A) is therefore the correct answer. The Court of Justice of the European Communities has a role aiding interpretation of the law, but does not propose new law.

Test your understanding 16

(a) The most superior domestic court is the Supreme Court. The High Court is a court made up of three divisions, the Queen's Bench, Family and Chancery divisions. The Court of Appeal is a court which has a civil division and a criminal division.

(b) Legislation is the supreme source of English law. However, if its provisions should contradict law of the European union, the latter will prevail.

Test your understanding 17

(a) In order to succeed in an action for negligence it is necessary first, to establish a duty of care owed, second, a breach of duty and finally, damage.

(b) In the tort of negligence, the principle of *res ipsa loquitur* means that 'the thing speaks for itself'. Where this principle applies the burden of proof is shifted on to the defendant who must show that he or she was not negligent in order to avoid liability.

(c) Under the doctrine of judicial precedent, the *ratio decidendi* of the case is binding upon lower courts whereas *obiter dicta* is not binding and is said to be of persuasive authority only.

Test your understanding 18

(a) When judges are interpreting legislation, application of the literal rule can result in an absurd outcome. By using the golden rule an absurd outcome can be avoided.

(b) The Rules of Language include *eiusdem generis* under which judges can identify the meaning of general words in a statute from the meaning of the particular words found.

(c) When interpreting legislation, the judiciary can rely on certain presumptions. These include the presumptions that the Crown will not be bound by the relevant legislation and that the legislation will not have retrospective effect.

chapter

2

The Law of Contract

Chapter learning objectives

After completing this chapter you should be able to:

- identify the essential elements of a valid simple contract and situations where the law requires the contract to be in a particular form
- explain how the law determines whether negotiating parties have reached agreement and the role of consideration in making that agreement enforceable
- explain when the parties will be regarded as intending the agreement to be legally binding and how an agreement may be avoided because of misrepresentations
- describe how the law controls the use of excluding, limiting and unfair terms
- explain the remedies which are available for serious and minor breaches of contract.

1 Contractual obligations

A contract is an agreement which the law will recognise. As will be seen throughout this text, it is of vital importance in business life, and forms the basis of most commercial transactions such as dealings in land and goods, credit, insurance, carriage of goods, the formation and sale of business organisations, and employment.

The essential elements of a valid simple contract

A contract is a legally enforceable agreement. It may be in writing or it may even be implied from the conduct of the parties. For example, all of the following everyday transactions are contracts: purchasing a newspaper, buying a bus or rail ticket, purchasing a sandwich and a drink at lunchtime, buying a book or a CD, going to the cinema, the theatre or a football game.

To amount to a valid contract, the following essential elements must be present:

(i) **Agreement**. The parties must be in agreement. Whether they are in agreement is usually determined by the presence of an offer by one party which has been accepted by the other.

(ii) **Consideration**. A contract in English law must be a two-sided bargain, each side providing or promising to provide some consideration in return for what the other is to provide. Only a promise made by deed can be binding if there is no consideration.

(iii) **Intention to create legal relations**. The parties must clearly have intended their agreement to be legally binding. For example, a mere social arrangement – such as an agreement with a friend to meet for a meal – will not normally be treated as a contract.

(iv) **Reality of the consent**. This element relates back to 'agreement'. The parties must have freely entered into their agreement.

(v) **Capacity to contract**. Each party must have the legal power to bind itself contractually. For example persons under the age of eighteen and persons of unsound mind or under the influence of alcohol have limitations on their power to contract.

(vi) **Legality**. Illegality can often invalidate a contract. Certainly some agreements which are *wholly* illegal – such as agreements to commit a murder – will not be recognised as valid contracts.

Form of the contract

There is a common misconception that a valid contract must be in writing. In fact, as stated above, most contracts are made verbally. A contract which does not need to be in a particular form is referred to as a **simple contract**.

It may be desirable to have a written agreement where a lot is at stake, or where the contract is to last for a long time, but this is only for purposes of proof and is not necessary for validity.

Certain contracts must be in writing or they will be *void.* These include bills of exchange, cheques and promissory notes, contracts of marine insurance, the transfer of shares in a company, and legal assignment of debts.

Hire purchase and other regulated consumer credit agreements may be unenforceable against a borrower unless they are made in writing and include the information required by the Consumer Credit Act 1974. Contracts of guarantee need not be in writing but they are unenforceable in the courts unless there is written evidence of the essential terms and they are signed by or on behalf of the guarantor.

Specialty contracts

Some transactions must be made by a formal document known as a deed. This must be signed, attested by a witness who also signs, and delivered. 'Delivery' means an intention to put the deed into effect rather than physically handing it over. Deeds are required for the validity of promises for no consideration, and some bills of sale (mortgages of goods).

Supplementary reading

Special rules apply to land where a transfer normally takes place in two stages. The parties will first contract to sell or lease the land. Under the Law of Property (Miscellaneous Provisions) Act 1989, this contract must be made in writing in a signed document which 'incorporates' all the terms which the parties have expressly agreed; the terms can either be set out in the document itself or be included by reference to other documents. In practice, two identical documents are prepared, each signed by one of the parties, and then handed over to the other party with a deposit paid by the purchaser. These formalities do not apply to sales by public auction.

The second stage is the completion of the transaction by conveying the title of the land to the purchaser in return for payment of (the rest of) the price. This conveyance must be by deed if the land is sold or leased for more than 3 years.

2 Agreement

Agreement is usually shown by the unconditional acceptance of a firm offer. It marks the conclusion of negotiations, and thereafter, any withdrawal will constitute a breach of contract. The rules governing offer and acceptance will be examined in turn.

Offer

An offer is a definite and unequivocal statement of willingness to be bound on specified terms without further negotiations.

An offer can be in any form – oral, written or by conduct. However, it is not effective until it has been communicated to the offeree. For example, if a reward is offered for the return of a lost item, it cannot be claimed by someone who did not know of the reward before they returned the item.

An offer can be made to a particular person, to a class of persons or even to the whole world – **Carlill v Carbolic Smoke Ball Co (1893)**.

What is not an offer?

Offers must be distinguished from other actions which may appear to be similar.

(1) An invitation to treat is not an offer.

An invitation to treat means an invitation to the other party to make an offer; e.g. 'we may be prepared to sell' – **Gibson v Manchester City Council (1979)**. An invitation to treat cannot be accepted to form a valid contract.

Examples of invitations to treat

Most advertisements

General rule – an advertisement is an invitation to treat, not an offer, as shown in:

Partridge v Crittenden (1968)

Facts: The defendant put the following advertisement in a magazine: 'Bramblefinch cocks and hens, 25s each'. The Protection of Birds Act 1954 made it an offence to offer such birds for sale.

Held: This was an invitation to treat and not an offer. The advertisement stated that the birds were for sale, not that the seller would sell to all comers. The defendant was therefore not in contravention of the Act.

Exception to an advertisement not being an offer

Note, however, that it would be an offer if no further negotiations were intended or expected. This is the position in **Carlill v Carbolic Smoke Ball Co (1893)**, where the advertisers made it clear that they would pay money to anyone complying with the terms of the advertisement.

Carlill v Carbolic Smoke Ball Co (1893)

Facts: The manufacturers of a medicinal 'smoke ball' advertised in a newspaper that anyone who bought and used the ball properly and nevertheless contracted influenza would be paid a £100 reward. Mrs Carlill used the ball as directed and did catch influenza. The defendant claimed that there was no enforceable contract because:

(i) this was not an offer but a "mere puff or boast" not intended to be taken seriously

(ii) even if it was an offer it was not made to an individual and it is not possible to make an offer to the whole world

(iii) even if it is possible to make an offer to the whole world, Mrs Carlill did not communicate her acceptance of the offer to the company.

Held: The court rejected the defendants argument on the basis that:

(i) normally advertisements are mere puffs or boasts but this advert was so detailed a reasonable person would consider it to contain an offer, particularly as it states "...£1,000 is deposited with the Alliance Bank Regent Street to show our sincerity in this matter." (The Alliance was a real bank – the advert is reproduced below)

(ii) it is possible to make an offer to the whole world, the contract being formed with the limited number of people who come forward and perform the condition on the faith of the advertisement

(iii) although the general rule is that acceptance of an offer must be communicated, there are exceptions where the offeror may expressly or impliedly waive the need to do so. This was a unilateral contract which was formed when the offeree carried out the required act (using the smokeball as prescribed) and there was no need to communicate acceptance.

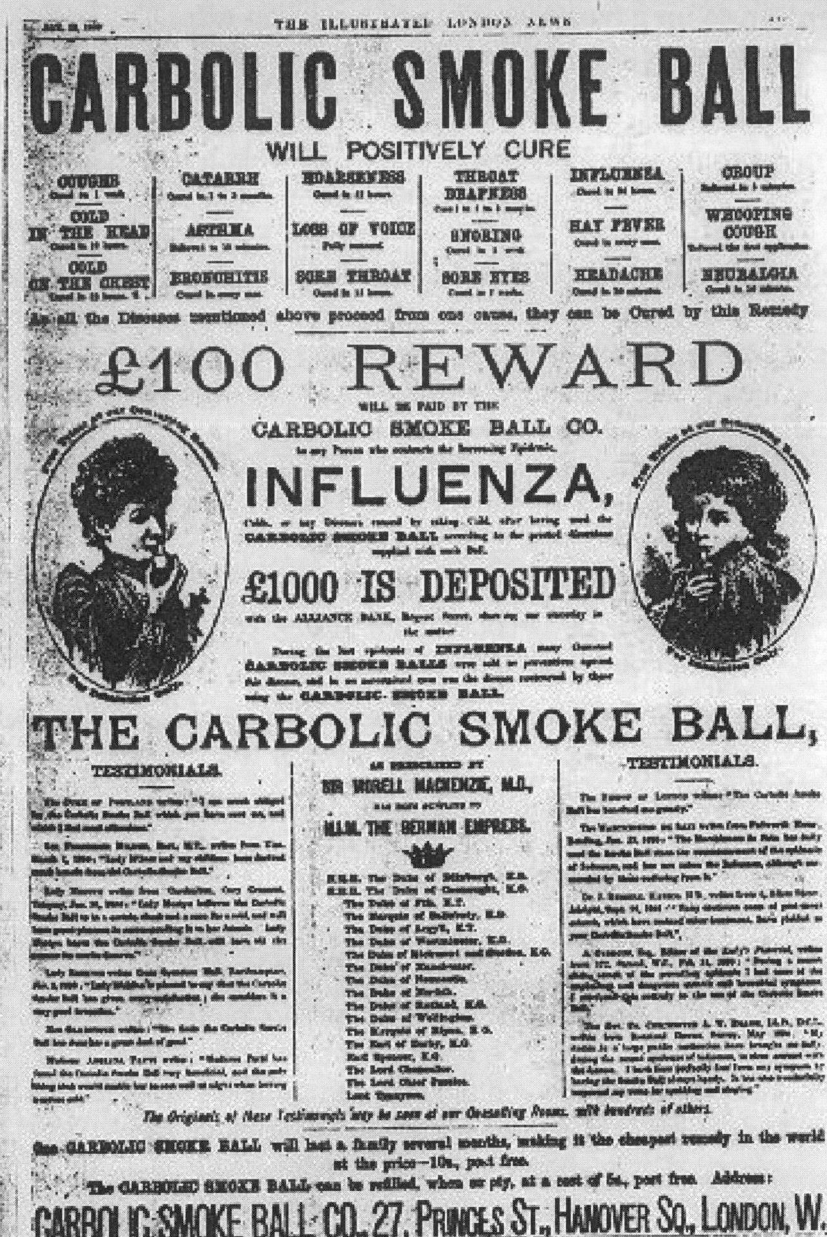

THE ILLUSTRATED LONDON NEWS

CARBOLIC SMOKE BALL

WILL POSITIVELY CURE

COUGHS — COLD IN THE HEAD — COLD ON THE CHEST — CATARRH — ASTHMA — BRONCHITIS — HOARSENESS — LOSS OF VOICE — SORE THROAT — THROAT DEAFNESS — SNORING — SORE EYES — INFLUENZA — HAY FEVER — HEADACHE — CROUP — WHOOPING COUGH — NEURALGIA

As all the Diseases mentioned above proceed from one cause, they can be Cured by this Remedy

£100 REWARD

WILL BE PAID BY THE

CARBOLIC SMOKE BALL CO.

INFLUENZA,

£1000 IS DEPOSITED

THE CARBOLIC SMOKE BALL,

TESTIMONIALS.

SIR MORELL MACKENZIE, M.D.,

H.I.M. THE GERMAN EMPRESS.

TESTIMONIALS.

CARBOLIC SMOKE BALL CO., 27, PRINCES ST., HANOVER SQ., LONDON, W.

Shop window displays

Fisher v Bell (1961)

Facts: The Restriction of Offensive Weapons Act 1959 creates a criminal offence of 'offering for sale' certain offensive weapons. A shopkeeper was prosecuted under this statute for displaying a flick knife in his shop window, and thus 'offering it for sale'.

Held: A window display was not an offer of sale, but only an invitation to treat. So the display did not infringe the law.

Goods on shop shelves

Pharmaceutical Society of Great Britain v Boots Cash Chemists (1953)

Facts: Statute requires that the sale of certain pharmaceuticals must be carried out under the supervision of a qualified pharmacist. Boots operated a store where the drugs were displayed on a self-service basis and the customers paid at a cash desk for the goods they had selected. A pharmacist was present at the cash desk but not at the shelves where the goods were displayed with a price tag. The Pharmaceutical Society claimed that the statute was being contravened.

Held: The display of goods in a shop was not an offer, but an invitation to treat. It was the customer who made the offer and Boots could either accept or reject this offer at the cash desk (in the presence of the qualified pharmacist). The act constituting the acceptance is the ringing up of the price on the till by the cashier and at that moment a binding contract of sale is made.

Supplementary reading

A **tender** arises where one party issues a statement asking interested parties to submit the terms on which they are willing to carry out work or supply goods. The person inviting the tender is simply making an invitation to treat. The person submitting a tender is the offeror and the other party is free to accept or reject the offer as they please.

The effect of acceptance depends upon the wording of the invitation to tender. If the invitation states that the potential purchaser **will require** a certain quantity of goods, acceptance of a tender will form a contract and they will be in breach if they fail to order the stated quantity from the person submitting the tender.

If, on the other hand, the invitation states only that the potential purchaser **may require** goods, acceptance gives rise only to a standing offer. In this situation there is no compulsion on the purchaser to take any goods, but they must not deal with any other supplier. Each order forms a separate contract and the supplier must deliver any goods required within the time stated in the tender. The supplier can revoke the standing offer, but they must supply any goods already ordered **(Great Northern Railway v Witham (1873))**.

(2) A **mere statement of selling price** in response to a request for information is not an offer.

Harvey v Facey (1893)

Facts: The claimant (H) sent the defendant (F) a telegram stating: "Will you sell us Bumper Hall Pen? Telegraph lowest cash price-answer paid." On the same day, F sent H a reply by telegram stating: "Lowest price for Bumper Hall Pen £900." H sent F another telegram agreeing to purchase the property at the asking price. F refused to sell and H sued for specific performance and an injunction to prevent the new buyer from taking the property.

Held: The court held that by replying to H's question regarding the lowest price of the property, F did not make an affirmative answer to the first question regarding his willingness to sell. The defendant's response to the query was simply a statement of information. It was not an offer capable of being accepted by the claimant.

(3) A **mere statement of intention to sell** is not an offer.

Harris v Nickerson (1873)

Facts: The defendant placed an advertisement in London papers that certain items, including some office furniture would be placed up for auction over three days. The claimant obtained a commission to buy the office furniture and expended time and expense to travel to bid for the office furniture. On the third day, the lots for the office furniture were withdrawn. The claimant sued for loss of time and expense.

Held: An advertisement that goods will be put up for auction does not constitute an offer to any person that the goods will actually be put up, and that the advertiser is therefore free to withdraw the goods from the auction at any time prior to the auction.

Termination of an offer

Once an offer has been terminated, it cannot be accepted. An offer can be terminated by:

- revocation
- rejection
- lapse.

Revocation

Revocation by the offeror can be made at any time before acceptance, even if the offeror has agreed to keep the offer open.

Routledge v Grant (1828)

Facts: G offered to buy R's horse and stated that the offer would remain open for six weeks. However, before the six-week period had elapsed, G withdrew the offer.

Held: G was entitled to withdraw the offer at any time before acceptance.

The revocation must be communicated to the offeree, i.e. it must be brought to his actual notice.

Byrne v Leon Van Tienhoven (1880)

Facts: An offer was posted on 1 October. It reached the claimant on 11 October. The claimant immediately cabled his acceptance. In the meantime, the defendant had changed his mind and posted a letter of revocation on 8 October. The revocation was received by the claimant after he had cabled his acceptance.

Held: The revocation did not take effect as it was not communicated to the claimant prior to his acceptance. The contract was therefore binding.

The revocation can be communicated by the offeror or a reliable third party.

Dickinson v Dodds (1876)

Facts: The defendant agreed to keep an offer open for two days. However, in the meantime the defendant sold the property to a third party. The offeree was told of the sale by a third party, but then attempted to accept the original offer.

Held: This was a reasonable way of communicating revocation. The offer was therefore properly revoked and could not be accepted.

There are two exceptions to the above rules on revocation:

- If the offeree pays the offeror to keep the offer open, any revocation will amount to a breach of that collateral contract. The offeree could claim damages for the loss of the opportunity to accept the offer, although he could not accept the offer itself.
- In the case of a unilateral/option contract, the offeror cannot revoke his offer once the offeree has begun to perform the acts which would amount to acceptance.

Errington v Errington (1952)

Facts: A father offered to transfer his house to his son if the son paid the mortgage. The son began to pay the mortgage but, when the father died, his personal representatives wanted to withdraw the offer.

Held: The offer could not be withdrawn because the son, by paying some of the instalments, had started acceptance.

Rejection

Rejection by the offeree may be outright or by means of a counter-offer. A counter-offer is an offer made in response to an offer.

Hyde v Wrench (1840)

Facts: Wrench offered to sell Hyde a farm for £1,000. Hyde made a counter-offer, by offering £950. Wrench rejected this. Later Hyde came back and said that he now accepted the original offer of £1,000. Wrench rejected it.

Held: Hyde could no longer accept the original offer. It had been terminated by the counter-offer and was no longer capable of acceptance. His 'acceptance' was merely a fresh offer which Wrench was free to turn down.

Note that a mere request for further details does not constitute a counter-offer.

Stevenson v McLean (1880)

Facts: M offered, in writing, to sell a quantity of iron to S at a given price. S replied querying delivery times, but before receiving a reply sent a further letter accepting the offer. This acceptance crossed in the post with a letter of revocation from M to S. M refused to supply the iron to S, arguing that S's query was a counter-offer.

Held: M could not treat the query as a counter-offer. S had not intended to prejudice M's position, just to establish the boundaries of the deal. Therefore M's offer was still open when S wrote accepting it.

Lapse

An offer will lapse on:

- the death of the offeror (unless the offeree accepts in ignorance of the death)
- the death of the offeree
- after the expiry of a fixed time (if any) or after a reasonable time. What is a reasonable time may depend on the subject matter of the contract.

Ramsgate Victoria Hotel Co v Montefiore (1866)

Facts: The defendant applied to the company to buy some shares in June and paid a deposit. He didn't hear anything until November when the company sent him a letter of allotment as acceptance and a request for the balance. By this time the defendant had changed his mind and no longer wanted the shares.

Held: The offer was for a reasonable time only and since five months had passed since the offer had been made the offer was deemed to have lapsed. The defendant was not bound to buy the shares. Their value could have changed dramatically in such a long period.

If the goods are perishable the time for lapse will be very short.

Acceptance

Acceptance is the unqualified and unconditional assent to all the terms of the offer.

It can be oral, written or by conduct – **Carlill v Carbolic Smoke Ball (1893)**.

The offeror can stipulate a particular mode of acceptance. However, if he merely requests a mode, the offeree is not limited to that mode.

Communication

As a general rule, acceptance is not effective until it is communicated to the offeror.

Entores v Miles Far Eastern (1955)

Facts: The claimants, who were based in London, made an offer by telex to the defendants in Amsterdam. The defendants accepted by telex. The point at issue was where the acceptance had taken place, i.e. in Amsterdam at the time the defendants sent the telex or in London when it was received. It can be important to know which country the contract was concluded in as different countries have different legal rules.

Held: Acceptance is not effective until it is communicated. Therefore the contract was made in London.

The following conclusions can be drawn from the **Entores** case:

- If a fax, telex or telephone message is received during normal business hours, that is when it is communicated even though it might not be read until later.
- If a fax, telex or telephone message is received outside normal business hours, it is deemed to be communicated when the business next opens.

Note, in addition, that the offeror can expressly or impliedly dispense with the need for communication – **Carlill v Carbolic Smoke Ball (1893)**. However, he cannot impose silence as the means of acceptance of an offer.

Felthouse v Bindley (1863)

Facts: The claimant was interested in buying a horse and had discussed with his nephew the purchase of a horse belonging to him. The claimant wrote to his nephew and stated in this letter that he assumed the horse was his for £30.15 if he did not receive a response from his nephew. The nephew did not reply, and instructed the defendant, an auctioneer he had engaged to conduct a sale of his farming stock, to withhold the horse from the auction. By mistake, the defendant allowed the horse to be put up and sold. The claimant sued the auctioneer in the tort of conversion in an attempt to recover the horse. He argued that the auctioneer had no power to sell the horse which has become his by a contract between himself and his nephew.

Held: An acceptance of an offer will not give rise to a binding agreement unless it is expressly communicated to the individual who makes the offer. Although the nephew had the intent to sell his horse to the claimant at the offered price, he did not communicate this intention to his uncle, or do anything to bind himself. Since ownership of the horse had not passed to the claimant he could not succeed in his action against the auctioneer.

The postal rule

The postal rule is an exception to the rule that acceptance must be communicated.

The postal rule states that acceptance is complete as soon as the letter is posted.

Adams v Lindsell (1818)

Facts: The case involved two parties in the sale of wool. On 2 September, the defendants wrote to the claimants offering to sell them certain fleeces of wool and requiring an answer in the course of post. The defendants, misdirected the letter so that the claimants didn't receive it until 5 September. The claimants posted their acceptance on the same day but it was not received until 9 September. Meanwhile, on 8 September, the defendants, not having received an answer by 7 September as they had expected, sold the wool to someone else.

Held: The question for the court was whether a contract of sale had been entered into before 8 September when the wool was sold to the third party. If the acceptance was effective when it arrived at the address or when the defendant saw it, then no contract would have been made and the sale to the third party would amount to revocation of the offer. However, the court held that the offer had been accepted as soon as the letter had been posted. The defendant was therefore liable in breach of contract.

However, the postal rule only applies if:

- the letter is properly stamped, addressed and posted, and
- post is a reasonable method of communication.

It applies even if the letter is never received by the offeror.

Household Fire Insurance v Grant (1879)

Facts: G applied for shares in HFI. HFI posted a share allotment letter to G, accepting his offer. The letter was not received.

Held: Once the letter was posted, HFI could not recall it. They had accepted G's offer to take shares.

However, the postal rule does not apply if the offeror states that he must receive 'notice in writing' or otherwise specifies that the acceptance must be received – **Holwell Securities v Hughes (1974)**.

Email communication

As seen above in **Entores v Miles Far Eastern (1955)** the postal rule does not apply to instantaneous communication. The now commonplace use of email raises the question of whether the "postal acceptance rule" applies to emailed acceptances. A consideration is whether an email constitutes instantaneous communication. Currently there is no definitive statutory law on this point.

The dangers of email exchange were highlighted in **NBTY Europe Ltd v Nutricia International BV(2005)** where the court upheld a binding agreement worth £2.5 million concluded by email, despite subsequent efforts by the defendant to withdraw its email acceptance.

3 Consideration

The basic rule

A contract must be a two-sided affair, each side providing or promising to provide some consideration in exchange for what the other is to provide. Each party must therefore provide consideration i.e. something of value to the other party.

It therefore stands that every simple contract must be supported by consideration from each party. This may take the form of an act, a forbearance to act, or a promise.

The exception is contracts made by deed (specialty contracts) which do not require consideration unless the terms of the agreement require it.

Types of consideration

Executory consideration is given where there is an exchange of promises to do something in the future.

For example, when a person agrees to pay for some goods 'cash on delivery'. Both the payment and the delivery are 'executory', i.e. to be completed at a later date.

Executed consideration means that the consideration is in the form of an act carried out at the time the contract is made.

For example, handing over 60p and receiving a newspaper. Both the payment and the handing over of the paper are executed at the time of the contract.

Sufficient consideration

Consideration must be sufficient but need not be adequate.

Sufficient means that:

- there must be some monetary value to the consideration
- it must be capable in law of amounting to consideration.

The words 'need not be adequate' mean that there is no need for each party's consideration to be equal in value.

Chappell v Nestle Co Ltd (1959)

Facts: Records were sold for 1s 6d plus three chocolate wrappers.
Held: The wrappers were part of the consideration even though they had minimal value.

Thomas v Thomas (1842)

Facts: A promise to lease a house to a widow for rent of £1 a year was binding.
Held: The consideration had some value, and so was sufficient at law, even though it was inadequate as a years rent.

Past consideration

Past consideration is insufficient and therefore is **not valid**.

Consideration is past if the consideration is an act which has been wholly performed before the other party gives his promise.

Re McArdle (1951)

Facts: A mother and her three grown-up children lived together in a house. One of the sons and his wife did some decorating in the house and later the other two children promised to pay towards the decorating costs and signed a document to this effect.
Held: It was held that the promise was unenforceable as all the work had been done before the promise was made and was therefore past consideration.

However, the situation in **Re McArdle (1951)** can be contrasted with that in **Re Casey's Patent (1892)**.

Facts: A and B owned a patent and C was the manager who had worked on it for two years. A and B then promised C a one-third share in the invention for his help in developing it. The patents were transferred to C but A and B then claimed their return.

Held: C could rely on the agreement. Even though C's consideration was in the past, it had been done in a business situation, at the request of A and B and it was understood by both sides that C would be paid and the subsequent promise to pay merely fixed the amount. There was an implied promise to pay as the development of the patent had been requested by A and B.

Performance of an existing duty

As a general rule, performance of an existing statutory duty is not sufficient consideration.

Collins v Godefroy (1831)

Facts: A witness was promised payment if he would attend court and give evidence.

Held: This did not amount to consideration as he was legally required to attend court.

Similarly, performance of an existing contractual duty is not consideration.

Stilk v Myrick (1809)

Facts: A captain promised to share the wages of the deserting seamen with the rest of the crew who had contracted to sail the ship home.

Held: The promise was not binding as there was no extra consideration from the seamen, they were merely doing what they had contracted to do.

However, there are three exceptions:

(1) If the existing contractual or statutory duty is exceeded, there is sufficient consideration.

Glasbrook Bros Ltd v Glamorgan County Council (1925)

Facts: Glasbrook Bros Ltd requested the police to provide protection in excess of the statutory requirement.

Held: The police had provided sufficient consideration to give entitlement to remuneration by providing the extra officers over and above the statutory requirement.

Leeds United Football Club Ltd v Chief Constable of West Yorkshire Police (2012)

Facts: The police argued that they could charge for 'special police services' carried out in respect of 'trouble spots' outside Leeds United's football ground.

Held: Policing such areas was part of the general duty of the police to keep the peace and the cost should be paid out of public funds and not by Leeds United.

Hartley v Ponsonby (1857)

Facts: A high number of desertions from a merchant ship rendered the vessel unseaworthy since it was now undermanned. Extra pay was offered to the crew if they remained loyal and sailed the ship home.

Held: The promise of extra money was recoverable by the seamen who remained loyal, since they were now working in a dangerous situation not contemplated by their original contractual undertaking (i.e. they were doing more than required by their original contract).

(2) The performance of an existing contractual duty may be sufficient if it confers some benefit of a practical nature on the other party.

Williams v Roffey Bros (1990)

Facts: W agreed to do some carpentry in a block of flats for R at a fixed price of £20,000, by an agreed date. The contract contained a 'time penalty' clause and R agreed to pay an extra £10,000 to ensure that the work was completed on time. If the work had not been completed on time, R would have suffered a penalty in his own contract with the owner of the flats.

Held: The Court of Appeal decided that, even though W was in effect doing nothing over and above the original agreement to complete the work by an agreed time, there was a new contract here for the £10,000. The court decided that both W and R benefited from the new contract. Two reasons were given:

- Even though W merely did what he was already contracted to do, this nevertheless conferred a practical benefit on R in that R not only avoided penalties under the head contract, but also the cost and aggravation of employing substitute contractors.

- R's promise to pay the extra £10,000 had not been extracted by fraud or pressure. (It was R who had approached W and had volunteered the extra money.) It would be inequitable to go back on his promise.

(3) The performance of an existing contractual obligation is sufficient consideration to support a promise from a third party.

Shadwell v Shadwell (1860)

Facts: The claimant was engaged to E (at this time an engagement was an enforceable contract). The claimant's uncle wrote him a letter saying "I will pay you £150 per year during my life until your income as a barrister shall reach 600 guineas pa" if you marry E. When the uncle died the claimant sought to recover outstanding amounts. The deceased's personal representatives argued that the claimant was already under a contractual obligation to marry when the uncle made the offer, and therefore the claimant supplied no consideration.

Held: There was sufficient consideration as the uncle had promised the claimant a reward and in return the uncle had received a promise to which he previously had no right. The contract was between the claimant and E. The uncle was a third party and the claimant promised to marry E in consideration of the payments.

Illegal acts

An illegal act cannot amount to consideration.

The part-payment problem

The problem – if A accepts £400 from B in full and final settlement of a debt of £500, can A sue for the remaining £100?

General rule – the rule in **Pinnel's case (1602)** states that payment of less than the amount due cannot satisfy the full debt at common law. It may seem unfair that a person may go back on his word having accepted an offer of part payment in satisfaction of a debt. Clearly there is agreement between the parties. However, in English contract law an agreement is unenforceable unless it is supported by consideration. As can be seen in Pinnel's case, the courts decided as long ago as 1602 that paying less that the amount due did not amount to consideration. This has been affirmed in **Foakes v Beer (1884)**.

Foakes v Beer (1884)

Facts: Mrs Beer obtained a judgement against Dr Foakes for a sum of £2,090 with interest. She agreed to payment of the debt in instalments and also promised that further proceedings on the judgement would not be taken. After receiving the £2,090, Mrs Beer sued for £360 interest on the judgement debt which Dr Foakes refused to pay.

Held: The interest was recoverable. Payment of the debt and costs, a smaller sum, was not consideration for the promise to accept this amount in satisfaction of a debt, interest and costs, a greater sum. The debtor had not provided any consideration for the promise not to claim interest.

Exceptions

There are four exceptions to the rule in **Pinnel's case**:

- where the part payment is made by a third party
- composition with creditors (i.e. the creditors all agree to accept a sum which is less than they are owed)
- accord and satisfaction
  - accord means that both the parties agree freely to the part payment.
  - satisfaction i.e. the debtor provides some additional consideration to the creditor such as payment before the due date, payment at a different place to that originally agreed or in a different currency etc.

D & C Builders v Rees (1966)

Facts: R owed money to D & C and knew that D & C were in financial difficulties. R offered to pay a smaller sum to be accepted in full and final payment of whole amount. R stated that if it was not accepted, the claimant would get nothing. The claimant reluctantly accepted the smaller sum but later sued for the balance.

Held: The claimant could successfully sue for the balance. Several reasons contributed to the court's decision, amongst them were:

(1) In view of the pressure put on the claimant and the claimant's reluctance there was no true accord

(2) Payment by cheque and cash are, in these circumstances, no different. Therefore the payment by cheque did not amount to consideration: it conferred no benefit over and above payment in cash.

- the equitable doctrine of promissory estoppel.

Promissory estoppel

The doctrine of promissory estoppel is based on the principles of fairness and justice. It prevents a person going back on his promise to accept a lesser amount.

The principle was established in **Central London Property Trust v High Trees House (1947)**.

Central London Property Trust v High Trees House (1947)

Facts: Claimants let a block of flats to the defendants in 1937 at an annual rent of £2,500 pa. The defendants were then going to sublet the flats. Owing to World War II and London being bombed, some of the flats became empty and it was impossible to re-let them. In addition the existing tenants had their rent reduced. The claimants agreed to accept half the rent for the rest of the war.

Held: The full rent would be payable from the end of the war. The doctrine of promissory estoppel would stop the claimants from recovering the full rent foregone during the war years. High Trees House were expected to reduce their rent as a result of the rent reduction by Central London Property Trust, which they did thereby proving their reliance on the waiver.

The principle is subject to the following conditions:

- There must be an existing contract between the parties.
- The claimants must voluntarily waive their rights under the contract.
- There must be an intention that the defendants should rely on the waiver.
- The defendants must alter their legal position because of the waiver.

The doctrine has a number of limitations:

- It is a shield not a sword, i.e. it is a defence not a cause of action.
- It may only have a suspensory effect, as shown in the **High Trees case**. (The claimant's rights were suspended during World War II, but reinstated for the future once the war had finished.)
- The party seeking to use it as an equitable defence must also have acted fairly in their dealings with the claimants.

In **D & C Builders v Rees** (above) Mrs Rees attempted to rely on promissory estoppel, but it was held that she could not do so as she had attempted to force the claimant to accept less and thus had not acted fairly herself i.e. she did not 'come to equity with clean hands'.

Privity of contract

The general rule

Only the parties to a contract:

- acquire rights and obligations under it
- can sue and be sued on it.

Exceptions

There are a number of exceptions to the general rule regarding privity of contract:

- The Contracts (Rights of Third Parties) Act 1999 allows a person who is not a party to a contract to enforce it so long as the contract was for his benefit and he was expressly identified, by name or description.
- Under the rules of land law, restrictive covenants run with the land to which they relate i.e. that a future owner will be subject to restrictions made in previous contracts.

Tulk v Moxhay (1848)

Facts: The owner of several pieces of land sold a plot to another party, making a covenant to keep a particular area "uncovered with buildings" such that it could remain a pleasure ground. Over the following years the land was sold several times over to new parties, eventually to the defendant. The defendant, who was aware of the covenant at the time of purchase, refused to abide by the covenant as he claimed he was not in privity of contract and so was not bound by it.

Held: An injunction was granted against the defendant to restrain a breach of the covenant.

- Insurance law allows a third party to take the benefit of a contract of insurance for example where the policy is for life insurance which will pay out to a third party in the event of the policy holder's death.
- Trust law allows a beneficiary to enforce a trust.
- Agency law allows an agent to make a contract between his principal and a third party, even though the third party may be unaware that he is acting as an agent.
- An executor can enforce contracts made by the deceased for whom he is acting.

Beswick v Beswick (1967)

Facts: A coal merchant sold his business to his nephew in return for a pension during his lifetime and the payment of a smaller pension to his widow, on his death. After the uncle died, the nephew stopped paying the widow. She sued the nephew in her own personal capacity and in her capacity as the administrator of her husband's estate.

Held: Although she was not a party to the contract and could not sue in her own personal capacity, she could sue in her capacity as the administrator of her husband's estate.

4 Intention that the agreement should be legally binding

Introduction

In order to create a contract, both parties must intend to enter into a legal relationship. If it is not clear from the contract that the parties intended legal consequences then the law presumes the intention of the parties based on the type of agreement.

Domestic or social agreements

It is presumed that there is no intention to be legally bound, unless it can be shown otherwise.

Balfour v Balfour (1919)

Facts: The defendant, who was about to go abroad, promised to pay his wife £30 per month in consideration of her agreeing to support herself without calling on him for any further maintenance. The wife contended that the defendant was bound by his promise.

Held: There was no legally binding contract between the parties. As it was a domestic agreement it was presumed the parties did not intend to be legally bound.

The usual presumption that agreements between spouses living happily together are not legally enforceable does not apply when they are about to separate, or have already separated. In such instances the circumstances of the case can be shown to rebut the presumption.

Merritt v Merritt (1970)

Facts: A husband, separated from his wife, wrote and signed a document stating that, in consideration of the wife paying off the outstanding mortgage debt of £180 on their matrimonial home, he would transfer the house standing in their joint names into her sole ownership. The wife paid off the outstanding mortgage debt, but the husband refused to transfer title in the house to her, alleging that his promise was a domestic arrangement and did not give rise to legal relations.

Held: The husband's promise was enforceable, the agreement having been made when the parties were not living together amicably. A legal relationship is contemplated where a husband deserts his wife and an agreement is concluded on ownership of the matrimonial home occupied by the wife and children. The circumstances of their separation was enough to rebut the presumption.

The presumption that there is no intention to be legally bound will also be rebutted where the evidence shows that the parties made formal and/or detailed financial arrangements.

Simpkins v Pays (1955)

Facts: Pays and her granddaughter, together with Simpkins, a paying lodger, submitted an entry each week in a fashion competition appearing in the Sunday Empire News. All three devised a separate solution to the competition, but they were submitted on one coupon only, in Pays' name. The entry fees and postage were shared equally. The granddaughter made a correct forecast and Pays received a prize of £750. Simpkins claimed a one-third share of the prize money.

Held: Although this was an arrangement in a domestic context the presumption was rebutted: it was a legally enforceable joint enterprise and the parties clearly intended to share any prize money. 'There was mutuality in the arrangements between the parties and an intention to create legal relations'. It was decided that on the facts this went beyond a mere friendly agreement and became a joint enterprise.

Commercial agreements

It is presumed that there is an intention to be legally bound, unless it can be shown otherwise.

This is a strong presumption that can only be rebutted by clear evidence to the contrary.

5 Misrepresentation

During the negotiations preceding a contract, statements are often made with a view to inducing the other party to enter into a contract. If any such statement is false, the party thereby misled is not agreeing to what is the true state of affairs and the contract may be voidable for misrepresentation.

Misrepresentation, therefore, may be defined as a false statement of fact or law (but not a mere expression of opinion), made by one party to the other before the contract, and made with a view to inducing the other party to enter into it.

The statement must have been intended:

- to be acted upon, and
- it must actually have deceived the other party and induced him to make the agreement.

As a **general rule**, silence cannot amount to misrepresentation and there is no duty to disclose facts. In contracts for the sale of goods, this rule is known as caveat emptor (let the buyer beware).

There are two exceptional instances when there is a duty to disclose.

The first is a duty to correct statements which were true when made but, because the facts have changed, they have subsequently become false and it would be unfair to let them stand.

With v O'Flanagan (1936)

Facts: At the start of negotiations in January a doctor, who wished to sell his practice, stated that its profits were £2,000 per year. Shortly afterwards he fell ill and as a result the practice was almost worthless by the time the sale was completed in May.

Held: The statement should have been corrected and it amounted to misrepresentation.

The other exception relates to contracts of the utmost good faith (uberrimae fidei), contracts where one party alone possesses full knowledge of the material facts and must disclose them. This applies:

- in contracts for the sale of land with regard to defects in title
- in a prospectus inviting subscription for shares as to matters required by statute
- in contracts for family arrangements.

Supplementary reading

Prior to the Consumer Insurance Act 2012 it used to be the case that in contracts of insurance there must be full disclosure of all material facts which ultimately affect the decision whether to insure and in fixing the amount of the premium.

The effect of the Act was to remove the obligation to disclose all material facts. The consumer no longer has to volunteer information but only has to respond honestly and with reasonable care to questions asked.

In all instances of misrepresentation, the contract is said to be voidable at the option of the party deceived.

The contract may be rescinded or ended, and the parties restored to their original positions, for example by returning property transferred and money paid.

The right to rescind will be lost if such restoration is not possible as when property has been resold or destroyed. The right will also be lost if the party deceived affirms the contract by going on with it, knowing of the misrepresentation.

The right of rescission is 'equitable', which means that the courts can refuse to grant it when they think that it would be unfair.

The courts will insist that rescission be exercised reasonably promptly once the misrepresentation has been or should have been discovered by reasonable diligence; this rule is necessary to avoid uncertainty as to the ownership of property which might or might not have to be returned. What is 'reasonably promptly' is a question of fact. For things that change rapidly in value, the time can be very short – sometimes only weeks or less.

A claim for damages is the other possible remedy for misrepresentation:

- Damages can be awarded if the claimant can prove that the misrepresentation was made deliberately and fraudulently. It is the claimant who must prove that there has been fraud and this is not easy. This is therefore not very common.
- A defendant may be liable for damages under the Misrepresentation Act 1967 s. 2(1) unless he can prove that he had reasonable grounds to believe and did believe up to the time the contract was made that the statements that he made were true. In other words the defendant must show that he was not negligent. Tactically it is advisable for a claimant to use this provision as he is not obliged to prove that the defendant was negligent. Rather the burden of proof is placed upon the defendant to prove he was not negligent.
- Under the Misrepresentation Act 1967s. 2(2), damages may also be awarded at the court's discretion, as an alternative to rescission, even for innocent misrepresentation. If the defendant can prove his innocence, however, the claimant has no right to damages. He can only ask the court to exercise its discretion in his favour. This is not common.

In addition to these civil remedies for misrepresentation, a false statement of fact may also give rise to criminal liability, for example under the Trade Descriptions Act 1968 or the Property Misdescriptions Act 1991.

Misrepresentations may later become incorporated as terms in the contract. If so, it will be more advantageous for the party deceived to sue for breach of contract which, if successful, gives an automatic right to damages.

Any term in the contract which tries to exclude liability for misrepresentation is void unless it can be shown to be reasonable.

6 The contents of the contract

Overview

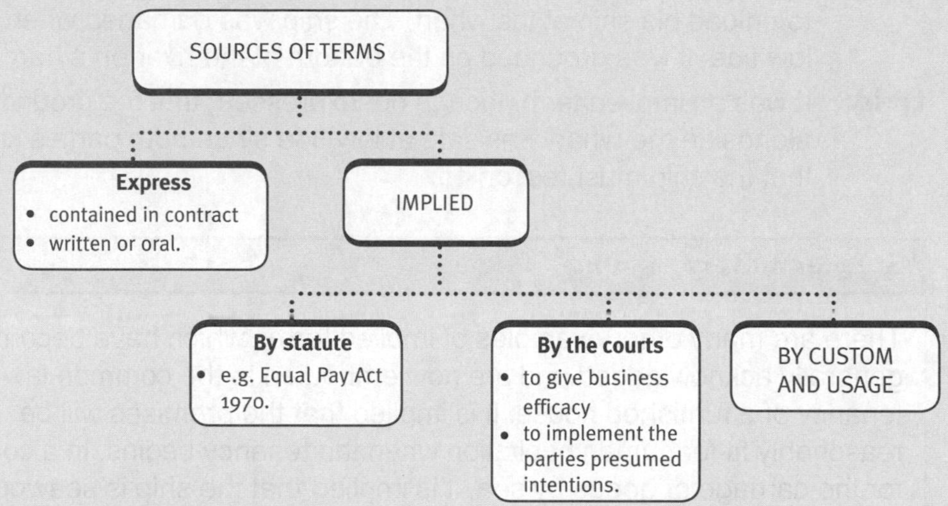

Express terms

Express terms are those specifically mentioned and agreed to by the parties at the time of contracting, either in writing or orally. They must be clear for them to be enforceable.

Scammel v Ouston (1941)

Facts: An agreement provided for the balance of the price to be paid 'on hire purchase terms over a period of two years'.

Held: The words 'hire purchase terms' were considered too imprecise as the seller had a range of such terms.

Implied terms

Implied terms are not expressly included in the contract, but they are nevertheless still part of the contract. They may be implied by statute or by the courts or rarely by custom.

Terms are implied by the courts to fill omissions and give business effect to the intentions of the parties. Such obligations will be imposed as the court feels the parties would have reasonably agreed to, had they considered the matter.

The Moorcock (1889)

Facts: There was an agreement by a wharf owner to permit a shipowner to unload his ship at the wharf. The ship was damaged when, at a low tide, it was grounded on the bottom of the river on a hard ridge.

Held: It was an implied term, though not expressed, that the ground alongside the wharf was safe at low tide since both parties knew that the ship must rest on it.

Supplementary reading

There are many other examples of implied terms which have become generally acknowledged and are now embodied in the common law. In a tenancy of a furnished house, it is implied that the premises will be reasonably fit for human habitation when the tenancy begins. In a contract for the carriage of goods by sea, it is implied that the ship is seaworthy and will proceed with reasonable despatch without unnecessary deviations. In a contract of employment, it is implied that the employer will provide a safe system of work and that the employee will exercise care and skill in carrying out his or her work.

Implied terms will generally be overridden by express terms. However, some statutory terms cannot be overridden by express agreement, for example the Sale of Goods Act 1979.

The Sale of Goods Act 1979 (as amended in 1994) provides a number of examples of terms implied by statute.

There are five important terms which can be implied into every contract of sale. These impose obligations upon a seller:

- that the seller has (or will have) the right to sell the goods; (S12)
- that the goods shall correspond with any description applied to them; (S13)
- where the sale is made in the course of business, that the goods shall be both, of satisfactory (formerly 'merchantable') quality and reasonably fit for the required purpose if the seller had been made aware of this; (S14) and
- that the bulk will correspond with any sample (S15).

Rogers v Parish (1987)

Facts: The claimant bought a new Range Rover for £16,000. It had defects in the engine gearbox and bodywork. After several attempts at repair, the car still didn't work properly, so the claimant sued.

Held: The car was of unsatisfactory quality. As the car was a new Range Rover, this gave rise to expectations above those relating to a more modest car.

The implied terms relating to the provision of services is contained in the Supply of Goods and Services Act 1982. The Act provides a statutory term that 'the supplier will carry out the service with reasonable care and skill'.

Under the Act, an accountant owes the following implied duties:

- obey client's instructions (but not illegal ones)
- demonstrate the level of skill that has been professed
- to take reasonable care – the standard of care is high
- to be honest
- to show good faith
- confidentiality
- to keep proper records.

7 The status of contractual terms

Types of terms

There are three types of terms:

- conditions
- warranties
- innominate terms.

The distinction between the types of term is important because it determines the remedies that may be available in the event of a breach.

Conditions

A condition is an important term going to the root of the contract.

Breach can result in damages or discharge or both. Discharge entitles the innocent party to repudiate the contract and claim damages.

Poussard v Spiers & Pond (1876)

Facts: A soprano, Madame Poussard, agreed to sing in a series of operas for Spiers. She failed to appear on the opening night and Spiers refused her services for subsequent nights.

Held: The obligation to appear on the opening night was a condition. Spiers was entitled to treat the contract as at an end and was therefore not himself in breach by refusing her services for the remaining nights.

Warranties

A warranty is a less important term, which is incidental to the main purpose of the contract.

Breach of warranty results in damages only.

Bettini v Gye (1876)

Facts: A tenor, Bettini, who agreed to sing in a series of concerts and to attend six days of rehearsals beforehand failed to appear for the first four rehearsal days. Gye in consequence refused Bettini's services for the balance for the rehearsals and performances.

Held: The obligation to appear for rehearsals was a warranty and therefore Bettini's breach did not entitle Gye to treat the contract as at an end. Gye was accordingly in breach of contract when he refused Bettini's services for the remainder of the contract.

Innominate terms

An innominate or indeterminate term is neither a condition nor a warranty.

The remedy depends on the effects of the breach:

- if trivial – damages only i.e. term is treated as if it were a warranty.
- if serious – damages, discharge or both i.e. term is treated as if it were a condition.

The Hansa Nord (1976)

Facts: Citrus pulp pellets for use in animal food had been sold for £100,000 under a contract which provided for "shipment to be made in good condition." Part of the goods had not been so shipped and in addition the market value in such goods had fallen at the delivery date. The buyers rejected the goods which were later resold pursuant to a court order and eventually reacquired by the original buyers for just under £34,000. The buyers then used the goods for the originally intended purpose of making cattle food.

Held: The Court of Appeal held that rejection was not justified. The term as to shipment in good condition was neither a condition nor a warranty but an innominate term; and there was no finding that the effect of its breach was sufficiently serious to justify rejection. The buyers seem to have tried to reject, not because the goods were impaired, but because they saw an opportunity of acquiring them at well below the originally agreed price. In these circumstances their only remedy was in damages: they were entitled to the difference in value between damaged and sound goods.

Consumer Rights Bill 2014

This legislation will bring about major changes to the law in 2015. Although the Bill is not examinable it will of course become so in due course assuming the Bill becomes an Act. It is intended to consolidate current consumer rights legislation in relation to goods, services, digital content and the law relating to unfair contract terms in consumer contracts, into one piece of legislation, whilst at the same time harmonising the different national and EU provisions. It is expected that the new law will show marked differences in relation to contracts not involving consumers (business contracts) and those which do involve consumers (consumer contracts).

The Consumer Rights Bill may be seen at the following site:

http://www.publications.parliament.uk/pa/bills/lbill/2014-2015/0029/lbill_2014-20150029_en_1.htm

The Explanatory Notes to the Bill may be accessed by going to the following site:

http://www.publications.parliament.uk/pa/bills/cbill/2013-2014/0161/en/14161en.htm

Supplementary reading

How to determine the status of contractual terms

In general, the law allows contracting parties freedom of contract in that they are free to classify terms as they choose. What may appear to be a minor issue to one person, may be of crucial importance to another. It follows that the overriding task of the courts is to determine the intention of the parties.

The status of terms may be determined by asking the following questions, which can almost be used as a flow chart:

(i) **Does the contract expressly state that breach of a particular term gives the innocent party the right to terminate the contract?**

- If the answer is yes, then the term must be a condition. This is so even if, when looked at objectively, the term appears to be of relatively minor importance.

- If the answer is no, it is necessary to ask additional questions.

(ii) **Does the contract describe a particular term as a condition or a warranty?** Even where the parties use the word condition or warranty to describe a particular term, the courts have stated that this will not in itself be conclusive. In Schuler AG v Wickman Machine Tools Sales Ltd (1974), a term described as a 'condition' required Wickman to make weekly visits over a four-and-a-half-year period to six named firms, a total of some 1,400 visits in all. A further clause allowed Schuler to terminate the agreement in the event of a 'material breach'. Wickman failed to make some of the weekly visits so Schuler terminated the contract. It was held that Schuler acted in breach by repudiating the contract. Even though the word 'condition' had been used to describe the term, the House of Lords did not believe that it was the parties' intention that a failure to make a single visit would give Schuler the right to terminate. It follows that even the use of the word condition or warranty by the parties is not conclusive.

(iii) **Does the law state that the term in question is a condition?** For example, suppose that a dispute should arise from the delivery of goods to the buyer which turn out to be different from their description in the seller's catalogue. Is this a breach of a condition or a warranty? The answer lies in Section 13 of the Sale of Goods Act 1979, which provides, 'in contracts for the sale of goods by description there is an implied condition that the goods shall correspond with their description.'

Clearly, the law states that the term is a condition. In this instance there is no room for any argument, and it follows that the innocent party is entitled to the options described above for breach of a condition.

(iv) **Has the innocent party been deprived substantially of what it was intended that he should receive under the contract?** This test has been criticised on the ground that the courts should be attempting to determine the intention of the parties at the time the contract was entered into, rather than looking at the effect of the breach. Consequently, it can be viewed as a test of last resort. Where the other questions have not produced a conclusive answer, and evidence of intention is unclear, a pragmatic way of resolving the dispute is to look at the seriousness or otherwise of the breach. If the effect of breaking a term was to deprive the innocent party of the main benefit of the contract, then that term must have been a condition. If not, it follows that the term must have been a warranty.

8 Exemption and limitation clauses

Definition

An exemption clause (or exclusion clause) is a term that seeks to exclude and a limitation clause is a term which seeks to limit, a party's liability for breach of contract.

Common law rules

In order to be valid an exemption clause must satisfy two conditions:

- it must be incorporated into the contract
- its wording must cover the loss.

An exemption clause can be incorporated into a contract by:

- signature
- notice
- previous dealings.

Signature

The case of **L'Estrange v Graucob (1934)** established that a clause is incorporated by signature even if the signatory did not read or understand the document.

L'Estrange v Graucob (1934)

Facts: The proprietess of a cafe bought a cigarette vending machine and signed a contract of sale, which she did not read, that contained a clause: 'Any express or implied condition, statement or warranty, statutory or otherwise not stated herein is hereby excluded'. The machine was defective.

Held: She was unable to recover the price or obtain damages because she was bound by the clause as she had signed the contract.

However, the situation in **L'Estrange v Graucob (1934)** can be contrasted with **Curtis v Chemical Cleaning (1951).**

Curtis v Chemical Cleaning (1951)

Facts: The claimant took a white satin wedding dress to the defendants for cleaning. She was asked to sign a document that contained a clause: 'that the dress is accepted on condition that the company is not liable for any damage howsoever arising' but, before she signed, she was told that the effect of the document that she was about to sign was to exclude liability for damage to beads or sequins. Without reading all the terms of the document the claimant then signed as she was asked. The dress was stained due to the negligence of the defendants.

Held: The defendants were liable and could not rely on the clause because of the misrepresentation as to the extent of the clause.

Notice

For an exclusion clause to be incorporated by notice, reasonable steps must have been taken to bring it to the attention of the other party at the time the contract was made. What are 'reasonable steps' depend on the circumstances.

Thompson v LMS Railway (1930)

Facts: T bought a railway ticket, which stated that she would travel subject to the company's standard conditions of carriage. These conditions could be inspected at the station; one of them excluded liability for injury to passengers. T was unable to read, and so was unaware of the clause. She was injured and claimed damages.

Held: The ticket was a document which should be expected to contain terms, being more than a mere receipt for payment. The railway company had taken reasonable steps to bring the exclusion clause to passengers' attention, by incorporating it into the contract document (the ticket). T was bound by the clause (even though she could not read: 'illiteracy is a misfortune, not a privilege') as were all other passengers.

A clause can be incorporated by notice, provided it was given before making the contract. In **Olley v Marlborough Court (1949)**, a notice in a hotel room did not exclude liability as the contract was made at the reception desk.

Previous dealings

For an exclusion clause to be incorporated by previous dealings, there must have been a consistent course of dealings between the parties.

Spurling v Bradshaw (1956)

Facts: The defendant had dealt with the claimant for a number of years. On the contract in question he delivered four full barrels for storage. As usual, he later received a document which acknowledged receipt and contained a clause excluding liability for negligence. When he came to collect the barrels, he found they were empty.

Held: The exclusion clause had been incorporated into the contract, even though it was received after the contract was made. It had been incorporated through the previous course of dealings whereby he had been sent copies of documents containing the clause, even though he had never read them.

However, **Spurling v Bradshaw (1956)** can be contrasted with **Hollier v Rambler Motors (1972)** in which three or four deals between a garage and a private customer over a five-year period were held to be insufficient to constitute a course of dealings.

The wording must cover the loss

Under the contra proferentem rule, the courts interpret the words narrowly against the interests of the person seeking to rely on the clause.

Photo Productions Ltd v Securicor (1980)

Facts: A security guard burned down the factory he was supposed to be guarding. The contract between his employers and the factory owners limited the employers' liability for injurious acts and defaults of guards.

Held: The clause was clear and unambiguous and effectively limited their liability even for this fundamental breach.

Statutory rules

Even if a clause passes the common law test, it must also satisfy the statutory rules. These are contained in:

- Unfair Contract Terms Act 1977 (UCTA)
- Unfair Terms in Consumer Contract Regulations 1999 (UTCCR).

The Unfair Contract Terms Act 1977

UCTA 1977 applies to exemption clauses in contracts made in the course of business.

It states that a clause exempting liability for:

- death or personal injury due to negligence is void
- other loss due to negligence is void unless reasonable.

Where there is any standard form contract (which could be between two businesses) or any contract between a business and a consumer, any attempt by a business to exclude or restrict liability for breach depends on whether the clause is reasonable.

The burden of proving reasonableness is on the party seeking to rely on the clause. In assessing whether a term is unfair or unreasonable, the court has regard to:

- the strength of the bargaining positions of the parties
- whether the buyer received an inducement to agree to the term
- whether the buyer knew or ought to have known of the existence and extent of the term
- the ability of the party to insure against the liability.

St Albans City and District Council v International Computers Ltd (1994)

Facts: The defendants had been hired to produce a computer system which would calculate population figures on which the claimants would base their community charges. The contract contained a clause restricting liability to £100,000. The database that the computer system produced was seriously inaccurate and as a result the claimant sustained a loss of £1.3m.

Held: The clause was unreasonable. The defendants could not justify the limitation of £100,000 which was small both in relation to the potential risk and the actual loss. In addition, the defendants had insurance of £50m themselves. Therefore, it was reasonable to expect that those who stood to make the profit, and had been well able to insure and had insured, should carry the risk.

In relation to the Sale of Goods Act 1979, UCTA 1977 provides that:

- S12 cannot be excluded in any contract for the sale of goods
- Ss13–15 cannot be excluded in any consumer sale (business to consumer – in fact it is a criminal offence)
- Ss13–15 can be excluded in a non-consumer sale 'where reasonable' (business to business).

The Unfair Terms in Consumer Contracts Regulations 1999

UTCCR 1999 applies to contracts where:

- the seller is acting in the course of business
- the other party is a consumer and
- the terms have not been individually negotiated.

The regulations apply to ALL terms of a contract not just exclusion clauses.

A term is unfair if:

- it is not expressed in plain, intelligible language
- contrary to the requirement of good faith, it causes a significant imbalance in the parties' rights and obligations and this is to the detriment of the consumer.

A term is unfair if it allows the seller to alter the terms of the contract unilaterally without a valid reason which is specified in the contract: Sched 3 UTCCR 1999.

If a term is unfair, it is not binding on the consumer, though the rest of the contract can stand.

As mentioned above, the Consumer Rights Bill 2014 will have a significant impact on the law relating to unfair terms assuming that it becomes law (see above).

Summary

Does the clause pass the common law rules? i.e.

- Is it incorporated into the contract?
- Does the wording cover the loss?
- If no, the clause is void.
- If yes, consider statutory rules.

If the contract is made in the course of business UCTA 1977 applies.

Void if exempts liability for death or personal injury. Other loss – void unless reasonable.

If one party is a consumer and the other is in business, UTCCR 1999 applies in addition to UCTA 1977.

Unfair (and not binding) if not expressed in plain language or if it causes a significant imbalance in parties' rights.

Supplementary reading

Other Acts which restrict unfair terms

Other statutes impose restrictions upon contractual terms in general and upon exemption clauses in particular. Under the Misrepresentation Act 1967, any term excluding liability for misrepresentation is void unless it is proved that the exemption was fair and reasonable, having regard to the circumstances which were known or ought reasonably to have been known to the parties when they contracted. This applies also to non-business liability as in Walker v Boyle (1982), where an exemption clause in the conditions of private sale of a house was held to be unreasonable and hence did not exclude liability for misrepresentations.

The Consumer Credit Act 1974 includes various provisions to protect the debtor during the credit period. Contractual terms cannot prevent the debtor paying off what he owes at any time, a prescribed procedure must be followed if the debtor is in default and this cannot be excluded. Any 'extortionate' bargain to the debtor's detriment in the past could have been reopened and varied by the court. 'The Consumer Credit Act 2006 contains amendments to the Consumer Credit Act 1974 and updates existing legislation. The new Act is aimed at establishing greater competition and fairness for consumers.' Now under Section 19 of the Consumer Credit Act 2006, he can challenge the credit agreement content on the basis of there being an unfair relationship between the contracting parties.

Section 19 of the Consumer Credit Act 2006 provides that borrowers will be able to challenge credit agreements before a court on the grounds that the relationship between the parties is unfair. This test replaces the present concept of extortionate credit bargains. Enforcement actions will be taken by the Office of Fair Trading. Other consumer bodies will be able to enforce the provisions under Part 8 of the Enterprise Act 2002 where unfair relationships are harming the collective interests of consumers.

The Office of Fair Trading has issued draft guidance on the new unfair relationship provisions, giving advice to consumer organisations and businesses on how the new powers will be used. The draft guidance, Unfair Relationships, can be accessed through the consultations section of the OFT's website at www.oft.gov.uk.

Another example is the Fair Trading Act 1973 which empowers the Department of Trade and Industry to make regulations prohibiting certain undesirable consumer trade practices. Exemption clauses which are unaffected by other legislation can thereby be invalidated. Criminal liability may also be imposed, for example, where a seller of goods uses a void exemption or other clause in a contract with a consumer who is not aware of this invalidity.

9 Discharge of the contract

A contract can be brought to an end in several ways:

- by performance
- by frustration
- by breach of contract.

Performance of the contract

A contract is usually discharged by the performance of both parties of their obligations under the contract.

Generally, the rule is that performance must be exact and precise and that a partial performance is no performance.

Cutter v Powell (1795)

Facts: C was employed on a ship sailing from Jamaica to the UK. He died before completing the journey. His wife tried to sue to recover part of the wages due to her husband.

Held: The widow was not entitled to anything because her husband had not completed the journey and there was no complete performance of the contract.

The following are exceptions to this rule:

- **Substantial performance.** If performance is substantial that will be a sufficient discharge. If a contractor has substantially performed the contract with only minor defects he is entitled to the contract price less the cost of remedying the defects.

  Hoenig v Isaacs (1952)

  Facts: The claimant was employed by the defendant to decorate his flat. The price was £750 to be paid in instalments. The defendant paid £400 but refused to pay the rest as he was dissatisfied with the claimant's work.

  Held: The defendant had to pay the outstanding amount less the cost of remedying the minor defects in the claimant's work.

  Bolton v Mahadeva (1972)

  Facts: The claimant agreed to install central heating in the defendant's house for £1,560. His work was defective: the system did not produce adequate heat, and it gave off fumes. It would have cost £174 to put the defects right. The defendant refused to pay and the claimant sued arguing that he had substantially performed the contract.

  Held: The contract had not been substantially performed so the claimant was not entitled to £1,560 less £174 to remedy the defects. He was entitled to nothing as he had not performed his obligations under the contract.

- **Severable (divisible) contracts.** The contract may provide for performance by instalments with separate payment for each of them. However, not all contracts with stage payments are severable in this manner. Thus, for example, in a contract to build a house for £100,000, the contract may provide for £30,000 to be paid on completion of the foundations; £30,000 on completion of the fabric of the house and the balance of £40,000 to be paid on completion of the house. It should be noted that despite these stage payments, there is only one contract and, if the builder should fail to complete the project, he would be liable to compensate the land owner.
- **Performance has been prevented**. This is where one party is prevented from performing his duties under a contract due to the actions of the other party. In these circumstances the offer of performance is sufficient to discharge contractual obligations, and enables the party to sue for damages or bring an action for quantum meruit (see the remedies section).

Planche v Colburn (1831)

Facts: C had agreed to write a book as part of a series of titles. He was to be paid £100 on completion. He did some research and started the book but the series for which the book was intended was cancelled.

Held: C was entitled to a payment of half of the agreed price as reasonable pay on a quantum meruit basis (explained later on in the chapter).

Frustration

A contract is frustrated if, after the contract is formed and through no fault of either party, something happens which renders the contract impossible to perform.

The following are examples of frustration.

One instance might be subsequent physical impossibility if the subject matter upon which the contract depends is accidentally destroyed or rendered unusable.

Taylor v Caldwell (1886)

Facts: A hall was let to the claimant for a series of concerts on specified dates. Before the date of the first concert the hall was accidentally destroyed by fire. The claimant sued the owner of the hall for damages for failure to let him have the use of the hall as agreed.

Held: Destruction of the subject matter rendered the contract impossible to perform and discharged the defendant from his obligations under the contract.

There might be some change in the law after the contract was made which rendered it illegal to perform the contract.

Avery v Bowden (1855)

Facts: There was a contract for a claimant to carry cargo for the defendant. The claimant arrived early to collect the cargo and the defendant told them to sail on as they did not have any cargo for them to carry and would not have by the agreed date. The claimant decided to wait around in the hope that the defendant would be able to supply some cargo. However, before the date the cargo was supposed to be shipped the Crimean war broke out.

Held: The breakout of war meant the contract was frustrated. The claimant therefore lost their right to sue for breach. Had they brought their action immediately they would have had a valid claim.

The non-occurrence of an event will also frustrate a contract if that event was the sole purpose of the contract.

Krell v Henry (1903)

Facts: A room belonging to the claimant, which overlooked the route of the coronation procession of Edward VII, was let out for the day of the coronation for the purpose of viewing the procession. The coronation was postponed owing to the illness of the King. The owner of the room sued for the agreed fee.

Held: As the coronation did not take place and the contract was made for the sole purpose of viewing the procession, the contract was frustrated.

Some other radical change in circumstances might occur which makes nonsense of the purpose of the existing agreement.

Metropolitan Water Board v Dick, Kerr & Co (1918)

Facts: Construction of a reservoir was stopped by the government for economic reasons throughout the war.

Held: The character and duration of this interruption, and the changed financial environment which affected everyone after the war, made nonsense of the original contract and ended it by frustration.

However, a contract will not be discharged by frustration where an alternative mode of performance is possible, even if that alternative is more expensive.

Tsakirooglou & Co v Noblee and Thorl GmbH (1962)

Facts: The defendant agreed to ship some Sudanese peanuts during November or December 1956 to Hamburg for a certain price. On 2nd Nov the Suez canal was closed to shipping. The defendant could still have transported the peanuts within the contractually agreed time but this would mean going via the Cape of Good Hope which would have taken four times as long and increased the cost of transport considerably. The defendant did not carry the goods and argued that the contract had been frustrated.

Held: The contract was not frustrated. It was still possible to perform the contract without any damage to the peanuts. The fact that it was more difficult or costly to perform is not sufficient to amount to frustration.

The Law Reform (Frustrated Contracts) Act 1943 regulates the rights and liabilities of each party following the frustration of a contract. The Act provides that where a contract has been frustrated:

- amounts paid by one party to another party under the contract are to be refunded
- amounts still outstanding are no longer due
- if a person has to repay sums he may set off expenses, provided they were incurred in carrying out the contract prior to the frustrating event.

This is at the discretion of the court.

Breach of contract

Breach of contract occurs where one of the parties to the agreement fails to comply, either completely or satisfactorily, with their obligations under it.

Types of breach

Actual breach is where the breach occurs on the due date for performance.

Anticipatory breach occurs where, before the due date for performance, a party shows an intention not to perform his contractual obligations. It is referred to as renunciation.

Anticipatory breach may be express or implied.

Express anticipatory breach occurs where one of the parties declares, before the due date for performance, that they have no intention of carrying out their contractual obligations.

Hochster v De La Tour (1853)

Facts: In April, De La Tour employed Hochster to act as a travel courier on his European tour, starting on 1 June. On 11 May De La Tour wrote to Hochster stating he would no longer be needing his services. Hochster started proceedings on 22 May. The defendant claimed there would be no cause of action until 1 June.

Held: The claimant was entitled to start the action as soon as the anticipatory breach occurred.

Implied anticipatory breach occurs where one of the parties does something which makes subsequent performance of their contractual undertaking impossible.

Omnium D'Enterprises v Sutherland (1919)

Facts: The defendant had agreed to hire a ship to the claimant but before the hire period was to commence, he actually sold the ship to someone else.

Held: The sale of the ship amounted to a clear repudiation of the contract. The claimant could sue for breach from that date.

What are the effects of anticipatory breach?

Anticipatory breach does not automatically bring the contract to an end. The innocent party has two options:

- treat the contract as discharged and bring an action for damages immediately, without waiting for the contractual date of performance as in **Hochster v De La Tour (1853)**
- elect to treat the contract as still valid, complete his side of the bargain and then sue for payment by the other side.

White & Carter (Councils) v McGregor (1961)

Facts: McGregor contracted with the claimants to have advertisements placed on litter bins which were supplied to local authorities. The defendant wrote to the claimants asking them to cancel the contract. The claimants refused to cancel, and produced and displayed the advertisements as required under the contract. They then claimed payment.

Held: The claimants were not obliged to accept the defendant's repudiation, but could perform the contract and claim the agreed price.

It should be noted that this case has been severely criticised and will only apply in very limited circumstances where the party not in breach has a 'legitimate interest in performing the contract rather than claiming 'damages'. (**Hounslow LBC v Twickenham Garden Developments Ltd (1971)**).

10 Remedies for breach of contract

Damages

Damages are a common law remedy. They are available as of right for breach of contract.

Damages are intended to be compensatory not punitive.

Liquidated damages and penalty clauses

Where a contract provides for the payment of a fixed sum on breach, it may either be a liquidated damages clause or a penalty clause.

Liquidated damages are a genuine pre-estimate of the expected loss. The amount stated is the amount of damages claimable. The clause is enforceable by the court.

Dunlop Pneumatic Tyre Co v New Garage and Motor Co (1915)

Facts: The claimant supplied the defendant with tyres, under a contract which imposed a minimum retail price. The contract provided that the defendant had to pay the claimant £5 for every tyre they sold in breach of the price agreement. When the defendant sold tyres at less than the agreed minimum price, they resisted the claim for £5 per tyre, on the grounds that it represented a penalty clause.

Held: The provision was genuine attempt to fix damages, and was not a penalty. It was, therefore, enforceable.

A penalty clause threatens large damages for breach. The amount is often very large in relation to the expected loss. It is unenforceable.

A clause is presumed to be a penalty clause if:

- the stipulated sum is extravagant in comparison with the maximum loss that could be incurred
- the same sum is payable in respect of one or more breaches, both trifling and serious
- the sum stipulated is larger than the amount which would actually be payable if the contract were performed.

Assessment of unliquidated damages

Where the contract does not make any provision for damages, the court will determine the damages payable. These are known as unliquidated damages.

There are two factors to consider in determining the amount of unliquidated damages:

- remoteness of loss (i.e. what losses can be claimed for?) and
- measure of damages (i.e. how much are those losses worth?).

Remoteness of loss

Damages cannot not be recovered for all losses suffered. Some losses are too remote.

A loss is not too remote:

- if it arises naturally from the breach (general damages or normal loss)
- it may reasonably be supposed to be within the contemplation of the parties, at the time they made the contract, as a probable result of the breach (special damages or abnormal loss).

Hadley v Baxendale (1854)

Facts: C owned a mill. One of the mill parts had broken and C made a contract with D for the transport of the old part to London as a pattern for making a replacement. D was responsible for a delay in delivering the part and as a result the mill was closed for a longer duration than would have been necessary if there had been no delay. C claimed for loss of profits during the period of delay.

Held: D did not know that the mill was inoperable without the part and whilst he was directly responsible for the delay itself, that stoppage was not a natural consequence of the delay in transportation. C could have had a spare part and did not alert D to the fact that the mill would be inoperable until the new part was made. Accordingly, D was not liable for the loss of profit.

Victoria Laundry v Newman Industries (1949)

Facts: A laundry required a new boiler to enlarge its plant. There was delay in the delivery of the boiler and as a result the laundry lost:

(a) a normal trading profit from the delay in bringing the new plant into use, and

(b) an extra large profit on certain government contracts.

Held: The boiler manufacturer was liable for the loss of normal profits; under the first branch of the rule, he or anyone else would know that an industrial boiler was essential to the operation of the plant and, therefore, to earning normal profits from it. He was not liable for the loss of profit on the government contracts, of which he had no information. (If, of course, he had known of them he would have been liable under the second branch of the rule.)

Jarvis v Swans Tours (1973)

Damages cannot usually be recovered for loss of enjoyment, unless the contract is one designed to give enjoyment. In this case, it was a holiday.

Measure of damages

The measure of damages is the amount which will put the claimant in the position he would have been in had the contract been properly performed.

This is sometimes described as damages for loss of bargain.

It is particularly difficult to measure damages in cases involving **building contracts** as there are two ways in which the damages could, in theory, be measured:

A the damages could be the difference in value between the building as it has been completed and its value if it had been properly completed, or

B the cost of rebuilding so that it meets the required specifications.

The usual measure of such damages is the cost of repairing the faulty work. However, this may not be the case where the costs of remedying the defects are disproportionate to the difference in value between what was supplied and what was ordered.

Ruxley Electronics and Construction Ltd v Forsyth (1995)

Facts: The parties had entered into a contract for the construction of a swimming pool. Although the contract stated that the pool was to be 7ft 6in deep at one end, the actual depth of the pool was only 6ft 9in. The total contract price was around £18,000. Fixing the error would have required a full reconstruction and would have cost about £21,000.

Held: The House of Lords considered that, as the costs of reinstatement would have been out of all proportion to the benefit gained, the difference in value only should be awarded. This was £0 as the pool as constructed was just as suitable for swimming and diving as one built to the original specification. However, the House of Lords did uphold the lower court's award of £2,500 for loss of amenity/enjoyment (although they commented that the amount was on the high side).

Reliance damages enable the claimant to recover compensation for expenses incurred in performing his part of the contract before its breach. Where applicable, they are given in place of damages for loss of bargain; the claimant cannot receive both.

Anglia TV Ltd v Reed (1972)

Facts: R was engaged to play the leading role in a TV play. The claimants incurred expenses in preparing for filming. R repudiated the contract. Anglia could not find a suitable replacement and had to abandon the project.

Held: Anglia could recover the whole of their wasted expenditure from R.

Further points:

- If there is no actual loss, the claimant can recover only nominal damages.
- The claimant must take reasonable steps to mitigate (i.e. reduce) their loss.

Brace v Calder (1895)

Facts: Brace was employed by a partnership for a fixed period of two years, but after only five months the partnership was dissolved, thereby prematurely terminating his contract of employment. He was offered identical employment with a reconstituted partnership which was immediately formed to replace the previous one. He refused the offer and sued for wages he would have earned had his job continued for the agreed two year period.

Held: Brace had not mitigated the loss he suffered by his employer's breach of contract, thus he could only recover nominal damages.

- A notional deduction may be made to reflect taxation.

BTC v Gourley (1956)

Facts: A civil engineer was awarded damages by the British Transport Commission in respect of a railway accident. The award included an amount for loss of earnings. The question was whether the amount of damages should be paid to the recipient gross or net of deductions that would have been suffered by the individual had he remained in employment.

Held: It was held that the award should be made net of an amount that would reflect the deductions that would have been made for tax and national insurance in arriving at the settlement figure. The broad general principle which should govern the assessment of damages in cases such as this is that the tribunal should award the injured party such a sum of money as will put him in the same position as he would have been in if he had not sustained the injuries.

- Difficulty in evaluating losses does not prevent their recovery. In **Chaplin v Hicks (1911)**, an amount was awarded representing the loss of opportunity to audition for a theatre role even though there was no guarantee of the claimant being awarded the role.

Other common law remedies

Action for the price

If the breach of contract arises out of one party's failure to pay the contractually agreed price, then the creditor should bring an action to recover that sum.

If the contract is for the sale of goods, the action may only be brought if the property has passed to the buyer, unless the price has been agreed to be payable in a specific date.

Quantum meruit

Under this remedy, the value of the contractual work which has already been performed is measured.

This remedy is likely to be sought where one party has already performed part of his obligations and the other party then repudiates the contract.

Remedies in sale of goods contracts

Where the seller is in breach of contract the buyer has the following remedies:

- reject the goods
- claim damages for the price of the goods.

Where the buyer is in breach of contract the seller has the following remedies:

- sue for the price
- damages for non-acceptance.

In addition the Sale of Goods Act 1979 gives an unpaid seller certain rights over the goods themselves:

- if the goods are in the seller's possession, they may hold onto them until payment is received.
- where the buyer is insolvent, the seller has the right to stop delivery whilst the goods are being transported so they can be recovered.
- if the contract allows, or if the buyer is notified, the seller may rescind the contract and resell the goods if payment is not received in a reasonable time.

Equitable remedies

Specific performance	Requires someone to perform their contractual obligations. Not available for personal service contracts. It enforces positive covenants within the contract.
Injunction	Orders someone to do something or not to do something. It enforces negative covenants within the contract.
Rescission	Restores the parties to their exact pre-contractual position.

Equitable remedies are only available at the discretion of the court. They are not granted if:

- damages are an adequate remedy
- the claimant has acted unfairly (i.e. he who comes to equity must come with clean hands)
- the order would cause undue hardship
- the order would require the constant supervision of the court
- there is undue delay in seeking the remedy (i.e. delay defeats the equities).

Warner Brothers Pictures Inc v Nelson (1936)

Facts: The film star, Bette Davis (Miss Nelson) entered into a contract with the claimants, whereby she agreed that she would not undertake other film work or any other occupation without the claimant's written consent. The claimant sought an injunction to restrain her from doing film work for another company in breach of this agreement.

Held: The injunction would be granted. However, no injunction would be granted to prevent her engaging in 'other occupations' as this would force her to work for the claimants.

Page One Records v Britton (Trading as The Troggs) (1967)

Facts: The claimants, as managers of a pop group (The Troggs), sought an injunction to restrain the group from breaching their contract by engaging another manager.

Held: As the group would have been unable to obtain an order of specific performance to compel the claimants to perform their personal services as managers, the claimants could not obtain an injunction against the defendants, as there was no mutuality between the parties.

Limitation of actions

Contractual obligations are not enforceable indefinitely. There must be an end to possible litigation if only because evidence becomes less reliable with the passage of time.

After a certain period, therefore, contracts become unenforceable. It is still possible to carry out such contracts and any dispositions of property under them are valid but, in the event of a dispute, the law bars any remedy.

The general periods within which an action must be brought are prescribed under the Limitation Act 1980.

Actions based on a simple contract will be barred within 6 years from the date when the cause of action accrued.

Where the action is based on a deed or the recovery of land, the period is extended to 12 years.

A right 'accrues' when a breach occurs and an action could begin. Thus, if a loan is made for a fixed time, the right will accrue when this time expires. If no time is agreed upon, it will be when a demand for payment is made.

Supplementary reading: Chapter summary

At the end of this chapter, students should make sure that they are familiar with the following material:

- The essential features of a valid contract, namely:
  (i) Agreement – shown by offer and acceptance.
  (ii) Consideration – the rule that a simple contract is a bargain where each side gives consideration to the other; and the exception that in a specialty contract a promise can be binding without consideration if it is made by deed.
  (iii) Intention to create legal relations.
  (iv) Reality of the consent.
  (v) Capacity of the parties to contract – the rule that, exceptionally, some parties' power to make a valid or/binding contract is limited: particularly (although not in detail):
    – infants
    – parties whose contracts may be ultra vires.
  (vi) Legality – not in detail.
- The rule that in general there are no requirements that the contract should be in any particular form, but that there are exceptional circumstances where written documents or even a deed may be required.
- The rules of misrepresentation which are required by the syllabus to be included here, and may often be the subject of examination questions. Students should pay particular attention to the Misrepresentation Act 1967.
- The normal terms of contract should be studied very carefully – in particular:
  – conditions and warranties, and the differences between them
  – express terms and implied terms, particularly implied terms in contracts between a professional person and his client; at this point, students should refer again to the situations where a professional person can also be liable to a non-client.
- Exemption clauses are important, and students should make sure that they know about the attitude of the courts, and the effect of legislation such as the Unfair Contract Terms Act 1977.
- Discharge of a contract by performance and by agreement.
- Discharge by frustration.
- The results of breach of contract (briefly).

- Breach of contract.
- Rescission for breach and rights to treat the contract as repudiated.
- Specific performance.
- Injunctions.
- Requiring payment of the price.
- Damages for breach of contract
  - remoteness and causation
  - measure
  - mitigation
  - exceptional cases where damages can be reduced for contributory negligence
  - liquidated damages and 'penalty' clauses.
- Limitation periods.

11 Test your understanding questions

Test your understanding 1

The vast majority of contracts are 'simple'. What is the meaning of the word 'simple' in this context?

A The terms of the contract are set out in writing

B The contract does not need to be in any particular form to be binding

C The contract contains fewer than ten provisions

D The contract is not supported by consideration

Test your understanding 2

Dennis wrote to Mark, offering to sell him a Renoir painting for £100,000. One week later, Mark wrote back saying he would pay that amount but not for another 2 months. Dennis did not respond and Mark, who decided that he wanted the painting, then heard that Dennis had sold the painting to Tom. Was there a contract between Dennis and Mark?

A Yes. Dennis has made a valid offer which Mark has accepted

B Yes. Mark's response was a request for further information and he was able to accept the offer afterwards

C No. Mark's response constitutes a counter-offer which effectively destroyed Dennis's original offer

D No. Dennis's letter to Mark constituted an invitation to treat, not an offer

Test your understanding 3

Which of the following is the correct limitation period for contracts (other than those made by deed)?

A 3 years

B 6 years

C 9 years

D 15 years

Test your understanding 4

In contract law, once an offer has been terminated it cannot be accepted.

Which of the following does not terminate an offer?

A A request for further information

B Revocation by the offeror

C Lapse of reasonable time

D Rejection by the offeree

Test your understanding 5

Which *one* of the following is *incorrect*?

A A term may be implied into a contract by statute

B A term may be implied into a contract by a court on the ground that the term is customary in the parties' trade

C A term may be implied into a contract by a court on the ground that it would make the contract more equitable

D A term may be implied into a contract by a court on the ground of business efficacy

Test your understanding 6

Which *one* of the following is *incorrect*?

A A condition is a term which the parties intend to be of fundamental importance

B A warranty is a term which the parties do not intend to be of fundamental importance

C If a condition is breached, then the contract must be terminated

D If a warranty is breached, then the injured party cannot terminate the contract

Test your understanding 7

Tom and Sarah visited Bath for the first time in their lives, and booked into a hotel for a night. On arriving in their room they noticed that there were many conditions of contract pinned to the back of the door, and that these included clauses purporting to exclude liability by the hotel for personal injuries or loss suffered by guests while at the hotel. Tom and Sarah had never seen these conditions before. Which *one* of the following is true?

A Tom and Sarah are not bound by the conditions

B Tom and Sarah are bound by the conditions if they are fair and reasonable

C Tom and Sarah are bound by the conditions relating to loss of property but not those relating to personal injuries

D Tom and Sarah are not bound by the conditions because a hotel is never allowed to exclude its own liability in contract

Test your understanding 8

Builder Ltd was under contract to build an extension for Land Ltd at a price of £40,000. Builder Ltd completed three-quarters of the extension, stopped work, and was then placed in creditors' voluntary liquidation, and failed to complete the extension. Which of the following is *correct*?

A Builder Ltd is entitled to nothing

B Builder Ltd has substantially performed the contract and is entitled to a reasonable sum in respect of the work done

C Builder Ltd has completed three-quarters of the work and is, therefore, entitled to £30,000

D The contract between Builder Ltd and Land Ltd is frustrated

Test your understanding 9

Which one of the following contracts might be specifically enforceable?

A Alan has contracted to sell his house to Bob but has changed his mind and no longer wishes to sell it

B Chris has contracted to buy a new Ford motor car but the garage is now refusing to honour the contract

C Diane has contracted to purchase a number of tins of fruit for her business but the seller has now stated that he no longer wishes to proceed with the contract

D Eduardo has contracted to sing at a concert organised by Fernando, but Eduardo has withdrawn as he has received a more lucrative offer from Giovanni

Test your understanding 10

In breach of contract, C Ltd refused to sell a motor car to D Ltd at the agreed price of £10,000. If the type of motor car is readily available on the market at a price of £9,000 which *one* of the following is *correct*?

A D Ltd is entitled to an order of specific performance, forcing C Ltd to carry out its contract

B D Ltd is entitled to damages of £1,000

C D Ltd is entitled to nominal damages only

D D Ltd is not entitled to damages

Test your understanding 11

In an action for breach of contract, the court will *never* award

A unliquidated damages

B nominal damages

C liquidated damages

D exemplary damages

Test your understanding 12

Farmer owns some land, part of which is woodland. He sells the land to B, who covenants in the contract that he will not cut down the trees. One year later, B does prepare to cut down the trees. Farmer seeks a remedy immediately. What remedy is appropriate at this stage?

A Damages

B Specific performance

C Injunction

D Rescission

Test your understanding 13

Beryl enters a shop to purchase a new dress. She tells the shop assistant that she would like to buy the blue dress which is displayed in the shop window and priced at £100. The assistant removes the dress from the window for Beryl, but when she tries to pay for it at the till, the manager informs her that it is not for sale. He tells her that the dress is for display purposes only.

Required:

Delete as appropriate and complete the following sentences:

Beryl is/is not **(1 mark)** entitled to the dress because the display of the dress in the shop window constitutes an …. (3 words) **(2 marks)** and not an ……… (1 word) **(2 marks).** It follows that Beryl does not have/has **(1 mark)** a contract with the shop owners who have/have not **(1 mark)** acted in breach of contract.

(Total: 7 marks)

Test your understanding 14

Vendor owned a factory. He persuaded Mr Purchaser to sign a contract to buy it, and to pay a deposit of £50,000. During negotiations he told Purchaser that the local authority had no plans to build a rumoured road nearby. In fact the local authority had decided to build the road and was about to commence work. This might have been discovered by checking at the Town Hall, but Vendor genuinely believed what he had said.

Required:

Delete as appropriate and complete the following sentences:

Vendor appears to have made a ……… (1 word) **(2 marks)** to Purchaser. This renders the contract ……… (1 word) **(2 marks)** and if Purchaser acts quickly, he will be able to ……… (1 word) **(1 mark)** the contract which means that Vendor and Purchaser will be returned to their pre-contract position. Purchaser will/will not **(1 mark)** be obliged to pay the rest of the price and he will/will not **(1 mark)** be able to recover his deposit. In addition, Purchaser may be able to recover damages from Vendor unless Vendor can show that he was not negligent under the ……… Act 1967 (1 word) **(1 mark).**

(Total: 8 marks)

Test your understanding 15

HIJ Ltd contracted with TUV plc for the latter to service the former's industrial machinery. HIJ Ltd agreed to sign a document headed *'TUV plc Service Agreement',* which contained a clause stating neither TUV plc nor its employees will accept any responsibility for any loss or damage arising from the servicing of customers' machinery, irrespective of the manner in which the loss was caused. An employee of TUV plc carelessly failed to replace certain parts of a machine which he had serviced. This error caused the machine to seize up, and HIJ Ltd lost several days' production and had to purchase a replacement machine.

Required:

Delete as appropriate and complete the following sentences:

The clause was/was not **(1 mark)** incorporated into the contract by the .... (1 word) **(2 marks)** of HIJ Ltd. The term is an .... (1 word) **(1 mark)** clause and, as such, is subject to the provisions of the .... (3 words) **(2 marks)** Act 1977. This Act provides that such a clause is .... (1 word) **(1 mark)** unless it can be shown to be .... (1 word) **(1 mark)**. A schedule to the 1977 Act sets down a .... (1 word) **(1 mark)** test. On balance, it would appear that the clause is/is not **(1 mark)** valid.

(Total: 10 marks)

Test your understanding 16

Delete as appropriate and complete the following sentences:

The remedy which requires a person to carry out his contract is known as .... (2 words) **(2 marks).** The remedy requiring a person not to act in breach of contract is known as an .... (1 word) **(2 marks).** These are both .... (1 word) **(1 mark)** remedies and, as such, are discretionary. If the contract contains a provision which is designed to frighten the other party into completing the contract by setting down a disproportionate sum payable in the event of a breach, the provision will be regarded as a .... (1 word) **(2 marks)** clause and will be treated as .... (1 word) **(2 marks),** that is, of no legal effect. If one party has completed his contractual obligations, all that remains is to sue for the price, in which case remoteness of damage and mitigation of loss are relevant/irrelevant **(1 mark).**

(Total: 10 marks)

Test your understanding answers

Test your understanding 1

B

Most contracts are binding irrespective of their form, and in this respect are described as 'simple', (A) which refers to written contracts is therefore inaccurate. The number of provisions as identified in (C) is of no relevance. Further, a contract is only recognised where consideration is provided by both parties, therefore (D) cannot be correct.

Test your understanding 2

C

(A) is not true, because Mark did not accept Dennis's offer in full, by the fact that he introduced a further term, that is that he would pay in 2 months' time. (B) is not true, because Mark did not request further information. (C) is the correct answer, because Mark is trying to impose his own terms, and thus is making a counter-offer which is capable in turn of acceptance, and which destroys Dennis's original offer. (*See Hyde v Wrench* (1840). (D) is not correct, because the language used indicates that a definite offer is being made by Dennis, indicating a definite intention to be bound.

Test your understanding 3

B

The limitation period for contracts made by deed is 12 years.

Test your understanding 4

A

This was established in Stevenson v McLean.

Test your understanding 5

C

(A) is correct. A good example of implied terms found in statute is the Sale of Goods Act 1979 as amended. Contract terms are implied into contracts on the basis of custom, therefore (B) is correct. Also, business efficacy is a basis for contract terms being implied into contracts, as seen in the Moorcock case (1889). (D) is a correct statement.

Test your understanding 6

C

(C) is the correct answer because whilst a breach of condition can result in the contract being terminated, it is wrong to say the contract must be terminated. A condition is of fundamental importance to a contract and a warranty is not of fundamental importance; therefore (A) and (B) are correct statements. Also, a contract cannot end as a result of a breach of warranty, so (D) is a correct statement.

Test your understanding 7

A

The question is concerned with offer and acceptance and also with exclusion of liability. (A) is true, and therefore the correct answer. Tom and Sarah are not bound by the conditions because they were not made aware of them before reaching agreement. Therefore, any questions about the fairness or otherwise of the conditions under the Unfair Contract Terms Act 1977 and the regulations are irrelevant, as in (B) and (C). (D) is untrue: the hotel could have excluded liability by contract or by notice for breach of contract or breach of duty, provided that the exclusion is fair and reasonable, and provided that it did not relate to liability for personal injuries or death.

Test your understanding 8

A

Performance must normally be total and precise for any entitlement to payment to arise. If a party *chooses* to accept part performance in circumstances where they are able to make such a choice, then they must pay for what they *choose* to take; but Land Ltd does not seem to have any option but to take the partially completed job here.

Test your understanding 9

A

Where goods such as motor cars and tins of fruit are identified as consideration, then the usual remedy on any breach of contract would be compensation as such items are available from any number of suppliers. (B) and (C) are therefore not the correct answers. Likewise, on the facts of (D), where Eduardo will sing at a concert organised by Giovanni rather than Fernando, compensation is the appropriate remedy. A house is unique in that it cannot be likened to cars or tins of fruit, where effectively the same product can be acquired from various sources. A specific performance order requiring Alan to sell to Bob might therefore be available.

Test your understanding 10

C

As the type of motor car is readily available on the market, a specific performance order would not be the appropriate remedy. (A) therefore is incorrect. (D) is incorrect as a breach of contract has occurred and the innocent party can look to the common law remedy of damages. As D Ltd can purchase the car on the market for less than the original contract price, nominal damages only can be recovered. Damages are provided to restore an injured party to the position they would have enjoyed had the contract been properly performed. (C) and not (B) is therefore the correct answer.

Test your understanding 11

D

Exemplary or punitive damages are not now awarded for breach of contract, although they were awarded in the past. Damages for breach of contract should do no more than compensate the plaintiff for his loss. Unliquidated damages (choice (A)) are damages which have not yet been quantified, and once they have been quantified, can be awarded by a court. Nominal damages (choice (B)) are awarded by courts where no actual loss has been suffered but there has been a breach of contract, and are sometimes awarded to recognise that there has been a breach. Liquidated damages (choice (C)) are agreed in advance by the parties as the measure of loss if there is breach of that contract, and are commonly agreed in the case of large construction works.

Test your understanding 12

C

Not (A) – the farmer has not really suffered any damage yet. It is probably too late to rescind the contract (D). Specific performance (B) is an order to do something; the farmer wants an order *not* to do something. An injunction (C) is appropriate and it can often be obtained very quickly.

Test your understanding 13

Beryl *is not* entitled to the dress because the display of the dress in the shop window with a price tag constitutes an *invitation to treat* and not an *offer to sell*. It follows that Beryl *does not have* a contract with the shop owners, who *have not* acted in breach of contract.

Test your understanding 14

Vendor appears to have made a *misrepresentation* to Purchaser. This renders the contract *voidable* and if Purchaser acts quickly, he will be able to *rescind* the contract which means that Vendor and Purchaser will be returned to their pre-contract position. Purchaser *will not* be obliged to pay the rest of the price and he *will* be able to recover his deposit. In addition, Purchaser may be able to recover damages from Vendor unless Vendor can show that he was not negligent under the *Misrepresentation* Act 1967.

Test your understanding 15

The clause *was* incorporated into the contract by the *signature* of HIJ Ltd. The term is an *exclusion* clause, and, as such, is subject to the provisions of the *Unfair Contract Terms* Act 1977. This Act provides that such a clause is *void* unless it can be shown to be *reasonable*. A schedule to the 1977 Act provides a *reasonableness* test. On balance, it would appear that the clause *is* valid.

Test your understanding 16

The remedy which requires a person to carry out his contract is known as *specific performance*. The remedy requiring a person not to act in breach of contract is known as an *injunction*. These are both *equitable* remedies and, as such, are discretionary. If the contract contains a provision which is designed to frighten the other party into completing the contract, by setting down a disproportionate sum payable in the event of a breach, the provision will be regarded as a *penalty* clause and will be treated as *void,* that is, of no legal effect. If one party has completed his contractual obligations, all that remains is to sue for the price, in which case remoteness of damage and mitigation of loss are *irrelevant.*

chapter

3

The Law of Employment

Chapter learning objectives

After completing this chapter you should be able to:

- explain the difference between employees and independent contractors
- explain how the contents of a contract of employment are established
- explain the distinction between unfair and wrongful dismissal
- explain how employers and employees are affected by health and safety legislation
- describe the consequences of a failure to comply with health and safety legislation.

1 Employed versus self-employed

Overview

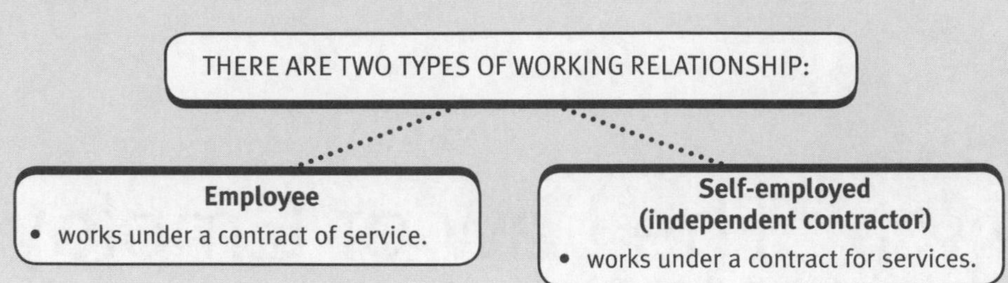

The employment relationship

The employment relationship arises when one person (the employee) supplies skill and labour to another (the employer) in return for payment; this may be for a fixed or indefinite period or to complete a particular job.

The relationship is primarily contractual and the rules outlined in the first two chapters relating to the formation and discharge of contracts apply equally to contracts of employment as to other types of contract.

In addition to the contractual rights enjoyed by an employee, there are a number of rights which are established by statute; for example, Employment Rights Act 1996.

Employees and contractors

We have so far been considering the close and continuing relationship which exists under a contract of employment. Another form of employment relationship may arise when an independent contractor is engaged for one particular job. For example, a builder, instead of employing joiners, may engage self-employed joiners as 'labour-only sub-contractors' for the woodwork on each new house.

This practice has advantages for an employer. Income tax and national insurance contributions need not usually be deducted from wages. The independent contractor has no statutory protection in respect of sick pay, required notice period, short-time working, unfair dismissal and redundancy, and has no preferential rights over other creditors if the employer becomes insolvent. Social security provisions are different.

Of special importance is the vicarious liability which an employer normally has for wrongful acts committed by employees in the course of employment, but not for those of an independent contractor. Vicarious liability will attach to an employer where an employee acting in the course of his employment commits a civil wrong. The courts will consider the wrongful act alongside the actual contract obligations of the employee, as a wrong committed outside such contract obligations, deemed as arising from 'a frolic of one's own', will not serve as a basis for employer vicarious liability.

The importance of the distinction

The type of working relationship has a number of consequences:

- employees receive statutory protection (e.g. unfair dismissal/redundancy)
- there are implied terms in a contract of employment (e.g. duty of obedience)
- an employer is vicariously liable for the acts of employees when they act in the course of the employer's business. The employer is not liable for the acts of independent contractors
- on the insolvency of the employer, an employee is a preferential creditor, whereas someone who is self-employed ranks as an ordinary unsecured creditor
- employees receive their pay net of income tax and national insurance under the PAYE system. Independent contractors are taxed under the trading income provisions
- certain state benefits (e.g. statutory sick pay) are only available to employees.

Supplementary reading

Agency workers: implied contract with end-user reinforced

The Court of Appeal reinforced a legal concept which states that, in appropriate circumstances, a tribunal can find an implied contract between an agency worker and the client or end-user, even where the contract between the agency and the worker states that the worker is to be considered as employed by the agency (see Cable & Wireless plc v Muscat (2006) 782 IRLB 14).

Mr Muscat was employed by Exodus Internet Ltd (EIL). EIL dismissed Mr Muscat but immediately engaged him as a contractor. He then continued to work for EIL as before, although he did set up a company called E-Nuff Comms Ltd to receive his pay and became responsible for his own tax and national insurance. Mr Muscat was transferred to Cable & Wireless under TUPE when the takeover of EIL by Cable & Wireless took place.

After this, he continued to work as a contractor for Cable & Wireless but was later required by them to supply his services through an agency, Abraxas plc, with whom Cable & Wireless had a contract for agency services. Mr Muscat continued to supply his services through his company arrangement and E-Nuff Comms Ltd made a contract with the agency, Abraxas plc, to supply Mr Muscat's services to Cable & Wireless. This set up a triangular situation between the agency, the service provider, and the end-user. Later, Mr Muscat was told by Cable & Wireless that his services would no longer be required and he claimed unfair dismissal, naming Cable & Wireless as his employer. The case eventually reached the Court of Appeal which ruled that:

- tribunals should always consider the possibility of an implied contract of employment between the worker and the end-user where there is this triangular worker, agency, and end-user arrangement
- on the facts of the case, there was an implied employment contract between Mr Muscat and Cable & Wireless, inferred or implied from their conduct. The fact that the worker's contract with the agency provided, as it did in this case, that the worker could not validly enter into a contract with the end-user did not prevent an implied contract from being construed from the facts of the case.

Vicarious liability

A House of Lords decision, in the case of Majrowski v Guy's and St Thomas' NHS Trust (2006) UKHL 34, confirmed that employers may now be held vicariously liable for breaches of statutory duties as well as other common law duties imposed upon employees.

Mr Majrowski's original action in the Central London County Court argued that he had been harassed and bullied during the course of his employment and that Guy's and St Thomas' had breached its statutory duties under the Protection from Harassment Act 1997. Mr Majrowski had been employed by the Trust as a clinical audit coordinator and, he alleged, had been bullied, harassed and intimidated by his manager. She had been excessively critical of his work, he claimed, strict about his time-keeping and rude and abusive to him even in front of other staff.

The 1997 Act is primarily intended to deal with stalking and other activities which constitute criminal harassment: prior to this case, it was not thought that it could be applied in an employment context. This judgement, however, effectively expands the scope of vicarious liability and confirms that employers can be vicariously liable for breaches of statutory duty, provided that the actions are committed in the course of employment.

The tests used to determine employment

The control test

The sole test that was used until about the 1940-50s to determine whether a person was an employee or an independent contractor was the 'control' test. This was set out in **Yewens v Noakes (1880)** – 'a servant is a person subject to the command of his master as to the manner in which he shall do his work'.

Thus a person was an employee if the employer could tell them not only what to do but how to do it. The test was based on the fact that in an agricultural or early industrial society the employer did have more knowledge and skill than the employees.

However, with developing technology and specialisation the control test became inappropriate as employers would hire people for particular skills, which the employer did not have sufficient knowledge or skill to instruct the manner in which they carried out their work.

The integration/organisation test

To deal with the shortcomings of the control test, the integration test was introduced to explain why professional and skilled workers with a large degree of personal autonomy could nevertheless be employees. The decisive factor was whether the individual became 'part and parcel' of the organisation.

The problem with this test was that someone could still be a contractor but also be an integral part of an organisation. For example a doctor could be a vital part of an organisation but still be a contractor at the same time.

Cassidy v Ministry of Health (1951)

Facts: Mr Cassidy went to hospital for a routine operation on his hand, but came away with stiff fingers because of the negligence of one of the doctors. He attempted to sue the Ministry of Health in its capacity as employer. The Ministry argued that it could not be held responsible and had no vicarious liability.

Held: The local authority was held to be vicariously liable. Although the hospital did not control the manner of his work he was nevertheless an employee because he was part of the institution of the hospital.

Beloff v Pressdam (1973)

Facts: B was a regular contributor to a newspaper. She had no regular hours, wrote for other newspapers, and had leave to write books. However, she wrote regularly for this newspaper, was an active member of the editorial staff, attending regular meetings and taking part in editorial decisions.

Held: She was an employee: her work was an integral part of the business.

The economic reality test (or multiple test)

Today under this test, the court takes all the surrounding factors into account. The test involves asking whether the person who is doing the work, is doing so as a person in business on his own account.

Market Investigations Ltd v Minister of Social Security (1969)

Facts: A market research interviewer worked on and off under a series of contracts whereby she interviewed for a company in accordance with interview instructions by the company. She had to complete the work within a specified period but otherwise had no specified hours of work. There was no provision for holiday or sick pay and she was free to work for others while working for the company.

Held: It was held that the company did have some control over the manner in which she did her work and the terms of the contract were consistent with her being an employee. The court emphasised that she did not provide her own tools and took no risk. She was therefore not 'in business on her account'. The court also emphasised that there was 'no exhaustive test compiled, nor strict rules laid down' as to the factors that identified a worker as being an employee.

The factors which will be considered include:

- the degree of control by the 'employer'
- ownership of tools and equipment
- the ability to provide a substitute
- degree of financial risk the worker undertakes
- whether there is a regular method of payment
- whether the person works regular hours
- whether there is mutuality of obligations.

No single test is really capable of determining employee status, therefore all of the above factors will be considered. The court will weigh up the factors and come to a decision accordingly.

2 The contract of employment

Contents

A contract of employment will consist of:

- express terms
- terms implied by the courts
- terms implied by statute.

Express terms

Express terms are those agreed by the parties themselves. The agreement may be written or oral.

The Employment Rights Act 1996 (ERA 1996) requires an employer to provide an employee with a written statement of certain particulars of their employment within two months of the commencement of employment.

The statement must include details of:

- pay rates and interval (i.e. weekly, monthly, etc.)
- job title
- hours of work
- place of work
- length of notice
- details of disciplinary and grievance procedures
- date of commencement of employment.

Any change must be notified by written statement within one month.

The statement is not a contract unless both parties agree and it is called a contract. It is strong prima facie evidence of the terms of the contract, but is not conclusive.

Terms implied by the courts

The courts have implied various duties into the employment contract.

Duties of the employee

Duty to obey lawful and reasonable orders

Pepper v Webb (1968)

Facts: A gardener refused to plant the plants where instructed by the employer.

Held: He was in breach of the duty of obedience and this, coupled with the fact that he was rude and surly, justified his summary dismissal.

Duty of mutual co-operation (or the duty to perform the work in a reasonable manner)

The duty of the employer to give, and the employee to obey, lawful instructions is often expressed as the duty of mutual co-operation. The courts have begun to imply a term that the employer must not act in a manner calculated to damage the mutual trust and confidence and this is taken into account in considering the reasonableness of the order. The courts have interpreted the duty to obey lawful and reasonable orders as a duty not to frustrate the commercial objectives of the employer.

Secretary of State for Employment v ASLEF (1972)

Facts: Railway workers 'worked to rule', i.e. obeyed the British Rail rule book to the letter. This resulted in considerable delays in the train service.

Held: There was an implied term that each employee in obeying instructions would not do so in a wholly unreasonable way which had the effect of disrupting the service he was there to provide.

Duty to exercise reasonable care and skill

The employee must act with reasonable care in performing his duties. The standard of care will depend on the circumstances. It is generally accepted that a single act of negligence, unless it is gross negligence, will not justify summary dismissal. There are certain occupations, such as airline pilots, where a single act of negligence in performing essential duties may warrant dismissal.

An extension of this duty of care is a duty to indemnify the employer for any damages which he has had to pay as a result of his vicarious liability for the employee's negligence.

Lister v Romford Ice & Cold Storage Ltd (1972)

Facts: An employee negligently ran over another employee with a fork-lift truck.

Held: He was liable in damages to his employer for breach of contract.

Duty of good faith – a duty to give honest and faithful service

The employee cannot use the employer's property as his own, and must account to his employer for any money or property which he receives in the course of his employment.

Sinclair v Neighbour (1967)

Facts: An employee secretly borrowed from the shop till. He repaid the money the next day.

Held: He was in breach of the duty of good faith and, since this was a serious breach of contract, the employer was justified in summarily dismissing him.

The employee may do other work in his own time. However, the law imposes a duty not to do spare time work which competes with that of his employer and may cause his employer damage.

An employee must not disclose trade secrets to a third party nor misuse confidential information he has acquired in the course of his employment. This implied duty may continue after the employment has ceased. Clearly an employee who uses or sells secret processes, such as chemical formulae, or photocopies list of customers and sells them or uses them for his own purposes will be in breach.

The real problem arises in drawing a line between trade secrets/confidential information and general knowledge and skill acquired by the employee in the course of his employment. An employee may always use skills he has learnt in his employment.

Hivac Ltd v Park Royal Scientific Instruments Ltd (1946)

Facts: Two employees of a company which manufactured sophisticated components for hearing aids worked at the weekends for a rival company.

Held: An injunction was granted as there was potential for misuse of the secret information.

Duty to render personal service

Employees may not delegate the performance of their work to someone else unless they have their employer's express or implied permission to do so.

Duties of the employer

Duty to pay reasonable remuneration

This will be implied in the absence of an express provision regarding pay.

Duty to indemnify the employee

The employer must indemnify his employee where the employee has incurred a legal liability or necessary expenses whilst acting on the employer's behalf.

Duty to provide a safe system of work

At common law the employer is under a duty to take reasonable care for the health and safety of his employees. Breach of this duty exposes the employer to liability in negligence to his employees.

In addition, the employer is under various statutory duties, e.g. the Factories Act 1961, the Offices, Shops and Railway Premises Act 1963, and the Health and Safety at Work etc. Act 1974 all regulate work conditions.

The requirement at common law is to take reasonable care to provide a safe system of work and this encompasses such matters as the selection of staff and provision for their supervision; and ensuring that premises, plant and materials are safe.

In assessing the reasonableness of the employer in these matters a number of factors must be considered. For example: what was the risk of injury? What was the cost of prevention? What were the characteristics of the employee?

If the employer has not acted unreasonably, he has not been negligent, and has no common law liability.

Latimer v AEC Ltd (1953)

Facts: Following flood damage, the employer carefully strewed sawdust over a factory floor to prevent employees slipping until the floor could be properly cleared. A small patch remained uncovered and L slipped and was injured.

Held: The employers had not acted unreasonably. They were not liable to L for his injuries.

Duty to give reasonable notice of termination of employment

In practice this implied duty rarely arises since most contracts of employment contain express provision stating the exact length of notice or stating that the contract is to be for a fixed term. Also there are statutory minimum periods of notice.

Duty of mutual co-operation

This duty has already been discussed in respect of employees' duties. The employer has a duty not to behave in a manner calculated to damage the relationship of trust and confidence, e.g. by abusively reprimanding an employee.

Provision of work

There is no general common law duty to provide work. However, such a term may be implied, under the business efficacy test, where failure to provide work would deprive the employee of a benefit contemplated by the contract. For example, if the contract expressly provides for remuneration on a piecework or commission basis it may be possible to imply a duty on the employer to provide sufficient work to enable the employee to earn a reasonable sum.

Similarly, where the employee is skilled and needs practice to maintain those skills, there may be an obligation to provide a reasonable amount of work.

William Hill Organisation Ltd v Tucker (1998)

Facts: T worked as a senior dealer (one of only five authorised to do so) operating in the field of spread betting. He served notice to terminate his contract in order to work for a competitor. WH insisted that he remain on the payroll for the notice period, but stayed at home 'on garden leave'. T sought to start his new job immediately, arguing that WH was in breach of contract in refusing to allow him to work.

Held: WH was in breach by not providing work because T had particular skills which must be exercised to maintain them.

Provision of a reference

There is no duty to provide a reference but, if one is provided, it must be truthful, as shown in:

Spring v Guardian Assurance (1994)

Facts: The claimant had worked as a representative for a company but was dismissed after their sale to Guardian Assurance. He applied to work for the insurance company Scottish Amicable. Guardian Assurance provided Scottish Amicable with a bad reference in respect of the claimant who claimed damages for negligent misstatement. The reference was, the judge said, 'so strikingly bad as to amount to . . . the 'kiss of death' to his career in insurance'.

Held: The defendants did owe the claimant a duty of care in providing a reference, knowing that a bad one might damage his prospects of employment, and that they were in breach of that duty.

Terms implied by statute

ERA 1996	Gives employees certain rights, such as a right not to be unfairly dismissed, a right to a redundancy payment if made redundant and a right to a minimum period of notice to terminate the contract.
Working Time Regulations 1998	Limit the **hours** of work to an average of **48 a week**. It also gives the right to **four weeks' paid leave** a year and **one day off each week**.
Employment Act 2002	Gives **parents of children under seventeen or disabled children under eighteen** the right to request **flexible working** arrangements. The employer must give serious consideration to such a request and can only reject it for clear business reasons. The Act also introduced paternity and adoption leave.
Equality Act 2010	Deals with protecting people from discrimination in the workplace (and in wider society). Recognises 'protected characteristics'.
Equal Pay Act 1970	Deals not only with pay, but other terms, e.g. holiday and sick leave. **Implies an equality clause** into all contracts of employment if workers of the opposite sex do the same job or a different job of equal value.
National Minimum Wage Act 1998	Imposes minimum levels of pay. https://www.gov.uk/national-minimum-wage-rates

Supplementary reading

The primary purpose of the Equality Act 2010 was to combine and simplify the various anti-discriminatory Acts and Regulations formerly referred to within the English Legal System. These were, primarily:

- The Equal Pay Act 1970
- Sex Discrimination Act 1975
- Race Relations Act 1976
- Disability Discrimination Act 1995
- The Equality Act 2006
- Sex Discrimination (Amendment of Legislation) Regulations 2008.

Now that the new Act has come into force, all earlier legislation is repealed. The Act has the same goals as the four major EU Equal Treatment Directives, whose provisions it mirrors and implements. With limited exceptions, the Act does not apply in Northern Ireland.

The Act identifies several characteristics as 'protected' characteristics:

- Age
- Disability
- Gender reassignment
- Marriage and civil partnership
- Pregnancy and maternity
- Race
- Religion or belief
- Sex; and
- Sexual orientation.

The Equality Act 2010 requires equal treatment in access to employment as well as private and public services, regardless of any of the protected characteristics listed above. It is also quite clear about the differences between direct and indirect discrimination.

A person directly discriminates against another if, because of a protected characteristic, an individual is treated less favourably than others would be treated.

A person indirectly discriminates against another if a provision is applied, or criterion or practice which is discriminatory in relation to a relevant protected characteristic.

In the case of disability, a person discriminates against a disabled person if they are treated unfavourably because of something arising in consequence of their disability and it cannot be shown that the treatment is a proportionate means of achieving a legitimate aim. This does not apply if an individual did not know, or could not have been expected to know, that a person has a disability. Further, employers and service providers are under a duty to make reasonable adjustments to their workplaces to overcome barriers experienced by disabled people, either by removing the physical feature in question, altering it or by providing a reasonable means of avoiding it.

In the case of gender reassignment, a person discriminates against a transsexual person if, in relation to an absence from work that is because of gender reassignment, the individual is treated less favourably than if the absence had been because of sickness or injury or for some other reason.

In the case of pregnancy and maternity matters, a person discriminates against a woman if she is treated unfavourably because of a pregnancy of hers, because of an illness suffered by her as a result of it, or if she is treated unfavourably within 26 weeks from the day of giving birth. Particular reference is made in the Act in relation to a woman being treated unfavourably because she is breast-feeding.

3 Notice and dismissal

Minimum notice periods

If a period of notice is not expressly agreed, the ERA 1996 imposes the following minimum notice periods:

Notice by employer

Continuous employment	Period of notice
1 month–2 years	1 week
2–12 years	1 week per complete year
12 years +	12 weeks

Notice by employee

An employee with at least four weeks' continuous employment must give his employer at least one week's notice of his terminating of the contract.

Wrongful dismissal

A claim for wrongful dismissal is a common law action for breach of contract. The claim is available to both employees and independent contractors. The usual rules of breach of contract will apply.

Wrongful dismissal occurs where the employer terminates the contract:

- without giving proper notice, or
- during its fixed term.

Dismissal without notice is known as summary dismissal.

Summary dismissal is usually wrongful dismissal unless the employee:

- waives their rights or accepts payment in lieu of notice
- repudiates the contract themselves or is in fundamental breach (e.g. wilful refusal to obey orders; failure to show professed skill; serious negligence; breach of duty of good faith).

Remedies

An individual who believes he has been wrongfully dismissed may sue in the County court or High Court for damages. The limitation period for such a claim is six years.

Alternatively, if he is an employee, he can bring a claim to the employment tribunal provided he does so within three months of his dismissal and the claim is for £25,000 or less.

Unfair dismissal

This is a statutory right under the Employment Rights Act 1996. Only employees can bring an action for unfair dismissal.

The employer terminates the contract without justifiable reason.

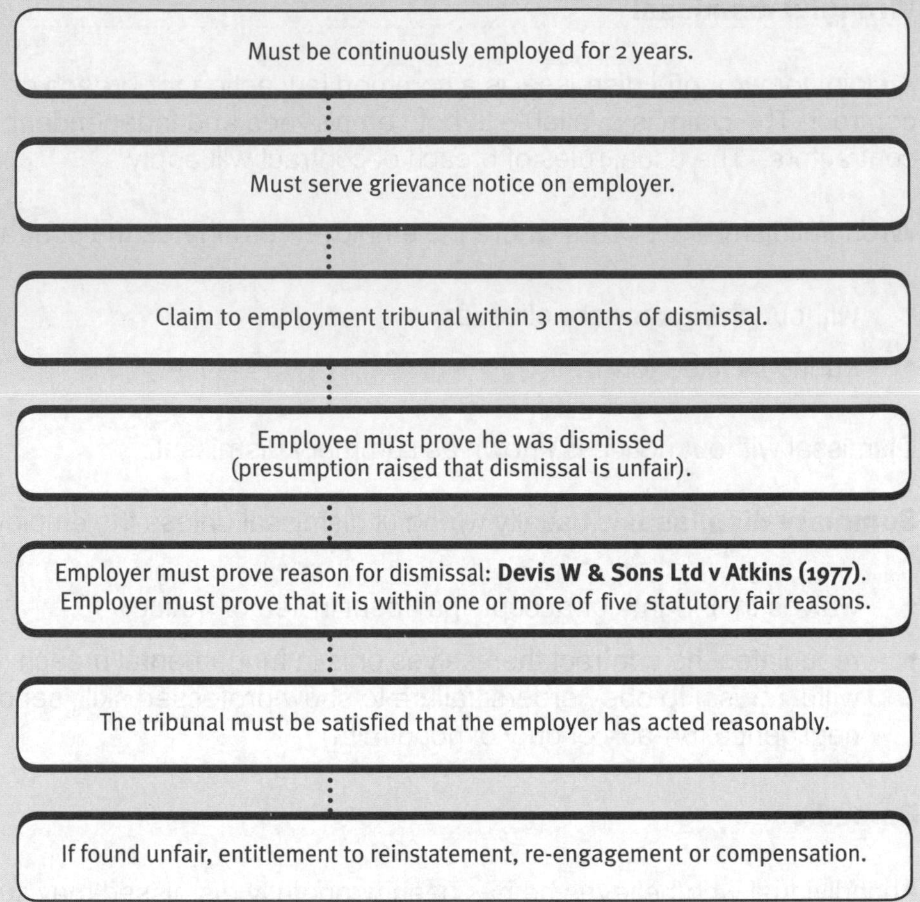

The requirement to be continuously employed for two years is for an employment contract which started on or after 6th April 2012. For employment contracts which started before this date the qualifying period is one year.

Types of dismissal

- Contract terminated by employer with or without notice.
- Fixed-term contract expired but not renewed.
- Constructive dismissal.

Constructive dismissal

Normally employees who resign deprive themselves of the right to make a claim for redundancy or unfair dismissal. However, s95 ERA 1996 covers situations where 'the employee terminates the contract with, or without, notice in circumstances which are such that he or she is entitled to terminate it without notice by reason of the employer's conduct'. This is known as constructive dismissal.

In **Western Excavating (ECC) Ltd v Sharp (1978)** it was held that an employee is entitled to treat himself as constructively dismissed if the employer is guilty of conduct which is a significant breach going to the root of the contract of employment, or which shows that the employer no longer intends to be bound by one or more of the essential terms of the contract. Whether the employee leaves with or without notice, the conduct must be sufficiently serious to entitle him to leave at once. However, he must act quickly, for if he continues for any length of time without leaving, he will be regarded as having elected to affirm the contract and will lose his right to treat himself as discharged.

Where such a repudiatory breach occurs the employee resigns and will have an action against the employer for wrongful dismissal.

Donovan v Invicta Airways (1970)

Facts: The employer put pressure on the employee, an airline pilot, to take abnormal risks on a flight. The employer did this three times in rapid succession. Each time the employee refused. Relations with management deteriorated and he left.

Held: The employer had committed a serious breach of contract amounting to constructive dismissal. The employee succeeded in an action for wrongful dismissal.

Simmonds v Dowty Seals Ltd (1978)

Facts: S had been employed to work on the night shift. When his employer attempted to force him to work on the day shift he resigned.

Held: He could treat himself as constructively dismissed because the employer's conduct had amounted to an attempt to unilaterally change an express term of the employment contract.

Kevin Keegan v Newcastle United Football Club Limited (2010)

Facts: A football club manager resigned from his position and claimed he was constructively dismissed. He contended that when he was appointed manager of the club it was agreed that he would have the final say regarding the transfer of players into the club. The club breached this term by signing a particular player against his express wishes and that he 'had no option but to resign'.

Held: The manager had been constructively dismissed and was awarded in the region of £2m in damages.

In **British Aircraft Corporation v Austin (1978)** a failure to investigate a health and safety complaint was held to be conduct sufficient to entitle the employee to treat the contract as terminated.

If the employee does not resign in the event of the breach, he is deemed to have accepted the breach and waived any rights. However, he need not resign immediately and may legitimately wait until he has found another job: **Cox Toner (International) Ltd v Crook (1981).**

Statutory fair reasons for dismissal

Dismissal for one of the following reasons is **fair unless the employer acted unreasonably** in dismissing for the reason given:

- capabilities/qualifications of employee
- conduct of employee
- redundancy
- continued employment would contravene statute
- some other substantial reason.

Reasons for dismissal

An employer can only rely on a given reason for dismissal where he knew of it at the date of the dismissal.

Devis W & Sons Ltd v Atkins (1977)

Facts: The employer dismissed the employee and afterwards discovered that the employee had been guilty of dishonesty.

Held: Dishonesty was not the reason for the dismissal and therefore the employer could not rely on it in order to justify the dismissal as fair.

Stevenson v Golden Wonder Ltd (1977)

Facts: A technical manager took part in an unprovoked assault on another employee at a company social function held outside working hours in the company canteen.

Held: This was a fair reason for the dismissal, it was serious misconduct.

An example of 'some other substantial reason' justifying dismissal is the case of **Singh v London Country Bus Services (1976)**, where an employee in a position of trust was convicted of a criminal offence of dishonesty (which he committed off duty).

Reasonableness of employer

Once the employee has shown they were dismissed and the employer has shown that it was for one or more of the five fair reasons it is then for the tribunal to decide whether the dismissal was fair or unfair.

S98(4) ERA 1996 states that the determination of this question 'depends on whether in the circumstances (including the size and administrative resources of the employer's undertaking) the employer acted reasonably or unreasonably in treating it (the reason) as a sufficient reason for dismissing the employee'. The question 'shall be determined in accordance with equity and the substantial merits of the case'.

Case law shows that this 'reasonableness test' involves two questions:

- Whether the reason given was sufficiently serious to justify dismissal.
- Whether the employer adopted reasonable procedures both in coming to the decision to dismiss and in the manner of the dismissal.

The Arbitration, Conciliation and Advisory Service (ACAS) has issued codes of practice for procedures to be followed in coming to the decision to dismiss an employee (e.g. warnings, proper inquiry into alleged misconduct, etc.) which the employment tribunal has regard to. These were illustrated by the House of Lords in **Polkey v Dayton (AE) Services (1987)** where it was stated that:

- in a case of incapability, the employer will normally not act reasonably unless he gives the employee fair warning and an opportunity to mend his ways and show he can do the job
- in a case of misconduct, the employer will normally not act reasonably unless he investigates the complaint fully and fairly and hears whatever the employee wishes to say in his defence or in explanation or mitigation
- in a case of redundancy (this was the situation in **Polkey**) the employer will normally not act reasonably unless he warns and consults any employees affected or their representative, adopts a fair basis upon which to select for redundancy and takes such steps as may be reasonable to avoid or minimise redundancy by redeployment within his own organisation.

Inadmissible reasons for dismissal

Dismissal for one of the following reasons is **automatically unfair**. This means that there is no need to meet the length of employment condition. The tribunal will also make an additional award of compensation.

The inadmissible reasons are:

- victimisation of health and safety complainants or whistleblowers. A whistleblower is a person who raises a concern about wrongdoing occurring in an organisation. The revealed misconduct may be classified in many ways; for example, a violation of a law, rule, regulation and/or a direct threat to public interest, such as fraud, health/safety violations, and corruption
- pregnancy or the exercise of maternity leave rights
- trade union membership/non-membership/activities
- assertion of a statutory right e.g. the exercise of paternity leave rights
- unfair selection for redundancy.

Remedies for unfair dismissal

The remedies for unfair dismissal are wide-ranging and will be more advantageous to an employee than an action for wrongful dismissal.

The remedies are:

- re-instatement
- re-engagement
- compensation.

Re-instatement

This is an order that the employee may return to the same job without any break in continuity. It will only be awarded if the applicant wishes it and if it is practicable.

Re-engagement

This is where an order is made to the effect that the employee must be given comparable employment.

The EAT has ruled that a re-engagement order will not be granted if there has been a breakdown of relationship and confidence between the two parties.

Compensation

This is the usual remedy in a case of unfair dismissal. There are three types of payment: the basic award, the compensatory award and the additional or special award.

Basic award	Compensatory award	Additional award
18–21 years of age – ½ week's pay for each year of service. 22–40 years of age – 1 week's pay for each year of service. 41 plus – 1½ weeks' pay for each year of service. Maximum – 20 years' service at £475 a week.	Discretionary award of up to £78,335. Based on employee's losses and expenses. Reduced if the complainant contributed to his dismissal.	Given where: • the employer ignores an order for reinstatement or re-engagement • the dismissal is unfair because of race, sex or disability discrimination • the reason cited for dismissal is an inadmissible one.

4 Occupational safety

Legislative controls

The common law was not directly concerned with preventing occupational accidents, but instead, principally through the tort of negligence, provided compensation for the victims of such occurrences. Preventive measures have come through legislation, slowly at first, and in a piecemeal fashion, with specific statutes directed at particular industries and particular types of industrial premises and processes.

The Health and Safety at Work Act 1974 (HSWA) marked an important step forward. Additional statutory obligations regarding safety were introduced and applied uniformly for the first time to almost all work situations. Increased use was to be made of codes of practice. Older statutes, notably the Factories Act 1961, have been largely replaced by regulations made under the HSWA 1974. The administrative machinery was improved.

The HSWA 1974 imposed a general duty not only upon employers but also on those in control of premises, manufacturers, suppliers, the self-employed and employees. The duty covers the health and safety of both employees and other people who may be in the workplace. It is a duty to take such measures with respect to materials, people and methods of working as are reasonably practicable in order to ensure safety. Breach of these duties is a criminal offence only and cannot give rise to a civil action. Maximum penalties that can be imposed by the courts for certain health and safety offences are increased under the Health and Safety (Offences) Act 2008.

More recent changes emanating from an attempt to harmonise health and safety requirements across the European Union means that the law here has been in a state of flux. Six directives became the first six regulations (the 'six-pack') in 1992. Made under the HSWA 1974, and, supplemented by codes of practice, these have come gradually into effect down to 1996 as existing workplaces made any necessary changes. Existing statutes, such as the Factories Act 1961 and the Offices, Shops and Railway Premises Act 1963, have, over the same period, been replaced.

Central to the new structure are the Management of Health and Safety at Work Regulations 1992. A duty is imposed upon employers to make a suitable and sufficient assessment of the risks likely to arise to health and safety. Appropriate measures must then be taken to eliminate or reduce these risks or, as a last resort, personal protective equipment should be issued. Other provisions cover safety training, the issue of comprehensible and relevant information to employees, and responsibility for shared workplaces – such as when a number of sub-contractors are working on a building site. A duty is also imposed on employees to cooperate and take reasonable care for the safety of themselves and others.

The other five regulations relate to the provision and use of work equipment, personal protective equipment, manual handling operations, display screen equipment, and the workplace. Many of the requirements included already existed, but they have now been consolidated and applied generally. A detailed scheme for health and safety applying to all workplaces has now therefore largely replaced the previous patchwork of assorted enactments.

The Health and Safety Commission, acting through the Health and Safety Executive and its inspectorate, is responsible for the enforcement of the HSWA 1974 and its related legislation. The inspectors have wide powers of entry and investigation, and may issue improvement notices requiring a defaulter to remedy the specified contravention of the legislation within a stated period. More serious offences may result in a prohibition notice ordering the cessation of certain activities until the breach has been remedied. As a last resort, the factory occupier may face a criminal prosecution.

Two other duties of the occupier must be mentioned. Records must be kept of such matters as the required testing of equipment and of more serious accidents which must be notified to the inspector. The occupier is also required to set up a safety committee if requested by safety representatives nominated by a trade union.

Supplementary reading

Risk assessments

The Management of Health and Safety at Work Regulations 1999 (MHSWR) require all employers to carry out a hazard analysis study of their business operation, identify risks through the appointment of competent persons, analyse them as to their degree of seriousness and put in place appropriate protective and preventative measures to guard against them.

There are many other regulations that deal with the requirement to carry out risk assessments and put in place appropriate protective and preventative measures in relation to specified hazards or workplaces.

However, the MHSWR are of fundamental importance in health and safety law. Most of the remaining legislative provisions, including other regulations made pursuant to the EC Framework Directive (known as the six-pack), should be read in conjunction with them. In any event, in many respects, the various sets of regulations overlap.

Each set of regulations will usually have an associated Approved Code of Practice and/or guidance notes provided by the Health and Safety Executive or others.

Vulnerable employees

Health and safety legislation requires employers to take greater care of the more vulnerable employees, whether that is because:

- they have a pre-existing injury (mental or physical)
- they are more susceptible to dangerous working conditions or processes (such as in the case of pregnant women)
- they cannot appreciate the dangers (because of lack of experience or maturity, such as in the case of young people)
- they have a disability that otherwise puts them at a disadvantage.

The Management of Health and Safety at Work Regulations 1999 specifically require employers to take account of individuals' capabilities when assessing risks, particularly so in the case of pregnant women and young people.

Civil liability for occupational injuries

In addition to any criminal liability for safety breaches, the employer must initially pay statutory sick pay to workers absent through injury caused by a breach. Later, he or she may be obliged to pay compensation following a common law claim for breach of an implied term in the contract of employment. Claims can also be for the torts of negligence or breach of statutory duty. Liability may arise for the employer's own acts or for the acts of other employees for whom he or she is vicariously responsible.

Claims for breach of contract or negligence are based on the principles outlined earlier. It is well established that an employer owes a duty of care to his employees in three respects:

(1) With regard to other staff, he must take care with their selection, give proper instructions and training and dismiss those whose behaviour is dangerous.

Hudson v Ridge Manufacturing Co Ltd (1957)

Facts: An employee, known to be a practical joker, took a prank too far and injured a fellow employee.

Held: The employer was liable to pay compensation for the employee's actions, as they knew his character and so should have taken action to either curb his behaviour, or dismiss him.

(2) He must be careful in providing and maintaining the materials, machinery and other equipment provided. By the Employers' Liability (Defective Equipment) Act 1969, he cannot escape liability by showing that the equipment was obtained from a reputable supplier.

Bradford v Robinson Rentals Ltd (1967)

Facts: The claimant was required by his employer to take an old van to collect a new one. The weather was very cold and the old van did not have a heater. The claimant suffered frostbite.

Held: The employer had failed to provide suitable plant and therefore was liable to the claimant.

(3) There is the duty to combine staff and equipment into a reasonably safe system of working.

The test of whether the duty has been broken is based upon what a reasonable and prudent employer would have done in the circumstances. Thus, it would be reasonable to take greater care where the consequences of an accident would be severe or where an employee at risk has a known disability.

Paris v Stepney Borough Council (1951)

Facts: A Local Authority employed Mr Paris as a garage mechanic. Mr Paris had lost the sight of one eye during the war. In order to loosen a stiff bolt he struck it with a hammer; a piece of metal flew off and, because he was not wearing goggles, struck him in his good eye, causing him to become totally blind.

Held: The employers, knowing of his disability, should have taken extra care to provide goggles for him. The more serious the possible damage, the greater the precautions that should be taken. Stepney Borough Council owed a special duty of care to Mr Paris and had been negligent in failing to supply him with goggles, even though sufficient equipment was not given to other employees.

The third requisite for a successful claim is that the employee's loss was suffered in consequence of the employer's breach and was not too remote.

Robinson v Post Office (1974)

Facts: The claimant slipped on a ladder at work because of oil on the step and suffered a minor injury. He went to hospital and was given an anti-tetanus injection, as a result of which he contracted encephalitis due to an allergy of which he was previously unaware.

Held: The defendants were legally responsible for the encephalitis as well as for the minor injury: if a wrongdoer ought to foresee that, as a result of his wrongful act, the victim may require medical treatment, then he is liable for the consequences of the treatment applied even though he could not reasonably foresee those consequences.

The Employer's Liability (Compulsory Insurance) Act 1969 now makes it compulsory for all employers to insure against liability so that any claims for compensation can be paid.

In the case of both negligence and breach of statutory duty, the employer may reduce the damages payable on the grounds of contributory negligence by proving that the employee was partially to blame for the accident. Where reasonable care only is required, the employer may defeat the claim by delegating the duty to an apparently responsible third party; these defences are not available where the duty is strict.

Supplementary reading

Social security compensation

More immediate compensation for an injured employee may be obtained through the social security scheme. While absent from work, statutory sick pay and incapacity benefit may be claimed. After return to work or after 6 months, if there are lasting effects of the injury, a claim may be made for disablement benefit – a pension paid on a sliding scale according to a medical assessment of 'loss of faculty'; the loss must be at least 14 per cent. There may also be entitlement to various supplements, for example for dependants, or to other benefits such as a disability living allowance. In order to claim disablement benefit, an employee must prove that loss arose either from personal injury caused by accident arising out of, or in the course of, employment or from a prescribed industrial disease.

An important change introduced by the Social Security Act 1989 allows the Department of Social Security to recoup almost all social security benefits received in the ensuing 5 years from compensation paid in respect of an injury or disease. Before an employer (or insurance company) pays any compensation, including out-of-court settlement, a certificate must be obtained from the Compensation Recovery Unit of the Department stating the amount of benefit to be deducted. This amount must then be deducted and paid over to the Unit and the balance paid to the injured employee.

Supplementary reading: Chapter summary

At the end of this chapter, students should make sure that they understand the following:

- the employment relationship, particularly the distinction between employees and independent contractors
- duties of employers/rights of employees, particularly regarding
  - wages
  - other general obligations, such as to provide a reasonably safe system of work
  - sex discrimination and race discrimination
- duties of employees, such as obedience, care and good faith
- notice and dismissal
- summary dismissal and wrongful dismissal
- unfair dismissal
- occupational safety:
  - legislative controls
  - judicial controls
  - liability and compensation for occupational injuries.

5 Test your understanding questions

Test your understanding 1

An employer always had an implied duty:

A To provide facilities for smokers

B To give employees who leave a reference

C To provide work

D To behave reasonably and responsibly towards employees

Test your understanding 2

Which of the following statements suggests that John is an independent contractor in relation to the work he carries out for Zed Ltd?

(i) He is required to provide his own tools.

(ii) He is required to carry out his work personally and is not free to send a substitute.

(iii) He is paid in full without any deduction of income tax.

A (i) and (ii) only

B (ii) and (iii) only

C (i) and (iii) only

D (i), (ii) and (iii)

Test your understanding 3

Which of the following does not constitute a duty owed by an employee towards his employer under the common law?

A A duty not to misuse confidential information

B A duty to provide faithful service

C A duty to maintain trust and confidence

D A duty to obey all orders given to him by his employer

Test your understanding 4

Gertrude, aged 61, had worked for Fabulous Fabrics for 25 years and the employment tribunal has ruled that she was unfairly dismissed.

Which of the following best illustrates the calculation of the basic award to which she will be entitled?

A 1.5 weeks' pay × 20

B 1.5 weeks' pay × 25

C 1 wook's pay × 20

D 1 week's pay × 25

Test your understanding 5

Which one of the following cannot justify the dismissal of an employee?

A The employee's incompetence

B The employee's misconduct

C The employee's inability to do the job without contravening a statute

D That the employee proposes to join an independent trade union

Test your understanding 6

An employee is entitled to a written statement of employment particulars:

A Immediately on commencing employment

B Within one month of commencing employment

C Within two months of commencing employment

D Within three months of commencing employment

Test your understanding 7

H plc carries on its business using both employees and independent contractors. It is important for H plc to be able to distinguish between its employees and its independent contractors for a number of reasons.

Which of the following is incorrect?

A Employers owe statutory occupational safety duties to employees but not to independent contractors

B Employees have a right not to be unfairly dismissed, but this does not apply to independent contractors

C H plc must deduct income tax and national insurance contributions from the wages of its employees, but not from the amounts paid to independent contractors

D H plc must give statutory notice of detailed terms of work to part-time employees but not to independent contractors

Test your understanding 8

Various tests have been developed for the purpose of distinguishing between employees and independent contractors.

Which one of the following is not an identifiable test applicable?

A The control test

B The liability test

C The organisation test

D The economic reality test

Test your understanding 9

Tom had in the past been employed as a technician by a television production company. He decided to work for himself and offered his services to a number of production companies.

The contracts he obtained never lasted for more than 10 days, and on one or two occasions, he sent a substitute when he was unable to attend personally.

One – Tom submitted invoices, which were paid in full without deduction of tax. He was registered for VAT, and bore the responsibility of dealing with his own accounts and chasing slow payers. Two – Tom provided no tools of his own, contributed no money to the cost of any of the productions, and the companies which employed him determined the time, place and duration of any assignment.

Required:

Complete the following:

In relation to the work that he undertakes, information provided in the scenario content numbered .... (1 word) **(2 marks)** supports the argument that he is an employee according to the .... test (1 word) **(1 mark)**. However, the fact that the scenario content numbered .... (1 word) **(2 marks)** applied to Tom is more consistent with his status as an independent contractor. That Tom may send along a substitute is more consistent with his status as an .... (2 words) **(1 mark).** On balance, Tom is likely to be regarded as an .... (2 words) **(1 mark).** The distinction is particularly important to issues including .... (1 word) **(2 marks)** protection, ... (1 word) **(2 marks)** liability and the payment of .... (4 words) **(3 marks)**

(Total: 14 marks)

Test your understanding 10

Nigel is employed by New Bank Limited as a clerk. He has worked for the bank for 3 years, and, until recently, the quality of his work was excellent. In the last few weeks, however, the quality of his work has deteriorated and he is often late for work. His manager, Supreet, has warned him informally on several occasions that his work is unsatisfactory, but to no avail. When Nigel joined the bank he undertook to study to obtain his banking qualifications within 3 years, but so far he has made little progress, passing only the first part of the examinations after several attempts.

Supreet has spoken to the bank's personnel manager about Nigel's poor performance and his failure to obtain the required qualifications within 3 years. He has advised Supreet that Nigel's employment should be terminated unless there is an immediate improvement in his performance and punctuality.

Supreet proposes to hold a formal disciplinary interview with Nigel, but is concerned about its content and structure.

Required:

(a) Delete as appropriate and complete the following:

Nigel's contract may be determined by giving him either .... **(2 marks)** weeks' notice or the length of notice specified in the contract, whichever is the .... (1 word) **(1 mark).** Failure to give Nigel the correct period of notice would constitute .... (2 words) **(2 marks).** A claim may be made before the court or .... (2 words) **(1 mark)** and must be made within .... (2 words) **(1 mark).** Only if the Bank can show that Nigel was guilty of gross misconduct can .... (1 word) **(1 mark)** dismissal be justified.

(8 marks)

(b) Nigel could alternatively claim .... (1 word) **(1 mark)** dismissal and he may make a claim within 3 months of his dismissal.

(1 mark)

(c) The Bank would have to show that the reason for the dismissal was for one of the following.

.... (1 word) **(1 mark)**

.... (1 word) **(1 mark)**

.... (1 word) **(1 mark)**

.... (4 words) **(1 mark)**

.... (3 words) **(1 mark)**

(5 marks)

Furthermore, the tribunal would have to be satisfied that the Bank acted reasonably in all the circumstances.

(d) The bank would probably rely on .... (1 word) **(1 mark)** as the potentially fair ground for Nigel's dismissal on the basis that his performance has been unsatisfactory and that he was recruited on the understanding that he would gain his banking qualification within 3 years.

(1 mark)

(Total: 15 marks)

Test your understanding answers

Test your understanding 1

D

This is an implied duty of an employer.

Test your understanding 2

C

Whilst an employee is required to carry out work personally, an independent contractor can use a substitute. A contractor is required however, to provide his own tools and pay income tax personally, having received the full contract price for the services provided. (C) is therefore the correct answer.

Test your understanding 3

D

An employee is only under an obligation to obey orders which are lawful and reasonable.

Test your understanding 4

A

An employee is entitled to 1.5 weeks' pay for each year of service over the age of 41, up to a maximum of 20 years. The week's pay element is subject to a statutory maximum.

Test your understanding 5

D

(A), (B) and (C) are all stated in the Employment Rights Act 1996 as being categories of potentially fair dismissal. Dismissal in category (D) is an automatically unfair dismissal.

Test your understanding 6

C

Test your understanding 7

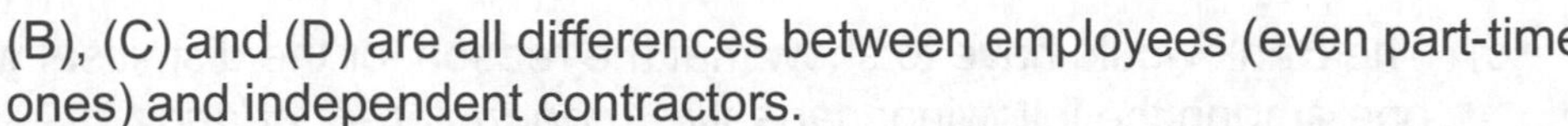

A

(B), (C) and (D) are all differences between employees (even part-time ones) and independent contractors.

Test your understanding 8

B

(A), (C) and (D) identify recognised tests applicable in distinguishing the employee from the independent contractor. (B) is false and therefore the correct answer.

Test your understanding 9

In relation to the work that he undertakes, information provided in the scenario content numbered *two* supports the argument that he is an employee, according to the *multiple* test. However, the fact that the scenario content numbered one applied to Tom is more consistent with his status as an *independent contractor*. That Tom may send along a substitute, is more consistent with his status as an independent contractor. On balance, Tom is an independent contractor. The distinction is particularly important to issues, including *statutory* protection, *vicarious* liability and the payment of *tax and national insurance*.

Test your understanding 10

(a) Nigel's contract may be determined by giving him either *3* weeks' notice or the length of notice specified in the contract, whichever is the *longer*. Failure to give Nigel the correct period of notice would constitute *wrongful dismissal*. A claim may be made before the court or *Employment Tribunal* and must be made within *6 years*. Only if the Bank can show that Nigel was guilty of gross misconduct can summary dismissal be justified.

(b) Nigel could alternatively claim *unfair* dismissal and he may make a claim within 3 months of the date of his dismissal.

(c) The Bank would have to show that the reason for the dismissal was one among the following: *capability, conduct, redundancy, contravention of statutory provisions, other substantial reason*. Furthermore, the tribunal would have to be satisfied that the Bank acted reasonably in all the circumstances.

(d) The bank would probably rely on capability as the potentially fair ground for Nigel's dismissal on the basis that his performance has been unsatisfactory and that he was recruited on the understanding that he would gain his banking qualification within *3* years.

chapter

4

Company Administration

Chapter learning objectives

On completion of their studies students should be able to:

- describe the essential characteristics of the different forms of business organisations and the implications of corporate personality
- explain the purpose and legal status of the articles of association
- explain the ability of a company to contract
- explain the use and procedure of board meetings and general meetings of shareholders
- identify the various types of shareholder resolutions.

1 Business organisations

Sole traders/practitioners

Under a sole tradership or practionership, as the name suggests, one person is fully responsible for putting in the capital and expertise of the business. If the business should fail, then that person is fully liable for the debts of the business and is subject to the rules of bankruptcy.

Sole traders are usually found in the retail trades or in smaller service businesses such as plumbers or electricians.

There are various advantages of running a business as a sole trader:

(1) They can be set up informally with no legal requirements.

(2) Business decisions are entirely those of the sole trader with no need for consultation or meetings.

(3) All the profits accrue to the sole trader personally.

Some disadvantages of the sole trader are as follows:

(1) The personal wealth of the sole trader is at risk if the business should fail. He is fully liable for all the debts of the business.

(2) The business is dependent on the continued health and strength of the sole trader.

(3) Other disadvantages lie with the size of the business, such as diversification, obtaining finance or offering choice.

Business name

Many traders and practitioners prefer to trade under a 'business name' that is in general, a name which does not consist solely of the surname and initials of the trader or professional. For example, a business called 'High Street Fashions' must be operating under a business name. First, this is clearly not the name of a real person, and second, it cannot be the name of a company as it does not end in 'Limited' or 'Ltd', 'public limited company' or 'plc'.

If a trader or a professional chooses to operate under a business name then he or she must comply with the rules contained in Part 41 of the CA 2006, Sections 1192–1208. Do not confuse a business name (which is not the name of a person or any legal entity) with a company name which is the name of a legal person.

The main controls under the Act are that the name of the owner of the business:

- must be stated on all business letters, written orders, receipts and invoices and so on, and
- must be stated prominently at all premises from which the business is carried on.

The reason for this requirement is that, to use the above example, High Street Fashions does not exist as a legal entity, and cannot therefore sue or be sued.

Partnerships

The Partnership Act 1890 sec.1 defines a partnership as 'the relation which subsists between persons carrying on a business in common with a view to profit'.

A partnership can be a small operation or as with some large firms of solicitors and accountants partnerships with several hundred partners.

Characteristics of a partnership

In order for a partnership to exist, a business must be carried on with a view to profit. This means that the persons involved in the partnership intend the business to yield a profit and they are all entitled to share in that profit.

The following do not necessarily create a partnership:

- joint ownership of property
- the sharing of gross returns
- the sharing of expenses.

Cox v Coulson (1916)

Facts: C agreed with M that M would put on a play at C's theatre. C was to have 60% and M 40% of the gross box office receipts. C paid the expenses of running the theatre and M paid the expenses of putting on the play. During a performance the claimant, who was in the audience, was accidentally shot by one of the actors. The claimant sued C alleging that C was M's partner and was jointly liable with M.

Held: C was not M's partner because they merely shared gross box office receipts.

A partnership begins as soon as the partners start their business activity. The actual agreement may be made earlier or later than that date.

No formalities are required to form general partnerships, no documentation and no registration. The reason for this is that The Partnership Act 1890 applies to every partnership whether written or oral. Many of the Act's provisions apply, unless they are excluded by a **partnership agreement**. The PA 1890 provides that partners shall share profits equally, but in cases where partners contribute different amounts of capital this may not be appropriate and partners will need to agree specific profit sharing arrangements within their partnership agreement.

The partnership agreement is a contract. Like any contract it may be:

- express (e.g. oral, in writing or by deed), or
- implied.

The partners are contractually bound by the terms they have agreed, even if they conflict with PA 1890.

Partnership name

If there are several partners (more than three or four usually), they will usually choose a 'firm name'. This may be an business name, for example Mobile Valeting, or it may comprise the names of one or more of the senior partners. Additions such as 'Company' or '& Co.' are allowed by the CA 2006, but not 'limited' or 'Ltd' or 'plc'.

The names of all partners must be shown beside letterheads, except for firms with more than twenty partners, where no names need to be given. Such a firm must display all partners' names at its business premises, and written disclosure must be given on request to those doing business with the firm.

Under the CA 2006, artificial names which are misleading, offensive or falsely suggest connection with another business are prohibited. In the UK a person may not carry on business under a name which is likely to give the impression that the business is connected with any of the following:

- Her Majesty's Government
- The Scottish Administration
- Her Majesty's Government in Northern Ireland
- Any local or public authority specified in regulations made by the Secretary of State.

If an application is made for the approval of a particular name the Secretary of State may require the applicant to seek the approval of a specified Government department (Section 1193 CA 2006).

When operating under a firm name, partners must also beware the tort of 'passing off'. This would occur if their chosen name and the nature of their business was so like those of a competitor that third parties might be deceived. If Mr A and Mr B choose to call their retail shop 'Marks and Spencers', the owners of the well-known Marks and Spencers retail chain could obtain an injunction against A and B by suing under the tort of passing off. The well-known Marks and Spencers could also claim compensation if it could be shown that use of that name by A and B had caused a loss of revenue.

Limited partnerships

Under the Limited Partnership Act 1907, a limited partnership is a partnership in which the liability of one or more partners is limited to their capital contribution.

A limited partnership must fulfil the following conditions:

- There must be at least one partner with unlimited liability.
- The partnership must be registered with the registrar of companies as a limited partnership.
- Limited partners may not participate in the management of the business. If they do, they forfeit their limited liability.
- A limited partner has no power to bind the firm to contracts, i.e. unlike the unlimited partners, he is not an agent of the firm.

Limited Partnerships should not be confused with Limited Liability Partnerships formed under the LLP Act 2000 (see later).

2 Authority of partners

Agency relationship

When entering into a contract to carry out the business, each partner is acting as the agent of all the partners:

- The actual authority of a partner is set out in the partnership agreement.
- The apparent authority is set out in s5 PA 1890.

S5 PA 1890 states that every partner is the agent of the firm and of the other partners. This means that each partner has the power to bind all partners to business transactions entered into within their actual or apparent authority.

Apparent authority

Under s5 every partner is presumed to have the implied or apparent authority to:

- sell the firm's goods
- buy goods necessary for, or usually employed in, the business
- receive payments of debts due to the firm
- engage employees
- employ a solicitor to act for the firm in defence of a claim or in the pursuance of a debt.

Trading partnerships

The above implied powers apply to both trading and non-trading partnerships. Partners in trading partnerships have additional powers, such as to borrow money.

In order to be acting within his implied authority, the individual partner must be acting within the usual scope of a partner's powers in the particular business concerned.

Mercantile Credit Co v Garrod (1962)

Facts: P and G entered into a partnership to let lock-up garages and repair cars. P ran the business and G was a sleeping partner. The partnership agreement expressly stated that the firm would not buy and sell cars. P sold a car to a finance company, M. M sued G to recover the £700 which it had paid to P for the car. G denied liability claiming that P when selling the car had been acting outside the agreed limits of the firm's business and therefore P had no actual or apparent authority to make the contract. Evidence was given that other garage businesses of the type carried on by P and G did deal in cars.

Held: The test of what is the firm's business is not what the partners agreed it should be but 'what it appears to the outside world' to be. Under that test P appeared to M to be carrying on business of a kind carried on by such a firm. This contract was within the apparent authority of P and therefore the contract was binding on G.

3 Liability for partnership debts

Is there liability in contract?

The firm is liable for contracts made by a partner if he was acting within his actual or apparent authority.

The firm is not bound by the apparent authority of a partner if:

- the third party knows the partner has no actual authority, or
- the partner has no actual authority and the third party does not know or believe him to be a partner.

Holding out

Every person who by his words or conduct represents himself (or knowingly allows himself to be represented) as a partner is liable as if he is a partner to anyone who thereby gives credit to the firm: s14 PA 1890.

Martyn v Gray (1863)

Facts: G went to Cornwall to discuss the possibility of investing in a tin mine belonging to X. Nothing came of the discussions, but while G was in Cornwall he was introduced by X to M as 'a gentleman down from London, a man of capital'. M later gave X credit believing he was in partnership with G.

Held: The introduction amounted to a representation that G was in partnership with X, and so G was liable for the debt incurred subsequent to the introduction. He should have made the true position clear by correcting the impression made.

Liability in tort

Where a tort is committed during the ordinary course of the partnership's business, or by a partner acting with the authority of the other partners, the partners are jointly and severally liable to the person who has suffered loss.

Misapplication of money or property

The partnership is liable to make good the loss where a third party's money or property is misapplied:

- after being received by a partner within his actual or apparent authority, or
- while it is in the custody of the firm, such as in the partnership bank account.

Which partners are liable (general partnership)?

General rule	Every partner is jointly and severally liable for the debts and contracts of the business. Outsiders can sue one partner alone or the firm.
New partners	A new partner is not personally liable for debts incurred before they became a partner.
Retiring partners	A retiring partner remains liable for any debts incurred while he was a partner. If no notice of the retirement is given, the firm continues to be bound by his actions as he is still being held out as a partner.
Change in partners	Where a third party deals with a partnership after a change in partners, all of the partners of the old firm are still treated as partners, until the third party receives notice of the change: • Previous customers require actual notice. • Third parties who were not existing customers can be notified by a notice in the London Gazette: s36 PA 1890. This is known as constructive notice. Notification must take place prior to retirement if the retiring partner is to avoid liability for contracts entered into after his retirement.
Novation	A creditor agrees with the outgoing, continuing and/or incoming partners that liability for an existing debt will be that of the continuing and incoming partners. (Thus the liability of the outgoing partner is removed and the incoming partner becomes liable for the debt even though it was incurred before he became a partner.)
Indemnity	The continuing and incoming partners may agree to indemnify the outgoing partner against debts incurred pre- and/or post-retirement.

4 Dissolution of a partnership

Without court order

The partnership will automatically end in the following situations:

- The expiry of a fixed term or the completion of a specific enterprise.
- One of the partners gives notice (unless the partnership agreement excludes this right).
- Death or bankruptcy of a partner (the partnership agreement will usually make provision for the partnership to continue if a partner should die).
- Where continuation of the partnership would be illegal.

Hudgell, Yeates and Co v Watson (1978)

Facts: Practising solicitors are required by law to have a practising certificate. One of the partners in a firm of solicitors forgot to renew his certificate which meant that it was illegal for him to practice.

Held: The failure to renew the practising certificate brought the partnership to an end, although a new partnership continued between the other two members.

By court order

Under s35 PA 1890, the court can bring a partnership to an end in any of the following situations:

- Partner has mental disorder or permanent incapacity.
- Partner engages in activity prejudicial to the business.
- Partner wilfully or persistently breaches the partnership agreement.
- Partner conducts himself in a way that it is no longer reasonably practicable for the others to carry on in business with him.
- Business can only be carried on at a loss.
- It is just and equitable to do so.

Distribution of assets

In the event of dissolution the assets of the partnership will be used to pay off the debts of the partnership. As a partnership does not have the advantage of limited liability status, if the proceeds on the sale of the assets does not cover the debts then the partners' personal wealth will be called upon to make up the shortfall.

The proceeds from the sale of the assets will be applied in the following order:

(i) paying debts to outsiders

(ii) paying the partners any advance they made to the firm beyond their capital contribution i.e. a loan

(iii) paying the capital contribution of the partners.

If there is a residue remaining this will be divided between the partners in the same proportion in which they share the profits of the partnership.

In the event that the assets are insufficient to meet the debts to outsiders then profits held back from previous years or partners' capital will be used to make good the shortfall. If these are also insufficient then the partners will individually contribute in the proportion to which they shared in the profits.

5 Corporations

The concept of incorporation

Corporations can come into existence in various ways. In England, the earliest surviving way is by Royal Charter. The Charter is issued by the Crown (the government) under the Royal prerogative on the advice of the Privy Council. Today, this form of incorporation is used almost entirely for non-trading bodies, such as the new universities, and professional bodies (including CIMA). The BBC is another example.

As the powers of Parliament and the functions of government increased in the last two centuries, it then became common to create corporate bodies by statute. Local government authorities are notable examples today.

For businesses, a relatively simpler procedure is possible. Corporate bodies – companies – can be created under the Companies Acts by registration with a public official, the Registrar of Companies and, provided that the requirements of the Acts have been met, it is he who issues the certificate of incorporation (see later). The position today is substantially governed by the Companies Act 2006 which consolidates many earlier Acts.

The doctrine and veil of incorporation

The company is a separate legal entity (i.e. separate from its shareholders, the owners, and its directors, the managers).

Salomon v Salomon & Co Ltd (1897)

Facts: The claimant, S, had carried on business for 30 years. He decided to form a limited company to purchase the business, so he and six members of his family subscribed for one share each in the company. The company then purchased the business from S for £30,000, the purchase price being payable to the claimant by the issue of 20,000 £1 shares, and £10,000 of debentures which was secured over the company's assets. The company became insolvent within twelve months and the company went into insolvent liquidation owing £10,000 to S and a lot of money to other creditors.

The liquidator claimed that the company's business was in effect still the claimant's. Therefore he should bear the liability for its debts, and that repayment of the debenture debt to him should be postponed until the company's trade creditors were paid.

Held: The House of Lords held that S and the company were two separate legal persons at law. The claimant was under no liability to the company or its creditors, his debentures were validly issued and the security created by them over the company's assets were effective.

Lee v Lee's Air Farming Ltd (1960)

Facts: This case concerned an aerial crop-spraying business. Mr Lee owned the majority of the shares (all but one) and was the sole working director of the company. He was killed while piloting the aircraft.

Held: Although Lee was the majority shareholder and sole working director of the company, he and the company were separate legal persons. Therefore he could also be an employee of the company for the purposes of the relevant statute with rights against it when killed in an accident in the course of his employment.

Macaura v Northern Life Assurance (1925)

Facts: M owned a forest. He formed a company in which he beneficially owned all the shares and sold his forest to it. He, however, continued to maintain an insurance policy on the forest in his own name. The forest was destroyed by fire.

Held: He could not claim on the policy since the property damaged belonged to the company, not him, and as shareholder he had no insurable interest in the forest.

Consequences of incorporation

There are a number of consequences of being a separate legal entity:

- Limited liability. A company is fully liable for its own debts. If a company fails, the liability of the shareholders is limited to any amount still unpaid on their share capital (or any amount they have agreed to contribute if the company is limited by guarantee).
- A company enters into contracts in its own name and can sue and be sued in its own name.
- A company owns its own property.
- A company has perpetual succession, irrespective of the fate of shareholders.
- The management of a company is separated from its ownership.
- A company is subject to the requirements of the Companies Act 2006 (CA06).
- Where a company suffers an injury, it is the company itself that must take the appropriate remedial action. This is known as the rule in **Foss v Harbottle**.

Foss v Harbottle (1843)

Facts: Two minority shareholders initiated legal proceedings against, among others, the directors of the company. They claimed that the directors had misapplied the company's assets.

Held: The court dismissed the claim and held that when a company is wronged by its directors it is only the company that has standing to sue.

Lifting the veil of incorporation

The phrase ‘lifting the veil of incorporation’ means that in certain circumstances the courts can look through the company to the identity of the shareholders.

The usual result of lifting the veil is that the members or directors become personally liable for the company’s debts.

Statutory examples

There are a number of occasions on which statute will intervene to lift the veil:

- S399 of CA06 requires accounts to be prepared by a group of related companies, therefore recognising the common link between them.

- Under the Insolvency Act 1986 (IA 1986), members and/or directors liable for wrongful or fraudulent trading may be personally liable for losses arising as a result. (See Chapter 5).
- If a public company starts to trade without first obtaining a trading certificate, the directors can be made personally liable for any loss or damage suffered by a third party: S767 CA06.
- Under the Company Directors Disqualification Act 1986, if a director who is disqualified participates in the management of a company, that director will be jointly or severally liable for the company's debts.

Case law examples

Sham companies

The veil will be lifted only where **'special circumstances** exist indicating that it is a mere facade concealing the true facts': **Woolfson v Strathclyde Regional Council (1978)**.

Gilford Motor Co Ltd v Horne (1933)

Facts: An employee had a covenant in his contract of employment which stated that he would not solicit his former employer's customers. After he left their employment he formed a company to solicit those customers and claimed it was the company approaching the customers and not him.

Held: The court held that the company could be restrained from competition, as the previous employee had set it up to evade his own legal obligations. An injunction was granted against him and the company.

Jones v Lipman (1962)

Facts: Mr. Lipman contracted to sell his land and thereafter changed his mind. In order to avoid an order of specific performance he transferred his property to a company.

Held: The veil was lifted in order to prevent the seller of a house evading specific performance. An order of specific performance was granted against him and the company to transfer the property to the buyer.

Nationality

In times of war it is illegal to trade with the enemy. It may be possible to lift the veil of incorporation so as to impute to a company the same nationality as its members.

Daimler v Continental Tyre & Rubber Co (1916)

Facts: C sued D for debts owing. C was a UK company, however all shareholders but one were German. D argued that they should not pay the debt to German individuals to prevent money going towards Germany's war effort.

Held: As C was German, D need not discharge their debt to C since effective control of the latter was in enemy hands and hence to do so would be to trade with the enemy.

Groups

Although each company within a group is a separate legal entity, there have been a number of cases where the courts have lifted the veil between a holding company and its various subsidiaries. This has generally been done in order to:

- benefit the group by obtaining a higher compensation payment on the compulsory purchase of premises
- benefit creditors of an insolvent company by making other companies within the group liable for its debts.

DHN Food Distributors v London Borough of Tower Hamlets (1976)

Facts: DHN carried on business from premises owned by a subsidiary. The subsidiary itself had no business activities. Both companies had the same directors. The local authority acquired the premises compulsorily but refused to pay compensation for disturbance of the business since the subsidiary, which owned the premises, did not also carry on the business.

Held: The companies were, in economic terms, mutually interdependent on each other and therefore they should be regarded as a single economic entity. Thus there was a valid claim for disturbance since ownership of the premises and business activity were in the hands of a single group.

The above case can, however, be contrasted with the more recent case of **Adams v Cape Industries (1990)** which represents the current position:

Adams v Cape Industries (1990)

Facts: Cape was an English registered company. One of its subsidiaries, CPC, a company incorporated and carrying on business in the United States, had a court judgement against it.

Held: It was unsuccessfully argued that the veil should be lifted between the companies so as to enable the judgement to be enforced against Cape. The Court of Appeal said there were no special circumstances indicating that CPC was a mere facade for Cape such as was the situation in **Jones v Lipman**.

There was no agency as CPC was an independent corporation under the control of its chief executive.

The DHN doctrine of economic reality would not be extended beyond its own facts to facts such as these where the effect would be to make a holding company liable for its subsidiary's debts.

Family investment companies

In recent years the use of family investment companies was diminishing due to the courts using the assets of such companies as part of the matrimonial pot for distribution following a divorce.

The case of **Prest v Petrodel Resources Ltd & Others (2013)** which went on appeal to the Supreme Court was a highly anticipated case as it would give a definitive answer to the circumstances in which the corporate veil can be lifted.

Prest v Petrodel Resources Ltd & Others (2013)

Facts: There were a number of properties owned by the Petrodel Group, a group of companies which were wholly owned by the husband. The issue was whether the corporate veil could be lifted so that the wife could seek financial relief from the properties owned by the companies.

Held: The Supreme Court concluded that the properties were held by the company on resulting trust for the husband. The properties had been funded with the husband's money rather than that of the Petrodel Group companies. As the husband was a beneficial owner of the properties they were deemed to form part of his estate and the wife would have financial recourse to the properties following divorce.

6 LLPs

Ordinary (or general) partnerships lack the characteristics of a company in the sense that they do not have limited liability or separate legal personality. Over time the government was pressurised to recognise the needs of some partnerships (especially professional partnerships such as solicitors, accountants and auditors) to limit their liability and have separate legal personality without having to form a company. This resulted in the Limited Liability Partnerships Act 2000 (LLPs).

LLPs have similar features to private limited companies, for example, their members (i.e. not called partners) are not directly responsible for the debts of the partnership.

Incorporation	• Incorporation document must be delivered to registrar stating name of LLP, location and address of registered office, names and addresses of members (minimum two). • Must send a declaration of compliance that LLP satisfies requirements of the Limited Liability Partnerships Act 2000. • Registrar issues a certificate of incorporation.
Membership	• First members sign incorporation document. Later members join by agreement with the existing members. • Membership ceases on death, dissolution or in accordance with agreement with other members. • Rights and duties are set out in membership agreement. If no agreement, governed by Limited Liability Partnership Regulations 2001. • Each member acts as an agent of the LLP.
Designated members	• Perform the administrative and filing duties of the LLP. • Incorporation document specifies who they are. • Must be at least two designated members. If there are none, all members will be designated members.
Name	• Must end with Limited Liability Partnership, llp or LLP. • Rules on choice are the same as for companies.
Taxation	• Members are treated as if they are partners carrying on business in a partnership, i.e. they pay income tax, not corporation tax.

Liability for debts	• The liability of a member of an LLP to contribute to its debts is limited to his capital contribution. However, there is no requirement for a capital contribution, and any contribution made can be withdrawn at any time. • If an LLP goes into liquidation, the court can order the members to repay any drawings made in the previous two years if it can be shown that the member knew or had reasonable grounds to believe that the LLP: – was unable to pay its debts at the date of withdrawal, or – would become unable to pay its debts because of the withdrawal: s214A Insolvency Act 1986 (IA 1986). The fraudulent and wrongful trading provisions of IA 1986 apply to members of LLPs in the same way as they apply to directors of companies.
Differences between LLP and partnership	• The liability of the members of an LLP is limited to the amount of capital they have agreed to contribute. • The LLP must file annual accounts and an annual report with Companies House. • LLP is an artificial legal entity with perpetual succession. It can hold property in its own right, enter into contracts in its own name, create floating charges (covered in Chapter 5), sue and be sued.

Company versus partnership

Company	General Partnership
Created by registration – with a written constitution.	No special formality required for creation.
Separate legal person, i.e. can own property, sue or be sued, and contract in own name.	Not a separate legal person – the partners own any property, are jointly liable on contracts and are liable if sued.
Shares are transferable. However, the articles of private companies usually restrict transfer.	Limits on transfer of shares (may require dissolution of partnership or consent of other partners to enable partners to realise their share).

Can create both fixed and floating charges as security for borrowing.	Can only create fixed charges as security for borrowing. More usual to have personal guarantees.
Managed by directors, who may or may not also be shareholders.	Managed by partners, who are also the owners of the business.
The company cannot usually return capital to its members (except on dissolution).	Partners may withdraw their capital.
The company is liable for its debts. (No personal liability for shareholders beyond any unpaid portion of the price of their shares or the amount they have agreed to contribute.)	The partners are personally liable for the debts of the firm. Their liability is joint and several.
Must make information about financial affairs and ownership publicly available.	Private business. No disclosure of results.
The business is run by the directors. Members have no right to participate.	Every partner has the right to take part in the management of the business.
Must comply with Companies Act requirements concerning meetings, special resolutions, filing accounts and annual return.	No administrative requirements regarding meetings.
Formal dissolution procedure (known as liquidation). Death/bankruptcy of any member/director does not dissolve the company.	May dissolve by agreement. Automatically dissolved on the death/bankruptcy of any partner.
Companies pay corporation tax.	Partners pay income tax.

7 Types of company

Introduction

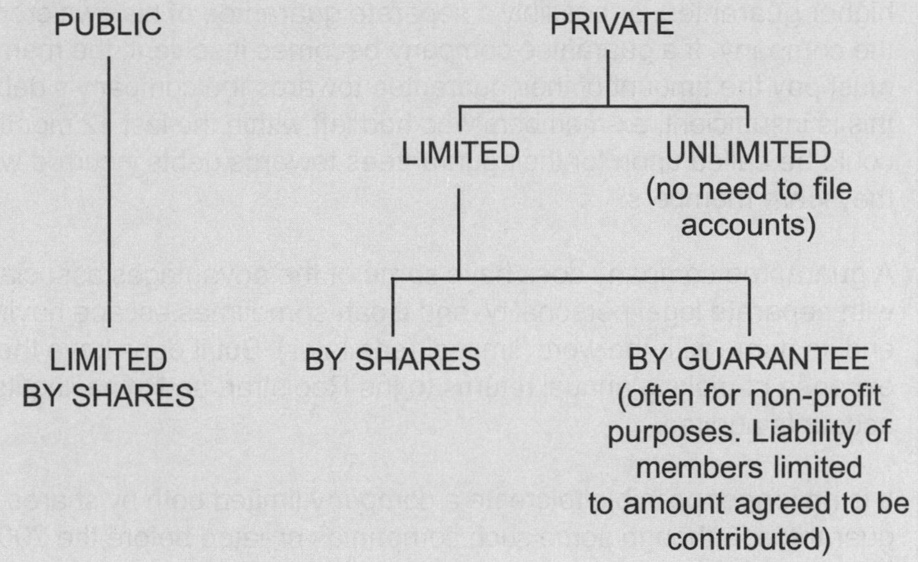

Supplementary reading

Classification by limitation of liability

Unlimited companies can be created by registration under the Acts. The company is a separate legal entity and, if it has assets, it will have the benefits arising from separate legal personality when membership changes. But if the company's assets are insufficient to meet its liabilities, all members are liable to contribute without limit towards paying its debts and the cost of liquidation. If the personal resources of present members are insufficient, then ex-members who had left within the last 12 months can be called upon for debts incurred while they were members.

Such companies do have the advantage that they need not have their accounts audited, and need not deliver annual copies to the Registrar of Companies. This exemption does not apply, however, if the unlimited company is a subsidiary or a holding company of a limited one.

A company may be registered as unlimited from the outset, with or without share capital. A limited company may be re-registered as unlimited: the Registrar must be sent a prescribed form of assent, signed by or on behalf of all members; a statutory declaration by the directors that the signatories constitute all members; and a copy of the new Memorandum and Articles. Because of the risks, unlimited companies are rare.

In companies limited by guarantee, a member must, when he joins, guarantee the company's debts, but only up to a limited amount. There is no statutory minimum, and the guarantee may be for only £1. If the company engages in trading, however, a potential creditor might want a higher guarantee, or possibly a separate guarantee of his own credit to the company. If a guarantee company becomes insolvent, the members must pay the amount of their guarantee towards the company's debts. If this is insufficient, ex-members who had left within the last 12 months could be called upon for their guarantees towards debts incurred while they were members.

A guarantee company does have some of the advantages associated with separate legal personality, and it can sometimes escape having to end its name with the word 'limited' (see later). But it does have the expense of making annual returns to the Registrar, and of having its accounts audited.

It is no longer possible to create a company limited both by shares and by guarantee, although some such companies created before the 2006 Act still exist. Guarantee companies are not very common, and are used substantially for non-trading associations and clubs.

Companies limited by shares comprise the vast majority of companies. The company's capital is divided into 'shares'. Each member holds one or more. Initially, the shares are issued by the company in return for a payment by the member. Each share will have a 'nominal' value of, say, 50p, but a company will often issue its shares at a premium, that is, for more than the nominal value. If 50p shares are issued for £2.50 each, they are issued at a premium of £2. Sometimes a company allows payment by instalments, for example £1 immediately and the remaining £1.50 in one year's time. During this time, the shares are said to be 'partly paid'. The shareholder can be called upon to pay the remaining £1.50 immediately if the company becomes insolvent. But once the remaining £1.50 has been paid, the share is 'fully paid', and the shareholder has no further liability for the company's debts. A share can be sold partly paid, and the above rules apply to the new holder in the same way as they would have done to the old holder had he kept the share.

There are some exceptions to the basic rule that the holder of a fully paid share has no further liability for the company but these are very much exceptions, and the basic rule normally applies.

Private company versus public company

The following table summarises the basic differences between public companies and private companies.

	Public companies	Private (limited) companies
Definition	Registered as a public company.	Any company that is not a public company.
Name	Ends with plc or public limited company.	Ends with Ltd or limited.
Capital	Must have allotted shares of at least the "authorised minimum" value of £50,000.	No minimum (or maximum) requirements.
Raising capital	May raise capital by advertising its securities (shares and debentures) as available for public subscription.	Prohibited from offering its securities to the public.
Start of trading	Must obtain trading certificate from registrar. Available when the company has allotted the above authorised minimum and been paid at least one quarter (£12,500) plus the whole of any premium.	Can begin from date of incorporation.
Directors	Minimum two.	Minimum one.
Company secretary	Must have one. Must be qualified.	Need not have one.
Accounts	Must file accounts within 6 months.	Need not lay accounts before general meeting. Must file within 9 months.
Audit	Accounts must be audited.	Audit not required if turnover below £6.5m.
AGM	Must be held each year.	Need not hold an AGM.
Resolutions	Can't pass written resolutions.	Can pass written resolutions.

Supplementary reading

Holding and subsidiary companies

It will already be apparent that one company can hold shares in another. Many large businesses consist of many companies. Although in law each of these companies is a separate person, in reality the members of the 'group' are closely related and (usually) are run as a coherent whole. In this context, a 'holding' company is one which controls another (the 'subsidiary') either by:

(a) being a member of the subsidiary and controlling the composition of the subsidiary's board of directors; or
(b) holding more than half the equity share capital in the subsidiary.

Where the subsidiary itself has similar powers over another company, that other company too is a subsidiary of the holding or 'parent' company.

The relations can be complex but, in general, a subsidiary must not be a member of (i.e. shareholder in) its holding company. However, a company can take over another which *already* holds shares in the parent, and the subsidiary can continue to hold those shares.

Quoted companies

These are public companies whose 'securities' (shares and/or debentures) are 'listed' for buying or selling on a recognised stock exchange. The company must apply to the exchange, and must satisfy the requirements of the exchange as to matters such as disclosure and total value of shares. 'Listing' of their securities is sought, in the main, by the largest public companies.

Community interest companies

Since 2004 it has been possible to form a 'Community Interest Company' for those wishing to establish social enterprises. The company's object must be considered by a reasonable person to be of benefit to the community and any surpluses made by the company should be re-invested for the purposes of the company. Such a company must first be registered as a company limited by guarantee or as a company limited by shares and then apply to the Regulator of Community Interest Companies for community interest company status. These companies may be used as vehicles for community interests such as a local crime prevention group. The company name must end in C.I.C. or Welsh equivalent (C.B.C.).

European companies

Since 8 October 2004 it has been possible to establish a European company ('Societas Europana' (SEs)). This is a public limited company formed under European law rather than the law of an individual member state. The founders must operate a business in at least two member states. For example, an SE could be formed by the merger of two companies operating in different member states. In practice, a number of problems remain with such companies, in particular the fact that the law which governs the SE largely depends upon the country in which it is registered. Rules relating to taxation, employment, insolvency, and so on are still not harmonised across the European Union and such harmonisation is not imminent. It follows that the establishment of such companies is unlikely to prove popular in practice at the present time.

'Small' companies

In general, companies must prepare annual reports and professionally audited accounts, which must then be filed with the Registrar of Companies and be open to public inspection. This can be a burden, and exceptions have therefore been made for 'small' companies. These are companies which have had for the present and previous financial years (or since incorporation) any two of the following: turnover not exceeding £6.5 million; balance sheet assets not exceeding £3.26 million; and on average, not more than 50 employees.

'Small' companies need not file their directors' report or profit and loss account with the Registrar. They need only file a shortened balance sheet, with no details of dividends or directors' remuneration. The accounts of companies with turnover of less than £6.5m do not need to be audited.

8 Promoters

Definition

There is no statutory definition of a promoter.

According to case law, a promoter is a person who 'undertakes to form a company and who takes the necessary steps to accomplish that purpose': **Twycross v Grant (1878)**.

The definition excludes people just acting in a professional capacity, such as accountant or solicitor.

Duties

A promoter is under a fiduciary duty to:

- disclose any interest in transactions to the company and not to make a 'secret profit'
- disclose any benefit acquired to an independent board and/or to the shareholders.

If a promoter does make a secret profit, the company may:

- Rescind the contract – but this is not always possible, e.g. if a third party has acquired rights under the contract.
- Obtain damages – but this requires the company to prove loss.
- Recover the profit – the company must prove that the promoter has failed to disclose his profit from a transaction.

Pre-incorporation contracts

A pre-incorporation contract is where a person enters into a contract before a company has been registered.

The position at common law is that a company, prior to its incorporation, does not have contractual capacity and after its formation it cannot ratify or formally adopt a pre-incorporation contract. The promoter is therefore personally liable under any such contract. (This is because a company does not legally exist until it is incorporated.)

Kelner v Baxter (1866)

Facts: A, B and C entered into a contract with the claimant to purchase goods on behalf of the proposed Gravesend Royal Alexandra Hotel Co. The goods were supplied and used in the business. Shortly after incorporation the company collapsed.

Held: As the Gravesend Royal Alexandra Hotel Co was not in existence when the contract was made it was not bound by the contract and could not be sued for the price of the goods. Neither could it ratify the contract after incorporation.

S51 CA06 reinforces the common law position by providing that, subject to any agreement to the contrary, the person making the contract is personally liable. Clear and express words are needed in order to negate liability: **Phonogram Ltd v Lane (1981)**.

The promoter can protect his position by:

- including a term in the contract giving the company the right to sue under the Contracts (Rights of Third Parties) Act 1999 (see Privity of Contract: **Chapter 2**)
- postponing finalising contracts until the company is formed
- entering into an agreement of novation (this involves discharging the original contract and replacing it with a new one) or assigning (transferring) the contract. All parties must agree
- agreeing with the company that there is no personal liability for the promoter
- buying an 'off-the-shelf' company, so it is ready to contract without waiting for incorporation.

Off-the-shelf companies

Rather than forming a new company themselves, those wishing to set up a company may buy one 'ready made' or 'off-the-shelf' from a company formation dealer.

The dealer will hold in stock a number of ready made companies with generally non-descriptive names. The company can either trade with an existing name, or have the existing name changed to one of the purchaser's choice, subject to availability.

Buying off the shelf has a number of advantages as follows:

- cheap and simple
- can trade immediately
- no problem of pre-incorporation contracts.

9 Company registration

Documents to register

The following must be submitted to the Registrar at Companies House in order to form a company.

Memorandum of association	• Used to be a more important document under previous company legislation. • Signed by all subscribers and stating that they wish to form a company and agree to become members of the company. • In relation to a company limited by shares, the memorandum provides evidence of the members' agreement to take at least one share each in the company. • Is not possible to amend or update the memorandum of a company formed under CA06.
Application for registration	S9 CA06 sets out the information that must be delivered to the Registrar when an application for registration is made. In all cases, the application form (IN01), must include: • the proposed name of the company • whether the members will have limited liability (by shares or guarantee) • whether the company is to be private or public • details of the registered office.
Documents to be sent with application: **Statement of capital and initial shareholdings**	Essentially is a 'snapshot' of a company's share capital at the point of registration. This must state: • the number of shares • their aggregate nominal value • how much has been paid up.

OR	
Statement of guarantee	This states the maximum amount each member guarantees to contribute in a winding up.
Statement of proposed officers	This gives details of the first directors (and company secretary, if applicable) and their consent to act.
Statement of compliance	This provides confirmation that CA06 has been complied with. It may be made in paper or electronic form.
Registration fee	Currently £20 approximately.

Note: As the model articles will apply if no articles are supplied, it is not a requirement that articles must be sent, although all companies will have articles.

Registrar's duties

On receipt of the above documents the registrar must:

- **Inspect the documents** and ensure that Companies Act requirements are fulfilled.
- **Issue certificate of incorporation** which is conclusive evidence that Companies Act requirements have been fulfilled: s15 CA06. The company exists from the date on the certificate of incorporation.

Trading certificate – public companies only

A plc cannot commence trading until the registrar has issued a trading certificate.

In order to obtain a trading certificate, an application must be made to the registrar which states:

- The nominal value of allotted share capital ≥ £50,000.
- That at least a quarter of the nominal value and all of any premium have been paid up (i.e. at least £12,500 of nominal capital).
- The amount of preliminary expenses and who has paid or is to pay them.
- Any benefits given or to be given to promoters.

If it trades before the certificate is issued:

- The company and any officers in default are liable to a fine.

- It is a criminal offence to carry on business, but any contracts are still binding on the company.
- The directors are personally liable if the company defaults within 21 days of due date.
- It is a ground for winding up if not obtained within one year: s122 IA 1986.

10 Articles of association

Introduction

The articles of association form the company's internal constitution. They:

- set out the manner in which the company is to be governed and
- regulate the relationship between the company, its shareholders and its directors.

There are no mandatory contents.

Contents of Articles

Companies Act 2006 states that the articles should be contained in a single document which is divided into consecutively numbered paragraphs.

Articles should contain rules on a number of areas, the most important of which are as follows:

- Appointment and dismissal of directors.
- Powers, responsibilities and liabilities of directors.
- Director's meetings.
- Member's rights.
- Dividends.
- Communication with members.
- Issue of shares.
- Documents and records.

Legal effect of company's constitutional documents

S33 CA06 states that the provisions of a company's constitution bind the company and its members to the same extent as if there were covenants on the part of the company and of each member to observe those provisions. This means that the articles form a statutory contract between the company and its members, and between the members themselves, even if they do not sign them.

(1) **The articles are enforceable by the company against the members.**

Hickman v Kent or Romney Marsh Sheepbreeders' Association (1915)

Facts: The company's articles included a clause to the effect that all disputes between the company and its members were to be referred to arbitration. A member brought court proceedings against the company.

Held: The proceedings were stopped. The company could enforce the arbitration clause against a member.

(2) **The articles are enforceable by the members against the company.**

Pender v Lushington (1877)

Facts: The articles provided for one vote per ten shares, with no member to have more than 100 votes. A member with more than 1,000 shares transferred the surplus to a nominee and directed him how to vote. The chairman refused to accept the nominee's votes.

Held: The right to vote was enforceable against the company and should have been recognised by the company as a breach of the articles.

(3) **The articles also operate as a contract between individual members in their capacity as members.**

Rayfield v Hands (1958)

Facts: The articles required the directors to be members, i.e. to hold qualification shares and to purchase shares from any member who wished to sell.

Held: This was enforceable against the directors in their capacity as members.

However, the articles do not bind the company to non-members nor do they bind the members in any other capacity.

Eley v Positive Government Security Life Assurance Co (1876)

Facts: The articles provided that Eley should be solicitor to the company for life.

Held: This was not a right given to him as a member and he could not rely on the articles as a contract for professional services. The right to be a director of a company has also been held to be an outsider right (i.e. a non-membership) right.

Beattie v EF Beattie (1938)

Facts: The company's articles contained an arbitration clause. B, a member and director of the company, was in dispute with the company concerning his rights as director. He brought court proceedings against the company.

Held: He was not bound by the arbitration clause since he was acting in his capacity as director, not a member.

However, even where the articles are not a relevant contract for this purpose, the terms may be evidence of another contract made independently.

New British Iron Co, ex parte Beckwith (1898)

Facts: The articles stated that directors were entitled to be paid £1,000 on taking office.

Held: The contract was implied from the directors' action in taking office. The provision in the articles was merely evidence of that separate contract.

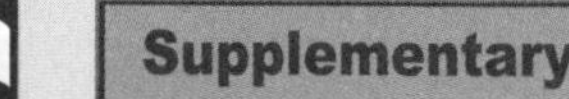

Supplementary reading

Although the articles indisputably forms a contract between the members (shareholders) and the company, and between the members themselves, the extent and force of this contract has always been a controversial topic amongst legal practitioners in practice, academics and the judiciary.

Bratton Seymour Service Co Ltd v Oxborough (1992)

A company involved in the management of a housing development which comprised a number of properties, sought amendment of an agreement (contained in the company's articles) by which an occupier of property within the developed site, a shareholder of the company, had agreed to contribute a pre-determined sum of money for the maintenance of specified parts of the common land attached to the developed property.

The company claimed that the amendment of the agreement would accord with the true intentions of the parties, namely that the shareholder concerned should be liable to contribute to all parts of the common areas of the developed property and not just those areas of common land specified in the agreement.

The Court of Appeal unanimously held that the amendment of the agreement would be inconsistent with the statutory nature of a company's articles.

Lord Justice Steyn said "I will readily accept that the law should not adopt a black-letter approach. It is possible to imply a term purely from the language of the document itself: a purely constructional implication is not precluded. But it is quite another matter to seek to imply a term into articles of association from extrinsic circumstances".

Towcester Racecourse Co Ltd v The Racecourse Association Ltd (2002)

The claimant, which was a member of the defendant, applied for final judgment on its claim for a declaration that it was entitled to a full copy of the defendant's report (and any appendices or other supporting material) into allegations that the chairman of a working party set up by the defendant to promote the broadcasting of horse-racing on television, who was also the chairman of a company which owned 13 racecourses in the UK, had made an inappropriate approach to a television company.

It was held, refusing the application, that the claimant's cause of action depended on the court finding a series of implied terms in the articles of association imposing duties upon the defendant in relation to its members; and that, while such a term could be implied from the language of the articles as a whole, it was not possible to do so wholly from extrinsic circumstances, especially where the implied terms contended for completely altered the way that the association would be run.

11 Alteration of articles

General rule

- The articles can usually be altered by a special resolution (75% majority).
- Copies of the amended articles must be sent to the Registrar within 15 days.

Exceptions

(1) **Entrenchment**

It is possible to entrench some of the articles. This means that a specified procedure (e.g. unanimous consent) may be required to change them.

(2) **Members increase liability**

S25 CA06 prevents a member being bound by any alteration made after he becomes a member that requires him to increase his liability or contribute further to the company.

(3) **Common law restriction**

Any change to the articles must be 'bona fide in interests of the company as a whole': **Allen v Gold Reefs of Africa (1900)**.

- It is for the members to decide whether the change is bona fide in the interests of the company as a whole.
- The court will not interfere unless no reasonable person would consider the change to be bona fide.
- If the change is bona fide, it is immaterial that it happens to inflict hardship or has retrospective operation.
- The change will be void if actual fraud or oppression takes place.
- An alteration is not invalid merely because it causes a breach of contract – but that does not excuse breach.

Greenhalgh v Arderne Cinemas Ltd (1950)

Facts: The issue was the removal from the articles of the members' right of first refusal of any shares which a member might wish to transfer; the majority wished to make the change in order to admit an outsider to membership in the interests of the company.

Held: The benefit to the company as a whole was held to be a benefit which any individual hypothetical member of the company could enjoy directly or through the company and not merely a benefit to the majority of members only. The test of good faith did not require proof of actual benefit but merely the honest belief on reasonable grounds that benefit could follow from the alteration.

In several cases the court has held that actual and foreseen detriment to a minority affected by the alteration was not in itself a sufficient ground of objection if the benefit to the company test was satisfied.

Brown v British Abrasive Wheel Co (1919)

Facts: The articles were altered to enable the majority to purchase at 'a fair value the shares of the minority'. The intention was to invoke the clause against some minority members who were refusing to inject further capital into the company. They objected to the alteration.

Held: This was not a bona fide alteration as it would benefit the majority shareholders, rather than the company as a whole.

Sidebottom v Kershaw, Leese & Co (1920)

Facts: The company altered its articles to empower the directors to require any member who carried on a business competing with that of the company, to sell his shares at a fair price to persons nominated by the directors. The minority against whom the new article was aimed did carry on a competing business and they challenged the validity of the alteration on the ground that it was an abuse of majority power to 'expel' a member.

Held: The Court of Appeal held that the evidence showed that the claimant might cause the defendant company loss by information which he received as a member, and as the power was restricted to expulsion for competing, the alteration was for the benefit of the company as a whole and was valid.

Allen v Gold Reefs of West Africa Ltd (1900)

Facts: Z held fully paid up and partly paid up shares in the company. The company's articles provided for a lien for all debts and liabilities of any member upon all partly paid shares held by the member. The company by special resolution altered its articles so that the lien was available on fully paid up shares as well.

Held: The company had power to alter its articles by extending the lien to fully paid shares.

Southern Foundries (1926) Ltd and Federated Foundries Ltd v Shirlaw (1940)

Facts: Following a merger the members of the new group of companies agreed to make alterations in the articles regarding directors. The amended articles gave the group the power to remove any director of the company and also stipulated that a managing director should cease to hold office if he ceased to be a director. Shirlaw was removed from office as a director which meant that he could no longer be a managing director, however, his contract still had some time to run.

Held: The House of Lords held that the company could not be prevented from altering its articles but that the only remedy for an alteration which has caused a breach of contract was damages.

12 The ability of a company to contract

Companies registered under the Companies Act 2006 have unrestricted objects (s31). In other words such companies may contract for any business purpose. If a company wishes to restrict the ability of its directors to enter into contracts this may be done by passing a special resolution to amend the articles.

If a company has restricted the ability of its directors to contract on behalf of the company and the directors cause the company to contract in a way which ignores the restrictions, this will have no effect on the outsiders who may enforce the contract. However, the shareholders may seek an injunction to stop the directors contracting in the first place and may sue the directors for breach of duty (see Chapter 5).

Most companies in existence today were registered under the Companies Act 1985. At that time companies were required to specify their objects in their memorandum of association. Obviously the memorandum has become a much less important document under the regime introduced by the Companies Act 2006. In order to ensure that companies are treated the same, no matter when they were registered, s28 of the Companies Act 2006 provides that the objects clause of all pre-existing companies is deemed to be part of the company's articles and subject to amendment by special resolution in the normal way.

13 Advantages and disadvantages of companies limited by shares

Supplementary reading

Advantages

(In practice, those who carry on business through the medium of such a company may enjoy a number of tax advantages, depending on the tax regime in force at any particular time. However, tax considerations are outside the scope of Business Law and will be covered in Business Taxation.)

The main advantages derive from the separate legal personality of companies.

- Limited liability is the main advantage. A shareholder whose shares are fully paid up is not liable for the debts of the company. If the business is owned by a company, therefore, it becomes much more attractive to entrepreneurs. An entrepreneur is more likely to start a business if he/she knows that potential liability is limited. Equally, people are much more likely to invest money in the business by becoming shareholders later if they know that liability is limited. Both commencement and expansion of the business can benefit. It must be noted, however, that although limited liability is always enjoyed by shareholders in public companies which are quoted on the Stock Exchange, in practice it may not be enjoyed by shareholders in a small private company. Whether the shareholders have limited liability depends on their particular circumstances. Thus, for example, persons who own shares in asset-rich companies may well enjoy limited liability, as the company is itself able to provide security for any borrowing. However, many companies are incorporated under capitalised, many with share capital of less than £100.

Example

X is the sole director and shareholder in X Ltd and holds 100 £1 shares. X wants to borrow £100,000 from the bank on behalf of X Ltd so that the company can purchase a house and rent it out to students. Clearly, the bank will require security for the loan and the company itself is unable to provide any as it only has £100.

It follows that if the loan is to proceed, it is likely that the bank will require (i) a charge over the property to be purchased and (ii) a personal guarantee from X that if the company does not repay the loan, he will. (The bank may also possibly require a charge over X's matrimonial home.) It follows that until the loan is repaid, X does not enjoy limited liability, because if the company fails to pay its debts, X can be called upon under his guarantee to pay them.

Assume that the loan is repaid from the rents X Ltd has received from students, and X wishes to repeat the process and buy another house to rent out. Now the company has an asset (the first property) and the bank may be persuaded to make a loan to the company taking security over the company's existing property and the property to be acquired without requiring X to enter into a contract of guarantee. If that is the case, X has now begun to enjoy limited liability.

- Perpetual succession indicates that a company, as a separate legal person, lasts forever until it is wound up by due legal process. If the business is owned by the company it remains the property of the company, whatever happens to ownership of the shares. Investors can come and go, buy shares and sell them, without any change in ownership of the business. This too can help to attract capital. A partnership only lasts as long as the agreement lasts, and ownership of the business may change and have to be transferred on the death or retirement of any partner. The assets of an individual practitioner can similarly have to be transferred on his death. All of this can involve complications and expense.
- Agreement to the transfer of interests is not needed in public companies. A member who wishes to transfer his shares does not need to obtain the permission of the other shareholders. A partner cannot normally transfer his share of the partnership without first obtaining the permission of all the other partners.
- Borrowing money might be easier and/or more convenient for a company than for an unincorporated business, because a company can offer a floating charge over such assets of a particular type as the company might have from time to time. This security leaves the company free to deal with its assets without having to redeem the charge each time. An unincorporated business cannot issue a valid 'floating' charge.

Disadvantages

- On formation, the detailed documents and administration procedures required on registration can deter a small business from forming a company.
- Disclosure requirements are imposed on companies. A great deal of information about the company and its officers must be kept at the registered office, and most of it must be available for public inspection. Much information must also be sent to the Registrar of Companies and be similarly available. Some disclosure requirements apply even to very small companies.
- Many administrative requirements are imposed, for example in preparing and keeping the accounts (which must be audited in all but very small companies) and registers which contain the above information. There are also detailed requirements as to the meetings to be held and the types of resolution which must be used (see later).

Generally, this does not apply to unincorporated businesses. The bureaucracy imposed on companies is largely the price to be paid for potential size, and disclosure provisions give outsiders some safeguard against the company's limited liability, in that they can at least find out who and what they are dealing with.

Other features of companies

- Taxation. In practice, the different tax treatment of companies on the one hand and sole traders and partnerships on the other, may be one of the main factors in deciding whether to carry on business in corporate or non-corporate form.

  Companies pay corporation tax on their profits, whether or not they are distributed to the shareholders by way of dividends. Directors are liable to pay income tax and national insurance contributions on salaries and fees paid by the company. The amounts are deducted monthly through the operation of PAYE (pay-as-you-earn).

  The separate legal personality of the company could be problematic for directors in small private companies, as they could find themselves in effect being subjected to a double charge to national insurance in that both the company as employer and the directors as officers/employees are liable to pay such contributions.

  On the other hand, dividends extracted by shareholders are not subject to national insurance contributions and the tax payable on them is not due until some 10 months after the income tax year in which they are received. Dividends are also currently taxed at rates below those applicable for employment income.

  Partnerships and sole traders/practitioners. Partners and sole traders extract profits from the business in the form of 'drawings'. Drawings are advance payments of profit extracted by the proprietor pending the determination of the annual profit on production of the accounts. Drawings (like dividends above), may be extracted from the business weekly or monthly without any tax being payable on the date of extraction. Rather income tax of the proprietor's share of profits for the year is payable following the determination of final accounts.

- Management systems differ. In a company the members elect the directors who are then responsible for the day-to-day management and policy-making of the corporation. The members have no right to intervene in normal management, although they may have some rights in the event of managerial misconduct. They also have the right to remove directors, and to exercise their rights to vote at general meetings.

  These divisions of function are inevitable in large companies. In very small companies they may not matter too much if the directors and the shareholders are the same persons.

  In a partnership, unless the partnership agreement provides otherwise, all the partners have a right to participate in management.

14 The use and procedure of board meetings and general meetings of shareholders

Directors' powers must generally be exercised as a board, acting at board meetings.

The actual way in which boards reach their decisions is governed by the Articles of Association. It follows that the company may adopt any rules that it chooses.

Usually the Articles permit directors to regulate proceedings at board meetings as they think fit.

In practice the chairman of the board will attempt to achieve unanimity. If this is not possible however, and the matter has to be put to the vote, most boards will reach their decisions by simple majority vote.

Each director will normally have one vote, apart from the chairman who is often given a casting vote so that a decision can be reached in the event of deadlock.

The members of a company are its shareholders. They do not, in their capacity of shareholders, take part in the day-to-day management of the company. They do, however, have considerable powers to control the management, and they also have some wider powers.

Shareholders' powers are exercised through voting on resolutions at general meetings of shareholders (members' meetings).

Two types of general meeting are recognised, annual general meetings (AGMs) and general meetings (GMs).

Where different classes of share have been created (**see Chapter 5**) there can also be class meetings for example a meeting of all the preference shareholders. Each of these is discussed below.

Board meetings

The board is the agent of the company and is responsible for management. The board determines the overall policy of the company and leaves the day-to-day management to appointed managers.

It follows that boards of directors do not meet every day or week but meet from time to time when the situation demands it. Thus, the board will meet to consider such matters as whether to diversify into another business area, to raise further capital, to make investments, to issue further shares, to change the constitution of the company, to purchase another business, and so on.

For some of these matters, the law requires shareholder approval so the board will have to call a GM in order to allow the shareholders to vote on the matter.

In the case of a private company, it may not be necessary to call a GM as, in most cases, the law allows a written resolution of the shareholders to be used as an alternative to an ordinary or special resolution of members voted at general meetings.

The powers of directors must generally be exercised as a board, except to the extent that they are validly delegated. The board normally operates at meetings, although it can agree unanimously by each member signing a written resolution without a meeting. Procedure is generally governed by the Articles.

A meeting can be called by any director, and must be called by the company secretary if any director so requires. Reasonable notice must be given to all directors, but not necessarily to those out of the United Kingdom or whose whereabouts are not known. No agenda need be sent.

The quorum is presumed to be two, but this may be varied by the directors themselves, as it will be in single-director private companies.

The board can appoint a chairman, and give him a second 'casting' vote if one should be needed. Otherwise, the rule is generally one vote per director, regardless of shareholding, and decisions are reached by a simple majority. Minutes of board meetings must be kept, and made available to directors but not to members generally.

If there are an equal number of votes for and against a particular resolution, there is deadlock and the negative view prevails. This means that the proposed resolution is defeated, unless the chairman chooses to exercise his/her casting vote.

Members meetings

Annual general meeting (AGM)

Timing	Public companies must hold an AGM within the six months following their financial year end: s336.
Failure to hold	The company and every officer in default can be fined if an AGM is not held. Any member can apply to the Department for Business, Innovation and Skills to convene the meeting.
Private companies	Private companies are not required to hold an AGM.
Notice	**21 days' notice** is required unless every member entitled to attend and vote agrees to a shorter period. The notice must state that the meeting is an AGM.
Business	Usual business includes: • consider accounts • appoint auditors • elect directors • declare dividends.
Resolutions	• Members holding at least 5% of the voting rights (or at least 100 members holding on average £100 paid-up capital) have the right to propose a resolution for the AGM agenda and to require the company to circulate details of the resolution to all members. • If the members' request is received before the financial year end, the members are not required to cover the costs of circulation. Otherwise, the members requesting the resolution must deposit a sum to cover the company's costs.

General meetings (GM)

Timing	Held **whenever required**. Must be held by a plc if a serious loss of capital has occurred, i.e. net assets have fallen to less than half of the called up share capital.
Notice	At least **14 days** (subject to short notice).
Business	The person who requisitions the meeting sets the agenda.

Class meetings

Purpose	Meeting of a class of shareholders, usually to consider a variation of their class rights.
Procedure	Notice, etc. as for general meetings.
Quorum	Two persons holding or representing by proxy at least one-third in nominal value of the issued shares of the class in question.

Who can call a meeting?

Directors	The articles usually delegate the power to the directors.
Members	Members may require the directors to call a GM if they hold at least 5% of the paid up voting capital. The directors must call a meeting within 21 days of receiving a requisition. The meeting must take place within 28 days of the notice convening the meeting. If the directors do not call a meeting, the members who requested the meeting (or any members holding over 50% of the total voting rights) may themselves call a meeting to take place within three months of the initial request and recover their expenses from the company.
Resigning auditor	A resigning auditor may require the directors to convene a meeting so he can explain the reasons for his resignation.
Court	A court can call a meeting on the application of a director or member where it would otherwise be impracticable e.g. to break a deadlock.

Notice

Who must receive notice?	Every member and every director: s310.
Failure to give notice	Accidental failure to give notice to one or more persons does not invalidate the meeting: s313.
Contents of notice	Date, time and place of the meeting. The general nature of the business to be transacted. The text of any special resolutions.

Length of notice period	**AGM – 21 days** Less if every member entitled to attend and vote agrees. **GM – 14 days**
Short notice	A private company can hold an AGM or GM in less than the above notice periods if a majority of members holding at least 90% of the voting shares agree (the percentage maybe increased to 95% by the company's articles).
Special notice	Requires 28 days' notice. Required for the removal of a director or auditor.

A **quorum** is the minimum number of members that needs to be present at a meeting in order to validate business. It is generally two persons who can be members or proxies: s318 CA06.

Voting is by a **show of hands** initially, unless a poll is demanded. A show of hands means one member one vote, irrespective of the number of shares held.

A **poll** may be demanded by members holding at least 10% of the total voting rights (or by not fewer than 5 members having the right to vote on the resolution). A poll means one vote per share. The result of a poll replaces the result of the previous show of hands. Quoted companies must publish the results of polls on their website: s341 CA06.

Members have a statutory right under s324 CA06 to appoint one or more persons as their ' **proxy** '. A proxy can attend meetings, vote and speak on behalf of the member for whom he is acting.

Companies (Shareholders' Rights) Regulations 2009

The Regulations made a number of amendments to the Companies Act 2006. The majority of changes made were in relation to "traded companies" i.e. public companies whose shares are traded on a regulated market in an European Economic Area country.

(1) **Amendments affecting all companies**

- Company articles may allow poll votes to be cast in advance of the meeting, rather than just providing for appointment of a proxy to vote at the general meeting.
- Meetings may be held in a way that allows persons not physically together in the same place to attend, speak and vote at the meeting by electronic means.

(2) **Amendments affecting "traded companies" only**

- Before a general meeting companies must publish on a website information about the business of the meeting and voting rights at the meeting.
- The notice of the meeting will need to give details of the website where the above information is available.
- At general meetings, companies must answer any question put by a member relating to the business dealt with at the meeting.
- Shareholders are entitled to ask for matters other than proposed resolutions to be included in the business to be dealt with at an AGM.
- The Chairman's casting vote has been abolished.

15 Resolutions

Resolutions are the way in which companies take decisions. They are voted on by the members in person or by proxy. There are three types of resolution.

Type	% required to pass	To Registrar?	Purpose of resolution
Special	75% approval of those present and voting at the meeting in person or by proxy.	Yes – within 15 days	• Alter name. • Wind up company. • Alter articles. • Reduce share capital.
Ordinary	50% plus 1 of those present and voting at the meeting in person or by proxy.	Only if required by statute	Used whenever the law or the articles do not require a special resolution.

Written (private companies only)	The same percentages for special and ordinary resolutions as above but the percentages in favour must be of **ALL** the membership and not just those present at the meeting.	Yes if a 75% majority is required	The purpose can be anything apart from resolutions requiring special notice. Members cannot revoke their agreement. The date of the resolution is the date when the necessary majority has been reached. The resolution must generally be passed within 28 days from its circulation.

Supplementary reading: Chapter summary

At the end of this chapter, students should make sure that they understand the following:

- the legal position of individual traders and practitioners
- partnerships: nature, structure and liabilities
- the concept of incorporation, especially in relation to companies
- in particular, the concepts of:
  - separate legal personality
  - limited liability
  - perpetual succession
  - ultra vires
- different types of company, especially public/private, single-member and quoted companies
- lifting the veil of incorporation, both by the courts and by statute

- the procedure for forming and registering companies, including the advantages and disadvantages of off-the-shelf companies. In particular, students should be familiar with:
  - the position of promoters
  - registration
  - Memorandum of Association – including alteration
  - Articles of Association – including alteration
  - shareholder agreements
  - details of directors, and so on
  - the certificate of incorporation
- the advantages and disadvantages of carrying on business through the medium of a company limited by shares
- the general legal structure of companies: directors and shareholders
- board meetings
- meetings of members – types of meeting:
  - annual general meeting
  - general meetings
  - class meetings
- resolutions at meetings:
  - ordinary (with or without special notice)
  - special
  - written
- calling a meeting
- conduct of meetings, including minutes, and so on.

16 Test your understanding questions

Test your understanding 1

Which one of the following is not an example of an artificial legal person?

A The chairman of a public company

B The BBC

C A company limited by guarantee

D A private company with only two shareholders

Test your understanding 2

DC, who had never been in business before, decided to rent a corner shop and open a food store which he named The All-Hours Food Mart. From this information it can be inferred that

(i) The All-Hours Food Mart is a legal person.

(ii) The All-Hours Food Mart is an unincorporated business.

(iii) DC is a sole trader.

(iv) DC is a director of a private company.

Which of the above are correct?

A (i) and (ii) only

B (ii) and (iii) only

C (i), (iii) and (iv) only

D (i), (ii) and (iii) only

Test your understanding 3

A partnership is a significant form of business organisation, particularly among providers of professional services such as architects and financial accountants.

Which one of the following statements is correct?

A A partnership is an example of an incorporated business organisation

B A partnership is recognised in law as an artificial legal person

C Partners generally benefit from limited liability for any debts incurred as a result of their business activities

D Professional codes of practice may require members of the profession to trade as partners or as sole traders rather than through companies

Test your understanding 4

All the following statements about the formation of a company in the United Kingdom are true except one. The exception is

A The company comes into existence when the Registrar of Companies issues a Certificate of Incorporation

B The company comes into existence when granted a listing by the Stock Exchange

C A company can have just one member

D A public company must have a certificate of incorporation and a trading certificate before it can commence business

Test your understanding 5

Which of the following is incorrect in relation to company names?

A In general, the name of a private or public company must end in 'limited', 'Ltd', 'public limited company' or 'plc' as appropriate

B The name must not be the same as that of an existing company

C The name cannot be changed without the unanimous approval of the shareholders

D The name of the company may be registered as a trade mark

Test your understanding 6

Which one of the following statements is incorrect?

A A private company can decide not to hold an Annual General Meeting

B An Annual General Meeting in a public company must be held within one year of incorporation

C Accounts of a public company must be laid before members for approval at an Annual General Meeting

D Articles of Association can be altered at an Annual General Meeting

Test your understanding 7

To dismiss a director under s.168 of the Companies Act 2006 requires:

A an ordinary resolution with 14 days' notice to the company

B a special resolution with 14 days' notice to the company

C an ordinary resolution with 28 days' notice to the company

D a special resolution with 28 days' notice to the company

Test your understanding 8

Which type of resolution from the list below cannot be used by a public company?

A Ordinary resolution

B Special resolution

C Written resolution

D Ordinary resolution with special notice

Test your understanding 9

Which one of the following statements is incorrect in relation to a shareholders' agreement?

A The agreement need not be open to public inspection

B It can validly provide that a particular director will remain a director for life

C It can be enforced simply by means of an action by one shareholder against another

D It can be changed by a simple majority of members

Test your understanding 10

Paul had been in business on his own account for a number of years, acting as a retailer of household goods and furnishings. In April 2010 Paul decided that he would incorporate his business by transferring it to Paul's Furnishings Ltd, a company which he proposed to register as soon as possible. Paul called to see his solicitor (Anne) who arranged for the necessary documents to be sent to the Registrar of Companies. In the meantime Paul notified his suppliers of the change and ordered some new furniture from Luxury Chairs Ltd. Paul signed the order 'Paul, for and on behalf of Paul's Furnishings Ltd'.

Required:

Delete as appropriate and complete the following:

At law Paul is a .... (1 word) **(2 marks)** of Paul's Furnishings Ltd. The company will not come into existence until Paul receives a .... (3 words) **(2 marks)** from the .... (3 words) **(2 marks)**. Paul has ordered goods on behalf of the company before it has been registered, and has therefore entered into a .... (1 word) **(2 marks)** contract. This contract is enforceable against .... (1 word) **(2 marks)**.

(Total: 10 marks)

Test your understanding 11

Required:

Delete as appropriate and complete the following:

In a general partnership the partners are .... (3 words) **(2 marks)** liable for the debts of the company. In contrast when business is carried on through the medium of a company limited by .... (1 word) **(1 mark),** the .... (1 word) **(2 marks)** is fully liable for any debts contracted rather than the shareholders. A company is a separate .... (1 word) **(1 mark)** at law and if the shareholders have fully paid the amount due on their .... (1 word) (**1 mark)** they cannot be called upon to make any further contribution. The relationship between the company and its shareholders is set down in the company's .... (2 words) **(2 marks)** Association.

(Total: 9 marks)

Test your understanding 12

A, B, C and D are the only directors and shareholders in ABCD Ltd, each holding 500 ordinary £1 shares.

Required:

Delete as appropriate and complete the following:

To propose an ordinary resolution .... (1 word) **(1 mark)** days' notice must be given to the shareholders. To pass a special resolution .... (1 word) **(1 mark)** days' notice must be given. If the shareholders wish to change the company's Articles of Association they will need to pass a .... (1 word) **(2 marks)** resolution. This resolution can be passed by the votes of any .... (1 word) **(2 marks)** of the shareholders. Alternatively, the Articles could be changed by a .... (1 word) **(2 marks)** resolution which would require the support of .... (percentage) **(1 mark)** the shareholders.

(Total: 9 marks)

Test your understanding 13

Required:

Delete as appropriate and complete the following:

A board meeting may be called by giving .... (1 word) **(2 marks)** notice of the meeting to all the directors. A board usually reaches its decisions by .... (1 word) **(2 marks)** vote. If the directors cannot attend a board meeting it may still make a decision by all the directors signing a .... (1 word) **(2 marks)** resolution. The procedure at board meetings and the voting rights of directors are set down in the company's .... (3 words) **(2 marks).** Sometimes the law will require the shareholders to support the board's proposals. In that event the board may call .... (2 words) **(2 marks)** on 14 days' notice.

(Total: 10 marks)

Test your understanding answers

Test your understanding 1

A

Human beings are 'natural' legal persons and not 'artificial' legal persons. The chairman of a public company is a human being; hence statement (A) is the answer. All the other statements relate to incorporated organisations which possess an artificial legal personality.

Test your understanding 2

B

Since DC is commencing business as an unincorporated individual proprietor or sole trader, only (ii) and (iii) of the statements in the question are correct. Being a 'natural person', DC is a legal person, but not his business. Statement (i) is therefore incorrect. And as his business is not a company, DC cannot be a director. Statement (iv) is the therefore also incorrect.

Test your understanding 3

D

Being unincorporated, a partnership does not possess a personality in law separate from the natural personality of each of the partners. Hence, statements (A) and (B) are incorrect. Statement (C) is also incorrect because most partners do not possess limited liability. This leaves statement (D) as the correct answer: as part of the professional ethic, many (though not all) professional bodies prevent their members from selling their services through the intermediary of a company.

Test your understanding 4

B

All the statements except (B) are correct. (B) certainly does not apply to private companies which are not allowed by law to market their shares. Many, but not all, public companies apply for a Stock Exchange listing so that a market may be created in their shares. However, even when a public company applies for a Stock Exchange listing, the granting of such a listing does not define when the company comes into existence. (B) is therefore the exception and the correct answer.

Test your understanding 5

C

(C) is incorrect as although the name may be changed by a written resolution of all the shareholders, it may also be changed by the shareholders passing a special resolution, which is achieved by at least 75 per cent of those present at the meeting voting in favour.

Test your understanding 6

B

(C) identifies what must be undertaken at the meeting as ordinary business. (D) identifies what also can be carried out at the meeting but as special business, in other words that which is done out of choice rather than necessity. Private companies are now able to dispense with the need to hold this meeting by passing an elective resolution. Some flexibility exists in the time allowed to companies following incorporation before they need to hold the meeting. The maximum period is 18 months, not 1 year.

Test your understanding 7

C

By s.168 Companies Act 2006, removal of a director before the expiry of his term of office requires an ordinary resolution on special notice, and the length of special notice is 28 days. Therefore (A), (B) and (D) are all incorrect.

Test your understanding 8

C

The written resolution procedure enables private companies only to dispense with the need to hold general meetings. Public and private companies will use the ordinary resolution where the law or the company's articles do not require another form of resolution. The use of special resolution and ordinary resolution with special notice by both private and public companies is determined by statute.

Test your understanding 9

D

A shareholders' agreement is a *contract* which, like any other contract, can only be changed by *all* of the parties to the contract ('members'). (A) (B) and (C) are all potential advantages of shareholders' agreements.

Test your understanding 10

At law Paul is a *promoter* of Paul's Furnishings Ltd. The company will not come into existence until Paul receives a *Certificate of Incorporation* from the *Registrar of Companies*. Paul has ordered goods on behalf of the company before it has been registered, and has therefore entered into a *pre-incorporation* contract. This contract is enforceable against *Paul.*

Test your understanding 11

In a general partnership the partners are *jointly and severally* liable for the debts of the company. In contrast, when business is carried on through the medium of a company limited by *shares,* the *company* is fully liable for any debts contracted rather than the shareholders. A company is a separate *person* at law and if the shareholders have fully paid the amount due on their *shares* they cannot be called upon to make any further contribution. The relationship between the company and its shareholders is set down in the company's *Articles of* Association.

Test your understanding 12

To propose an ordinary resolution *fourteen* days' notice must be given to the shareholders. To pass a special resolution *fourteen* days' notice must be given. If the shareholders wish to change the company's Article of Association, they will need to pass a *special* resolution. This resolution can be passed by the votes of any *three* of the shareholders. Alternatively, the Articles could be changed by *written* resolution which would require the support of 75 per cent the shareholders.

Test your understanding 13

A board meeting may be called by giving *reasonable* notice of the meeting to all the directors. A board usually reaches its decisions by *majority* vote. If the directors cannot attend a board meeting it may still make a decision by all the directors signing a *written* resolution. The procedure at board meetings and the voting rights of directors are set down in the company's *Articles of Association*. Sometimes the law will require the shareholders to support the board's proposals. In that event the board may call a *General Meeting* on 14 days' notice.

chapter

5

Company Finance and Management

Chapter learning objectives

After completing this chapter you should be able to:

- explain the nature of different types of shares, the procedure for the issue of shares and acceptable forms of payment
- explain the ability of a company to take secured and unsecured loans, the different types of security and the registration procedure
- explain the procedure for the appointment, retirement, disqualification and removal of directors
- explain the powers and duties of directors when in office
- explain the qualifications, powers and duties of the company secretary.

1 Shares and share capital

Definition of a share

A share is 'the interest of a shareholder in the company measured by a sum of money, for the purpose of a liability in the first place, and of interest in the second, but also consisting of a series of mutual covenants entered into by all the shareholders': **Borland's Trustee v Steel Bros & Co Ltd (1901)**.

A shareholder is a member of the company and therefore has voting rights, depending on the class of shares held. They are also entitled to dividends depending on the availability of profits.

In the event of liquidation, depending on the type of share, a shareholder receives payment after all other creditors, but can participate in surplus assets.

Supplementary reading

In the great majority of companies, which are small and private, the main shareholders and the directors (who are responsible for management) will be the same persons. In large companies the majority of shares are usually held by institutional investors such as the pension funds. Although such shareholders can influence management they are often criticised for not participating more actively in their companies affairs and thus giving the directors too much freedom to run the companies as they see fit. (This is dealt with more fully in Chapter 8, 'Corporate Governance'). Finally it should be noted that there is no *legal* obligation upon any director to own any shares in his/her company as such.

Terminology

Companies issue shares to raise capital, usually in the form of cash although shares may be issued in exchange for assets. This is known as non-cash consideration, and public companies particularly are subject to strict rules regarding the valuation of this non-cash consideration (covered in more detail later in this chapter).

Issued share capital	Issued share capital comprises share capital that has actually been issued, released or sold by the company.
Paid up share capital	The amount which shareholders have actually paid on the shares issued.
Called up share capital	The amount of unpaid share capital which has been called for from shareholders but not yet paid.
Uncalled share capital	The amount of unpaid share capital that has not yet been called for from shareholders and therefore also remains unpaid.

Types of shares

Type of share	General characteristics
Ordinary	• Shareholders have full voting rights. • Dividends will be paid after preference dividends. They are not fixed. • Shareholders will be entitled to share surplus assets after payment of liabilities and preference shares.
Preference	• Shareholders either have restricted voting rights or none at all. • Fixed dividends will be paid in priority to other dividends (usually cumulative). • Shareholders receive a prior return of capital, but cannot participate in any surplus assets.
Deferred	• Shares with no right to dividends either for a set period or until certain conditions are met, for example, a certain level of profitability is achieved. • Usually do not carry voting rights but will depend on the Articles of association and the terms of issue.

Treasury	• A company which purchases its own shares out of distributable profits may hold the shares purchased 'in treasury'. • The directors may reissue the shares without the formalities associated with a new issue of shares. • The company can hold up to 10% of its shares as treasury shares. • The company cannot exercise any rights in respect of the shares, such as voting and receiving dividends. • They can only be sold for cash.
Redeemable	• Shares which under their terms of issue must be bought back by the company at a certain time. • The redemption must be in accordance with the Articles of association. • The shares must be fully paid for and cancelled on redemption.

Supplementary reading

When deciding whether to issue preference shares or not, the directors have a range of choices as they can issue different types of preference shares. If they wish to raise capital for a period of time and then repay it, as an alternative to borrowing they could offer redeemable preference shares. These will be issued for a specified period of time and then bought back by the company at the time agreed. Once bought back, the shares have to be cancelled so they cannot be re-issued (but see 'treasury shares' below).

In times of high interest rates or the current difficulties associated with obtaining credit/finance, redeemable preference shares may be particularly attractive to companies. This is so because if a company borrows money, interest at the agreed rate must be paid whether or not the company is making a profit. However, dividends to the preference (and ordinary) shareholders are only paid if the company has available profits. At the time of writing these notes, with the recovery from the global recession, and potential imminent hikes in the Bank of England base rate, this makes it particularly difficult for businesses to obtain necessary finance. It may be therefore, that obtaining additional finance from the company's membership is a more attractive proposition than attempting to obtain it by way of bank loans.

Clearly the share issue must be made attractive to the participating preference shareholders. It is likely therefore that the company will provide an additional return, perhaps in the form of a premium payable on redemption, or allowing the shareholders the right to share in any surplus profits which remain after a certain percentage has been paid to the ordinary shareholders.

The courts have held that possession of a share certificate is only prima facie evidence of ownership of the shares described in the certificate. It is not conclusive because the share certificate could have been stolen, copied or forged. Conclusive evidence is obtained by looking at the name of the person who has been allotted the shares in the company's register of shareholders.

It follows that a shareholder will be issued with a share certificate to evidence that he/she has a certain number of shares in the company. Ownership of shares, however, depends on the company's register of shareholders.

2 Class rights

What are they?

Class rights are the special rights attached to each class of shares, such as dividend rights, distribution of capital on a winding up and voting. (See above concerning the different rights that normally attach to ordinary shares and preference shares.)

How can they be varied?

The procedure for varying class rights depends on whether any procedure is specified in the articles:

Is procedure to vary specified?	Method of variation
Yes	Procedure set out in articles must be followed.
No	Variation needs special resolution or written consent of 75% in nominal value of the class: S630 CA 2006.

Minority protection

Under s633 CA 2006, the holders of 15% of the nominal value of that class who did not consent to the variation, may ask the court to cancel the variation within 21 days of the passing of the resolution.

The court may confirm or cancel the variation. However, it will only cancel the variation if the petitioner proves it is unfairly prejudicial.

The court draws a distinction between:

- a variation that affects the value, enjoyment or power derived from the rights and
- a variation that changes the rights themselves.

The court will only intervene in the latter case.

White v Bristol Aeroplane Co (1953)

Facts: The company made a bonus issue of new ordinary and preference shares to the existing ordinary shareholders who alone were entitled to participate in bonus issues under the articles. The existing preference shareholders objected on the basis that this reduced their voting power within the company and was a variation to which they had not consented.

Held: The bonus issue was not a variation of the preference shareholders rights. They had exactly the same votes before the issue as they did after. This was an alteration of the power that came with their shares and not a variation of the rights themselves.

In **Cumbrian Newspapers Group Ltd v Cumberland & Westmorland Herald (1986)** the court stated that rights or benefits contained in articles of association fell into 3 categories:

(1) Rights or benefits attached to particular shares (e.g. dividend and voting rights)

(2) Rights or benefits conferred on individuals not as shareholders/ members but for some other reason (i.e. "outsider rights" for example as in **Eley v Positive Government Security Life Assurance Co (1876)** above)

(3) Rights conferred on particular individuals in their capacity as shareholder/member (e.g. weighted voting rights as in **Bushell v Faith (1970)** below).

It was held that categories (i) and (iii) only constitute class rights.

Greenhalgh v Arderne Cinemas Ltd (1950)

Facts: The company had two classes of ordinary shares, 50p and 10p shares, with every share carrying one vote. A resolution was passed to subdivide each 50p share into five 10p shares, thereby multiplying the votes of that class by five.

Held: The subdivision of shares is not a variation of class rights. The rights of the original 10p shares had not been varied since they still had one vote per share as before.

3 Issuing shares

Allotment of shares

This is where the shares are allocated to a person under a contract of allotment. Once the shares are allotted and the holder is entered in the register of members, they become a member of the company.

Authority

(1) **Private companies with only one class of shares.** The directors have automatic authority to issue new shares unless restricted by the articles.

(2) **Private companies with more than one class of shares and public companies.** The directors must be authorised to issue shares either in the articles or by an ordinary resolution in general meeting.

(3) **If authority is necessary it must:**

- State the maximum number of shares to be allotted; and
- State the period for which the authority is to last (maximum five years).

Types of issue

Statutory pre-emption rights	New shares must first be offered to existing shareholders in proportion to their shareholdings. Raises new funds. Purpose is not to dilute individual member shareholding. Only applies to ordinary shares which must be paid for in cash. The offer is open for 21 days. Pre-emption rights can be disapplied by provision in the articles of association or by a special resolution being passed by the members.

Bonus issues	Also referred to as scrip issue or capitalisation issue. Are normally issued at no cost to the shareholders in which case do not raise any new funds. Sometimes the company issues partly paid-up bonus shares in which case the shareholders may have to make some contributions in the future. Carried out by using some of the company's non-distributable reserves to issue shares to existing shareholders in proportion to their shareholdings. Must never be funded from a company's ordinary capital.
Rights issues	New shares offered to existing shareholders in proportion to their shareholdings to raise new funds. Can be used where the statutory pre-emption rights have been disapplied. Shares usually offered at discount to current market value (but not at discount to nominal value). Shareholders who do not want to buy the new shares themselves may sell the rights to a third party.

Supplementary reading

New issues of shares may be by:

- **Prospectus**. The Prospectus Directive (203/71/EC) specifies that where there is a public offer of shares or a request for admission of securities to trading on a regulated market a prospectus must be issued which contains all the information necessary to enable investors to make an informed choice. A prospectus could be published in a glossy brochure or could be contained in the pages of the financial press. Members of the public respond by applying to purchase shares and the offer is accepted by the company allotting shares into the applicants name. A person induced to purchase securities on the basis of a false or misleading prospectus may have remedies in misrepresentation and under the FSMA 2000.

- **A public offer**. In this case, the public subscribes directly to the company for the shares.
- **A placing**. This where the shares are offered to (placed with) a small number of persons. It could well be that this is the cheapest way of issuing the shares as there are only a small number of persons involved, usually some of the major financial institutions.
- **An offer for sale**. In this case, an issuing house will acquire a company's new issue of shares and then offer them for resale to the public.

Factors to take into account when issuing shares

Obviously, when the company's directors are deciding that they need to raise money and are considering doing so through a share issue, they have to take into account:

- the costs involved, and the more people they have to reach the more costly it will be
- other major share issues that have recently occurred or are occurring, as they will be competing against these to the extent that there is only so much investors' money to go round
- the price at which the shares are to be offered. If it is too high then they will find that shares are not taken up. If they have had the issue underwritten then the shares not taken up will be purchased by the underwriter. Conversely, if the share price is too low, they will find themselves inundated with demands for shares exceeding those which they have on offer, involving a costly procedure to return cheques and so on
- The type of share to issue and the conditions attaching to the shares
- The expertise within the company relating to share offers and the facility the company has to cope.

In the end, the offer has to be attractive to potential investors, whether existing shareholders or not, otherwise they will not apply for the shares.

Issue at discount

Every share has a **nominal value** which is fixed at the time of incorporation of the company in the statement of capital and initial shareholding. The nominal value of the share represents the extent of a shareholders potential liability.

The common law rule is that a company cannot issue its shares for a consideration which is at a discount on their nominal value.

Ooregum Gold Mining Co of India v Roper (1892)

Facts: Shares in a company which had a nominal value of £1 were trading at a market price of 12.5p. In an honest attempt to refinance the company, new £1 preference shares were issued and credited with 75p as already paid, so the purchasers of the shares only had to pay 25p per share. The company subsequently went into liquidation.

Held: The holders of the shares were required to pay a further 75p per share.

The common law rule is given statutory effect in S580 CA06. In addition S582 CA06 states that shares are only treated as paid up to the extent that the company has received money or money's worth.

If this rule is breached the issue is still valid, but the allottee must pay up the discount plus interest. This applies to any subsequent holder of such a share who was aware of the original underpayment: S588 CA06.

Issue at premium

Where a share is allotted at a value greater than its nominal value, the excess over the nominal value is share premium. This is where the market value of the share is greater than the fixed nominal value.

S610 CA06 requires any premium to be credited to a share premium account, which may only be used for:

- writing off the expenses of the issue of new shares
- writing off any commission paid on the issue of new shares
- issuing bonus shares.

Paying for shares – private companies

Private companies may issue shares for non-cash consideration. The court will interfere with the valuation only if there is fraud or the consideration is 'illusory, past or patently inadequate'.

Paying for shares – public companies

There are a number of additional rules relating to the issue of shares in public companies contained in CA06:

S584	Subscribers to the memorandum must pay cash for their subscription shares.
S585	Payment for shares must not be in the form of work or services.
S586	Shares cannot be allotted until at least one-quarter of their nominal value and the whole of any premium have been paid.
S587	Non-cash consideration must be received within five years.
S593	Non-cash consideration must be independently valued and reported on by a person qualified to be the company's auditor. The valuation must be carried out in the six months prior to the allotment.

Supplementary reading

Finding buyers

Private companies cannot invite the public generally to purchase the company's shares. Rather share capital is obtained from the family, friends or business associates who have decided to combine their resources into a business venture. In the case of private companies, loan capital is usually obtained from a bank.

Public companies however, may indeed raise share capital by inviting members of the public to subscribe for shares. Such companies may also raise loans from the public. In fact there are a number of ways in which public companies may raise share capital. Most public companies aim to be 'listed' in other words to have their shares quoted on a stock exchange, the largest in the UK being the London Stock Exchange which in fact operates two markets, the Stock Exchange and the Alternative Investment Market ('AIM'). However, not all public companies are quoted on the London Stock Exchange or the AIM which require the companies to be listed on either market to be of a certain size and to comply with stringent regulations.

Listing

In order to obtain a listing, on the London Stock Exchange (known as a 'flotation'), a company must be registered as a public company or have re-registered as such. In addition to raising finance, a flotation allows the founders of the business to obtain a public valuation of the business and thus to sell out to new owners if that is desired. The listing of securities is governed by the Financial Services and Markets Act 2000 ('FSMA') and the regulatory authority is the Financial Services Authority which is known as the UK Listing Authority ('UKLA') when acting in this regard. UKLA is responsible for drafting the rules which are designed to provide a level of protection for investors and to maintain the integrity of the Exchange. Conditions which must be satisfied to obtain a listing include:

- the company is properly incorporated and is not a private company
- the company has published or filed audited accounts for the previous 3 years
- the company must be able to carry on business at arms length from any shareholder with a controlling interest, which generally means 30% of the voting rights in this context.

In addition the company must be applying to have securities listed which:

- are freely transferable
- the expected market value of the securities being listed must be at least £700,000 (usually much more); and
- usually at least 25% of the shares being listed must be distributed to the public.

It is also a condition for admission to the official list of any new securities that have not been offered to the public before, that a prospectus in the form and containing the information which has been specified by UKLA. Please note these conditions are not exhaustive but are designed to demonstrate some of the factors involved.

4 The issue of shares for an improper purpose

Obviously, shares are usually issued to raise capital. However, when a person purchases a share in a company he/she not only holds an investment in that company but also becomes a member of it and usually has the right to vote.

The power to issue shares vests in the directors and the fact that shares carry the right to vote has tempted them, particularly directors of private companies, to issue shares in order to change the power structure within the company.

Bamford v Bamford (1969)

Facts: The directors allotted shares to a company which they knew would vote against a threatened takeover bid. At least one reason was to ensure that the directors remained on the board. It is very common for a company which is taking over another to appoint its own directors and remove the existing board.

Held: Although it was accepted that the directors were acting in what they believed to be the best interests of the company, it was held that since the shares were issued for a collateral purpose it was an improper exercise of the directors' powers. The fact is that shares are supposed to be issued to raise capital and not to manipulate the voting power of the existing shareholders. Nevertheless, ratification of the directors' actions by the shareholders other than the company was held to be valid.

Again in **Hogg v Cramphorn Ltd (1967)**, it was held to be an improper use of the directors' powers when they issued shares with the objective of destroying the voting control of the existing majority.

It should be noted that a number of statutory provisions now governs the issue of shares.

5 Variation and maintenance of share capital

Variation

So long as the articles of a company with a share capital permit, S617 CA 2006 currently provides that it may:

(i) increase its share capital by allotting new shares

(ii) consolidate all or any of its share capital (e.g. by changing five 20p shares into one £1 share), in accordance with S618

(iii) subdivide its shares, or any of them, into shares of a smaller amount, in accordance with S618 (e.g. changing one £1 share into five 20p shares)

(iv) reduce its share capital in accordance with S626 (see later).

The powers in S617 may be exercised by an ordinary resolution of the shareholders in a general meeting or in a private company, by written resolution.

Maintenance of capital

As a basic principle of company law, a limited company's share capital must normally be maintained. The expression 'maintenance of capital' means that the company cannot simply give back its share capital to its members. It can and will be actively used to finance the company's business.

The capital maintenance rule manifests itself in various ways. As a general rule:

- Shares must not be issued at a discount, that is, for less than their nominal value. This is capital maintenance at the very outset – at least the nominal value must arrive at the company.
- No dividends should be paid to shareholders except out of profits, although profits set aside from earlier years can be used if the company is not at present profitable.
- The CA 2006 S656, requires that a general meeting of shareholders be held within 56 days of any director in a public company becoming aware that the value of the company's net assets has fallen to half or less of the company's called up share capital. This is intended to give some protection against loss of the real value of a company's capital. At the meeting, measures to remedy the situation should be considered (including possible changes of directors).
- A company must not buy its own shares, because to do so would effectively be to pay off those shareholders. This is based on the case of **Trevor v Whitworth (1887)**. There are important exceptions to this rule today, and these are discussed below.
- A company must not give financial assistance to help anyone to acquire its shares, or reward anyone for doing so. Again, there are exceptions discussed below.
- A company must not hold its own shares.

The last four of these general rules are discussed more fully below.

Reduction of capital

As a **general rule**, a limited company cannot reduce its share capital. There is, however, an exception to this general rule.

Under S641 CA06, a company can reduce its capital at any time, for any reason. The section suggests the following three situations where it may be useful for the company to reduce capital.

Method	**Process**	**Effects**
Reduce or cancel liabilities on partly-paid shares.	Where shares are only partly paid up the company could either: • reduce the nominal value to the amount paid up, or • reduce the nominal amount to a figure between the original nominal value and the amount paid up.	The company gives up its claim on the amount not paid up.
Return capital in excess of the company's needs.	The company reduces the nominal value of fully paid up shares.	The company returns the reduction in nominal value to the shareholders.
Cancel the paid-up capital that is no longer represented by the assets.	Where the company has fully paid shares with a nominal value in excess of the net assets, the nominal value may be reduced.	If the company has a debit balance on its reserves, it can write this off by reducing capital and thereby does not need to make good past losses.

Procedure:

Pass a special resolution

Apply to the court to confirm the special resolution.

If reduction involves one of the first two methods above, court must require company to settle a list of creditors entitled to object.

The court must not confirm the reduction until it is satisfied that all creditors have either consented to the reduction or had their debts discharged or secured.

The company must file documents with the Registrar. If the share capital of a public company falls below £50,000, it must re-register as a private company.

Simplified procedure for private companies:

Pass a special resolution supported by a solvency statement.

The solvency statement is a statement by each of the directors that the company will be able to meet its debts within the following year.

A solvency statement made without reasonable grounds is an offence punishable by fine and/or imprisonment.

Copies of the resolution, solvency statement and a statement of capital must be filed with the Registrar within 15 days.

Acquisition of new shares

Generally, a company may not acquire its own shares except in accordance with Companies Act 2006. Contravention of this rule:

- is an offence which render the company and defaulting officers liable to a fine and/or imprisonment of up to two years, and
- renders the acquisition void.

There are a number of exceptions to this prohibition:

- a company can acquire its own fully paid shares otherwise than for valuable consideration
- an acquisition in a lawful reduction of capital
- an acquisition pursuant to a court order, or
- a forfeiture of shares for failure to pay any sum in respect of them.

Redemption of shares

A company may redeem its shares provided:

- the articles of a public company authorise the redemption. (A private company may redeem shares subject to any restriction in its articles)
- the company must have some non-redeemable shares still in issue after the transaction
- the shares to be redeemed must be fully paid and provide for payment on redemption
- the redeemed shares must be cancelled, and
- the company must make a return to the Registrar within one month, accompanied by a revised statement of capital.

The redemption must be financed out of:

- distributable profits – a transfer equivalent to the nominal value of redeemed shares must be made to the capital redemption reserve (this is a non-distributable reserve)
- the proceeds of a new issue
- a permissible capital payment (private co only) – only to the extent that the distributable profits and the proceeds of a new issue are insufficient. (See below for further details).

Permissible capital payment

Private companies can purchase or redeem shares out of capital, subject to any restriction or prohibition in their articles.

The following formalities must be complied with:

The directors must make a statutory declaration stating that the company will be able to pay its debts as they fall due over the next year.

The auditors must make a statement supporting the directors' declaration

A copy of the directors' statement and auditor's report must be available to members before the resolution approving the payment is passed, otherwise it will be ineffective.

A special resolution must be passed within one week of the directors' statement

A public notice (in the Gazette) must be made within one week of the resolution, inviting creditors to apply to the courts to prevent the payment within five weeks if they object.

The payment out of capital must be made between five and seven weeks following the resolution

The documents must be filed with the Registrar

Purchase of own shares

The procedure and finance are the same as for redemption of shares.

There are two types of purchase:

Market purchase = purchase on the Stock Exchange	**Off market purchase** = purchase directly from a shareholder
• an **ordinary resolution** is required stating the maximum number of shares and the maximum and minimum prices.	• an **ordinary resolution** is required.
• the authority to purchase lasts for a specified time – the maximum is 5 years.	• a contract of sale must be available for inspection by members for at least **15 days** before the meeting and at the meeting.
	• vendors may not vote on the resolution with the shares which are to be purchased.

A return giving details of any purchase of own shares must be delivered to the Registrar within 28 days. Default is again an offence and subject to a fine.

Financial assistance

A public company may not give financial assistance to a third party to enable them to purchase shares in the company. Private companies are exempt from the provisions relating to financial assistance (s682 CA 2006).

Financial assistance includes:

- a gift, loan or indemnity
- a guarantee or security of third party loan
- any other financial assistance whereby the net assets of the company are materially reduced.

Financial assistance does not include:

- dividends or bonus shares
- a distribution upon winding-up
- a capital reduction under the Act, or
- a purchase or redemption of shares.

Financial assistance is not prohibited if:

- its principal purpose is not to enable the acquisition of shares but the assistance is incidental to some larger purpose and it is given in good faith in the interests of the company
- the company lends money in the ordinary course of its business
- it is for the purpose of an employee's share scheme, or
- it is given to an employee (not a director) to enable them to purchase fully paid shares.

If unlawful assistance is given, the company/officer commit a criminal offence punishable by a fine and/or imprisonment for up to two years.

A company holding its own shares

In almost all of the situations where a company can validly acquire its own shares, it must then go on to cancel or dispose of them. A company holding its own shares would be particularly susceptible to the objections that a company cannot be a member of itself, and that it should not be in a position to create a false market in the shares.

Treasury shares are a major exception to this rule. However, protection exists in so far as the company cannot exercise the voting or other rights attaching to the shares.

Similarly, as a general rule, a subsidiary company must not be a shareholder in its holding company. Any allotment or transfer of shares in a company to its subsidiary is void. However, a company can validly take over another which already holds shares in the (new) holding company, and the subsidiary can continue to hold those shares.

6 Loan capital

All companies have the implied power to borrow for the purpose of business.

Loan capital comprises all the longer term borrowing of a company such as:

- permanent overdrafts at the bank
- unsecured loans either from a bank or other party
- loans secured on assets either from a bank or other party.

Companies often issue long-term loans in the form of **debentures**.

Debentures

A debenture is a document issued by a company containing an acknowledgment of its indebtedness whether charged on the company's assets or not.

There are three main types of debentures:

- a single debenture e.g. a company obtains a secured loan or overdraft facility.
- debentures issued as a series and usually registered.
- debenture stock subscribed to by a large number of lenders.

Advantages of debentures

- The board does not (usually) need the authority of a general meeting to issue debentures.
- As debentures carry no votes they do not dilute or affect the control of the company.
- Interest is chargeable against the profit before tax.
- Debentures may be cheaper to service than shares.
- There are no restrictions on issuing debentures at a discount or on redemption.

Disadvantages of debentures

- Interest must be paid out of pre-tax profits, irrespective of the profits of the company. If necessary must be paid out of capital.
- Default may precipitate liquidation and/or administration if the debentures are secured.
- High gearing will affect the share price.

Fixed charge

A fixed charge is a charge over specific company assets such as land. By the terms of the charge the company is not able to deal freely with the asset charged in the ordinary course of business. Thus, in the case of land, the company would need to obtain the permission of the lender before granting a lease over the land.

A fixed charge has three main characteristics:

- It is on an identified asset.
- The asset is intended to be retained permanently in the business.
- The company has no general freedom to deal with (e.g. sell) the asset.

In certain circumstances a fixed charge can be set aside by a liquidator or an administrator if it can be shown that the company sought to put a creditor in a preferential position.

Floating charge

The judge in **Re Yorkshire Woolcombers' Association (1903)** stated that a floating charge has three main characteristics:

- It is on a class of assets, present and future.
- The assets within the class will change from time to time.
- The company has freedom to deal with the charged assets in the ordinary course of its business.

A floating charge cannot be created by a partnership.

Crystallisation

A floating charge does not attach to any particular asset until crystallisation.

Crystallisation means the company can no longer deal freely with the assets. It occurs in the following cases:

- liquidation
- the company ceases to carry on business
- any event specified (e.g. the company is unable to pay its debts; the company fails to look after its property; the company fails to keep stock levels sufficiently high).

Advantages of a floating charge

A floating charge has the following advantages for the company:

- The company can deal freely with the assets.
- A wider class of assets can be charged.

Disadvantages of a floating charge

A floating charge has a number of disadvantages for the chargee:

- The value of the security is uncertain until it crystallises.
- It has a lower priority in order of repayment than a fixed charge (see below).
- It may be challenged by a liquidator if it was created within 12 months preceding a winding up. This is to prevent a company from giving preference to one of its unsecured creditors by giving a floating charge over its assets.

A floating charge ranks after all of the following if the company is wound up:

(a) The costs and expenses of the winding up.

(b) Fixed charges created before the floating charge. A fixed charge created after the floating charge will also rank higher than the floating charge unless the company has contractually agreed in the debenture document not to create any new charges ranking equally or in priority to the charges already created. Major lenders such as the main banks always insist upon such a term (known as a 'negative pledge clause') being included in the debenture. It should be noted that any new lender is only bound by the clause if given actual notice of it.

(c) Preferential creditors. If the assets comprised in the floating charge are sold, the proceeds must first be used to pay off the preferential creditors. However, a number of important changes to this area of law have been made by the Enterprise Act 2002 which was enacted on 7 November 2002 and came into force on 15 September 2003. In particular the Act has abolished the preferential status of debts due to the Crown such as the taxes payable to Her Majesty's Revenue and Customs, ('HMRC') which are now reduced to the status of unsecured creditors.

Following the changes made by the Act the following are the only remaining preferential creditors: (i) contributions to occupational pension schemes; (ii) arrears of employee remuneration; and (iii) coal and steel levies.

Although this may appear beneficial to the floating charge holders in that there are now fewer prior claims, the Insolvency Act 1986 (Prescribed Part) Order 2003 which also came into force on 15 September 2003, provides that out of a company's 'net property', that is, the property which would have been available for satisfaction of the claims of floating charge holders before the Order was enacted, the following amounts shall be set aside for the benefit of unsecured creditors:

(1) where the company's net property does not exceed £10,000, 50 per cent of that property.

(2) where the company's net property exceeds £10,000 the sum of
   (i) 50 per cent of the first £10,000 and
   (ii) 20 per cent of the property exceeding £10,000 up to a maximum of £600,000.

Illustration 1

PQR Ltd is in liquidation. Wye Bank plc has made a loan of £70,000 to PQR Ltd secured by a floating charge over the company's stock. The company's stock has raised £100,000 and there are preferential creditors who are owed £20,000.

The amount available for the floating charge holder is

	£	£
Proceeds from sale of stock	100,000	
Less preferential creditors		20,000
		80,000
'Prescribed part' for unsecured creditors		
50% × 10,000	5,000	
20% × 70,000	14,000	19,000
Available for the floating charge holder		£61,000

It follows that £9,000 is still owed to the bank, which must stand as an unsecured creditor for that amount. This appears to be a tremendous step forward for the rights of the unsecured creditors who, prior to the introduction of these rules, were often left with nothing in a company's liquidation.

(d) A landlord's execution and distress for rent completed before crystallisation.

(e) The interests of a judgment creditor (who has obtained judgment in the court against the company) if, to enforce the judgment, the creditor has had the company's goods seized and sold by the sheriff; similarly if he has obtained a garnishee order over money in the company's bank accounts. A garnishee order is a legal procedure by which a creditor can collect what a debtor owes by reaching the debtor's property when it is in the hands of someone other than the debtor.

(f) The owners of goods supplied to the company under a hire-purchase agreement (i.e. usually the finance company).

(g) The owners of goods supplied under a contract containing a reservation of title clause (sometimes called a 'Romalpa clause'). In fact, a supplier of goods who is able to rely upon such a clause will obtain priority over all creditors of the company, including those holding fixed charges. The reason for this is that such clauses commonly state words to the effect that '... ownership of the goods supplied does not pass to the buyer until the goods have been paid for.' It follows that if the company fails to pay for the goods, the supplier is entitled by law to recover them as the supplier remains the legal owner of them.

Furthermore, a floating charge may be invalid if it was created within certain periods before either the commencement of a liquidation or the presentation of a petition for an administration order.

The Insolvency Act 1986 s.245 provides that a floating charge may be invalid if:

(a) It was created in favour of a connected person within 2 years of the company becoming insolvent – for example, in favour of a relative of a director of the company.

(b) It was created in favour of any other person within 1 year of the company becoming insolvent. This applies only if, at the time the charge was created, the company was unable to pay its debts as a result of the transaction.

(c) It was created at a time between the presentation of a petition for the making of an administration order and the making of the order.

Registration

The company must also notify the Registrar within 21 days of the creation of the charge.

Registration can be undertaken by:

- the company
- the chargeholder.

Failure to register:

- renders the charge void against the liquidator
- renders the money secured immediately repayable.

If the charge relates to land it must also be registered with the Land Registry.

The company must also include all charges in its own register of charges. However, failure to include the charge in the company's own register does not invalidate the charge.

Supplementary reading

Debentures and debenture stock

Debentures can take many forms. The main debenture for a small company may be a loan agreement with its bank. This may be unsecured, but for any substantial amount it will normally give the bank some security, such as a floating charge over all the company's undertaking and assets.

A larger business might wish to seek capital from public subscription without having to dilute its share capital. A public company can do this by a prospectus offering a series of debentures, usually for a fairly small amount each and ranking equally between themselves for sale to the public, or by offering debenture stock. Buyers will receive a debenture or debenture stock certificate, and can usually sell on their investment to other holders, as with shares. Unlike shares, debentures can be issued at a discount. A private company cannot issue debentures for public subscription.

Usually, a public company will issue debentures or stock through a financial institution such as a bank or insurance company, which will hold legal title to the debentures as trustee for the eventual buyers, and generally carry out the necessary administration.

Debentures are often long term, and can even be 'perpetual', in that the company is not bound to repay the loan until the company is wound up (although it usually reserves the *right* to redeem). The contract contained in the terms by which the debentures are issued will give the holders a right to interest payments, usually at stated intervals such as twice per year.

Trust deed

When debentures are issued by a public company to investors, it is usual for them to be issued under a trust deed. Where the loan stock is to be quoted on the Stock Exchange, the company must, to comply with the requirements of the Stock Exchange, establish a trust for the duration of the loan and appoint trustees to safeguard the interests of the stockholders. One of the trustees appointed (or the sole trustee) must be a trust corporation (e.g. a bank).

This arrangement has the following advantages:

(a) The trustees can take action to protect the interests of the investors – for example, the appointment of a receiver when interest on the loan stock is in arrears.

(b) The company need deal only with the trustees, on matters relevant to the issue – instead of having to deal with large numbers of individual investors.

(c) It facilitates the holding of meetings with investors and the passing of resolutions by those investors.

(d) Any security given by the company to secure the debentures can be vested in the trustees who, where appropriate, can enforce that security on behalf of all the investors.

(e) It satisfies the requirements of the Stock Exchange that the trustees represent the holders of the listed debt securities.

The trust deed will, inter alia, specify the amount and terms of issue of the debentures; the date and amount of redemption, including details of any sinking fund established by the company for that purpose; the circumstances in which the security (if any) may be enforced by the trustees – for example, on the company's failure to pay interest on the debentures, or the failure of the company's business.

Rights of debenture holders on default by the company

If the company defaults in paying interest or in repaying the loan, a debenture holder will have a variety of possible remedies, under the terms of issue, at common law, and by statute. For example:

(1) He or she can sue the company for the amount due under the terms of the loan agreement.

(2) The terms of the debenture will usually give the lender a charge over the company's property and will set out the right of the lender to sell the property in the event of the company defaulting in repaying the debt.

(3) He or she may be entitled to appoint a receiver in order to achieve the sale. Any surplus after the debt has been repaid will go to the company.

(4) In the absence of express powers, there are various statutory powers to have a receiver appointed and to realise any security.

(5) If the assets are substantial (e.g. a floating charge over the entire undertaking), the holder of the floating charge would often be entitled by the terms of the debenture to appoint an administrator. Usually, the holder of a fixed charge will appoint a receiver in relation to the piece of property charged.

(6) Any of this may result in a petition for a winding-up of the company.

Supplementary reading

Shares and debentures compared

(1) A shareholder is a member of the company, and can normally therefore attend and vote at meetings. A debenture holder is not a member but a creditor of the company.

(2) Debenture interest must be paid, even if the company has current trading losses. Dividends can generally only be paid if (after debenture interest and all other expense has been paid) there are still available profits.

(3) Directors and members have a discretion over whether to declare a dividend on shares. Debenture interest is a contractual debt which *must* be paid.

(4) Loan interest is deducted before the company's profits are assessed for tax, but dividends paid on shares are payable out of company profits after they have been assessed for tax. The tax laws make it advantageous for the owners of a company to extract profits in the form of dividends as opposed to salaries or loans. This is so because (a) dividends are taxed at a lower starting rate than salaries, and (b) national insurance contributions are payable by the company and the director/employee on salaries, but are not payable on dividends.

(5) Shares may well vary substantially in value, according to whether or not the company is successful.

(6) Debentures can be repaid while the company still exists; shares, generally, cannot (see 'capital maintenance' earlier).

(7) Debenture (loan) capital must be repaid on a winding-up before the shareholders receive anything. Secured debentures will have even earlier claims on the assets given as security.

(8) Directors need little or no special authority to borrow money and issue debentures, unlike the detailed authority which may be required to issue further shares.

7 Corporate management – directors

Definition of director

The term 'director' includes 'any person occupying the position of director, by whatever name called': s250 CA 2006.

The decision as to whether someone is a director is therefore based on their function, not their title.

There must be at least one director who is a 'natural person'. In addition, a director must normally be aged at least 16.

De Jure Director

A person who is formally and legally appointed or elected as director in accordance with the articles of association of the company and gives written consent to hold the office of a director.

De Facto Director

A person who is not a de jure director but performs the acts or duties of a director.

Any person, who is not technically a director, but according to whose directions and instructions other directors and employees are accustomed to act, is legally deemed a de facto director.

A de facto director owes the same duties to the company as a de jure director, i.e. he is subject to both statutory duties and prohibitions, and he also owes fiduciary duties to the company.

Types of director

Managing director (MD)	• A director appointed to carry out overall day-to-day management functions. • The model articles allow the board to delegate to the MD any powers they see fit. • The MD has a dual role – member of board and also executive officer. • **Freeman & Lockyer (A Firm) v Buckhurst Park Properties (Mangal) Ltd (1964)** – the MD has the apparent authority to enter into all contracts of a commercial nature.
Shadow director	• 'A person in accordance with whose directions or instructions the directors of a company are accustomed to act': s251 CA06. As discussed earlier this means that it is the person's function rather than their title that defines them as a director. • Used to regulate activity by those who exercise control over a company but try to evade their responsibilities and potential liabilities as a director. • All the rules of company law are equally applicable to shadow directors. • Not a shadow director if advice is given only in a professional capacity e.g. accountants and lawyers.
Executive director	• Likely to be a full-time employee involved in management. • Performs a specific role under a service contract. • May be distinguished by a special title such as 'Sales Director' or 'Finance Director'.
Non-executive director (NED)	• Part-time. • Not an employee. • Brings outside expertise to board. • Contributes an independent view. • Exerts control over executive directors. • Subject to the same duties, controls and potential liabilities as executive directors.

Chairman of board	• Chairs meetings of board. • Acts as spokesman for the company. • Has a casting vote.
Chief Executive	• Responsible for leadership of the company and managing it within authorities delegated by the board. • Develops strategy proposals for recommendation to the board. • Be responsible to the board for the performance of the company consistent with agreed plans, strategies and policies.
Alternate director	• Appointed by a director to attend and vote for them at board meetings which they are unable to attend. • Can be another director within the same company or more usually an outsider.

Appointment

First Directors	• Appointed in Statement of Proposed Officers. • Public companies need a minimum of two; private companies need one. • There is no statutory maximum, but the articles may specify a maximum number.
Appointment procedure	• Usually appointed by the existing directors or by ordinary resolution. • Directors of public companies should generally be voted on individually: s160 CA06. • A director's actions are valid notwithstanding that his appointment was defective: s161 CA06.
Model articles for public companies	• At the first annual general meeting (AGM) all the directors retire and offer themselves for re-election by ordinary resolution. • At each AGM one-third retire (those most senior). They can be re-elected. • Casual vacancies are filled by the board until the next AGM when the new directors must stand for election.
Publicity	• The company must notify Companies House within 14 days of new appointments and any changes in particulars. It must also enter details in the register of directors.

Disqualification

Model articles – Directors must vacate their office if they become bankrupt or insane.

Company Directors (Disqualification) Act 1986 (CDDA 1986)

The CDDA 1986 was introduced to prevent the misuse of the limited liability status of companies by directors who would set up a new company to carry on essentially the same business as an old company which had ceased trading with unpaid debts.

A disqualified director cannot be concerned in the management of a company directly or indirectly or act as a liquidator, receiver or promoter.

The CDDA 1986 identifies three distinct categories of conduct:

(1) General misconduct in connection with companies. This includes:

- Conviction of a serious offence in connection with the management of a company (maximum fifteen years disqualification).
- Persistent breaches of CA06, e.g. failure to file returns (maximum five years disqualification).

(2) Disqualification for unfitness. This includes:

- Where an investigation by the Department for Business, Innovation and Skills finds the director unfit to be concerned in the management of the company.
- Where a liquidator's report finds the director unfit to be concerned in the management of a company (minimum two years, and maximum fifteen years, disqualification).

(3) Other cases for disqualification. This includes:

- participation in fraudulent or wrongful trading (maximum 15 years disqualification)
- where an undischarged bankrupt has been acting as a director.

Breach of a disqualification order:

- This is a criminal offence, which could result in a fine and imprisonment.
- The disqualified director (or any person who acts on his instructions) is personally liable for the debts of the company while so acting.

Removal

Under s168 CA06, a company may by ordinary resolution remove a director before expiration of his period of office notwithstanding anything in:

- its articles, or
- any agreement between him and it.

Thus a director can be removed despite any provision to the contrary in his service contract, although he can sue for damages if the removal is in breach of his contract. The company must follow this procedure to remove a director:

Special notice (28 days) is required of the resolution by persons wishing to remove a director.

The company must forward a copy of the resolution to the director concerned.

Notice of the meeting goes to the director and all members entitled to attend and vote.

The director in question can require the company to circulate written representations to members.

At the meeting, the director can read out representations if there was no time for prior circulation.

The director must be allowed to attend the meeting and to speak.

An ordinary resolution is needed to remove the director.

The power of the members to remove a director may be limited:

Bushell v Faith (1970)

Facts: A provision in the articles tripled the number of votes of shares held by directors on a resolution to remove them. Statute only required an ordinary resolution and made no provision as to how it could be obtained or defeated.

Held: The weighted voting rights provided in the articles were valid. (Note that this decision applies to private companies only).

Registers and information concerning directors

The company itself must keep a register of directors at its registered office: S162 CA2006.

The company's register of directors should contain details of each director as their name, nationality, business occupation, other directorships and should include a service address. This register must be available for inspection by shareholders (free) and by the public (for a small fee).

A company will also be required to keep a register of director's residential addresses which must be notified to the Registrar of Companies. However, this information, with a few exceptions, will not be disclosed.

The Registrar of Companies must be given the same details of directors on Form IN01 when the company is formed, and later within 14 days of any change. This is open to public inspection.

Copies of directors' service contracts (if any), or terms of employment (if any), must be available to members, normally at the registered office.

8 Powers and duties of directors

Powers of directors

The function of the directors is to manage the company. They must make management decisions on most matters, and they are responsible for ensuring that those decisions and the decisions of shareholders are executed. The exact powers will be determined by the Articles.

Exercise of directors' powers must generally be by the board, acting collectively at board meetings. Unless there has been delegation, individual directors have no authority. Board resolutions can be reached without a meeting if a written resolution is signed by all directors.

Limits and controls over the powers of directors

Various common law precedents and statutory provisions aim to prevent abuse of power by the directors. Some transactions are prohibited as criminal offences. Others can only take place if approved by the shareholders. The prohibitions often have the effect of limiting the situations where there is a potential conflict between the personal interests of the director, and his fiduciary duties to the company.

Property transactions between the company and its own directors are controlled by S190–196 CA 2006. If a director wishes to buy, sell or deal with a non-cash asset of the 'requisite value' from or to his company, he must first obtain the approval of the shareholders by ordinary resolution. The 'requisite value' is £100,000; or 10 per cent of the company's net assets, subject to a £5,000 minimum. The rule extends to dealings between the company and persons 'connected with' a director.

If approval of the shareholders is not obtained, any directors who made or authorised the transaction must indemnify the company against any loss, and the director or connected person who actually contracted with the company must normally account to it for any profit which he has made. The contract is often voidable by the company.

Directors' service contracts for over 2 years must be approved by ordinary resolution of shareholders; similarly if an existing contract is extended for more than 5 years (see S188). A director must not vote on the terms of his own service contract. A copy must be kept at the registered office. The term 'service contract' has now been extended to cover letters of appointment and also contracts for services, for example consultancy contracts.

Loans and quasi loans to directors

The Companies Act 2006 has removed criminal penalties in relation to loans to directors. There is now a general provision whereby any loan to a director must be approved by the shareholders, so long as they are informed of the amount of the loan, the nature of the transaction, its purpose and the extent of the company's liability (Ss197–214 CA 2006).

In relation to quasi loans, shareholder approval is only required in the case of public companies. A quasi loan is a payment of a director's debts or expenses on terms that the payment must be repaid by the director. A quasi loan to a connected person, such as the director's spouse, must be approved by the shareholders.

Duties of directors to the company

Prior to the Companies Act 2006, common law rules, equitable principles and fiduciary duties made up the law on directors' duties. A fiduciary duty is a duty imposed upon certain persons because of the position of trust and confidence they are in.

These have now been replaced by the specific statutory duties provided in the Companies Act 2006. However, the old case law still has relevance in interpreting the new legislation and illustrating its application.

Duty to act within powers: s171

A director must act in accordance with the company's constitution and only use his powers for the purpose which they were given. They have a fiduciary duty to the company to exercise their powers bona fide in what they honestly consider to be the interests of the company.

If this rule is not adhered to the transaction will be void, unless it is approved by the shareholders.

Hogg v Cramphorn (1967)

Facts: The directors issued further shares and gave financial assistance for their purchase in an attempt to fight off a takeover bid, believing it to be in the best interests of the company.

Held: The directors had acted in what they believed to be the best interests of the company, but were in breach of the duty to act within their powers. Therefore, it was open to the members to ratify their actions, which they did.

Duty to promote the success of the company: s172

A director must act in good faith, in a way which promotes the success of the company and for the benefit of the members as a whole.

The Act requires the directors to have regard to:

- the likely consequences of any decision in the long term
- the interests of the company's employees
- the need to foster the company's business relationships with suppliers, customers and others
- the impact of the company's operations on the community and the environment
- the desirability of the company maintaining a reputation for high standards of business conduct and
- the need to act fairly as between members of the company.

Companies may have wider purposes than just the benefit of members such as charitable companies and community interest companies. S172(2) provides that where that is the case, then the duty of the director is to act in a way that would be most likely to achieve that purpose.

S172(3) provides that the general duty is subject to any specific enactment or rule of law requiring directors to consider or act in the interests of creditors of the company. This provision therefore formally recognises that the duty to the shareholders is displaced when the company is insolvent or heading towards insolvency.

Duty to exercise independent judgment: s173

A director of a company must exercise independent judgment.

This duty is not infringed by a director acting:

- in accordance with an agreement duly entered into by the company that restricts the future exercise of discretion by its directors, or
- in a way authorised by the company's constitution.

Duty to exercise reasonable care, skill and diligence: s174

The standard expected of a director is that of a reasonably diligent person with:

- the general knowledge, skill and experience that could reasonably be expected of a director, and
- the actual knowledge, skill and experience held by the director.

The reasonableness test therefore consists of two elements:

(1) *An objective test*

A director in carrying out his functions, must show such care as could reasonably be expected from a competent person in that role. It is not a defence for a director to claim lack of expertise.

(2) *A subjective test*

A director is expected to show the degree of skill which may reasonably be expected from a person of his knowledge and experience.

Re City Equitable Fire Insurance Co (1925)

Facts: The company was in liquidation and it was discovered there was a shortage of funds mainly due to the deliberate fraud of the chairman, for which he had been convicted. The liquidator brought an action against the other directors of the company for negligence on the basis that they had left the management of the company entirely in the hands of the chairman.

Held: The liquidator failed and the judge laid down the duties of care and skill to be expected of a director:

(a) A director need not exhibit in the performance of his duties a greater degree of skill than may reasonably be expected from someone of his knowledge and experience.

(b) A director is not bound to give continuous attention to the affairs of the company.

(c) Where duties may properly be left to some other official, a director is justified, in the absence of grounds for suspicion, in trusting that official to perform his duties honestly.

The low level of care shown in **Re City Equitable Fire Insurance Co (1925)** was raised in:

Dorchester Finance Co Ltd v Stebbing (1989)

Facts: The company was a money-lending company and had three directors, Parsons, Hamilton and Stebbing. All three had considerable accountancy and business experience (Parsons and Hamilton were chartered accountants). No board meetings were ever held and Parsons and Hamilton left all the affairs of the company to Stebbing. Parsons and Hamilton did, however, turn up from time to time and signed blank cheques on the company's account which they left Stebbing to deal with. Stebbing loaned the company's money without complying with statutory regulations applying to money lending, such that the loans were unenforceable.

Held: All three were liable in negligence. If a director has a special skill (e.g. as an accountant) he is expected to use it for the benefit of the company.

Duty to avoid conflicts of interest: s175

A director must avoid any situation which places him in direct conflict with the interests of the company or the performance of any other duty.

IDC v Cooley (1972)

Facts: Cooley, the managing director of IDC, had been negotiating a contract on behalf of the company, but the third party wished to award the contract to him personally and not to the company. Without disclosing his reason to the company (or its board) he resigned in order to take the contract personally.

Held: He was in breach of fiduciary duty as he had profited personally by use of an opportunity which came to him through his directorship: it made no difference that the company itself would not have obtained the contract. He was therefore accountable to the company for the benefits gained from the contract.

The IDC case also illustrates that an individual may still be subject to the duties even after he ceases to be a director.

The accountability arises from the mere fact of having made a profit, it is not a question of loss to the company.

Regal (Hastings) Ltd v Gulliver (1942)

Facts: The claimant company owned one cinema and wished to buy two others with the object of selling all three together. They formed a subsidiary to buy the cinemas but could not provide all the capital needed to finance the purchase. The directors bought some of the shares in the subsidiary to enable the purchases to be made and later sold their shares at a profit.

Held: The directors must account to the claimant company for the profit on the grounds that it was only through the knowledge and opportunity they gained as directors of that company that they were able to obtain the shares and consequently to make the profit.

Duty not to accept benefits from third parties: s176

A director must not accept any benefit from a third party which arises by reason of him being a director or performing/not performing an act as a director, unless acceptance cannot reasonably be regarded as likely to give rise to a conflict of interest.

Boston Deep Sea Fishing & Ice Co v Ansell (1888)

Facts: Ansell was managing director of the claimant company. He accepted a 'commission' (bribe) from a supplier to order goods from that supplier, on behalf of the company. When the company found out, he was dismissed.

Held: The defendant was in breach of his fiduciary duty as the agent of the company. Therefore the company could recover the commissions paid to him.

Duty to declare interest in proposed transaction or arrangement: s177

A director is required to declare the nature and extent of any interest, either direct or indirect through a connected person, that they have in relation to a proposed transaction or arrangement with the company. Even if the director is not a party to a transaction, the duty may apply if they are aware or ought reasonably to have been aware, of the interest.

This declaration can be made in writing, at a board meeting or by a general notice that he has an interest as a third party.

Aberdeen Railway v Blakie (1854)

Facts: A company bought some chairs from a firm. At the time of the contract, one of the company's directors, unknown to the company, was a partner in the firm.

Held: The company, could avoid the contract, because of this undisclosed interest in the transaction.

The consequences of a breach of director's duty

As a general rule, the company must bring the action against the director in question. This is therefore consistent with the rule in **Foss v Harbottle (1843)**. It follows that the previous difficulties, i.e. the fact that it may be difficult for shareholders to persuade a board to cause the company to take action against a particular director, still remain. The problem becomes particularly acute where it is alleged that the whole board has acted in breach of duty, as the board is unlikely to cause the company to sue themselves!

The CA 2006 introduced a procedure in relation to so-called 'derivative' actions which may enable shareholders to take action in appropriate situations (covered in details later on in this chapter).

9 Liability of directors

To shareholders

As stated above, directors (and the company secretary) owe their duties to the company, not to individual shareholders. Therefore, it is only in exceptional circumstances that a director can be liable to legal action by members. Certainly, negligent directors whose conduct causes the value of the shares to fall are not liable to pay damages to the shareholders. Generally, directors will only become personally liable to a shareholder if they make a contract between themselves and the shareholder which is separate from the directors' duties to the company.

Allen v Hyatt (1914)

Facts: Some directors made what amounted to an agency agreement with some of the shareholders. The directors took an option on the shares with a view to selling them for the benefit of the shareholders during takeover negotiations. The directors abused this option. They bought the shares for themselves, sold them at a profit and kept the profit.

Held: The directors had to account to the shareholders for this profit, for breach of the agency contract.

To the company's creditors

As a general rule, directors are not personally liable to the company's creditors or to other outsiders. The debts, etc., are the debts of the company, which is a separate legal person from its members or officers. However, there are some exceptional situations where a director may be personally liable to outsiders.

While the company is still operating

In this case, the exceptions are few.

(a) If a director claims to make a contract on behalf of the company in circumstances where the company is not bound, the director is personally liable to the other party for breach of warranty of authority. This will not often occur today because, by s40 CA 2006 Act, the company will almost always be bound by the acts of directors on its behalf.

(b) Under the Company Directors Disqualification Act 1986, if a person who has been disqualified by a court order from acting as a director then disobeys the order, he can be personally liable for company debts while he does so. Similar rules apply to undischarged bankrupts.

(c) By the Insolvency Act 1986, s216, someone who was a director of an insolvent company during the last 12 months of an insolvent company during the last 12 months before it was wound up must not without court consent be a director in a new company with a name too similar to that of the old company for the next 5 years. To do so is a criminal offence, and makes him personally liable for the debts of the new ('phoenix') company. Section 216 also applies to unincorporated businesses.

(d) Exceptionally, it seems that a director may be vicariously liable for torts committed by the company, if he had had extensive control over the company's conduct in connection with the tortious activity. In **Evans & Sons Ltd v Spritebrand Ltd (1985)**, a director was held personally liable for a company's breach of copyright.

(e) If the directors of a very small company seek credit from a large lender (e.g. an overdraft for the company from the bank), the lender may insist that the directors personally guarantee repayment. This is probably the most common situation in which directors will be personally liable.

(f) If an officer or other person signs any bill of exchange, cheque, and so on, or order for money or goods on the company's behalf, in which the company's name is not properly given, then he is personally liable if the company does not pay.

The name must be stated fully and accurately. Officers have several times been held personally liable where the word 'limited' was omitted (although 'ltd' is sufficient, as is 'co' for 'company'). Even the omission of '&', so that 'L & R Agencies Ltd' appeared as 'LR Agencies Ltd' rendered directors who had signed the cheque personally liable: **Hendon v Adelman (1973)**.

In the course of winding-up

In this case there are further possibilities.

- Fraudulent trading may occur. By the Insolvency Act 1986, s213, if it appears in the course of a winding-up that any business has been carried on with intent to defraud creditors, or for any fraudulent purpose, the liquidator may ask the court to declare that persons knowingly party to the fraudulent trading must make such contribution to the company's assets (and therefore indirectly to the creditors) as the court thinks proper.

  This can take place even if the company was solvent when wound up, and the section applies to managers as well as to directors. Persons guilty of the fraud also commit a criminal offence. In practice, fraudulent trading is very difficult to prove. Fraud is a subjective test, and it must be shown beyond reasonable doubt (which is the criminal standard of proof) that the individual intended to defraud the creditors. For this reason liquidators, who are primarily interested in obtaining a monetary contribution from the wrongdoers, would tend to pursue wrongful rather than fraudulent trading.

- Wrongful trading was introduced by the Insolvency Act 1986, s214, because of the difficulty in proving fraud. It is an objective test in that the directors are judged against what they ought to have known rather than what they actually knew.

  When a company has financial difficulties, and a director knows or ought to conclude that it has no reasonable prospect of recovery, he should take immediate steps to minimise the loss to creditors. For example, he should apply as soon as possible for a winding-up order.

  A director who wrongfully carries on trading in these circumstances may be ordered to contribute personally to the company's assets in the eventual liquidation. Unlike s213 above, wrongful trading only applies to directors, and only if the liquidation is insolvent. In effect the directors lose the benefit of limited liability from the period when they should have known that insolvency was inevitable.

In summary form, the following must be established.

(i) Whether the director(s) knew or ought to have known that there was no reasonable prospect of avoiding insolvent liquidation

(ii) The date which they knew or should have known this

(iii) Whether they took 'every step' after that date to minimise the loss to the creditors (in which case that is a complete defence); and, if not

(iv) how much they should contribute to the assets of the company.

It follows that neither fraud nor dishonesty needs to be proved, the over-optimistic folly of directors can be enough.

Re Produce Marketing Consortium Ltd (1989)

Facts: Two directors insisted on trading after auditors had warned them that the company was insolvent.

Held: They were ordered to pay £75,000 with interest in the eventual winding-up. If directors carry on trading when insolvency is inevitable, they are, in effect, using the creditors' money to finance their trade.

10 Division of powers between directors and shareholders

The powers of a company are exercised by the board of directors and by members in general meetings. Who can do what depends partly on statute and partly on the Articles.

Some decisions must be made by a resolution of shareholders, which will normally involve a general meeting. The most important of these are changes to the company's name, nominal capital or Articles.

Some transactions by the board must specifically be approved by a resolution of shareholders, again normally at a general meeting. Examples include property transactions between a company and any of its directors which fall within Ss. 190–196 (see earlier).

The board is the agent of the company, not the shareholders. It is the board which has the authority to carry on the day-to-day management of the company and the shareholders cannot interfere unless the Articles permit them to do so. Therefore, a general meeting cannot by ordinary resolution dictate to or overrule the directors in respect of matters entrusted to them by the Articles. Moreover a special resolution, even one altering the Articles for the future, cannot retrospectively invalidate something which was valid at the time when the board did it.

Supplementary reading

Duty of the board to report to a general meeting

The boards of public companies have to report annually to their shareholders at an AGM. However, as stated above, private companies are only obliged to do so if they so wish. In respect of each financial year of a company, the directors must lay before the company in general meeting copies of the accounts for that year. These 'accounts' must comprise:

(a) the company's profit and loss account and balance sheet

(b) the directors' report, and

(c) the auditors' report

(d) where the company has subsidiaries, it may also have to lay the company's group accounts.

As we have seen, the company's accounts must be prepared and audited each year. Copies must be sent to members and debenture holders at least 21 days before the date of the AGM.

The company must also send a copy of the above documents to the Registrar of Companies.

The Companies Act 2006 provides that private companies must file their annual report within 9 months of the year end and public companies within 6 months. Another change is that auditors will be able to limit their liability to such as is fair and reasonable in the circumstances (with a monetary cap permitted) by agreement with the company and subject to approval by the shareholders. In addition there will be a criminal offence in respect of auditors knowingly or recklessly including materially misleading information in an audit report.

The Companies Act 2006 also provides that quoted companies must ensure that they include a 'business review' in the directors' report which includes a commentary on (a) the main trends and factors likely to affect its future business; (b) information about the environment, the employees and social community issues; and (c) information about persons who have contractual or other arrangements with the company which are essential to its operations – unless this would be seriously prejudicial to that person or to the public interest. Directors will be liable to the company for misleading statements made in bad faith or recklessly.

Exemption clauses for directors

By Ss532–533 CA 2006, any provision, whether in the Articles or in any contract with the company or elsewhere, which tries to exempt a director from liability which would otherwise attach to him for negligence, will be deemed void.

Such a provision can, however, entitle the company to pay the costs of a director if the proceedings find him not liable (or not guilty in a criminal case).

Majority rule and minority protection

Minority shareholders who are unhappy with a decision have the following remedies:

Requirement	Remedy
Any member	Can apply to court to prohibit a payment out of capital by a private company.
>5% of voting rights	Can force the inclusion of a resolution on the agenda of the AGM.
>5% voting rights	Can require the directors to call a GM.
>15% voting	Can apply to court to cancel a variation of class rights.
>25% voting rights	Can defeat a special resolution to alter name, alter articles, reduce share capital or wind up company.

The rule in Foss v Harbottle

As a general rule, if a wrong has been done to a company, then the proper claimant is the company. If the minority is unhappy with a decision, then they have no recourse as a company is a separate legal person.

Foss v Harbottle (1843)

Facts: Foss, a shareholder, sued the directors of the company alleging that they had defrauded the company by selling land to it at an inflated price.

Held: The action must be dismissed. The company was the proper claimant, not the shareholders.

Derivative actions

Under s260 CA 2006, a member may bring a 'derivative' claim on behalf of the company against a director where there has been a breach of duty or negligence. The claim requires the permission of the court.

In deciding whether to refuse or grant permission for the action, the court will consider:

- whether a member is acting in good faith
- whether the company has decided not to pursue the claim
- the views of the members with no personal interest in the matter; and
- whether the member has the ability to pursue the matter in his own right, rather than on behalf of the company.

Protection against unfairly prejudicial conduct

Under s994 CA 2006, any member may apply to the court for redress on the grounds that 'the company's affairs are being or have been conducted in a manner that is unfairly prejudicial to the interests of the members generally or of some part of the members...or that an actual or proposed act or omission of the company is or would be so prejudicial'.

In order to claim relief:

- the petitioner must be a member of the company, and
- the complaint must be based on prejudice to them as a member.

Just and equitable winding up: Insolvency Act 1986, s122(g)

A minority shareholder may petition the court to wind up the company on the ground that it is just and equitable to do so. The member must show that there is no other suitable remedy available.

Orders tend to be made for winding up if:

- the company was initially formed for an illegal or fraudulent purpose
- there is a complete deadlock in the management of the company's affairs, or
- shareholders have lost confidence in the company's management.

Ebrahimi v Westbourne Galleries (1973)

Facts: The company was formed in 1958 to take over a business founded by N. From 1945, however, the business had been carried on in partnership with E, sharing the management and profits equally. When the company was formed N and E were the only shareholders and directors, holding 500 £1 shares each. N's son, G, was then made a director and N and E each transferred 100 shares to him. Shortly after there were disputes and N and G passed an ordinary resolution in general meeting removing E from office. E petitioned for a winding-up order on the just and equitable ground: s122 IA 1986.

Held: The company would be wound up on the just and equitable ground. The company was founded on the basis that the character of association would remain, i.e. a matter of personal relation and good faith. This had failed and thus by analogy to partnership law the court made a wounding up order.

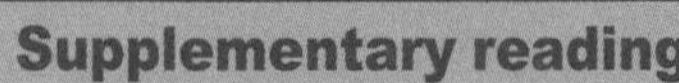

Supplementary reading

Other statutory rights and remedies

Many statutory provisions, mentioned at various places in this book, give rights and remedies to minorities of varying sizes. For example, in this chapter we have seen that:

- a minority of 25 per cent plus can protect itself against anything which has to be done by special resolution
- 15 per cent of shareholders of a particular class can petition against variation of class rights
- one-tenth of registered members can require the directors to call an general meeting
- 5 per cent can require the inclusion of a resolution at the next AGM
- two members may demand a poll
- and one member may petition under s994 above.

11 The company secretary

Introduction

Every public company must have a qualified company secretary. Private companies may choose to appoint a secretary, but are not obliged to do so.

The secretary is usually appointed and removed by the directors.

Qualifications

The secretary of a **public** company must be **qualified** under one of the following conditions:

- They must have held the office of company secretary in a public limited company (plc) for at least three out of the preceding five years.
- They must be a solicitor, barrister or member of ICAEW, ACCA, CIMA, ICSA, CIPFA.
- They must appear to be capable of discharging the functions by virtue of another position or qualification.

Duties

There are no statutory duties, therefore the duties will be whatever the board decides. The company secretary will typically undertake the following:

- check that documentation is in order
- make returns to the registrar
- keep registers
- give notice and keep minutes of meetings
- countersign documents to which the company seal is affixed.

Powers

The company secretary has the authority to bind the company in contract. There are two types of authority:

- actual authority – this is the authority delegated by the board
- apparent authority regarding contracts of an administrative nature.

Panorama Developments (Guildford) v Fidelis Furnishing Fabrics (1971)

Facts: B was company secretary of the defendant. Without authority from the directors he ordered from the claimants, a car hire firm, self-drive limousines stating that they were for the business purposes of the company. In fact he used the cars for his personal purposes. The company refused to pay for the cars.

Held: The contract was binding on the company as the contract was of the sort that a company secretary should be able to carry out.

However, two other cases indicate that there is a limit to the company secretary's authority:

- It does not extend to making commercial as opposed to administrative contracts: **Re Maidstone Building Provisions (1971)**.
- It does not usually carry the authority to borrow money: **Re Cleadon Trust Ltd (1938)**.

Supplementary reading: Chapter summary

At the end of this chapter, students should make sure that they understand the following matters:

- the nature of shares
- meaning of 'share capital', including issued, called up and paid up share capital
- types of share, particularly ordinary, preference, deferred and redeemable shares
- class rights
- issuing shares: authority to issue; finding buyers (e.g. by prospectuses or listing particulars); types of share issue (public offer, placing, etc)
- the issue of shares for an improper purpose
- variation of share capital
- maintenance of share capital: general rule; exceptions such as:
  - redeemable shares
  - purchase by a company of its own shares
  - reduction of share capital with confirmation of the court or by court order
  - limits on a company holding its own share
- loan capital, including whether to borrow and how to borrow. In particular, students must understand secured and unsecured debentures
- security for debentures, particularly the difference between fixed charges and floating charges
- registration of charges
- priority of charges
- rights of debenture holders on default by the company
- trust deeds
- shares and debentures compared and contrasted

- directors: company's general requirement; appointment; retirement; disqualification; possible removal; registration and keeping of information about directors
- duties of directors: to the company; to employees; to report to a general meeting
- possible liability of directors
  - to the company's creditors
  - to shareholders
  - effect of attempted exemption clauses for directors
- protection of minority shareholders
  - general position: majority rule
  - 'derivative' actions
  - wrongs to members personally
  - Companies Act 2006 s.994 – unfairly prejudicial conduct
- petition for winding up the company
- the company secretary: appointment, functions and status, removal.

12 Test your understanding questions

Test your understanding 1

Ethel is unsure whether to invest in shares or debentures.

Which one of the following statements is incorrect?

A Debenture holders are members of the company whereas shareholders are not

B Shareholders are members of the company whereas debenture holders are not

C Maintenance of capital rules apply to shares but not to debentures

D Shareholders are controllers of a company while debenture holders are creditors

Test your understanding 2

Which one of the following statements is incorrect?

A No company may issue shares at a discount

B A public company may issue shares for an undertaking to do work or perform services

C A company need not require full payment for shares immediately

D When a public company issues shares for a non-cash consideration, such consideration must be independently valued by a person qualified to be the auditor of the company

Test your understanding 3

Once a company has raised capital, it must be maintained.

In which one of the following is it permissible for this principle to be breached?

A Purchase by a private company of its own shares

B Purchase by a public company of its own shares

C By a private company when paying a dividend

D By a public company when paying a dividend

Test your understanding 4

HIJ Ltd has borrowed money from K Bank plc and has provided security by executing a fixed charge debenture in favour of the bank.

A fixed charge is:

A a charge over specific company property which prevents the company from dealing freely with the property in the ordinary course of business

B a charge over a class of company assets which enables the company to deal freely with the assets in the ordinary course of business

C a charge over specific company property which enables the company to deal freely with the assets in the ordinary course of business

D a charge over company land enabling the company to deal freely with the land in the ordinary course of business

Test your understanding 5

Big plc, a manufacturing company, has just taken over Small plc by buying all of Small plc's shares. At the time of the takeover, Small plc owned 2 % of Big plc's ordinary shares.

Which of the following steps can Big plc take?

A Let Small plc keep the shares in Big plc

B Buy and retain these shares itself

C Allow Small plc to buy more shares in Big plc on the open market

D Lend money to a director of Big plc to help him to buy the Big plc shares from Small plc for himself

Test your understanding 6

Which of the following statements concerning the role of non-executive directors of public companies is correct?

A A non-executive director cannot own shares in the company

B A non-executive director inevitably lacks any expertise in the company's main line of business

C A non-executive director may have an important role in determining the pay of the executive directors

D A non-executive director bears no responsibility to the company's shareholders

Test your understanding 7

Joe is a director of Abe Ltd, and has been sued by the company on the grounds of having made a secret profit.

Which one of the following could not arise?

A Joe could be ordered to account to the company for the secret profit

B Joe could be dismissed as a director

C The breach of fiduciary duty could be ratified by the company in general meeting

D The articles could validly provide an exemption for directors from liability for breach of duty

Test your understanding 8

HIJ plc is proposing to purchase some of its own shares.

Which of the following is incorrect?

A HIJ plc must have authority to purchase its own shares in its Articles of Association

B If the purchase is a market purchase, the shareholders of HIJ plc must give authority by ordinary resolution

C If the purchase is an off-market purchase, the shareholders of HIJ plc must give authority by ordinary resolution

D The purchase must be sanctioned by the court

Test your understanding 9

An application to the court under the Companies Act 2006, s.994, claiming that the company's affairs have been conducted in unfairly prejudicial manner can be made:

A By any shareholder, irrespective of the size of his/her/its shareholding

B Only by a member or members holding at least 5 % in number of the company's issued shares

C Only by a creditor or creditors

D Only after an ordinary resolution of shareholders

Test your understanding 10

Removal of the company secretary in a public company can be done:

A By the board of directors by a majority decision

B By the board of directors, but only by a unanimous decision

C By the board, but only after a petition by a member or members holding at least 25 % in number of the company's issued shares

D Only after an ordinary resolution of shareholders of which 28 days' notice has been given to members and the secretary

Test your understanding 11

Section 175 (1) of the Companies Act 2006 provides that a director owes a duty to avoid a situation in which he has an interest which conflicts or may conflict with the interests of the company. Bill is a non-executive director of Exe plc and has been offered an investment opportunity in his personal capacity which he wishes to take up.

Which of the following is correct?

A The duty does not apply to Bill in this situation as the investment opportunity was offered to him personally and not to the company

B The duty does not apply to Bill if Exe plc was not itself in a position to take advantage of the investment opportunity

C The duty can apply to Bill unless he ceases to be a director of Exe plc before taking up the opportunity

D The duty can apply to Bill as the situation can reasonably be regarded as being likely to give rise to a conflict of interest

Test your understanding 12

Required:

Complete the following sentences:

Under the .... (3 words) **(2 marks)** rule a company cannot return its .... (1 word) **(1 mark)** capital to its members. However, a company may reduce its capital if it has power in its .... (3 words) **(2 marks)** and it passes a .... (1 word) **(2 marks)** resolution and obtains the permission of .... (2 words) **(2 marks)**. In addition, in certain circumstances, a company may purchase or redeem its own shares using its authorised funds which are its .... (2 words) **(2 marks)** or the proceeds of .... (4 words) **(2 marks).**

(Total: 13 marks)

Test your understanding 13

B plc obtained a substantial loan from A Bank plc on 1 January 2002. The loan is secured by the following charges, which are set out in the bank's standard form of debenture document:

(i) A charge over the company's freehold land. The company is not free to sell, lease or in any way deal with the land without the bank's express permission.

(ii) A charge over all the company's other assets and undertakings. The company may deal freely with these in the ordinary course of business.

Required:

Complete the following sentences:

The charge over the land is a .... (1 word) **(2 marks)** charge and the charge over the company's other assets and undertaking is a .... (1 word) **(2 marks)** charge. If the charges were not registered at .... (2 words) **(2 marks)** within .... **(2 marks)** days of the creation of the charges they will be .... (1 word) **(2 marks)** against the liquidator. In addition the charges will need to be registered in the company's .... (4 words) **(2 marks).** If the charges had been created after 15 September 2003, A Bank plc would have been required to appoint an … … . .(1 word) **(2 marks).**

(Total: 14 marks)

Test your understanding 14

Dee Ltd was incorporated to purchase and resell a large estate. The company had three directors – D, E, and F – who each held one-third of the company's issued share capital.

The Articles of Association of Dee Ltd provided that all three directors had to be present to constitute a quorum and thus a valid board meeting. E and F had to travel abroad on other business, and, although they did not formally appoint D managing director, they agreed he should carry out the day-to-day management of the company in their absence, and that the company should attempt to sell the estate on their return.

While E and F were abroad, D decided to develop the estate, and on behalf of Dee Ltd instructed Gee Ltd, a property development company, to produce a major development plan and to secure the necessary planning consents. Following the return of E and F, Dee Ltd refused to pay Gee Ltd on the ground that D had no authority to engage the latter company. Gee Ltd has now advised Dee Ltd of its intention to initiate court proceedings to recover the amount due.

Required:

Delete as appropriate and complete the following sentences:

The .... (1 word) **(1 mark)** is the agent of the company. Individual directors have no/also have **(1 mark)** power to contract on behalf of the company unless power has been/irrespective of whether power has been **(1 mark)** delegated by the board. In this case Dee Ltd will/will not **(1 mark)** be liable to Gee Ltd, as D has acted within his apparent authority/without any authority **(1 mark).** E and F have no power to/may dismiss D **(1 mark)** by passing .... (2 words) **(2 marks)** resolution with .... (1 word) **(1 mark)** notice under section 168 of the Companies Act 2006.

(Total: 9 marks)

Test your understanding 15

Jane is a member of the board of Retailer Ltd and holds 51 % of the company's issued share capital. The company has a number of shops situated at holiday resorts around the country. One particular shop has traded at a loss for a number of years and the board has decided that it should be sold. The shop has been valued at £120,000 to include the premises and the stock. Jane wishes to buy the shop for her own use and is willing to pay the £120,000 valuation.

Required:

Complete the following sentences:

As a director Jane owes a .... (1 word) **(1 mark)** duty to the company not to place herself in a conflict of .... (1 word) **(1 mark)** and duty situation. As a result she is required to formally .... (3 words) **(2 marks)** to the board. In addition, as the value of the property being sold to Jane exceeds .... (state the amount) **(1 mark)** this is a '............ (2 words) **(2 marks)** transaction' and it follows that the .... (1 word) **(1 mark)** must approve the sale by passing .... (2 words) **(2 marks)** resolution which requires a simple majority to vote in favour.

(Total: 10 marks)

Test your understanding answers

Test your understanding 1

A

Debenture holders are not members of a company, and shareholders are members. (B), the opposite, is therefore true. (C) is true: maintenance of capital rules are rules to prevent capital being returned to members without the consent of the court, except in the course of a liquidation. (D) is also true: debenture holders are creditors of the company and cannot vote on company resolutions.

Test your understanding 2

B

(A) is true. This is forbidden, to ensure that the company receives the whole of the nominal value of the issued share capital from shareholders. (B) is the right answer. A public company is *prohibited* from accepting as consideration an obligation to do work or perform services in exchange for shares. (C) is true. (D) is true: this requirement is to make sure that the consideration received by public companies is actually the full worth of the shares.

Test your understanding 3

A

In all the other instances, capital must be maintained. But a private company is allowed to purchase its own shares out of capital, provided that it is authorised to do so in its articles, and that it first exhausts distributable profits (and any proceeds of a fresh share issue). There are other safeguards to ensure that members and creditors are not prejudiced.

Test your understanding 4

A

Assets subject to fixed charges (as opposed to floating charges) cannot be dealt with while subject to the charge, except with the consent of the creditor holding the charge.

(B) is not correct because the assets subject to a fixed charge cannot be dealt with freely in the course of business. (C) and (D) are likewise incorrect for the same reason.

Assets subject to a fixed charge are identified at the time of creation of the charge, and the assets subject to the charge will not fluctuate over time, unlike a floating charge.

Test your understanding 5

A

(B) and (C) both contravene the *general* rule that a company (Big plc) must not directly or indirectly own shares in itself. (A) is a statutory exception.

There is a general rule that a company (particularly public) must not give financial assistance for the purchase of its own shares (D).

Test your understanding 6

C

There is no law which prevents non-executive or independent directors on a company's board from owning shares in the company. And although non-executives may lack expertise in the company's business activities, this is not inevitable. All the directors on the board – executive and non-executive – bear a responsibility to the shareholders who own the business. (A), (B) and (D) are therefore untrue, leaving (C) as the correct answer. An increasingly important function of non-executive directors is to serve on the board's 'remuneration committee' which determines the pay of the executive directors.

Test your understanding 7

D

Outcome (A) could arise, since this is a remedy for the breach of duty which Joe has committed – *Regal (Hastings) Ltd v Gulliver* (1967). Outcome B could also arise, since a director can always be dismissed by rules under s.168 of the Companies Act 2006, whatever else the articles may provide. Outcome (C) is possible, provided the act was not done in bad faith. Outcome (D) could not arise, because by s.310 of the Companies Act 1985 such a provision would be void.

Test your understanding 8

D

Do not confuse purchase of shares (no court involvement) with capital reduction (requiring court sanction).

Test your understanding 9

A

The actual shareholding of the member is irrelevant, therefore (B) and (D) are incorrect. Further, the section provides protection to minority shareholders, not creditors, therefore (C) is inaccurate.

Test your understanding 10

A

A company secretary is normally appointed by the directors of a company and is an employee. As such, no shareholder involvement in the removal is necessary. (C) and (D) are therefore inaccurate. A board of directors usually makes decisions on a majority vote and that is applicable here. (B) is therefore incorrect.

Test your understanding 11

D

The duty can apply to Bill as the investment opportunity may be such that it involves a competitor of Exe plc or it may require Bill to give of his time which should be available to Exe plc.

Test your understanding 12

Under the *maintenance of capital* rule a company cannot return its *share* capital to its members. However, a company may reduce its capital if it has power in its *Articles of Association* and it passes *a special* resolution and obtains the permission of *the court*. In addition, in certain circumstances a company may purchase or redeem its own shares using its authorised funds which are its *distributable profits* or the proceeds of *a new share issue.*

Test your understanding 13

The charge over the land is a *fixed* charge and the charge over the company's other assets and undertaking is a *floating* charge. If the charges were not registered at *Companies House* within *21* days of the creation of the charges they will be *void* against the liquidator. In addition the charges will need to be registered in the company's *register of debenture holders.* If the charges had been created after 15 September 2003, A Bank plc would have been required to appoint an *administrator.*

Test your understanding 14

The *board* is the agent of the company. Individual directors have no power to contract on behalf of the company *unless power has been* delegated by the board. In this case Dee Ltd will be liable to Gee Ltd, as (D) has acted *within his apparent authority*. (E) and (F) *may* dismiss (D) by passing an *ordinary* resolution with special notice under Section 168 of the Companies Act 2006.

Test your understanding 15

As a director Jane owes a *statutory* duty to the company not to place herself in a conflict of *interest* and duty situation. As a result she is required to formally *declare her interest* to the board. In addition, as the value of the property being sold to Jane exceeds £100,000 this is a '*substantial property* transaction', and it follows that the shareholders must approve the sale by passing *an ordinary* resolution which requires a simple majority to vote in favour.

chapter

6

Ethics and Business

Chapter learning objectives

After completing this chapter, you should be able to:

- apply the values and attitudes that provide professional accountants with a commitment to act in the public interest and with social responsibility
- distinguish between detailed rules-based and framework approaches to ethics
- explain the ethical principles of integrity, objectivity, professional competence, due care, confidentiality and professional behaviour
- identify concepts of independence, scepticism, accountability and social responsibility
- explain the reasons why CIMA and IFAC each have a 'Code of Ethics for Professional Accountants'.

1 Introduction

In this chapter we will be considering:

- what is ethics?
- why is ethics important?
- why can ethics not be enforced by law?
- what is the code of ethics?

2 What is ethics

The ethics of a profession can be simply the description of the prevailing standards of ethical behaviour.

Ethics reflect principles and ideals of behaviour that ought to be adhered to, rather than merely describing and conforming to current professional practice. In short, just because some people bend the rules **in practice**, does not mean that they **should** do so.

Ethics is therefore a matter of what we ought to do and of having the confidence to do it. 'Ethics' is often used interchangeably with the term 'morals.' However, there is an important difference between them. Both concern questioning what is the right thing to do in a problem situation. Morals resolve problems with reference to the individual's personal belief system about what might be right or wrong. They are linked to the safety valve of personal conscience, and may additionally be linked to religious or other convictions.

3 Why ethics are important

A management accountant's role is to provide the crucial information that forms the basis of decision-making within an organisation. If work is undertaken badly or in bad faith there can be wide-ranging consequences. Unethical behaviour can affect not only the accountant (perhaps resulting in disciplinary action against the employee or by CIMA), but may also affect the jobs, financial viability and business efficacy of an organisation in which the accountant works. Management accountants in the public sector are also dealing with tax-payer's money which, if poorly stewarded, might be wasted or misused.

Supplementary reading

The current world financial crisis once again shows the relationship between those who manage and account for finance and social responsibility. Increasingly, there is global pressure to add tougher ethical regulation to existing regimes. This was evidenced by proposals by the International Federation of Accountants in 2007 to add tougher restrictions and even fee-setting to the International Code. This pre-dates the current economic crisis which highlighted complex investment instruments and practices such as fair-value accounting. Inevitably, there will be growing political pressure on governments to make law to regulate financial practices.

Because there are always choices in the way in which accounting information is prepared and presented, and because of the close working relationship between managers, whose performance is measured or reflected in accounting reports, there are numerous temptations to present a particular bias and many other factors that might influence the professional judgement of management accountants. The exercise of good judgement is a fundamental attribute of a competent accountant. An example of such a problem was highlighted during a CIMA roadshow (reported by Danielle Cohen in the May 2007 *issue of Financial Management*):

[The accountant] CI has been the finance director of his company – a clothing retailer – for ten years. He's responsible for the financial accounts and has identified some slow-moving stock that's over nine months old, which would usually be written down. The shareholders are trying to sell the firm and the managing director (the majority shareholder) has told him that it's not necessary to write down the stock this time. CI is sure that this is because the managing director wants to inflate the stock valuation. The managing director has found a prospective buyer and has indicated to CI that, if the deal is done, all employees will keep their jobs and CI will receive a pay rise.

In this real life example, as well as the pressure from the manager on the accountant to comply, there appears to be moral value in doing the wrong thing (saving people's jobs) as well as a personal incentive of a pay rise. However, misrepresenting the value of stock would be a threat to the integrity of the accountant, and also threatens the financial viability of the enterprise in the longer term. Resolving these issues is sometimes taxing and complex. Often it is simply a question of accepting that there is a right way to act and a wrong way. Understanding the standards for professional behaviour and also having the skills to identify where difficult questions of ethical conflict arise and how to address them are both areas of required professional knowledge.

4 The role of law in ethics

Legal and disciplinary frameworks do provide an effective means of challenging serious wrong-doing. They can provide deterrents to bad practice, through punishment and censure and remedies for some of the damage that results, for example by means of compensation. However, these means of controlling behaviour set the threshold for what amounts to unacceptable accounting practice at a fairly high level.

Thus, relying solely on the law and disciplinary frameworks to 'police' accounting ethics is not the most desirable way of preventing and detecting undesirable practices. Law by nature can be inflexible, therefore causing difficulty when trying to apply it to cases of ethical misconduct.

5 The CIMA and IFAC Codes of Ethics

In June 2005, IFAC published their Code of Ethics for Professional Accountants which was prepared by the International Ethics Standards Board of the International Federation of Accountants. That Committee was charged with developing and issuing **high-quality ethical standards and other pronouncements for professional accountants around the world**. This reflected what has been seen as a growing crisis of confidence in accounting ethics internationally, following financial scandals with global implications. Revised codes were issued in 2010 and 2014.

In 2006, the CIMA Code of Ethics for Professional Accountants' was launched. Revised codes were issued in 2010 and 2015.

The CIMA Code reflects the standards CIMA expects of its members and students. It is aligned with global standards across the profession.

The CIMA Code reflects its status as a Chartered Institute and as a basis for any complaints or cases under CIMA's disciplinary procedures.

The CIMA Code of Ethics aims to:

(i) identify the nature of the personal responsibility that the management accountant takes on as part of the price for getting a reasonable salary and status

(ii) provide guidance on how to identify the practical situations where particular care might need to be taken because of the ethical pitfalls involved

(iii) provide general guidance on how to address those difficult questions.

The CIMA Code itself is split into three parts with a list of definitions at the end:

Part A – General Application of the Code

This covers an introduction and the fundamental principles of integrity, objectivity, professional competence and due care, confidentiality and professional behaviour.

Part B – Professional Accountants in Public Practice

This covers particular issues identified as being of relevance to accountants in public practice such as professional appointment, conflicts of interest, second opinions, fees and other types of remuneration, marketing professional services, gifts and hospitality, custody of client assets, objectivity in all services and independence in assurance engagements.

Part C – Professional Accountants in Business

This covers issues such as potential conflicts, preparation and reporting of information, acting with sufficient expertise, financial interests and inducements.

The Code establishes ethical requirements for professional accountants and applies to all member firms or bodies of IFAC. Any such firm or **body may not apply less stringent standards than those stated in this Code**.

There is an override, should any firm or body be prohibited by law or regulation in complying with any parts of the Code. The expectation is that all parts of IFAC Code will be complied with otherwise. Professional accountants need to familiarise themselves with any differences if there are any, but to comply with the more stringent requirements and guidance unless prohibited.

Fundamental principles

CIMA's code lists five fundamental principles with which its members are expected to comply.

The fundamental principles are presented in Section 100.5.

Fundamental principles

100.5 A professional accountant shall comply with the following fundamental principles:

(1) **Integrity** – to be straightforward and honest in all professional and business relationships.

(2) **Objectivity** – to not allow bias, conflict of interest or undue influence of others to override professional or business judgments.

(3) **Professional Competence and Due Care** – to maintain professional knowledge and skill at the level required to ensure that a client or employer receives competent professional services based on current developments in practice, legislation and techniques and act diligently and in accordance with applicable technical and professional standards.

(4) **Confidentiality** – to respect the confidentiality of information acquired as a result of professional and business relationships and, therefore, not disclose any such information to third parties without proper and specific authority, unless there is a legal or professional right or duty to disclose, nor use the information for the personal advantage of the professional accountant or third parties.

(5) **Professional Behaviour** – to comply with relevant laws and regulations and avoid any action that discredits the profession.

By 'fundamental' it is meant that these form the very foundations of reasoning and professional practice. The accountant should therefore not only know them, but use them as tools of reasoning and decision-making when judging their own work and that of fellow-professionals. Alongside checking the technical competence of a piece of work, the management accountant should ask, for example 'am I being objective and impartial in the way I am presenting these figures?'

Because they are fundamental, they merit further, deeper explanation, which you will find later on in this chapter. However, to sum up: CIMA has produced a Code of Ethics that states the fundamental values that accountants should work by, and a framework by which they can put these into practice in challenging practical situations, where there may be more than one course of action which may have undesirable consequences. For the time being, we need to understand the different tools available for regulating ethical behaviour.

Supplementary reading

Integrity

Integrity is a holistic term implying other values too. So, in addition to being straightforward and honest in all professional and business relationships, this principle implies fair dealing and truthfulness. It particularly relates to reporting where a false or misleading statement might be made, or provided without care or attention, or a report might omit information, or be obscure and dense such that the report becomes misleading.

Integrity also denotes an attitude of personal and professional consistency in the way in which the accountant acts. It may be denoted by things as simple as the way in which the accountant interacts with different people. If he or she shows an inclusive and open attitude to one colleague and is formal and distant with another, it may lead to the inference that he or she nurtures a professional bias. This would certainly undermine the perception of the individual's integrity. Similarly, if an individual is willing to compromise principles and values that he or the profession espouses, in order to avoid conflict or challenge, then this too would be the sort of inconsistency that may give rise to questions about integrity.

Objectivity

Objectivity is contrasted with subjectivity. Subjective decisions are taken from the point of view of the individual concerned, taking into account the things that matter to them. These considerations might be friendship, loyalty or the instinct for self-preservation. While these subjective considerations are vital to making life go on, they have no place in professional decision-making. The management accountant should assemble all the relevant information available, account for what is not available (rather than guessing), and base decisions only on that data and the guiding principles of the profession.

This is of course easier said than done, because in the exercise of professional judgement, personal decision-making is the key. The accountant needs to be ever-vigilant, questioning himself whether other factors, such as self-interest or personal preference, are guiding a decision. Objective decision-making is the true value of the accountant within the management process, but it will frequently expose the accountant to difficult situations because others may not always like what they hear or appreciate a dispassionate analysis of a situation.

It is important for students and members to avoid putting themselves in positions where they or their work could become compromised. This might be through bias, conflicts of interest or through the undue influence of others. In these types of situations, an individual's objectivity may be impaired.

The sorts of situation that could arise are numerous, from forming an illicit relationship that may cause embarrassment, to accepting lavish hospitality which is later used to influence behaviour. It is impracticable to define and prescribe all such situations, but students need to be aware of, and resist, any such potential compromises on their objectivity.

If a threat to objectivity is identified, safeguards should be considered and applied to eliminate or reduce the threat to an acceptable level. Such safeguards could include withdrawing from the engagement, introducing more supervision into the process, terminating the relationship giving rise to the threat, and discussing the issue with the higher management and those reviewing the governance of the client relationship.

Professional competence and due care

Professional competence implies knowledge, skill, diligent delivery and an awareness of all the relevant issues in performing tasks. The professional is expected to maintain the competence and their capabilities to act responsibly at all times through continuing professional development.

There is also an expectation of acting diligently, which encompasses acting in accordance with the requirements of an assignment carefully, thoroughly and on a timely basis. Due care covers the wider responsibility the professional accountant has to ensure that those working under their authority have the necessary skills and capabilities to do so, and in particular have the professional capacity and appropriate training and supervision.

In accordance with the other principles and virtues expected of a professional accountant, they should ensure that clients or employers are aware of limitations inherent in services being provided to them so as to avoid the misinterpretation of an expression of opinion as an assertion of fact.

Confidentiality

The professional accountant is bound by the principle of confidentiality in all that they do unless required by law, professional right or duty to disclose. Such confidentiality covers disclosing information outside the firm or employing organisation and using information for personal or third party gain. Confidentiality extends to situations in a social environment too, where the professional accountant should be alert to the possibility of inadvertent disclosure to a close friend or family member.

Confidentiality also extends after the end of a relationship between a professional accountant and a client or employer. The professional accountant may use prior experience but not prior information gained in a previous role. In the Code, in Section 140.7, instances are explained when it would be appropriate to disclose confidential information, such as the requirement to produce documents as evidence in the course of legal proceedings.

Professional behaviour

Every professional accountant needs to be mindful that their behaviour will not bring the profession and CIMA into disrepute. The profession defines this as including actions which a reasonable and informed third party, having knowledge of all relevant information, would conclude negatively affects the good reputation of the profession.

It is to be remembered as Benjamin Franklin once said 'Glass, china and reputations are easily cracked and never well mended'. It is a constant challenge to management to maintain a good reputation. Without it, an organisation be it a professional body, a company or public sector body will become demoralised. Staff will not take pleasure in their work, the better qualified and able ones will leave and a downward spiral may develop. In addition, customers may be lost, the ability to raise finance made more difficult, and perhaps the 'licence to operate' from society also lost with many other consequences too.

6 Regulations, legislation, guidelines, codes and other standards: what do they all mean?

There is a complex relationship between legal and ethical duties because often they are dealing with different consequences of the same behaviour or more or less serious examples of behaviour that are to be discouraged. Thus, management accounting ethics can be regarded as being controlled and directed by a variety of means with a variety of consequences for a variety of purposes.

The following table indicates the broad differences in the approaches. Note that each does different things and that they are overlapping. It is not simply a case that breach of the criminal law is more serious than breach of ethical guidance.

Different approaches to controlling ethical behaviour

Approach	Deals with	Created by	Format	Enforced by	Consequence	Purpose
Criminal law (e.g. fraud laws)	Direct and serious threat to the public or to public administration	National authorities through Parliament or court	Acts of Parlia-ment, Principles in court cases	Police, Statutory, regulators	Fine, Imprisonment, Confiscation of assets	To deter, protect and stigmatise
Civil law (e.g. prof-essional negligence laws)	Damage or loss caused to other members of society Failure to comply with legal duties that have been voluntarily assumed (e.g. breaking a contract)	National authorities through Parliament of court	Acts of Parlia-ment, Principles in court cases	Lawsuits initiated by injured parties	Compensation, Compulsion to comply with legal obligations and enforceable agreements	To undo damage or to compensate where someone has not met their legal obligations to other private members of society
Regulations	Anything where further detail of actual practice needs to be spelled out	National authorities through Parliament, regulatory bodies or professional bodies	Rules made under powers stated in Acts of Parliament	Regulatory body or professional body	Anything from fine, through compensation to professional disciplinary hearing	To provide detailed rules of practice specific to a particular activity
Codes of practice	Guidance on how to undertake tasks as a practitioner	Regulatory or professional bodies	Guidance, rules, examples and principles	Regulatory or professional body or self-enforced	Disciplinary or development	To provide working guidance on how to perform tasks

7 Regulatory bodies

In the United Kingdom, the ethical lead for financial reporting has been taken by the Financial Reporting Council (FRC). The FRC is the United Kingdom's independent regulator for corporate reporting and governance, with the aim of promoting confidence in these areas.

A further body forming part of the FRC is the Conduct Committee.

The Conduct Committee is responsible for overseeing the FRC's Conduct Division in its work promoting high quality corporate reporting.

Supplementary reading

The Conduct Committee's responsibilities include overseeing:

- Monitoring of Recognised Supervisory and Recognised Qualifying bodies
- Audit Quality Reviews
- Corporate Reporting Reviews
- Professional discipline
- Oversight of the regulation of accountants and actuaries.

8 Rules-based and framework approaches to ethics

There are two different approaches to formulating a code of ethics:

- a rules-based approach
- a framework approach.

Rules-based ethics

A rules-based approach to ethics is sometimes referred to as a compliance approach. It explicitly sets out what individuals can and cannot do, and specifies the sanctions that will be imposed for non-compliance.

A rules-based approach works because it instils a sense of fear. Individuals comply because they are required to and because they fear the consequences. However, the main disadvantage of this approach is the fact that the rules cannot cover every particular situation and rules may become out of date as circumstances change.

Supplementary reading

Rules tend to be characterised by three things:

(1) In theory, you are either inside a rule (compliant) or have broken it. This sometimes provides a harsh divide which is often more about the precise interpretation of the rule than the human activity it regulates

(2) Because of these attempts to make sharp distinctions in rules (so people know where the boundaries of self-preservation lie), there is always argument about the precise meaning of rules

(3) Rules require enforcement by an objective party to decide on things like interpretation and to ensure that breach of the rule has a consequence.

These factors make rules expensive, the source of contention and inflexible. Moreover, in ethics, rules seldom are capable of encompassing the rather difficult questions about behaviour that are involved, without becoming incredibly complicated. The Code-based approach blends the mandatory requirement to take account of the Code with a principles or values-based approach.

Framework approach

A framework approach to ethics provides a set of principles to help individuals arrive at the correct decision. It attempts to instil the idea of the 'correct' thing to do.

Its main advantage is that it can be applied more easily to new developments in business practice or to unique cases. However, its disadvantage is that it is left to the member to decide how best to deal with an ethical question within the framework laid down.

It is also much more difficult to monitor compliance in a rules-based approach.

Supplementary reading

There has been a change in public and private attitudes to the performance of duties over the last five years that has moved against the idea of just doing what you can get away with towards continually striving to do the right thing. It is mirrored in the changes in management accounting trends from variance accounting, through activity-based to lean accounting. In management, it is reflected in the idea of performance management, rather than the management of labour. In public life, it is reflected in the change from a culture of trust and deference to those with authority, to a requirement for standards in public life and accountability.

The management accountant finds him or herself pushed by all three strands. Trends in management accounting look towards a more transparent approach to representing the life cycle of accounts. As an employee, the accountant is not there just to do a job and go home, but to do it well and continually improve. Ultimately, whether or not the accountant is employed in the public sector, the role of the accountant is to perform a public function in providing the truthful and independent account of finances that will be the basis of judgements by owners, shareholders, regulators, the government and so on.

Ultimately, whether or not the accountant is employed in the public sector, the role of the accountant is to perform a public function in providing the truthful and independent account of finances that will be the basis of judgements by owners, shareholders, regulators, the government and so on.

The publicly employed accountant is explicitly subject to the 'The Seven Principles of Public Life' issued by the 'Committee of Standards in Public Life', which arose out of the perceived crisis in public ethics of the 1990s in the United Kingdom. They are reflected to a great extent in the professional standards for all accountants.

Selflessness

Holders of public office should act solely in terms of the public interest. They should not do so in order to gain financial or other benefits for themselves, their family or their friends.

Integrity

Holders of public office should not place themselves under any financial or other obligation to outside individuals or organisations that might seek to influence them in the performance of their official duties.

Objectivity

In carrying out public business, including making public appointments, awarding contracts, or recommending individuals for rewards and benefits, holders of public office should make choices on merit.

Accountability

Holders of public office are accountable for their decisions and actions to the public and must submit themselves to whatever scrutiny is appropriate to their office.

Openness

Holders of public office should be as open as possible about all the decisions and actions that they take. They should give reasons for their decisions and restrict information only when the wider public interest clearly demands.

Honesty

Holders of public office have a duty to declare any private interests relating to their public duties and to take steps to resolve any conflicts arising in a way that protects the public interest.

Leadership

Holders of public office should promote and support these principles by leadership and example.

Given the trends towards less trust and more desire for accountability, it is therefore of little surprise that management accountants are now expected to do more than merely follow the rules.

9 Contrasting compliance driven and principles based codes

The following table, contrasting the characteristics of a compliance-driven framework versus one primarily driven by values, principles and ethics.

Feature	Ethics	Compliance (Rules)
Objective	Prevention	Detection
Approach	Principles	Law based
Motivation	Values driven	Fear driven
Standards	Implicit	Explicit
Measure	Principles (values)	Rules
Choices	Judgement	Obedience/disobedience
Enforceability	Discretionary	Mandatory

An example of applying the different approaches above would be a company which has a strong rules-based culture, where individuals clearly have a sense of what they can and cannot do (letter of the law, black and white, mandatory, explicit) and what will happen if they do not (fear-driven, requires obedience, mandatory). However, if an employee is faced with a situation not covered by the 'rule book' they will be required to use their own judgement as to what to do. In most instances, the decision they take will be the right one but any potential for the wrong decision being made will be reduced if the employee has guiding values and principles which will underpin that difficult decision-making. So, an ethical framework of guidance is likely to be more wide-ranging in its applicability than a fully rules-based one.

A key aspect of compliance is measurement in addition to 'ticking boxes' that all is well. This, of course, is difficult with ethical issues which tend not to be conveniently black and white. There is therefore a need to develop and use proxy indicators by those assuring themselves that individuals are acting in a proper fashion.

In a wider context, the same is true in the public and private sectors, where organisations equally, as though they were individuals, seek to build trust with their employees, customers, suppliers, shareholders and all others who have a legitimate interest in how they perform.

But the essential question remains: Is trust better engendered by principled behaviour based on 'doing it because it is the right thing to do' or because the individual, the company or the public body has to?

10 Personal development and life-long learning

Supplementary reading

Every professional person has a duty in maintaining their role of acting in public interest by keeping themselves up to date professionally, that is technically as well developing their competencies to be better informed. It is also essential in a dynamic area of practice, where failure to keep oneself aware of developments may fundamentally undermine basic professional competence and leave the accountant open to accusations of negligence.

This has grown in importance as the pace of change develops and the role of the professional accountant grows more complex. It is now regarded as one of the fundamental principles in the CIMA 'Code of Ethics' (see Appendix for the complete code), where the professional accountant has the duty to maintain professional knowledge and skill at the level required to ensure that a client or employer receives competent professional service based on current developments in practice, legislation and techniques.

The concept of competent professional service is thus based not only on attaining professional competence but also in maintaining it. This requires a continuing awareness of up-to-date developments in the profession. This can be met through continuing professional development. CIMA has developed the CIMA Professional Development framework which addresses both the requirements on members and the institute regarding CPD, and the ways in which CIMA is supporting members in their professional development.

For example, the public expectation is that all accountants are 'up to speed all the time' which requires commitment from all those in the profession. This is because the issues a professional faces do change over time. For instance, given the rapid advance in technology, returns may be filed electronically putting greater emphasis on professional review. In matters of security of customer/client data, where confidential information is transferred via e-mail, there is always the potential for that information to be corrupted if the computer system does not have up-to-date firewall and virus protection and so forth.

In areas of public service, there are increasing developments in the way in which information is made available to the public and in transparent costing processes. Similarly, in the private sector, the way in which data and private commercial and financial information is constantly evolving as are the means by which this is regulated.

Personal qualities

Members of the profession need, or need to develop, certain qualities and virtues in order to meet the expectations of CIMA and the public, served in the wider context. In upholding the highest standards of ethical behaviour, members are contributing to the promotion of the integrity of CIMA's qualification and supporting CIMA's purpose.

The underlying reason has been explained earlier, in the context of 'virtue ethics'. The professional attitude being encouraged provides the ethical compass and personal motivation to act in accordance with the values of the profession and to make ethically sound decisions in everyday practice.

The particular qualities and virtues sought are reliability, responsibility, timeliness, courtesy and respect. These are taken from 'Approaches to the Development and Maintenance of Professional Values, Ethics and Attitudes in Accounting Education Programs,' published by the International Accounting Education Standards Board.

Reliability

This is the concept of being able to be trusted by others and to be dependable through the ability to deliver what and when it has been agreed with another. It is linked to the idea of providing a consistent approach to work, both in quality and in dependability. It is fairly clear that an unreliable accountant would almost certainly also be falling short of other basic standards of professional competence.

Responsibility

This is the concept of being accountable for one's actions and decisions. This also entails an individual's assumption of authority for making decisions. A responsible accountant addresses the decision-making processes that he needs to engage with and is willing and able to personally answer for those decisions. A management accountant is in a position of responsibility because he is being employed for his expertise in making professional judgements and will need to be able to explain and answer for their exercise to colleagues who may or may not share that expertise.

Timeliness

This is the concept of delivering in a timely manner without delay and meeting the expectations of others. The practical implications of poor time-keeping are self-evident, however there is a further reflection of the ethics of diligence in addressing tasks and responsibility in prioritising and managing work.

Courtesy

This is the virtue of demonstrating politeness and good manners towards others. While respect for clients and others is regarded as appropriate and professional, the increasing seriousness with which unacceptable forms of address (racist, sexist, homophobic and the like) are being tackled by law mean that it underpins a more fundamental set of societal values.

Respect

This is the virtue demonstrating an attitude of esteem, deference, regard or admiration of others in dealing with them, especially where their attitudes might differ. It is not to be mistaken for undue deference, merely that the accountant should listen to others, take account of their views and ideas, and if for no other reason than these may provide a broader base for making informed judgements.

Like a number of these qualities, it is easy to see reasons why respect might be practically useful and help avoid problems that might lead to sanction or censure, but the utility of respecting people is not the reason why you should respect them; it is not simply a case of respecting those who you think might have something useful to say, like each of these qualities they are aspects of professionalism to be cultivated for their own sake.

Independence

It is in the public interest, and required in CIMA's Code of Ethics that members of assurance engagement teams and their firms (and when applicable extended network firms too) be independent of the assurance clients.

There are two key attributes to independence used in connection with the assurance engagement:

(1) Of mind

It is required that the professional accountant has a state of mind that permits a conclusion to be expressed without being affected by influences that would compromise their professional judgement.

This allows the individual to act with integrity and exercise objectivity and professional scepticism. Bias is an insidious thing, and sometimes we are not fully aware of the influencing factors on our mind. Second opinions of close judgement calls can often help, but the accountant is ultimately responsible for his or her decisions. Keeping a clear, professional attitude and focusing on objective information, rather than over-relying on intuitions is a useful means of maintaining some independence of mind.

(2) In appearance

This is a test reliant on the view that a reasonable and informed third party would conclude that a member of the assurance team's integrity, objectivity or professional scepticism was compromised if significant facts and circumstances were avoided or overlooked. The accountant often exercises judgements that have impacts on people's jobs, pay and progression. It is therefore of paramount importance that the exercise of professional judgement not only be just, but manifestly and undoubtedly be seen to be so.

It is impossible to define all situations where independence might be compromised, so it is in the public interest to prepare a conceptual framework requiring firms and member of assurance teams to identify, evaluate and address threats to independence. This can be based on identifying relationships between all the parties. For any threats so identified, safeguards can be introduced to eliminate or significantly reduce them to an acceptable level.

Accountability

The concept of accountability is that of the professional accountant being responsible to someone and for something or an action, and being able to explain those actions. It is an important aspect of the profession and of leadership in the wider business environment.

It is acknowledged that the professional accountant through CIMA, as a Chartered Institute, is accountable to the public in performing a public interest duty. That accountability is monitored by the FRC in the United Kingdom through the Professional Oversight Board for Accountancy (POBA) and the Accounting Standards Board (ASB).

Accountability is also to every client and employer too for whom the professional accountant is providing services. If that accountability fails then the client or employer can seek redress through complaint or disciplinary procedures.

Social responsibility

The professional accountant has a wider role in fulfilling their public duty, which is to be aware of their social or corporate responsibility. This is their role within the community, be it defined as their profession, their firm or place of work, where their place of work or home is located or howsoever the individual cares to define community.

Corporate Responsibility (CR) is the outward manifestation of an ethical policy. CR policies state the nature of the interaction between the company and its stakeholder base, employees, customers, suppliers and so forth (covered in more detail in Chapter 7). These CR policies need to be factored into risk management, which the better companies will report on in their reporting, internally and externally.

Many companies now prepare Social or Corporate Responsibility Reports for their shareholders and stakeholders. There are new methodologies developing to monitor non-financial impacts. Some CR activities can be measured, such as environmental impact, where a company can relatively easily evaluate its carbon footprint. But, evaluating ethical behaviour is more difficult and proxy indicators, such as staff turnover, may need to be used.

Typically, this is in relation to stakeholders listed as shareholders, employees, customers, suppliers and the wider community, to whom the company pays taxes and with whom it has a relationship as part of society. In upholding the principles of CIMA's 'Code of Ethics', the individual has a social responsibility to behave with integrity, courtesy, respect and with due care.

11 Ethical conflict: confidentiality

The following are circumstances where professional accountants are or may be required to disclose confidential information or when such disclosure may be appropriate:

(a) **Disclosure is permitted by law and is authorised by the client or the employer:**
An example of this might be personal data. Personal data held by an accountant (for example, bank details of an individual) is covered by the Data Protection Act 1998. This gives rise to particular responsibility on the accountant to maintain that data accurately and not to disclose it, except for the purposes it was disclosed. There are, however, some exceptions. One important one is that the person to whom that data pertains may have been given an authorisation for disclosure to third parties for marketing purposes. This would still need authorisation by the employer, but falls within the category of permissible disclosure.

(b) **Disclosure is required by law, for example:**

(i) Production of documents or other provision of evidence in the course of legal proceedings – numerous pieces of legislation allow investigative bodies, ranging from the national taxation authorities through to the police, the power to gain access to documents in the process of investigation. Strictly speaking, such access is limited to circumstances where the investigating agency has specific authorisation by a court, normally in the form of a warrant. In such circumstances, there is a duty to disclose that overrides any others.

(ii) Disclosure to the appropriate public authorities of infringements of the law that come to light – accountants are under some professional and ethical responsibility to disclose information which they believe tend to show illegal activity. This is a problematic area because such disclosures frequently run in the face of what an employer considers to be a duty of trust and confidence. A misplaced belief that an employer is doing wrong, which leads to an unauthorised disclosure will often end up as an acrimonious employment dispute.

The Public Interest Disclosure Act in the United Kingdom provides a means by which these two issues can be balanced. The accountant should first draw their manager's attention to the wrongdoing, or if it is inappropriate in the circumstances, a senior manager's attention may be drawn to it. If there is no adequate response or there is serious malfeasance which the accountant believes may be 'covered up', they may alert a professional body or an agency such as the police. Going to press is a risky and inadvisable course of action and carries with it few of the protections that are offered to those disclosing to professional bodies. In such circumstances, it is advisable to contact CIMA's Ethics Helpline. UK members and students of CIMA can contact the whistleblowing Advice the for advice on whether and how to make a public interest disclosure. CIMA's Ethics Helpline can help any member or student facing an ethical conflict.

(c) **There is a professional duty or right to disclose, when not prohibited by law:**

(i) To comply with the quality review of a member body or professional body

(ii) To respond to an inquiry or investigation by a member body or regulatory body

(iii) To protect the professional interests of a professional accountant in legal proceedings; or

(iv) To comply with technical standards and ethics requirements.

All these examples in (c), above, relate to the regulation and disciplinary functions of CIMA and the profession more generally. It is important that disclosures are not only those necessary for the achievement of purpose of the inquiry but that they also cover all relevant aspects of the subject matter being inquired into. Partial disclosure is tantamount to deception and may give rise to disciplinary or legal penalties or consequences.

Disclosure is generally a question of professional discretion, as much as the application of rules. In identifying whether confidential information can be disclosed, it is necessary to consider whether any parties would be harmed by such disclosure, whether all relevant information is known and substantiated, and the type of disclosure and to whom it is to be made. Once again, being well-intended when disclosing or not disclosing is part of the pavement to perdition.

12 Test your understanding questions

Test your understanding 1

Are these statements true or false?

A Professional accountants are expected to have regard to the public interest in performing their duties

B Professional accountants are not expected to have regard to the public interest in performing their duties

C Ethical values describe what an entity does, not how it does business

D Ethical values describe how entity does its business, not what it does

Test your understanding 2

Are these statements true or false?

A A rules based approach provides a set of principles

B A framework approach explicitly sets out what individuals can or cannot do

C 'The Seven Principles of Public Life' govern only professional accountants

D The CIMA 'Code of Ethics' includes reference to how a professional accountant can raise a concern about unprofessional or unethical behaviour

Test your understanding 3

Are these statements true or false?

A An ethically based code is based on principles

B A compliance based code is a rules-based framework

C A characteristic of a compliance based code is that it takes a tick box approach

D Compliance with legislation is mandatory

Test your understanding 4

Are these statements true or false?

A The five qualities and virtues sought by CIMA are reliability, accountability, fairness, responsibility and timeliness

B The five qualities and virtues sought by CIMA are reliability, responsibility, timeliness, courtesy and respect

C The professional accountant is not bound by the principles of confidentiality after the end of the relationship with a client or employer

D The professional accountant is bound by the principles of confidentiality after the end of the relationship with a client or employer

Test your understanding 5

Are these statements true or false?

A Professional accountants are expected to exercise professional scepticism

B Professional accountants are not expected to exercise professional scepticism

C The IFAC code is mandatory for all member firms or bodies of IFAC

D The IFAC code is a guide for all member firms or bodies of IFAC

Test your understanding 6

Which of the following is incorrect?

A The IFAC Code of Ethics takes a rules-based approach

B The CIMA Code of Ethics takes a framework-based approach

C Company codes of ethics can take a framework-based or a rules-based approach

D Code of ethics are often based on core values or principles

Test your understanding questions 7–9 are reflective questions and should be discussed or thought over. Answers to these have not been provided.

Test your understanding 7

Consider your work and, separately, everyday life. In what circumstances do you find the following compromised?

A Objectivity

B Courtesy

C Confidentiality

D The Appearance of Independence

Test your understanding 8

In relation to 7, above, consider whether each is because of:

A Something you have done

B Something you have failed to do

C Something you believe in

D Something outside your control

Test your understanding 9

Drawing on the discussions above, consider how and whether application of the ethical principles outlined might help you identify problems, and whether they might help you avoid them if you put them into practice.

Test your understanding answers

Test your understanding 1

A **True.** Professional accountants, whether practicing in public or private practice have a leadership role and are expected to behave and act in the public interest. This is laid down in the Royal Charter which governs CIMA – the *Chartered Institute of Management Accountants.*

B **False.**

C **False.**

D **True.**

Test your understanding 2

A **False.** This applies to a framework approach.

B **False.**

C **False.** The Seven Principles of Public Life apply to all holders of public office.

D **True.**

Test your understanding 3

A **True.**

B **True.**

C **False.** A characteristic of compliance is detection.

D **True.** Compliance with the law is mandatory.

Test your understanding 4

A **False.**

B **True.**

C **False.**

D **True.**

Test your understanding 5

A **True.**

B **False.**

C **True.**

D **False.**

Test your understanding 6

A

The CIMA and IFAC Codes both take a framework-based approach.

Test your understanding 7

There is no suggested solution.

Test your understanding 8

There is no suggested solution.

Test your understanding 9

There is no suggested solution.

chapter

7

Ethical Conflict

Chapter learning objectives

After completing this chapter you should be able to:

- explain the relationship between ethics, governance, the law and social responsibility
- describe the consequences of unethical behaviour to the individual, the profession and the society
- identify situations where ethical dilemmas and conflicts of interest occur
- explain how ethical dilemmas and conflicts of interest can be resolved.

1 The relationship between ethics, governance, the law and social responsibility

Ethical Codes vs Legislation

If the question of ethics is 'what to do for the best?' then the next natural question is 'why should I take responsibility for deciding what to do?' In effect, the key issues for all accountants are the linked questions of who should take responsibility for doing the right things and who picks up the pieces when it all goes wrong.

If there are problems of global or national significance that arise from a systematic failure, which in turn pressurises the individual into facing unpleasant choices, shouldn't the government or the profession step in to deal with the problem? The answer has to be 'yes'. This is why some aspects of professional conduct are regulated not by the profession, but by law.

The corporate and social responsibility agenda means that adherence to the ethics of the professions that support the business and the more general promotion of professionalism in the workplace is of paramount importance in the determination of the culture of organisations.

Supplementary reading

If the problem is too big or the temptations are too great or the professional body is too weak, then the law steps in. A classic example of this was the tightening of insider dealing laws in the 1980s; because of the signal failure of financial authorities to control their employees' use of advantageous privileged information.

Laws do not, of themselves, help you out of general ethical problems. For example, you might feel that it is unethical to obey an immoral law. However, such difficulties do not arise in management accounting. If there is a conflict between a professional duty, such as confidentiality, and statute law, the CIMA Code explicitly states that the law is to be preferred. In the hierarchy of obligations, law overrides everything.

Ethical Codes v Contracts

But what about other legal obligations? Surely the contract you sign with your employer is a legal obligation and the contracts with clients have legal effects? Of course this is true. However, voluntarily assumed legal obligations are exactly that. You have made a choice to enter into that obligation. You have a choice not to comply with a contractual obligation and take instead the penalty for breach of that contract. This might be the appropriate course of action when performing the contract would bring you into serious breach of the CIMA Code.

Supplementary reading

An example of where you might break with a contractual duty is where your employer instructed you to act in a way that is professionally unacceptable. Another might be where you are directed to follow a corporate policy that was devised to apply to general situations, but which you feel is inappropriate in a particular context because there are special ethical considerations.

From a purely ethical standpoint, if you are confronted by a choice of breach of professional ethics and a breach of your contract of employment, you are ultimately supposed to favour your profession over your employer.

Supplementary reading

This is easier said than done. Nobody wishes to directly confront the person who pays their wages, and refusal to do your job because of ethical conflict can sound very much like being uncooperative, idealistic, unrealistic or ill-disciplined. There is some small comfort to be had here. An employer who victimises a professional because of the professional's sense of duty to their profession and public is likely to be given little time by an Employment Tribunal, should you need to challenge them or should they dismiss you! The law will not enforce obligations that are unconscionable or contrary to public policy (the enforcement of a contract to force someone to breach their professional duty would easily fall into this category), but legal rights ultimately rely on the Employment Tribunal to enforce, rather than good faith.

However, most people consider that a problem that gets them into court is already a bigger problem than they wish to take on. Spotting the ethical problems before they turn into personal nightmares or planning to avoid them in the first place is obviously the most desirable course of action.

A different, but possibly equally difficult situation arises when you are expected to do something which is part of a contract with an outside client. Often, the management accountant has no direct relationship with the client. However, the repercussions of refusing to act in a certain way on your employer's client relationships can be considerable. Often, clients will simply take their business elsewhere, if they feel that your employer will not accommodate them. It may not cause a direct confrontation between you and your employer, but if clients won't work with your employer because of you, there is always the chance that you may feel that it is you who will be the first in line for redundancy!

Often, you will be trying to do the right thing, not for you, but for someone else. Resolving ethical conflict seldom has much more reward to the individual than the feeling that you know you have done the right thing. However, the accountant is not on his or her own. CIMA provides support for individuals faced with ethical conflict situations and the law 'helps' accountants and employers to make the right choice, often by imposing personal liability for the individual who acts unprofessionally or forces another to do so.

Corporate governance and responsibility

Much more pressure is being directed at employers to subscribe to ethical values and practice at an corporate level. There is greater willingness to use the word 'ethics' within the context of business, which perhaps a few years ago was not the case. The 'ethical consumer' and the impact of corporate scandals have redirected corporate attentions to how they operate on an organisational level.

Increasingly, professional bodies, firms, companies and other types of organisations are producing values-based codes and building values into their corporate strategies. The first and foremost reason is that by stating its values, it is setting the tone of the business. It clearly states the standard expected of employees and it encourages a sense of pride and loyalty. It has great marketing value as well.

The terms 'corporate responsibility' and 'social responsibility' have ceased to be words of challenge by external critics of corporate practice and have become part of mainstream management thinking. In this context, these organisational values are often ones that the professional can hitch his or her own ethical standards to in order to avoid the immediate conflict with employers.

Corporate values are important for giving guidance to staff about what the expectations an employer has of them with regard to their behaviour. They seek to ensure a consistency of conduct across the entity, including conduct that relates to personal probity and professionalism. This in turn underpins the risk management strategies of organisations.

Consistent conduct will reduce the risk of someone behaving inappropriately and the organisation potentially suffering a 'hit' to its reputation and credibility. Such codes are often voluntary and will be monitored through a variety of means, such as assurance, audit, through employee surveys, development and performance reviews, exit interviews and so forth.

Supplementary reading

'Governance' on its own is a term in common use in many types of organisations, from companies to charities, schools, local authorities and the National Health Service in the United Kingdom. In the United Kingdom, it was developed by the Committee on the Financial Aspects of Corporate Governance in 1992 (the Cadbury Report) with a code of best practice attached. It was aimed at listed companies but looked especially at standards of corporate behaviour. It also referred to ethics.

Taken from the Committee on the Financial Aspects of Corporate Governance 1992 (the Cadbury Report). 'It is important that all employees should know what standards of conduct are expected of them. We regard it as good practice for boards of directors to draw up codes of ethics or statements of business practice and to publish them both internally and externally.'

Governance has come to denote the generic way that an organisation is run, with particular emphasis on accountability, integrity and in many instances risk management. There are clear lines of responsibility for ethics that lead directly to Board level, with corresponding penalties for Board members for malfeasance. It is not surprising therefore that ethical compromises are counted as risk factors in an increasing number of organisations.

Social responsibility

'Social responsibility' is another newly popular term in management. It refers to how an organisation manages its relationships in the wider community. The range of issues is broad and encompasses many aspects of the current political agenda. For instance: How 'green' is the organisation? How much recycling of waste and paper is undertaken? Is low energy lighting used in the offices? Does the organisation support the local community in providing mentors or reading assistants at the local school, for instance? There are many possibilities.

It has long been accepted that all organisations have responsibilities beyond their shareholders or paymasters. Nowadays, the broader community has been reclassified as potential stakeholders or groups to whom a corporation might owe responsibilities.

Many organisations seek to express their social responsibility policies by identifying their stakeholders, those people or bodies who have either a financial or interested/influential relationship with the entity. It is now seen as part of good governance to have such policies.

Supplementary reading

An organisation has two types of stakeholder. The first are those with a financial relationship with the body, if anything were to happen to that entity then these groups would suffer. This group includes the shareholders, the employees, customers and suppliers, and the community in the sense that the company pays its taxes to support the community, both at local and national level.

The second group are those with an interest in how the organisation behaves. They may actually have an influence (greater than the financial stakeholders at times) over the entity. This group includes the media, non-governmental organisations (NGOs), activist groups, competitors and even the regulator (unless it has power to set prices, when it becomes a financial stakeholder).

The corporate and social responsibility agenda means that adherence to the ethics of the professions that support the business and the more general promotion of professionalism in the workplace is of paramount importance in the determination of the culture of organisations.

All policies for governance and social responsibility are ultimately rooted in the organisation's values and code of ethics.

There is a separate issue when an organisation spends its money; guided by issues other than pure profit and loss, which is usually referred to as its corporate social responsibility policy. Typically, there will be policies as to how communities are supported in which it operates, and a list of charities it will support.

In both respects though, the organisation needs to tie these policies back to its core values. If it does not, they may not be sustainable if there is a downturn in income and it has to make difficult decisions about continuing to support its community work and charities.

Ultimately, employers are coming round to building their own infrastructure of ethics, codes of ethics to give guidance to members, staff and employees to reduce the risk of problematic occurrences happening.

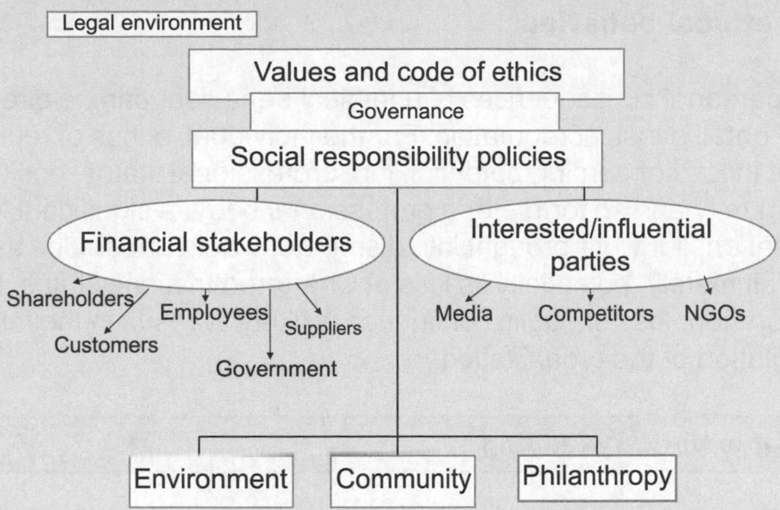

Figure 7.1 Interrelationship between ethics, governance, law and social responsibility in an organisation. *Source*: Institute of Business Ethics

Ethics programme

Three things are essential in developing an effective ethics programme.

(1) The first need is active leadership from the top. Not only should a senior member of the organisation's board act as a champion, but organisations should encourage all senior executives to lead by example.

(2) Secondly, that champion needs to get buy-in, which can be best done through consultation, information and encouraging transparency of decision-making.

(3) Thirdly, there needs to be a programme of training everyone covered by the code to embed the message.

The message is a simple one: the corporation's code of ethics expresses the values by which people are expected to behave and to assist them in dealing with dilemmas which emerge day to day in the course of business activities. These dilemmas are the tests of individual responses to carrying out the spirit of the code. To quote Carly Fiorina in 2003, the then CEO of Hewlett Packard: 'it is doing the right thing when no-one is watching'. Codes amplify what is the 'right thing' and help to reduce instances of unethical behaviour.

2 Unethical behaviour

The personal consequences of unethical behaviour can be dire, as typically it will entail a loss of reputation. For the individual, a loss of reputation may result in loss of earning potential, job, professional status, position in the community and so forth. For a professional body, a significant loss of reputation, if it were brought into disrepute, would undermine its credibility and, ultimately, potentially its loss of Chartered Institute status. For a corporation, loss of public confidence is likely to result in the failure and dissolution of the organisation.

Supplementary reading

These are dire consequences and there are many gradations in between, for instance when the Barings Bank scandal in the United Kingdom happened, the individual went to jail but the Bank was 'saved' as it was purchased by ING Bank. In the Maxwell case, the Mirror Group survived, though Polly Peck did not survive the scandals that were linked to its chief executive. Worldcom survived and reinvented itself but Arthur Andersen did not.

In the wider context, when such unethical behaviour is identified there is a greater damage, as trust is undermined not only in the people and organisations directly affected but also in similar bodies or institutions on the fear that they also may be targeted or affected by scandal. This is the trust that society bears for its organisations.

Often however, the true economic and human consequences of unethical behaviour are diffuse and hard to pinpoint. Like a lot of 'victimless crimes', the indirect global effects of one person who is discourteous, slow and unreliable might be minimal, but the impact on the profession of a few thousand practitioners who are like that can be considerable, as the legal profession would have to acknowledge.

3 Ethical dilemmas and conflicts of interest

Introduction

There is an expectation in wider society that professional accountants have a leadership role in ensuring that companies, institutions, public bodies and all types of organisations where they work will behave ethically in carrying out their activities. Demonstrating such leadership by example can be achieved only if the individual professional concerned is sensitive enough to spot and to tackle ethical dilemmas. Without an 'inner guide' to ethical behaviour an individual may easily trip up.

For instance, a leader who fails to follow company procedures by deciding to appoint a friend to the board of the company is vulnerable to accusations of a conflict of interest if the appointment fails, or if there is a lack of transparency in making the appointment in the first instance. Governance procedures can add rigour to the appointment process, but it should be natural instinct to realise that business cannot be run without a core ethical values.

All individuals need to be able to recognise an ethical dilemma and deal with it appropriately. Pressures challenge personal integrity as well as business skills, which is why ethical acumen is an essential ingredient for a professional accountant.

Identifying ethical dilemmas

In identifying ethical dilemmas, it is important to understand how they arise.

Conflict can arise from any number of sources, however common ones include:

- societal values
- professional values
- personal values
- corporate values.

Individuals will recognise tensions if they are asked to condone the behaviour by their company which they feel to be wrong or inappropriate. If the tension is too great, they will leave the company. Before doing so, however, they may try to speak up, to voice their concerns. An example is where an employee is asked to 'overlook' improprieties carried out by their company, which would be counter to their professional code.

There are also tensions between corporate values and the values of society. If companies or individuals are deemed by society to be behaving or conducting their business inappropriately, then laws will be introduced to enforce minimum levels of behaviour. Such laws are wide ranging in order to cover the wide ranging activities of a business from employment practices to disposal of products in an environmentally friendly way, to banning cartels and unfair competitive activities and fraud, and the prevention of bribery and corruption.

Supplementary reading

Moves towards an ever-increasing body of business-related law represent a breakdown of trust by society in individuals, companies and professionals. Criminal Law is then introduced on the basis that 'if you don't behave, we'll introduce a law to make you do so'. The corollary is better enforced self-regulation in order to stamp out bad practice. This encourages companies to act with a higher standard of behaviour rather than the minimum level of behaviour set by law. Organisations therefore need to pay attention to society's agenda, if only to protect themselves from more legislation.

Ethical dilemmas arise in many guises within an organisation – from those related to strategy and policy as faced by those running the organisation to those faced by middle managers or individuals in the course of their work. Dilemmas can occur at all levels.

How to identify an ethical dilemma

The boundaries of right and wrong as defined in the Criminal Law are clear. However, behaving ethically or choosing how one wants to undertake business and achieve business goals is discretionary. Therefore, companies, as represented by the board, may or may not choose to encourage ethical behaviour by their staff.

Dilemmas arise when the boundaries of right and wrong are not clear; when an individual is faced with two options – the choice between making a better choice, or the least wrong. The individual must choose what to do. What makes ethical decisions hard is that they often are such unpalatable choices.

It is clear that what is not an ethical dilemma is when there is a choice between what is good for me and what is prescribed by professional standards. Doing what I want for my own reasons is not a professional choice but a personal preference, and therefore has no place in ethical reasoning.

Personal compromises include when friendships, families, loyalties and affiliations to organisations, political and other belief systems are involved. None of these are relevant to decision-making, except when they so strongly colour your perceptions that they make you incapable of objective judgement or where they so taint the outside perception of you that others think that you lack objectivity.

Supplementary reading

Here are some examples of dilemmas which might occur:

- My wife has just got a great job as managing director of a successful business, which also happens to be one of my biggest clients. Does it matter?
- I have taken over a new account from my manager. In re-evaluating their work, I have come across a significant error, which nobody seems to have picked up on. I don't want to jeopardise my relationship with my manager. What should I do?
- I have had a client for many years who has always taken me for dinner after his year end to celebrate and say thank you. This year he says he's done rather well so he's offered to take me golfing for the weekend in St Andrews. Should I accept?
- Our firm has taken out an advert in the local paper to promote our services. However, it says that we are experts in tax and none of the partners have that expertise. I feel uncomfortable, but what can I do?
- Our firm is being taken over and there is talk of redundancies being made. I've been asked to review the accounting policies and see if I could 'make things look more favourable'; it was implied that my job would depend upon it. What should I do?
- I'm tendering for new business, and I bumped into the current accountants at a conference. They said they wouldn't be re-tendering for the business because of 'certain difficulties' with the client, but when pressed said that the information was confidential. What should I do?

In response to each of these instances, the CIMA Code gives guidance on how to avoid conflicts of interest and threats to independence, and how to deal with confidential issues.

Conflicts of interest

Individuals can often find that they face a conflict of interest between their professional and business lives. In such instances, it is important to follow guidelines laid down in the Code of Ethics. Some instances are obvious, others are subtle so the individual needs to be sensitive in spotting them.

Illustration 1: Conflicts of interest

Steve is the Management Accountant at the Head Office of EnviroServices Group. One of his best friends, Dan, works in another part of the group. They've been friends since university, their wives are also great friends and their families have been on holiday together once or twice. Steve and Dan often talk about work when their wives aren't listening, keeping each other abreast of developments in the respective parts of the group, although neither of them puts pressure on the other to divulge any sensitive information.

Restructuring is taking place throughout EnviroServices. Steve is a member of an internal working party mandated to ensure that the internal communications policies and practices of the group fully support the changes that will take place in the course of the restructuring. As a member of the working party, Steve is privy to plans for the restructuring. This is price-sensitive information available only to a few people apart from top management. This includes information about the proposed selling off of one part of the group, which is no longer seen as core business. It is the part of the group where Dan works.

There are bound to be redundancies, especially at Dan's middle manager level. When Steve and Dan had last got together, he'd been talking about moving his house, taking on a substantial new mortgage in the process, in order to be able to send his daughter to a special school for children with learning disabilities.

In training, the following three questions would be asked:

(1) What is the ethical issue?

(2) What are the options to resolve this issue?

(3) What is the appropriate response?

Conflicts of interest are not wrong in themselves, but they do become a problem when a professional continues to engage in a course of action being, aware of that conflict. When you think you may have a conflict of interest, it is always a sensible idea to declare it. It is normal that an individual will withdraw from a course of dealing when a conflict arises.

Resolving ethical dilemmas

A professional accountant may be called upon to resolve a dilemma in the application of the CIMA Code of Ethics' Fundamental Principles. Guidance is given in the Code in Sections 100.19–100.24.

Ethical Conflict Resolution

100.19 – A professional accountant may be required to resolve a conflict in complying with the fundamental principles.

100.20 – When initiating either a formal or informal conflict resolution process, the following factors, either individually or together with others, may be relevant to the resolution process:

(a) Relevant facts
(b) Ethical issues involved
(c) Fundamental principles related to the matter in question
(d) Established internal procedures; and
(e) Alternative courses of action.

Having considered the relevant factors, a professional accountant shall determine the appropriate course of action, weighing the consequences of each possible course of action. If the matter remains unresolved, the professional accountant may wish to consult with other appropriate persons within the firm or employing organisation for help in obtaining resolution.

100.21 – Where a matter involves a conflict with, or within, an organisation, a professional accountant shall determine whether to consult with those charged with governance of the organisation, such as the board of directors or the audit committee.

100.22 – It may be in the best interests of the professional accountant to document the substance of the issue, the details of any discussions held, and the decisions made concerning that issue.

100.23 – If a significant conflict cannot be resolved, a professional accountant may consider obtaining professional advice from the relevant professional body or from legal advisors. The professional accountant generally can obtain guidance on ethical issues without breaching the fundamental principle of confidentiality if the matter is discussed with the relevant professional body on an anonymous basis or with a legal advisor under the protection of legal privilege. Instances in which the professional accountant may consider obtaining legal advice vary. For example, a professional accountant may have encountered a fraud, the reporting of which could breach the professional accountant's responsibility to respect confidentiality. The professional accountant may consider obtaining legal advice in that instance to determine whether there is a requirement to report.

100.24 – If, after exhausting all relevant possibilities, the ethical conflict remains unresolved, a professional accountant shall, where possible, refuse to remain associated with the matter creating the conflict. The professional accountant shall determine whether, in the circumstances, it is appropriate to withdraw from the engagement team or specific assignment, or to resign altogether from the engagement, the firm or the employing organisation.

Supplementary reading

In essence, the resolution process entails several stages of investigation. First, the relevant facts need to be established and the ethical issues identified. The issue has to be tested against the Fundamental Principles. As a practical matter, the resolution process entails several stages of investigation.

- The relevant facts need to be established.
- The ethical issues are identified.
- Test the issue against the Fundamental Principles and Code of Ethics.

Once the relevant facts have been ascertained, then a course of action will need to be identified. Options would include:

(a) **Do nothing:** Sometimes it is impossible to ascertain or verify facts, for example when there is a dispute over matters discussed in a telephone call between two parties. In such an instance, it may not be possible to adjudicate, so nothing can be done.

(b) **Avoidance:** Where a dispute has arisen in which both parties are at fault, for instance, it might be prudent to separate them by introducing an intermediary through whom they will work thereby avoiding direct contact between the parties.

(c) **Modifying behaviours:** Sometimes it will be necessary to suggest that individuals modify or adjust their behaviours towards others. This is often the case where innocent banter in the office has been misinterpreted by other staff members.

(d) **Arbitration:** In difficult and complex situations, the professional accountant might wish to seek the advice or assistance of a professional mediator. This might happen where the allegations are of a more serious nature, such as bullying and harassment of one colleague by another but there is no third party corroboration of it.

In preparation for handling investigations, internal procedures for handling such dilemmas need to have been established so they can be referred to. During the course of such investigations, the professional accountant may well need to refer or discuss the issue with others within the organisation. All investigations should be documented in case any subsequent action has to be taken, as should all conversations held in connection with the issue.

Where there is a requirement to report, such as in cases of suspected or identified fraud, the professional accountant should obtain legal advice.

Supplementary reading

In many organisations, the procedures laid down for resolving ethical issues will refer to three initial tests for an ethical decision.

- **Transparency:** Do I mind who knows about my decision? Can I openly defend my stance?
- **Effect:** Have I identified whom the decision affects or hurts? Have I taken everything into account, including mitigating circumstances?
- **Fairness:** Will my decisions be judged by others to be fair?

Ethical dilemmas may be raised with a professional accountant through a number of routes:

(i) directly through an enquiry

(ii) via an in-house speak-up/help/whistleblower line

(iii) from an external customer, supplier or other agent to the organisation

(iv) anonymously.

In each case, the same rigorous process should be applied to ensure a consistent approach and consistent application of CIMA's Code of Ethics.

Ultimately, the existence of CIMA and the management accountant's subscription to their Code of Ethics and to their membership entitles the individual to support and guidance in resolving ethics. While confidentiality means details cannot be discussed, ethical conflicts are really matters of principle. The outside objective viewpoint can often highlight what is really at stake and produce an analysis which might not be what we want to hear, but nonetheless provides a clear and definitive resolution to the problem.

4 Test your understanding questions

Test your understanding 1

Which of the following are possible consequences to the accounting profession if unethical behaviour is widespread?

(i) The introduction of legislation.

(ii) Loss of its reputation.

(iii) Loss of its chartered institute status.

A (i) and (ii) only

B (ii) and (iii) only

C (i) and (iii) only

D (i), (ii) and (iii)

Test your understanding 2

Which statements are true or false?

A Unethical behaviour will lead to financial loss

B Codes of ethics are voluntary

C Governance refers to how an organisation is run

D Social responsibility refers to a company's relationship with its shareholders

Test your understanding 3

Which of the following is not an example of a familiarity threat?

A Accepting gifts or preferential treatment from a client

B Having a close business relationship with a client

C Having a close family relationship with a director of a client

D A former partner of the company being a director of the client

Test your understanding 4

An old friend has asked you to tender for accounting work. You are keen to assist. From an ethical as well as a business perspective, what is the most appropriate action for you to take?

A Tender for the work

B Suggest to your friend that they approach more than one company to create a competitive tender

C Suggest to your friend that they assign the work to a different company instead

D Ask a colleague to handle the client

Test your understanding answers

Test your understanding 1

D

They are all possible outcomes.

Test your understanding 2

A **False.** Unethical behaviour may have consequences when it is highlighted. Not all ethical behaviour is highlighted.

B **True.** A company may require its employees to comply with its code of ethics as part of the employee's contract of employment, but it is a voluntary decision of a company to set up a code of ethics initially.

C **True.** This is the generic manner in which the term governance is used.

D **False.** A company's social responsibility is a wider responsibility to ALL stakeholders of the company, not just the shareholders.

Test your understanding 3

B

Having a close business relationship with a client is an example of a self-interest threat.

Test your understanding 4

D

Accountants need to demonstrate both independence of mind and independence in appearance. You should therefore declare the potential conflict of interest and ask a colleague to handle the client.

chapter

8

Corporate Governance

Chapter learning objectives

On completion of their studies, students should be able to:

- define corporate governance
- explain the interaction of corporate governance with business ethics and company law
- describe the history of corporate governance internationally
- distinguish between detailed rules-based and principles based approaches to governance.

1 Introduction

As you have seen, companies have always been subject to quite strict regulation. Despite this, a number of issues have continued to cause considerable unrest and political controversy. The main concerns have centred on the apparent lack of effective control of directors of public listed companies, which have manifested themselves in perceived excessive remuneration packages and mismanagement leading to a number of high-profile corporate collapses.

Public listed companies employ thousands of employees and are the recipients of billions of pounds in investment by individuals and institutional investors such as pension funds. It follows that all governments, in the United Kingdom, in Europe and throughout the world, consider it crucial that public confidence in such companies is maintained.

The attempts to effectively control the remuneration of directors and the activities of directors in their management of public companies are known as 'corporate governance'.

Supplementary reading

The US President at the time of writing, Barack Obama, described as 'shameful' reports that employees in financial companies in New York collected an estimated $18.4 billion ($12.9 billion) in bonuses at a time when billions of dollars of American taxpayers' money was injected into the banking system so that money could be made available for loans to businesses and consumers during a period of recession.

2 What is corporate governance?

The term 'corporate governance' is neither defined by legislation nor has it been defined by the courts. As Farrar notes in his text book on company law, 'corporate governance is a term which has been much in vogue in the last 10 years. It suffers, nevertheless, from a lack of precision.' The Cadbury Committee defined corporate governance in its Report on the Financial Aspects of Corporate Governance (see below) as 'the system by which companies are directed and controlled'.

Corporate governance is primarily concerned with the effective control, business efficacy and accountability of the management of public listed companies for the benefit of stakeholders.

Supplementary reading

'Stakeholders' in this context means all those who are affected directly or indirectly by a company's activities. It follows that the expression includes directors, shareholders, investors, subsidiaries, joint venture partners, employees, customers, communities, local neighbourhoods, suppliers, and the environment.

3 Governance, ethics and company law

Clearly, there is an overlap between business ethics, company law and corporate governance. Company law is made up of ethical principles and standards of behaviour which legislators and the courts have thought it right and proper to enshrine within the law of the land.

Supplementary reading

Thus, for example, company law provides that directors owe a number of statutory duties including the duties to promote the success of the company under s172 CA 2006, to avoid conflicts of interest under s175 CA 2006 and not to accept benefits from third parties under s176 CA 2006.

It may be questioned therefore, if the law is so stringent, why has it proved necessary to have an additional body of rules and standards known as corporate governance? Why is it that the law has not prevented directors from paying themselves excessive salaries and/or involving their companies in major scandals?

The answer lies in the fact that, in many instances, the law provides for internal regulation of the activities of directors by:

(i) requiring directors to fully disclose their dealings to the shareholders and

(ii) by giving the shareholders the power to regulate the activities of the directors through their control of the company's constitution and, of course, by giving the shareholders the ultimate power, of appointing and dismissing the directors.

Why then does the law need to be supplemented? The short answer is that quite clearly these rules have not proved watertight, and in a number of high-profile instances directors have been able to circumvent the law. In general, this has happened for the following main reasons.

Firstly, persons and institutions who invest in shares in public limited companies mainly do so in order to achieve good capital growth, a good return on their investment in the form of dividends or a combination of the two. If that is what the investor is receiving, then he is less likely to be interested in the way that the company is being managed. In any event, the investors, particularly institutional investors, will be likely to have invested in a large number of companies throughout the world. It appears unrealistic in the extreme therefore, to suppose that fund managers will have the time to actively participate in the internal affairs of all the companies in which they invest.

Secondly, shares in public companies are potentially held by hundreds or even thousands of shareholders. It follows that shareholders in any particular company tend to be a disparate body, not united by any common objectives other than good returns on their investments. Such a group is likely to be difficult to organise behind a coherent policy and thus in a poor position to take on a relatively small powerful group like a board of directors. Even the ultimate power to remove directors may be difficult to use in practice. For example, it may be that the shareholders are concerned that if the market becomes aware of internal conflict within the company, that may have a detrimental effect on the share price. Additionally it may be that dismissing directors can be expensive in the extreme. Many directors of public companies would be entitled to large compensation payments in the event of their removal.

Supplementary reading

Morality and ethical behaviour are also enshrined in the criminal law. For example, as it is considered wrong and unethical that directors and other insiders should be able to benefit from inside information, it has been made a criminal offence for them to benefit from inside knowledge by making a profit or avoiding a loss in connection with share dealings under 'insider dealing' legislation (see Part V of the Criminal Justice Act 1993). Despite the fact that insider dealing is a criminal offence, there seems little doubt that it still goes on. Like any other branch of the criminal law, its effectiveness or otherwise depends upon a number of factors, including how well the law has been drafted and the efficiency of those who police it. As Gower notes: 'It is difficult to make a wholly accurate assessment of the extent of the use of the criminal process in this area but the figures for the numbers of prosecutions and convictions initiated by the DTI are not encouraging' (Gower and Davies Principles of Modern Company Law, 7th edition 2003 at page 775).

4 The history of corporate governance internationally

The United States

Supplementary reading

Writing in the United States in the 1930s, Berle and Means noted that:

"The shift of powers from the individual to the controlling management combined with the shift from the interests of the individual to those of the group have so changed the position of the stockholder that the current conception with regard to him must be radically revised. (The stockholder) becomes simply a supplier of capital on terms less definite than those customarily given or demanded by bondholders; and the thinking about his position must be qualified by the realisation that he is, in a highly modified sense, not dissimilar in kind from the bondholder or lender of money (The Modern Corporation and Private Property 1932)."

A major development since the work by Berle and Means has been the growth of the institutional investor both in the United States and United Kingdom. Although the directors of public companies may well own shares in the company, the vast majority of the shares, on an average some 60 per cent, are owned by institutional investors such as the pension funds and insurance companies. Originally, the criticism of fund managers was that they too were only interested in shares as investments rather than as shareholders as such. It followed that even though they were seen to hold considerable power it was said that if they become aware of any likely problem with the company, they were more likely to offload the investment as soon as possible rather than involve themselves in controlling management. Today, fund managers are under legal obligations to actively manage investments on behalf of their clients and are more likely than before to take an active interest in the way companies are managed.

Despite this development, problems have continued to arise in relation to the effective control of the directors of public listed companies. In more recent times, corporate governance issues arose first in the United States in the 1980s when company boards adopted protective measures to ward off what they considered to be undesirable takeover bids. Some shareholders, particularly institutional investors, saw this as being against their interests and, as they had a legal obligation to manage their assets, they began to take more interest in how the companies in which they invested were managed. This in turn led to the activities and practices of companies and their managers being brought to the attention of the public at large by the media.

The recent collapse of Enron and WorldCom in the United States has given renewed impetus to governments to take action in order to restore public confidence in the corporate sector.

Enron's problems came about because of unsustainable growth which had to be financed through increased borrowing. Following an investigation by the Securities and Exchange Commission, it became clear that in order to hide its excessive borrowing and thus maintain confidence in its stock, Enron effectively created a number of subsidiaries, each a legal entity in its own right, for the purpose of keeping Enron's borrowing off its balance sheet and thus maintaining its creditworthiness. In December 2001, Enron filed for protection under Chapter 11 of the United States Bankruptcy Code with debts of approximately $3 billion. The investigation has also revealed that the persons primarily responsible for Enron's fraud and subsequent collapse were the directors, chief executives and the company's auditors. To date there have been guilty pleas in relation to fraud, money laundering and insider dealing by Enron executives and a plea of guilty to obstructing justice by destroying Enron-related documents by Arthur Andersen, Enron's lead auditor. As may be imagined, the collapse of such a large corporation as Enron and the criminal activities revealed have led to renewed attention being given to the effectiveness of corporate governance measures.

The Sarbanes-Oxley Act was passed in July 2002 seeking to protect investors by improving the accuracy of corporate disclosure and reporting procedures and increasing corporate openness.

In addition, it had become clear that in many cases the relationship between corporations and their auditors was far too close. Auditors are required to carry out their work independently of the interests of the company's board or senior executives and to provide a check for the benefit of the shareholders. However, the auditors of Enron had conspired with the company in attempts to remove excessive debt from the Enron accounts. In practice, the independence of the auditors was compromised by the fact that they also received fees from the company for acting as financial consultants. As a result, the Sarbanes-Oxley Act created the Public Company Accounting Oversight Board which is charged with the task of policing the auditing of public companies in the United States. All auditors of public companies must be registered with the board which is required to set up quality assurance procedures, ethics and independent standards to which auditors are required to adhere. The Act also prohibits auditors from providing certain non-audit services to the companies for which they act. In addition, the Act requires the separate disclosure of the fees received by auditors for audit and all other fees. It follows that the independence of the scrutineers is now also subject to scrutiny!

Europe

Supplementary reading

In 2003, the European Commission announced that it did not believe it necessary to formulate a separate code of European corporate governance. Rather such matters could safely be left to individual member states. However, it did see the need for a common approach to be taken in regard to fundamental governance issues throughout the European Union. These are to be developed over time through the issue of Directives. Thus such matters as the greater involvement in management of independent non-executive directors, more information regarding directors' remuneration and greater disclosure of and access to other financial information should form the basis of the corporate governance of all EU member states.

In furtherance of this common approach, the European Union established an EU Corporate Governance Forum in October 2004. The forum has 15 members representing various stakeholders from across the European Union and its overall objective is to 'co-ordinate corporate governance efforts of member states' (DTI publication 'Promoting Competitiveness: The UK approach to EU company Law and corporate governance').

The United Kingdom

In the United Kingdom, there have been a number of scandals involving the likes of Guinness and Robert Maxwell and these highlighted the continuing ability of directors to involve public companies in mismanagement. These scandals and high-profile company frauds made it clear that effective control of the directors of public companies was not being carried out by the shareholders, with the result that governments and regulators have had to look to other means for effective control mechanisms.

Corporate governance of public listed companies was the subject of the following reports prepared for the Stock Exchange in the 1990s.

The Cadbury Committee Report 1992

The Cadbury Committee was set up by the Financial Reporting Council, the London Stock Exchange and the accountancy professions in 1991. The Cadbury Committee Report was published in 1992 and recommended that the boards of public companies should be required to comply with a code of best practice as a condition of continuing to be listed on the Stock Exchange. Listed companies were required to include a statement in their annual reports confirming that they had complied with the code or, where appropriate, detailing instances of non-compliance and the reasons for it.

Supplementary reading

The code recommended:

- Independent non-executive directors should be appointed to the boards of listed companies.
- The appointment of all executive directors should be vetted by a nomination committee made up of the company's non-executive directors.
- Executive directors should not be offered service contracts for more than 3 years, unless approved by the shareholders in a general meeting.
- The remuneration packages of executive directors should be agreed by a remuneration committee, wholly or mainly comprising non-executive directors.
- An audit committee consisting of a majority of non-executive directors should be established to oversee the company's finances.
- In order to promote the independent nature of the board the same person should not act as both chief executive and chairman.

The Greenbury Committee Report 1995

Despite the introduction of the code of practice as recommended by the Cadbury Committee, the issue of the excessive remuneration of directors of listed companies became a political embarrassment for the government of the day, following the privatisation of the nationalised utility companies such as the Gas Board. As a result, the Greenbury Report contained a new code of best practice for the directors of public listed companies.

Supplementary reading

The recommendations were:

- The remuneration committee should consider the interests of both the shareholders and the directors when determining the level of directors' remuneration.
- Directors should never be given discounted share options and annual bonuses should not be pensionable.
- Any long-term incentive schemes to be offered to directors should first be approved by the shareholders.
- Executive directors' service contracts should not provide notice periods exceeding 1 year.
- The remuneration committee should prepare an annual report to be included in the annual accounts and placed before the shareholders. The report should contain a statement that full consideration has been given to the Greenbury code and should explain any instances of non-compliance.

With effect from December 1995, the recommendations of the Greenbury Report were incorporated within the Stock Exchange listing rules. It follows that compliance with the Report became a necessary prerequisite to obtaining a listing.

The Hampel Committee Report 1998

This report was published on 28 January 1998. The report seeks to give effect to and, where necessary, add to the work done by the Cadbury and Greenbury committees.

Supplementary reading

The conclusions of the Hampel Report which were primarily related to public listed companies were as follows:

- Executive and non-executive directors should owe the same corporate duties and should be provided with more information and instruction as to their responsibilities.
- Executive directors should have the necessary experience to be able to understand the nature and extent of the interests of the company for which they are acting.
- The majority of non-executive directors should be independent and make up at least one-third of the board.

- One person should not occupy the role of Chairman and Chief Executive.
- All companies should have nomination committees for recommending new board appointments. Directors should be obliged to seek re-election for every 3 years.
- The remuneration of executive directors should not be excessive and should be based upon the recommendations of a remuneration committee made up entirely of non-executive directors.
- Directors' contracts should not exceed 12 months.

The Combined Code (now the UK Corporate Governance Code)

On 25 June 1998, the London Stock Exchange published a general code of good practice which was based upon the Hampel Report. The code became compulsory for all listed companies after 31 December 1998. Although it did not have the force of law, non-compliance could lead to the imposition of a fine by the London Stock Exchange and potentially lead to a refusal to list. The code is covered in more detail in section 7 of this chapter.

The Turnbull Report

The Turnbull Report was published in 1999. The report concluded that the board of directors should include within its responsibilities:

- An evaluation of the likely risks and categories of risk facing the company
- Ensuring that effective safeguards and internal controls were put in place to prevent or reduce risk
- Internal controls including an annual assessment of risk should be made transparent.

The Higgs Report 2003

The Higgs Report was a response to the collapse of Enron (see above). The main thrust of the report was to emphasise collective board responsibility.

The Smith Report on Audit Committees 2003

Sir Robert Smith, Chairman of the Weir Group plc and a member of the FRC was asked to prepare a report on the role and responsibilities of audit committees. He stated that his report and recommendations would build on current best practice. It was intended to reinforce the independence of the auditor and raise British corporate governance standards and help to maintain the UK's position among the leaders in the field.

5 The effect of corporate governance on directors' behaviour and their duties of care and skill

Supplementary reading

Directors' powers and duties can be determined by reference to the company's constitution, Articles of Association and the shareholder agreement (if any – private companies only). In addition, they may be derived from individual contracts of service (executive directors) and contracts for services (non-executive directors), the Companies Acts and case law.

Directors owe statutory duties contained in the Companies Act 2006. One of the duties is to 'promote the success of the company' (section 172 CA 2006). This duty has replaced the former equitable duty to act in good faith in the best interests of the company. Nonetheless the new statutory duties must be interpreted in the light of previous common law and equitable principles. Another duty requires directors (a) to act in accordance with the company's constitution and (b) to only exercise powers for the purposes for which they are conferred. This means that if directors ignore the company's Articles of Association they have acted in breach of duty. In addition part (b) effectively restates the rule that directors must not use their powers for an improper purpose. It follows, for example, that even if the board of a target company considers itself to be more suited to manage that company than a board which would be appointed following a successful takeover bid, that does not justify the issue of shares to supporters of the target company board so as to enable them to outvote those in favour of the bid. This is so even though the directors have the legal right to issue shares (*Hogg v. Cramphorn* [1967] Ch 254). In addition, a director may be held to have acted in breach of his statutory duty where it is obvious that he could not have been acting in the best interests of the company. For example, a director in poor health entered into a new service contract with his company and one of the terms provided that a generous pension should be paid to his widow in the event of his death.

The director died shortly after entering into the agreement and it became clear that he had not disclosed the poor state of his health to the company. It was held that the director had acted in the interests of his wife rather than of the company as a whole (Re W & M Roith Ltd [1967] 1 WLR 432). Further examples of fiduciary duties may be seen in Chapter 5.

As also considered in Chapter 5, directors also have a duty to exercise reasonable care, skill and diligence. Section 174 CA 2006 provides that a director must exercise the same care, skill and diligence that would be used by a reasonably diligent person with the general knowledge, skill and experience that may reasonably be expected of a person carrying out the functions that are being carried out by the director. This is a change from the previous common law which did not seek to judge the director by reference to the skills etc of a reasonable person. The important change lies in the inclusion of the expression 'reasonably diligent person' as it follows that the director is imputed with the general knowledge, skill and experience that may reasonably be expected of the holder of the position in question. If a director's standard of care should fall below that which could be expected of a reasonably diligent person, then the director could no longer rely on his/her own inadequacies to argue that he/she did not breach the duty of care. In short, today a director's behaviour is judged against an objective standard, that is that of the reasonably diligent person, rather than against his/her own standards. The duty is now comparable with that set down by statute, that is in Section 214 of the Insolvency Act 1986 which relates to 'wrongful trading'. A director owes the above duty of care to the company, that is the shareholders as a body. The duty is enforceable by the company, that is the legal entity.

The duty of care is largely concerned with expressing the standard of behaviour expected of directors when they are carrying out their duties of management. Thus, the duty enables the shareholders to proceed against a negligent director; for example, where his negligent actions have caused loss to the company. The rules and standards which make up corporate governance are aimed at a much wider audience than just the shareholders. As mentioned above, the rules are intended to benefit 'stakeholders', that is all those who are affected directly or indirectly by a company's activities. It follows that the expression includes directors, shareholders, investors, subsidiaries, joint venture partners, employees, customers, communities, local neighbourhoods, suppliers and the environment. It can be seen, therefore, that (a) the law setting down the duty of care and (b) the rules and standards which make up corporate governance have different aims. Corporate governance is much wider than the duty of care. A director could act in breach of the duty of care and yet could still be complying with the principles of corporate governance.

6 Board structures

(1) The role of the Board

According to the UK Corporate Governance Code (2010):

'The board's role is to provide entrepreneurial leadership of the company within a framework of prudent and effective controls which enables risk to be assessed and managed. The board should set the company's strategic aims, ensure that the necessary financial and human resources are in place for the company to meet its objectives and review management performance. The board should set the company's values and standards and ensure that its obligations to its shareholders and others are understood and met.'

It follows that the board is responsible for the policy and direction of the company. Although executive power is vested in the board as a whole, in practice the board delegates executive authority to the Chief Executive Officer (or Managing Director). The board retains overall responsibility for management, however, and must monitor, intervene and even dismiss the managing director if necessary.

(2) Board structures

(a) Board structures in the United Kingdom

The following is largely derived from the Institute of Directors. In the United Kingdom, boards are usually **'unitary'**. This means that there is one board which is responsible for management and governance. Tricker (1996) classified unitary board structures into the following three groups:

(i) *The all-executive board.* This structure is commonly found in private and subsidiary companies. All the directors have a managerial role. The main criticism of such a board is that the directors appear to be monitoring and supervising their own performance.

(ii) *The majority executive board.* This structure is more sophisticated than (i) above and comprises a mixture of executive and non-executive directors. Such a board structure would tend to be found in a company that has been in existence for some time. An executive director is effectively an employee of the company and operates under a contract of service. Non-executive directors are not employees but operate under a contract for services. They often provide additional expertise or are appointed as nominees by investors of loan or share capital.

(iii) *The majority non-executive board.* This structure is found in some UK companies but is more commonly found in public companies in Australia and the United States.

There are no rules as to maximum or minimum numbers of directors. The role of executive directors at board level can give rise to problems because of the so-called 'two hat syndrome'. In other words, the executive directors are responsible for both management and governance. According to the Institute of Directors: 'This can give rise to some conflicts and complexities about what hat the director is wearing at a particular time. That is why the role of director needs to be clearly differentiated from that of the executive and the board meetings need to concentrate on governance issues – NOT management tasks.'

(b) **Board structures in the United States**

Boards are generally unitary in structure. For large public companies, the trend is towards the appointment of more independent outside directors in a similar way to the increase in importance of independent non-executive directors in the UK.

Supplementary reading

Board structures in France

In general, there are three types of board structures in France:

(i) Unitary boards (Conseil D'administration) with a combined Chairman and Chief Executive Officer (President Directeur General (PDG)). The roles may now be separated.

(ii) Unitary boards with separate functions for the Chairman and Chief Executive Officer.

(iii) Two-tier boards comprising a supervisory board (Conseil De Surveillance) with a Chairman and a management committee (Directoire) with a Chief Executive Officer (Directeur General).

A board must have at least three and not more than eighteen directors. In listed companies at least two-thirds of the board must be non-executive directors.

Board structures in Germany

In Germany, the two-tier board structure is used in many limited liability companies (GmbH) and all joint stock companies (AG). The two-tier board structure comprises:

(i) A Supervisory Board that supervises the management of the company (Aufsichstrat); and
(ii) A Management Board that manages the company (Vorstand).

The Supervisory Board must have at least 20 members who are elected by the shareholders. A major distinction between UK boards and German boards is the fact that in Germany employees are represented at board level. In many cases, the shareholders elect two-thirds of the board and the employees (and trade unions) one-third. In AG companies which employ 2000 or more, the employees elect one-half of the board and the shareholders the other half. The Chairman of the Supervisory Board is elected by the shareholders and usually has a casting vote.

The members of the Management Board are usually appointed for 5 years and are appointed, advised, supervised and dismissed by the Supervisory Board. The largest public listed companies have between five and ten members and the smaller companies three to five members.

The Management Board, as the name suggests, is responsible for independently managing the company, and undertakes to increase the value of the enterprise. It reports to the Supervisory Board in respect of business policy and future strategy, profitability, the state of the business and transactions which have a material impact upon profitability or liquidity.

Both the Supervisory and the Management Boards report on the company's corporate governance in the annual report.

7 Best practice – policies and procedure

Obviously, best practice is intricately tied up with the size and resources of the company in question. For listed companies, the most important issues of best practice are contained in the UK Corporate Governance Code. This was first issued in 1998 and has been updated at regular intervals since then, most recently September 2012.

The UK Corporate Governance Code can be seen in full on the FRC website at

https://www.frc.org.uk/Our-Work/Codes-Standards/Corporate-governance/UK-Corporate-Governance-Code.aspx

The Code is not a rigid (or enforced) set of rules. Instead it consists of principles (main and supporting) and provisions. In the UK all companies quoted on the stock exchange have to comply with the FSA listing rules and these include a requirement that all companies include in their annual report:

- a statement of how the company has applied the main principles set out in the Code; and
- a statement as to whether the company has complied with all relevant provisions set out in the Code.

The main provisions of the Code are:

Leadership

- Every company should be headed by an effective board with collective responsibility
- There should be a clear division of responsibilities between the Chairman and the Chief Executive
- No one individual should have unfettered powers of decision; and
- Non-executive directors should constructively challenge and help develop proposals on strategy.

Effectiveness

- The board should have the appropriate balance of skills, experience, independence and knowledge
- There should be a formal, rigorous and transparent procedure for the appointment of new directors
- All directors should receive induction and should regularly update and refresh their skills and knowledge
- The board should be supplied with quality and timely information to enable it to discharge its duties
- The board and individuals should be subject to a formal and rigorous annual evaluation of performance; and
- All directors should be submitted for re-election at regular intervals.

Accountability

- The board should present a fair, balanced and understandable assessment of the company's position and prospects
- The board is responsible for determining the nature and extent of the significant risks it is willing to take in achieving its strategic objectives
- The board should maintain sound risk management and internal control systems; and
- The board should establish formal and transparent arrangements for corporate reporting and risk management and internal control principles and for maintaining an appropriate relationship with the company's auditor.

Remuneration

- This should be sufficient to attract, retain and motivate directors of the quality required to run the company successfully, but should not be excessive
- This should be structured so as to link a significant proportion of the rewards to corporate and individual performance
- There should be a formal and transparent procedure for developing policy on executive remuneration; and
- No director should be involved in deciding his or her own remuneration.

Relations with Shareholders

- There should be a dialogue with shareholders based on the mutual understanding of objectives
- The board as a whole has responsibility for ensuring that a satisfactory dialogue with shareholders takes place; and
- The board should use the AGM to communicate with investors and to encourage their participation.

8 The Regulatory Governance Framework for UK Companies

The regulatory governance framework for UK companies consists of a combination of law (statutes, statutory instruments and case law) and codes of practice.

The law

The main UK statutes are the Companies Act 2006 ('The Act') the Company Directors Disqualification Act 1986 ('CDDA'), the Insolvency Act 1986 ('IA') and the Financial Services and Markets Act 2000.

Supplementary reading

The Insolvency Act 1986 (as amended by the Enterprise Act 2002 and supplemented by the Insolvency Rules which are contained in a statutory instrument) provides for individual and corporate insolvency, including methods of liquidation and alternatives such as administration orders. Other Acts provide for particular types of behaviour, such as the Criminal Justice Act 1993 which contains the rules relating to 'insider dealing'.

In addition, there is a growing body of European legislation which seeks to harmonise aspects of company law throughout the European Union. Examples are Council Directive 2004/25 on takeover bids and Council Directive 2004/109 on transparency requirements in relation to companies which are listed on a regulated stock exchange. The Stock Exchange Listing Regulations 1984 implemented three EU Directives in addition to the Exchange's existing listing rule. A company wishing to be admitted to the Official List of the Stock Exchange must first comply with the Stock Exchanges' requirements as to admission and disclosure, and thereafter the listing rules of the Financial Services Authority to regulate the listing of securities.

Supplementary reading

The Stock Exchange website states as follows:

"All companies are subject to Company Law, but publicly listed companies have to abide by additional regulations called the 'Listing Rules'. These were traditionally set by the Stock Exchange itself but are now administered by the Financial Services Authority (FSA) and effectively have the force of law."

The Listing Rules dictate such matters as the contents of the prospectus on an IPO, and on-going obligations such as the disclosure of price sensitive information, and communications on new share offers, rights issues, and potential or actual takeover bids for the company. The UK Corporate Governance Code is also now the responsibility of the FSA but is more advisory. Go to the FSA web site at www.fsa.gov.uk for more information.

A note on our response in June 2006 to the FSA consultation on the EU Transparency Directive and the UK Listing Rules is present in FSA_Listing_Rules_June2006.

A note on our submission to the proposed changes to the Listing Rules for Investment Companies made in February 2007 is present in Listing_Rules_CP06_21 – a press release on this subject is present at Press038_ListingRules.

Codes of practice

For the reasons explained above, the law is supplemented by a number of codes of practice. The most important of these for the purposes of this chapter is the UK Corporate Governance Code 2012. Other codes of practice also directly concern corporate governance such as the City Code on Takeovers and Mergers. As seen in Chapter 6, codes of practice are also produced by the professional bodies, in particular the CIMA Code of Ethics and Fundamental Principles which are discussed in detail in that chapter.

Supplementary reading: Chapter summary

At the end of this chapter, students should make sure that they understand the following:

- how corporate governance interacts with the law and ethics
- the history of corporate governance in the United Kingdom and overseas
- the distinction between director's duties and corporate governance
- know the different types of board structure
- know what constitutes best practice according to the UK Corporate Governance Code
- be able to describe the regulatory governance framework for companies in the United Kingdom.

9 Test your understanding questions

Test your understanding 1

Which of the following is *correct*?

A It is a criminal offence for listed companies to fail to comply with the UK Corporate Governance Code

B A listed public company has complied with the UK Corporate Governance Code if it produces a report explaining why it has not implemented its recommendations

C The UK Corporate Governance Code has no status and may be ignored by all companies

D A public company may be sued for breach of statutory duty if it fails to comply with the UK Corporate Governance Code

Test your understanding 2

To which of the following does a director owe duties of care and skill?

(i) The public at large.

(ii) The company's creditors.

(iii) The shareholders as a body (the company).

A (i) only

B (ii) only

C (i) and (iii) only

D (iii) only

Test your understanding 3

Which of the following are not represented at board level in the United Kingdom?

(i) Creditors.

(ii) Shareholders.

(iii) Employees.

A (i) only

B (i) and (ii) only

C (iii) only

D (i) and (iii) only

Test your understanding 4

Which of the following types of committee are not recommended by UK best practice?

A Planning Committee

B Nominations Committee

C Remuneration Committee

D Audit Committee

Test your understanding 5

Which of the following are examples of unitary board structures?

(i) An all-executive board.

(ii) A majority executive board.

(iii) A majority non-executive board.

A (i) only

B (i) and (ii) only

C (ii) and (iii) only

D (i), (ii) and (iii)

Test your understanding answers

Test your understanding 1

B

The UK Corporate Governance Code is not contained in any statute. The code is effectively a 'comply or explain' code. It follows that a company which explains why it has not taken up the recommendations of the Code would nonetheless be complying wlth lt.

Test your understanding 2

D

Directors' owe duties of care and skill to the shareholders as a body. The duty is enforceable by the company. Although the duties are not owed to the company's creditors, if the company should become insolvent then directors would owe fiduciary duties of good faith to creditors. Directors do not owe duties of care to the public at large.

Test your understanding 3

D

In the United Kingdom, directors are mainly concerned with the short- and long-term interests of the company's owners, that is the shareholders. In Germany, up to one-third of the board may be elected by the employees. In the United Kingdom, directors must take account of the interests of employees, but the latter are not represented as such.

Test your understanding 4

A

UK best practice, identified through various incarnations of corporate governance since the Cadbury Report of 1992, recommends the use of board committees made up wholly or mainly of non-executive directors. Audit, remuneration and nominations committees are recommended, but not planning committees.

Test your understanding 5

D

In the United Kingdom, companies generally utilise the unitary board system. The examples given, that is an all-executive board, a majority executive board and a majority non-executive board, are all types of unitary boards.

chapter

9

Appendix 1: CIMA Code of Ethics for Professional Accountants

Supplementary reading: Preface

CIMA CODE OF ETHICS FOR PROFESSIONAL ACCOUNTANTS

CIMA PREFACE

As Chartered Management Accountants CIMA members (and registered students) throughout the world have a duty to observe the highest standards of conduct and integrity, and to uphold the good standing and reputation of the profession. They must also refrain from any conduct which might discredit the profession. Members and registered students must have regard to these guidelines irrespective of their field of activity, of their contract of employment or of any other professional memberships they may hold.

CIMA upholds the aims and principles of equal opportunities and fundamental human rights worldwide, including the handling of personal information. The Institute promotes the highest ethical and business standards, and encourages its members to be good and responsible professionals. Good ethical behaviour may be above that required by the law. In a highly competitive, complex business world, it is essential that CIMA members sustain their integrity and remember the trust and confidence which is placed on them by whoever relies on their objectivity and professionalism. Members must avoid actions or situations which are inconsistent with their professional obligations. They should also be guided not merely by the terms but by the spirit of this Code.

CIMA members should conduct themselves with courtesy and consideration towards all with whom they have professional dealings and should not behave in a manner which could be considered offensive or discriminatory.

To ensure that CIMA members protect the good standing and reputation of the profession, members must report the fact to the Institute if they are convicted or disqualified from acting as an officer of a company or if they are subject to any sanction resulting from disciplinary action taken by any other body or authority.

CIMA has adopted the following code of ethics. Parts A and B of this code are based on the IFAC* Code of Ethics, that was developed with the help of input from CIMA and the global accountancy profession. Part C of the Code was developed in cooperation with the American Institute of Certified Public Accountants (AICPA).The AICPA and CIMA joined together to create a designation for management accountants, the Chartered Global Management Accountant (CGMA). The CGMA designation is designed to elevate management accounting and further emphasize its importance for businesses worldwide. Part C of the Code is designed to provide guidance to all CIMA members around the world who are members in business and professional accountants in business and, those who hold the CGMA credential. When a CGMA is also a member in public practice the CGMA should also comply with the applicable guidance of the CIMA Code of Ethics and apply the most restrictive provisions.

If a member cannot resolve an ethical issue by following this Code by consulting the ethics information on CIMA's website or by seeking guidance from CIMA's ethics helpline, he or she should seek legal advice as to both his or her legal rights and any obligations he or she may have. The CIMA Charter, Byelaws and Regulations give definitive rules on many matters.

For further information see: www.cimaglobal.com/ethics

Note: The CIMA Code of Ethics is a Law of the Institute (to which all members and registered students are required to comply) for the purpose of the definition of "misconduct" in Byelaw 1.

*International Federation of Accountants.

Parts A and B of the CIMA Code of Ethics are based on the IFAC Handbook of the Code of Ethics for Professional Accountants, of the International Ethics Standards Board of Accountants (IESBA), published by IFAC in July 2014 and is used with permission by IFAC.

Supplementary reading: Contents

CIMA CODE OF ETHICS FOR PROFESSIONAL ACCOUNTANTS

Contents

Supplementary reading: Sections 100 and 110

PART A – GENERAL APPLICATION OF THE CODE

SECTION 100

Introduction and fundamental principles

100.1 A distinguishing mark of the accountancy profession is its acceptance of the responsibility to act in the public interest. Therefore, a professional accountant's responsibility is not exclusively to satisfy the needs of an individual client or employer. In acting in the public interest, a professional accountant shall observe and comply with this Code. If a professional accountant is prohibited from complying with certain parts of this Code by law or regulation, the professional accountant shall comply with all other parts of this Code.

100.2 This Code contains three parts. Part A establishes the fundamental principles of professional ethics for professional accountants and provides a conceptual framework that professional accountants shall apply to:

(a) Identify threats to compliance with the fundamental principles

(b) Evaluate the significance of the threats identified; and

(c) Apply safeguards, when necessary, to eliminate the threats or reduce them to an acceptable level.

Safeguards are necessary when the professional accountant determines that the threats are not at a level at which a reasonable and informed third party would be likely to conclude, weighing all the specific facts and circumstances available to the professional accountant at that time, that compliance with the fundamental principles is not compromised. A professional accountant shall use professional judgement in applying this conceptual framework.

100.3 Parts B and C describe how the conceptual framework applies in certain situations. They provide examples of safeguards that may be appropriate to address threats to compliance with the fundamental principles. They also describe situations where safeguards are not available to address the threats, and consequently, the circumstance or relationship creating the threats shall be avoided. Part B applies to professional accountants in public practice. Part C applies to professional accountants in business. Professional accountants in public practice may also find Part C relevant to their particular circumstances.

100.4 The use of the word 'shall' in this Code imposes a requirement on the professional accountant or firm to comply with the specific provision in which 'shall' has been used. Compliance is required unless an exception is permitted by this Code.

Fundamental principles

100.5 A professional accountant shall comply with the following fundamental principles:

(a) Integrity – to be straightforward and honest in all professional and business relationships.

(b) Objectivity – to not allow bias, conflict of interest or undue influence of others to override professional or business judgements.

(c) Professional Competence and Due Care – to maintain professional knowledge and skill at the level required to ensure that a client or employer receives competent professional services based on current developments in practice, legislation and techniques and act diligently and in accordance with applicable technical and professional standards.

(d) Confidentiality – to respect the confidentiality of information acquired as a result of professional and business relationships and, therefore, not disclose any such information to third parties without proper and specific authority, unless there is a legal or professional right or duty to disclose, nor use the information for the personal advantage of the professional accountant or third parties.

(e) Professional Behaviour – to comply with relevant laws and regulations and avoid any action that discredits the profession.

Each of these fundamental principles is discussed in more detail in Sections 110 –150.

Conceptual framework approach

100.6 The circumstances in which professional accountants operate may create specific threats to compliance with the fundamental principles. It is impossible to define every situation that creates threats to compliance with the fundamental principles and specify the appropriate action. In addition, the nature of engagements and work assignments may differ and, consequently, different threats may be created, requiring the application of different safeguards. Therefore, this Code establishes a conceptual framework that requires a professional accountant to identify, evaluate, and address threats to compliance with the fundamental principles. The conceptual framework approach assists professional accountants in complying with the ethical requirements of this Code and meeting their responsibility to act in the public interest. It accommodates many variations in circumstances that create threats to compliance with the fundamental principles and can deter a professional accountant from concluding that a situation is permitted if it is not specifically prohibited.

100.7 When a professional accountant identifies threats to compliance with the fundamental principles and, based on an evaluation of those threats, determines that they are not at an acceptable level, the professional accountant shall determine whether appropriate safeguards are available and can be applied to eliminate the threats or reduce them to an acceptable level. In making that determination, the professional accountant shall exercise professional judgement and take into account whether a reasonable and informed third party, weighing all the specific facts and circumstances available to the professional accountant at the time, would be likely to conclude that the threats would be eliminated or reduced to an acceptable level by the application of the safeguards, such that compliance with the fundamental principles is not compromised.

100.8 A professional accountant shall evaluate any threats to compliance with the fundamental principles when the professional accountant knows, or could reasonably be expected to know, of circumstances or relationships that may compromise compliance with the fundamental principles.

100.9 A professional accountant shall take qualitative as well as quantitative factors into account when evaluating the significance of a threat. When applying the conceptual framework, a professional accountant may encounter situations in which threats cannot be eliminated or reduced to an acceptable level, either because the threat is too significant or because appropriate safeguards are not available or cannot be applied. In such situations, the professional accountant shall decline or discontinue the specific professional activity or service involved or, when necessary, resign from the engagement (in the case of a professional accountant in public practice) or the employing organisation (in the case of a professional accountant in business).

100.10 Sections 290 and 291 contain provisions with which a professional accountant shall comply if the professional accountant identifies a breach of an independence provision of the Code. If a professional accountant identifies a breach of any other provision of the Code, the professional accountant shall evaluate the significance of the breach and the impact of the accountant's ability to comply with the fundamental principles. The accountant shall take whatever actions that may be available, as soon as possible, to satisfactorily address the consequences of the breach. The accountant shall determine whether to report the breach, for example, to those who may have been affected by the breach, a member body, relevant regulator or oversight authority.

100.11 When a professional accountant encounters unusual circumstances in which the application of a specific requirement of the Code would result in a disproportionate outcome or an outcome that may not be in the public interest, it is recommended that the professional accountant consult with a member body or the relevant regulator.

Threats and Safeguards

100.12 Threats may be created by a broad range of relationships and circumstances. When a relationship or circumstance creates a threat, such a threat could compromise, or could be perceived to compromise, a professional accountant's compliance with the fundamental principles. A circumstance or relationship may create more than one threat, and a threat may affect compliance with more than one fundamental principle. Threats fall into one or more of the following categories:

(a) Self-interest threat – the threat that a financial or other interest will inappropriately influence the professional accountant's judgement or behaviour

(b) Self-review threat – the threat that a professional accountant will not appropriately evaluate the results of a previous judgement made or activity or service performed by the professional accountant, or by another individual within the professional accountant's firm or employing organisation, on which the accountant will rely when forming a judgement as part of providing a current activity or providing a current service

(c) Advocacy threat – the threat that a professional accountant will promote a client's or employer's position to the point that the professional accountant's objectivity is compromised

(d) Familiarity threat – the threat that due to a long or close relationship with a client or employer, a professional accountant will be too sympathetic to their interests or too accepting of their work; and

(e) Intimidation threat – the threat that a professional accountant will be deterred from acting objectively because of actual or perceived pressures, including attempts to exercise undue influence over the professional accountant. Parts B and C of this Code explain how these categories of threats may be created for professional accountants in public practice and professional accountants in business, respectively. Professional accountants in public practice may also find Part C relevant to their particular circumstances.

100.13 Safeguards are actions or other measures that may eliminate threats or reduce them to an acceptable level. They fall into two broad categories:

(a) Safeguards created by the profession, legislation or regulation; and

(b) Safeguards in the work environment.

100.14 Safeguards created by the profession, legislation or regulation include:

- Educational, training and experience requirements for entry into the profession.
- Continuing professional development requirements.
- Corporate governance regulations.
- Professional standards.
- Professional or regulatory monitoring and disciplinary procedures.
- External review by a legally empowered third party of the reports, returns, communications or information produced by a professional accountant.

100.15 Parts B and C of this Code discuss safeguards in the work environment for professional accountants in public practice and professional accountants in business, respectively.

100.16 Certain safeguards may increase the likelihood of identifying or deterring unethical behaviour. Such safeguards, which may be created by the accounting profession, legislation, regulation, or an employing organisation, include:

- Effective, well-publicised complaint systems operated by the employing organisation, the profession or a regulator, which enable colleagues, employers and members of the public to draw attention to unprofessional or unethical behaviour.
- An explicitly stated duty to report breaches of ethical requirements.

Conflicts of interest

100.17 A professional accountant may be faced with a conflict of interest when undertaking a professional activity. A conflict of interest creates a threat to objectivity and may create threats to the other fundamental principles. Such threats may be created when:

- The professional accountant undertakes a professional activity related to a particular matter for two or more parties whose interest with respect to that matter are in conflict; or
- The interests of the professional accountant with respect to a particular matter and the interests of a party for whom the professional accountant provides a professional activity related to that matter are in conflict.

100.18 Parts B and C of this Code discuss conflicts of interest for professional accountants in public practice and professional accountants in business, respectively.

Ethical conflict resolution

100.19 A professional accountant may be required to resolve a conflict in complying with the fundamental principles.

100.20 When initiating either a formal or informal conflict resolution process, the following factors, either individually or together with other factors, may be relevant to the resolution process:

(a) Relevant facts

(b) Ethical issues involved

(c) Fundamental principles related to the matter in question

(d) Established internal procedures; and

(e) Alternative courses of action.

Having considered the relevant factors, a professional accountant shall determine the appropriate course of action, weighing the consequences of each possible course of action. If the matter remains unresolved, the professional accountant may wish to consult with other appropriate persons within the firm or employing organisation for help in obtaining resolution.

100.21 Where a matter involves a conflict with, or within, an organisation, a professional accountant shall determine whether to consult with those charged with governance of the organisation, such as the board of directors or the audit committee.

100.22 It may be in the best interests of the professional accountant to document the substance of the issue, the details of any discussions held, and the decisions made concerning that issue.

100.23 If a significant conflict cannot be resolved, a professional accountant may consider obtaining professional advice from the relevant professional body or from legal advisors. The professional accountant generally can obtain guidance on ethical issues without breaching the fundamental principle of confidentiality if the matter is discussed with the relevant professional body on an anonymous basis or with a legal advisor under the protection of legal privilege. Instances in which the professional accountant may consider obtaining legal advice vary. For example, a professional accountant may have encountered a fraud, the reporting of which could breach the professional accountant's responsibility to respect confidentiality. The professional accountant may consider obtaining legal advice in that instance to determine whether there is a requirement to report.

100.24 If, after exhausting all relevant possibilities, the ethical conflict remains unresolved, a professional accountant shall, where possible, refuse to remain associated with the matter creating the conflict. The professional accountant shall determine whether, in the circumstances, it is appropriate to withdraw from the engagement team or specific assignment, or to resign altogether from the engagement, the firm or the employing organisation.

Communicating with those charged with governance

100.25 When communicating with those charged with governance in accordance with the provisions of this Code, the professional accountant or firm shall determine, having regard to the nature and importance of the particular circumstances and matter to be communicated, the appropriate person(s) within the entity's governance structure with whom to communicate. If the professional accountant or firm communicates with a subgroup of those charged with governance, for example, an audit committee or an individual, the professional accountant or firm shall determine whether communication with all of those charged with governance is also necessary so that they are adequately informed.

SECTION 110

Integrity

110.1 The principle of integrity imposes an obligation on all professional accountants to be straightforward and honest in all professional and business relationships. Integrity also implies fair dealing and truthfulness.

110.2 A professional accountant shall not knowingly be associated with reports, returns, communications or other information where the professional accountant believes that the information:

(a) Contains a materially false or misleading statement

(b) Contains statements or information furnished recklessly; or

(c) Omits or obscures information required to be included where such omission or obscurity would be misleading.

When a professional accountant becomes aware that the accountant has been associated with such information, the accountant shall take steps to be disassociated from that information.

110.3 A professional accountant will be deemed not to be in breach of paragraph 110.2 if the professional accountant provides a modified report in respect of a matter contained in paragraph 110.2.

Supplementary reading: Sections 120 to 150

SECTION 120

Objectivity

120.1 The principle of objectivity imposes an obligation on all professional accountants not to compromise their professional or business judgement because of bias, conflict of interest or the undue influence of others.

120.2 A professional accountant may be exposed to situations that may impair objectivity. It is impracticable to define and prescribe all such situations. A professional accountant shall not perform a professional service if a circumstance or relationship biases or unduly influences the accountant's professional judgement with respect to that service.

SECTION 130

Professional competence and due care

130.1 The principle of professional competence and due care imposes the following obligations on all professional accountants:

(a) To maintain professional knowledge and skill at the level required to ensure that clients or employers receive competent professional service; and

(b) To act diligently in accordance with applicable technical and professional standards when providing professional services.

130.2 Competent professional service requires the exercise of sound judgement in applying professional knowledge and skill in the performance of such service. Professional competence may be divided into two separate phases:

(a) Attainment of professional competence; and

(b) Maintenance of professional competence.

130.3 The maintenance of professional competence requires a continuing awareness and an understanding of relevant technical, professional and business developments. Continuing professional development enables a professional accountant to develop and maintain the capabilities to perform competently within the professional environment.

130.4 Diligence encompasses the responsibility to act in accordance with the requirements of an assignment, carefully, thoroughly and on a timely basis.

130.5 A professional accountant shall take reasonable steps to ensure that those working under the professional accountant's authority in a professional capacity have appropriate training and supervision.

130.6 Where appropriate, a professional accountant shall make clients, employers or other users of the accountant's professional services or activities aware of the limitations inherent in the services or activities.

SECTION 140

Confidentiality

140.1 The principle of confidentiality imposes an obligation on all professional accountants to refrain from:

(a) Disclosing outside the firm or employing organisation confidential information acquired as a result of professional and business relationships without proper and specific authority or unless there is a legal or professional right or duty to disclose; and

(b) Using confidential information acquired as a result of professional and business relationships to their personal advantage or the advantage of third parties.

140.2 A professional accountant shall maintain confidentiality, including in a social environment, being alert to the possibility of inadvertent disclosure, particularly to a close business associate or a close or immediate family member.

140.3 A professional accountant shall maintain confidentiality of information disclosed by a prospective client or employer.

140.4 A professional accountant shall maintain confidentiality of information within the firm or employing organisation.

140.5 A professional accountant shall take reasonable steps to ensure that staff under the professional accountant's control and persons from whom advice and assistance is obtained respect the professional accountant's duty of confidentiality.

140.6 The need to comply with the principle of confidentiality continues even after the end of relationships between a professional accountant and a client or employer. When a professional accountant changes employment or acquires a new client, the professional accountant is entitled to use prior experience. The professional accountant shall not, however, use or disclose any confidential information either acquired or received as a result of a professional or business relationship.

140.7 The following are circumstances where professional accountants are or may be required to disclose confidential information or when such disclosure may be appropriate:

(a) Disclosure is permitted by law and is authorised by the client or the employer

(b) Disclosure is required by law, for example:

  (i) Production of documents or other provision of evidence in the course of legal proceedings; or

  (ii) Disclosure to the appropriate public authorities of infringements of the law that come to light; an

(c) There is a professional duty or right to disclose, when not prohibited by law:

  (i) To comply with the quality review of a member body or professional body

  (ii) To respond to an inquiry or investigation by a member body or regulatory body

  (iii) To protect the professional interests of a professional accountant in legal proceedings; or

  (iv) To comply with technical standards and ethics requirements.

140.8 In deciding whether to disclose confidential information, relevant factors to consider include:

(a) Whether the interests of all parties, including third parties whose interests may be affected, could be harmed if the client or employer consents to the disclosure of information by the professional accountant

(b) Whether all the relevant information is known and substantiated, to the extent it is practicable; when the situation involves unsubstantiated facts, incomplete information or unsubstantiated conclusions, professional judgement shall be used in determining the type of disclosure to be made, if any

(c) The type of communication that is expected and to whom it is addressed; and

(d) Whether the parties to whom the communication is addressed are appropriate recipients.

SECTION 150

Professional behaviour

150.1 The principle of professional behaviour imposes an obligation on all professional accountants to comply with relevant laws and regulations and avoid any action that the professional accountant knows or should know may discredit the profession. This includes actions that a reasonable and informed third party, weighing all the specific facts and circumstances available to the professional accountant at that time, would be likely to conclude adversely affects the good reputation of the profession.

150.2 In marketing and promoting themselves and their work, professional accountants shall not bring the profession into disrepute. Professional accountants shall be honest and truthful and not:

(a) Make exaggerated claims for the services they are able to offer, the qualifications they possess, or experience they have gained; or

(b) Make disparaging references or unsubstantiated comparisons to the work of others.

Supplementary reading: Sections 200 and 210

PART B – PROFESSIONAL ACCOUNTANTS IN PUBLIC PRACTICE

Section 200 Introduction
Section 210 Professional appointment
Section 220 Conflicts of Interest
Section 230 Second opinions
Section 240 Fees and other types of remuneration
Section 250 Marketing professional services
Section 260 Gifts and Hospitality
Section 270 Custody of client assets
Section 280 Objectivity – All services
Section 290 Independence – Audit and Review engagements: see Annex 1
Section 291 Independence – Other assurance engagements: see Annex 1

NOTE: CIMA Code of Ethics: Annex 1

Sections 290 and 291 address the independence requirements for audit, review and other assurance engagements and apply a conceptual framework approach. They also include commentary on the independence requirements and the effective date and transitional provisions for public interest entities, partner rotation, non-assurance services, fees and compensation and evaluation policies.

SECTION 200

Introduction

200.1 This Part of the Code describes how the conceptual framework contained in Part A applies in certain situations to professional accountants in public practice. This Part does not describe all of the circumstances and relationships that could be encountered by a professional accountant in public practice that create or may create threats to compliance with the fundamental principles. Therefore, the professional accountant in public practice is encouraged to be alert for such circumstances and relationships.

200.2 A professional accountant in public practice shall not knowingly engage in any business, occupation, or activity that impairs or might impair integrity, objectivity or the good reputation of the profession and as a result would be incompatible with the fundamental principles.

Threats and Safeguards

200.3 Compliance with the fundamental principles may potentially be threatened by a broad range of circumstances and relationships. The nature and significance of the threats may differ depending on whether they arise in relation to the provision of services to an audit client and whether the audit client is a public interest entity, to an assurance client that is not an audit client, or to a non-assurance client.

Threats fall into one or more of the following categories:

(a) Self-interest
(b) Self-review
(c) Advocacy
(d) Familiarity; and
(e) Intimidation.

These threats are discussed further in Part A of this Code.

200.4 Examples of circumstances that create self-interest threats for a professional accountant in public practice include:

- A member of the assurance team having a direct financial interest in the assurance client.
- A firm having undue dependence on total fees from a client.
- A member of the assurance team having a significant close business relationship with an assurance client.
- A firm being concerned about the possibility of losing a significant client.
- A member of the audit team entering into employment negotiations with the audit client.
- A firm entering into a contingent fee arrangement relating to an assurance engagement.
- A professional accountant discovering a significant error when evaluating the results of a previous professional service performed by a member of the professional accountant's firm.

200.5 Examples of circumstances that create self-review threats for a professional accountant in public practice include:

- A firm issuing an assurance report on the effectiveness of the operation of financial systems after designing or implementing the systems.

- A firm having prepared the original data used to generate records that are the subject matter of the assurance engagement.
- A member of the assurance team being, or having recently been, a director or officer of the client.
- A member of the assurance team being, or having recently been, employed by the client in a position to exert significant influence over the subject matter of the engagement.
- The firm performing a service for an assurance client that directly affects the subject matter information of the assurance engagement.

200.6 Examples of circumstances that create advocacy threats for a professional accountant in public practice include:

- The firm promoting shares in an audit client.
- A professional accountant acting as an advocate on behalf of an audit client in litigation or disputes with third parties.

200.7 Examples of circumstances that create familiarity threats for a professional accountant in public practice include:

- A member of the engagement team having a close or immediate family member who is a director or officer of the client.
- A member of the engagement team having a close or immediate family member who is an employee of the client who is in a position to exert significant influence over the subject matter of the engagement.
- A director or officer of the client or an employee in a position to exert significant influence over the subject matter of the engagement having recently served as the engagement partner.
- A professional accountant accepting gifts or preferential treatment from a client, unless the value is trivial or inconsequential.
- Senior personnel having a long association with the assurance client.

200.8 Examples of circumstances that create intimidation threats for a professional accountant in public practice include:

- A firm being threatened with dismissal from a client engagement.
- An audit client indicating that it will not award a planned non-assurance contract to the firm if the firm continues to disagree with the client's accounting treatment for a particular transaction.
- A firm being threatened with litigation by the client.
- A firm being pressured to reduce inappropriately the extent of work performed in order to reduce fees.

- A professional accountant feeling pressured to agree with the judgement of a client employee because the employee has more expertise on the matter in question.
- A professional accountant being informed by a partner of the firm that a planned promotion will not occur unless the accountant agrees with an audit client's inappropriate accounting treatment.

200.9 Safeguards that may eliminate or reduce threats to an acceptable level fall into two broad categories:

(a) Safeguards created by the profession, legislation or regulation; and

(b) Safeguards in the work environment.

Examples of safeguards created by the profession, legislation or regulation are described in paragraph

100.14 of Part A of this Code.

200.10 A professional accountant in public practice shall exercise judgement to determine how best to deal with threats that are not at an acceptable level, whether by applying safeguards to eliminate the threat or reduce it to an acceptable level or by terminating or declining the relevant engagement. In exercising this judgement, a professional accountant in public practice shall consider whether a reasonable and informed third party, weighing all the specific facts and circumstances available to the professional accountant at that time, would be likely to conclude that the threats would be eliminated or reduced to an acceptable level by the application of safeguards, such that compliance with the fundamental principles is not compromised. This consideration will be affected by matters such as the significance of the threat, the nature of the engagement and the structure of the firm.

200.11 In the work environment, the relevant safeguards will vary depending on the circumstances. Work environment safeguards comprise firm-wide safeguards and engagement-specific safeguards.

200.12 Examples of firm-wide safeguards in the work environment include:

- Leadership of the firm that stresses the importance of compliance with the fundamental principles.
- Leadership of the firm that establishes the expectation that members of an assurance team will act in the public interest.
- Policies and procedures to implement and monitor quality control of engagements.

- Documented policies regarding the need to identify threats to compliance with the fundamental principles, evaluate the significance of those threats, and apply safeguards to eliminate or reduce the threats to an acceptable level or, when appropriate safeguards are not available or cannot be applied, terminate or decline the relevant engagement.
- Documented internal policies and procedures requiring compliance with the fundamental principles.
- Policies and procedures that will enable the identification of interests or relationships between the firm or members of engagement teams and clients.
- Policies and procedures to monitor and, if necessary, manage the reliance on revenue received from a single client.
- Using different partners and engagement teams with separate reporting lines for the provision of non-assurance services to an assurance client.
- Policies and procedures to prohibit individuals who are not members of an engagement team from inappropriately influencing the outcome of the engagement.
- Timely communication of a firm's policies and procedures, including any changes to them, to all partners and professional staff, and appropriate training and education on such policies and procedures.
- Designating a member of senior management to be responsible for overseeing the adequate functioning of the firm's quality control system.
- Advising partners and professional staff of assurance clients and related entities from which independence is required.
- A disciplinary mechanism to promote compliance with policies and procedures.
- Published policies and procedures to encourage and empower staff to communicate to senior levels within the firm any issue relating to compliance with the fundamental principles that concerns them.

200.13 Examples of engagement-specific safeguards in the work environment include:

- Having a professional accountant who was not involved with the non-assurance service review the non-assurance work performed or otherwise advise as necessary.
- Having a professional accountant who was not a member of the assurance team review the assurance work performed or otherwise advise as necessary.
- Consulting an independent third party, such as a committee of independent directors, a professional regulatory body or another professional accountant.

- Discussing ethical issues with those charged with governance of the client.
- Disclosing to those charged with governance of the client the nature of services provided and extent of fees charged.
- Involving another firm to perform or re-perform part of the engagement.
- Rotating senior assurance team personnel.

200.14 Depending on the nature of the engagement, a professional accountant in public practice may also be able to rely on safeguards that the client has implemented. However it is not possible to rely solely on such safeguards to reduce threats to an acceptable level.

200.15 Examples of safeguards within the client's systems and procedures include:

- The client requires persons other than management to ratify or approve the appointment of a firm to perform an engagement.
- The client has competent employees with experience and seniority to make managerial decisions.
- The client has implemented internal procedures that ensure objective choices in commissioning non-assurance engagements.
- The client has a corporate governance structure that provides appropriate oversight and communications regarding the firm's services.

SECTION 210

Professional appointment

Client acceptance

210.1 Before accepting a new client relationship, a professional accountant in public practice shall determine whether acceptance would create any threats to compliance with the fundamental principles. Potential threats to integrity or professional behaviour may be created from, for example, questionable issues associated with the client (its owners, management or activities).

210.2 Client issues that, if known, could threaten compliance with the fundamental principles include, for example, client involvement in illegal activities (such as money laundering), dishonesty or questionable financial reporting practices.

210.3 A professional accountant in public practice shall evaluate the significance of any threats and apply safeguards when necessary to eliminate them or reduce them to an acceptable level. Examples of such safeguards include:

- Obtaining knowledge and understanding of the client, its owners, managers and those responsible for its governance and business activities; or
- Securing the client's commitment to improve corporate governance practices or internal controls.

210.4 Where it is not possible to reduce the threats to an acceptable level, the professional accountant in public practice shall decline to enter into the client relationship.

210.5 It is recommended that a professional accountant in public practice periodically review acceptance decisions for recurring client engagements.

Engagement acceptance

210.6 The fundamental principle of professional competence and due care imposes an obligation on a professional accountant in public practice to provide only those services that the professional accountant in public practice is competent to perform. Before accepting a specific client engagement, a professional accountant in public practice shall determine whether acceptance would create any threats to compliance with the fundamental principles. For example, a self-interest threat to professional competence and due care is created if the engagement team does not possess, or cannot acquire, the competencies necessary to properly carry out the engagement.

210.7 A professional accountant in public practice shall evaluate the significance of threats and apply safeguards, when necessary, to eliminate them or reduce them to an acceptable level.

Examples of such safeguards include:

- Acquiring an appropriate understanding of the nature of the client's business, the complexity of its operations, the specific requirements of the engagement and the purpose, nature and scope of the work to be performed.
- Acquiring knowledge of relevant industries or subject matters.
- Possessing or obtaining experience with relevant regulatory or reporting requirements.
- Assigning sufficient staff with the necessary competencies.

- Using experts where necessary.
- Agreeing on a realistic time frame for the performance of the engagement.
- Complying with quality control policies and procedures designed to provide reasonable assurance that specific engagements are accepted only when they can be performed competently.

210.8 When a professional accountant in public practice intends to rely on the advice or work of an expert, the professional accountant in public practice shall determine whether such reliance is warranted. Factors to consider include: reputation, expertise, resources available and applicable professional and ethical standards. Such information may be gained from prior association with the expert or from consulting others.

Changes in a professional appointment

210.9 A professional accountant in public practice who is asked to replace another professional accountant in public practice, or who is considering tendering for an engagement currently held by another professional accountant in public practice, shall determine whether there are any reasons, professional or otherwise, for not accepting the engagement, such as circumstances that create threats to compliance with the fundamental principles that cannot be eliminated or reduced to an acceptable level by the application of safeguards. For example, there may be a threat to professional competence and due care if a professional accountant in public practice accepts the engagement before knowing all the pertinent facts.

210.10 A professional accountant in public practice shall evaluate the significance of any threats. Depending on the nature of the engagement, this may require direct communication with the existing accountant to establish the facts and circumstances regarding the proposed change so that the professional accountant in public practice can decide whether it would be appropriate to accept the engagement. For example, the apparent reasons for the change in appointment may not fully reflect the facts and may indicate disagreements with the existing accountant that may influence the decision to accept the appointment.

210.11 Safeguards shall be applied when necessary to eliminate any threats or reduce them to an acceptable level. Examples of such safeguards include:

- When replying to requests to submit tenders, stating in the tender that, before accepting the engagement, contact with the existing accountant will be requested so that inquiries may be made as to whether there are any professional or other reasons why the appointment should not be accepted

- Asking the existing accountant to provide known information on any facts or circumstances that, in the existing accountant's opinion, the proposed accountant needs to be aware of before deciding whether to accept the engagement; or
- Obtaining necessary information from other sources.

When the threats cannot be eliminated or reduced to an acceptable level through the application of safeguards, a professional accountant in public practice shall, unless there is satisfaction as to necessary facts by other means, decline the engagement.

210.12 A professional accountant in public practice may be asked to undertake work that is complementary or additional to the work of the existing accountant. Such circumstances may create threats to professional competence and due care resulting from, for example, a lack of or incomplete information. The significance of any threats shall be evaluated and safeguards applied when necessary to eliminate the threat or reduce it to an acceptable level. An example of such a safeguard is notifying the existing accountant of the proposed work, which would give the existing accountant the opportunity to provide any relevant information needed for the proper conduct of the work.

210.13 An existing accountant is bound by confidentiality. Whether that professional accountant is permitted or required to discuss the affairs of a client with a proposed accountant will depend on the nature of the engagement and on:

(a) Whether the client's permission to do so has been obtained; or

(b) The legal or ethical requirements relating to such communications and disclosure, which may vary by jurisdiction.

Circumstances where the professional accountant is or may be required to disclose confidential information or where such disclosure may otherwise be appropriate are set out in Section 140 of Part A of this Code.

210.14 A professional accountant in public practice will generally need to obtain the client's permission, preferably in writing, to initiate discussion with an existing accountant. Once that permission is obtained, the existing accountant shall comply with relevant legal and other regulations governing such requests. Where the existing accountant provides information, it shall be provided honestly and unambiguously. If the proposed accountant is unable to communicate with the existing accountant, the proposed accountant shall take reasonable steps to obtain information about any possible threats by other means, such as through inquiries of third parties or background investigations of senior management or those charged with governance of the client.

Supplementary reading: Sections 220 to 280

SECTION 220

Conflicts of Interest

220.1 A professional accountant in public practice may be faced with a conflict of interest when performing a professional service. A conflict of interest creates a threat to objectivity and may create threats to the other fundamental principles. Such threats may be created when:

- The professional accountant provides a professional service related to a particular matter for two or more clients whose interests with respect to that matter are in conflict

  or

- The interests of the professional accountant with respect to a particular matter and the interests of the client for whom the professional accountant provides a professional service related to that matter are in conflict.

A professional accountant shall not allow a conflict of interest to compromise professional or business judgement.

When the professional service is an assurance service, compliance with the fundamental principle of objectivity also requires being independent of assurance clients in accordance with Sections 290 or 291 as appropriate.

220.2 Examples of situations in which conflicts of interest may arise include:

- Providing a transaction advisory service to a client seeking to acquire an audit client of the firm, where the firm has obtained confidential information during the course of the audit that may be relevant to the transaction.
- Advising two clients at the same time who are competing to acquire the same company where the advice might be relevant to the parties' competitive positions.
- Providing services to both a vendor and a purchaser in relation to the same transaction.
- Preparing valuations of assets for two parties who are in an adversarial position with respect to the assets.
- Representing two clients regarding the same matter who are in a legal dispute with each other, such as during divorce proceedings or the dissolution of a partnership.

- Providing an assurance report for a licensor on royalties due under a license agreement when at the same time advising the licensee of the correctness of the amounts payable.
- Advising a client to invest in a business in which, for example, the spouse of the professional accountant in public practice has a financial interest.
- Providing strategic advice to a client on its competitive position while having a joint venture or similar interest with a major competitor of the client.
- Advising a client on the acquisition of a business which the firm is also interested in acquiring.
- Advising a client on the purchase of a product or service while having a royalty or commission agreement with one of the potential vendors of that product or service.

220.3 When identifying and evaluating the interests and relationships that might create a conflict of interest and implementing safeguards, when necessary, to eliminate or reduce any threat to compliance with the fundamental principles to an acceptable level, a professional accountant in public practice shall exercise professional judgement and take into account whether a reasonable and informed third party, weighing all the specific facts and circumstances available to the professional accountant at the time, would be likely to conclude that compliance with the fundamental principles is not compromised.

220.4 When addressing conflicts of interest, including making disclosures or sharing information within the firm or network and seeking guidance of third parties, the professional accountant in public practice shall remain alert to the fundamental principle of confidentiality.

220.5 If the threat created by a conflict of interest is not at an acceptable level, the professional accountant in public practice shall apply safeguards to eliminate the threat or reduce it to an acceptable level. If safeguards cannot reduce the threat to an acceptable level, the professional accountant shall decline to perform or shall discontinue professional services that would result in the conflict of interest; or shall terminate relevant relationships or dispose of relevant interests to eliminate the threat or reduce it to an acceptable level.

220.6 Before accepting a new client relationship, engagement, or business relationship, a professional accountant in public practice shall take reasonable steps to identify circumstances that might create a conflict of interest, including identification of:

- The nature of the relevant interests and relationships between the parties involved; and
- The nature of the service and its implication for relevant parties.

The nature of the services and the relevant interests and relationships may change during the course of the engagement. This is particularly true when a professional accountant is asked to conduct an engagement in a situation that may become adversarial, even though the parties who engage the professional accountant may not initially be involved in a dispute. The professional accountant shall remain alert to such changes for the purpose of identifying circumstances that might create a conflict of interest.

220.7 For the purpose of identifying interests and relationships that might create a conflict of interest, having an effective conflict identification process assists a professional accountant in public practice to identify actual or potential conflicts of interest prior to determining whether to accept an engagement and throughout an engagement. This includes matters identified by external parties, for example clients or potential clients. The earlier an actual or potential conflict of interest is identified, the greater the likelihood of the professional accountant being able to apply safeguards, when necessary, to eliminate the threat to objectivity and any threat to compliance with other fundamental principles or reduce it to an acceptable level. The process to identify actual or potential conflicts of interest will depend on such factors as:

- The nature of the professional services provided.
- The size of the firm.
- The size and nature of the client base.
- The structure of the firm, for example, the number and geographic location of offices.

220.8 If the firm is a member of a network, conflict identification shall include any conflicts of interest that the professional accountant in public practice has reason to believe may exist or might arise due to interests and relationships of a network firm. Reasonable steps to identify such interests and relationships involving a network firm will depend on factors such as the nature of the professional services provided, the clients served by the network and the geographic locations of all relevant parties.

220.9 If a conflict of interest is identified, the professional accountant in public practice shall evaluate:

- The significance of relevant interests or relationships; and
- The significance of the threats created by performing the professional service or services. In general, the more direct the connection between the professional service and the matter on which the parties' interests are in conflict, the more significant the threat to objectivity and compliance with the other fundamental principles will be.

220.10 The professional accountant in public practice shall apply safeguards, when necessary, to eliminate the threats to compliance with the fundamental principles created by the conflict of interest or reduce them to an acceptable level. Examples of safeguards include:

- Implementing mechanisms to prevent unauthorised disclosure of confidential information when performing professional services related to a particular matter for two or more clients whose interests with respect to that matter are in conflict. This could include:
  - Using separate engagement teams who are provided with clear policies and procedures on maintaining confidentiality.
  - Creating separate areas of practice for specialty functions within the firm, which may act as a barrier to the passing of confidential client information from one practice area to another within a firm.
  - Establishing policies and procedures to limit access to client files, the use of confidentiality agreements signed by employees and partners of the firm and/or the physical and electronic separation of confidential information.
- Regular review of the application of safeguards by a senior individual not involved with the client engagement or engagements.
- Having a professional accountant who is not involved in providing the service or otherwise affected by the conflict, review the work performed to assess whether the key judgements and conclusions are appropriate.
- Consulting with third parties, such as a professional body, legal counsel or another professional accountant.

220.11 In addition, it is generally necessary to disclose the nature of the conflict of interest and the related safeguards, if any, to clients affected by the conflict and, when safeguards are required to reduce the threat to an acceptable level, to obtain their consent to the professional accountant in public practice performing the professional services. Disclosure and consent may take different forms, for example:

- General disclosure to clients of circumstances where the professional accountant, in keeping with common commercial practice, does not provide services exclusively for any one client (for example, in a particular service in a particular market sector) in order for the client to provide general consent accordingly. Such disclosure might, for example, be made in the professional accountant's standard terms and conditions for the engagement.
- Specific disclosure to affected clients of the circumstances of the particular conflict, including a detailed presentation of the situation and a comprehensive explanation of any planned safeguards and the risks involved, sufficient to enable the client to make an informed decision with respect to the matter and to provide explicit consent accordingly.

- In certain circumstances, consent may be implied by the client's conduct where the professional accountant has sufficient evidence to conclude that clients know the circumstances at the outset and have accepted the conflict of interest if they do not raise an objection to the existence of the conflict.

The professional accountant shall determine whether the nature and significance of the conflict of interest is such that specific disclosure and explicit consent is necessary. For this purpose, the professional accountant shall exercise professional judgement in weighing the outcome of the evaluation of the circumstances that create a conflict of interest, including the parties that might be affected, the nature of the issues that might arise and the potential for the particular matter to develop in an unexpected manner.

220.12 Where a professional accountant in public practice has requested explicit consent from a client and that consent has been refused by the client, the professional accountant shall decline to perform or shall discontinue professional services that would result in the conflict of interest; or shall terminate relevant relationships or dispose of relevant interests to eliminate the threat or reduce it to an acceptable level, such that consent can be obtained, after applying any additional safeguards if necessary.

220.13 When disclosure is verbal, or consent is verbal or implied, the professional accountant in public practice is encouraged to document the nature of the circumstances giving rise to the conflict of interest, the safeguards applied to reduce the threats to an acceptable level and the consent obtained.

220.14 In certain circumstances, making specific disclosure for the purpose of obtaining explicit consent would result in a breach of confidentiality. Examples of such circumstances may include:

- Performing a transaction-related service for a client in connection with a hostile takeover of another client of the firm.
- Performing a forensic investigation for a client in connection with a suspected fraudulent act where the firm has confidential information obtained through having performed a professional service for another client who might be involved in the fraud.

The firm shall not accept or continue an engagement under such circumstances unless the following conditions are met:

- The firm does not act in an advocacy role for one client where this requires the firm to assume an adversarial position against the other client with respect to the same matter

- Specific mechanisms are in place to prevent disclosure of confidential information between the engagement teams serving the two clients; and
- The firm is satisfied that a reasonable and informed third party, weighing all the specific facts and circumstances available to the professional accountant in public practice at the time, would be likely to conclude that it is appropriate for the firm to accept or continue the engagement because a restriction on the firm's ability to provide the service would produce a disproportionate adverse outcome for the clients or other relevant third parties.

The professional accountant shall document the nature of the circumstances, including the role that the professional the professional accountant is to undertake, the specific mechanisms in place to prevent disclosure of information between the engagement teams serving the two clients and the rationale for the conclusion that it is appropriate to accept the engagement.

SECTION 230

Second opinions

230.1 Situations where a professional accountant in public practice is asked to provide a second opinion on the application of accounting, auditing, reporting or other standards or principles to specific circumstances or transactions by or on behalf of a company or an entity that is not an existing client may create threats to compliance with the fundamental principles. For example, there may be a threat to professional competence and due care in circumstances where the second opinion is not based on the same set of facts that were made available to the existing accountant or is based on inadequate evidence. The existence and significance of any threat will depend on the circumstances of the request and all the other available facts and assumptions relevant to the expression of a professional judgement.

230.2 When asked to provide such an opinion, a professional accountant in public practice shall evaluate the significance of any threats and apply safeguards when necessary to eliminate them or reduce them to an acceptable level. Examples of such safeguards include seeking client permission to contact the existing accountant, describing the limitations surrounding any opinion in communications with the client and providing the existing accountant with a copy of the opinion.

230.3 If the company or entity seeking the opinion will not permit communication with the existing accountant, a professional accountant in public practice shall determine whether, taking all the circumstances into account, it is appropriate to provide the opinion sought.

SECTION 240

Fees and other types of remuneration

240.1 When entering into negotiations regarding professional services, a professional accountant in public practice may quote whatever fee is deemed appropriate. The fact that one professional accountant in public practice may quote a fee lower than another is not in itself unethical. Nevertheless, there may be threats to compliance with the fundamental principles arising from the level of fees quoted. For example, a self-interest threat to professional competence and due care is created if the fee quoted is so low that it may be difficult to perform the engagement in accordance with applicable technical and professional standards for that price.

240.2 The existence and significance of any threats created will depend on factors such as the level of fee quoted and the services to which it applies. The significance of any threat shall be evaluated and safeguards applied when necessary to eliminate the threat or reduce it to an acceptable level. Examples of such safeguards include:

- Making the client aware of the terms of the engagement and, in particular, the basis on which fees are charged and which services are covered by the quoted fee.
- Assigning appropriate time and qualified staff to the task.

240.3 Contingent fees are widely used for certain types of non-assurance engagements. They may, however, create threats to compliance with the fundamental principles in certain circumstances. They may create a self-interest threat to objectivity. The existence and significance of such threats will depend on factors including:

- The nature of the engagement.
- The range of possible fee amounts.
- The basis for determining the fee.
- Whether the outcome or result of the transaction is to be reviewed by an independent third party.

240.4 The significance of any such threats shall be evaluated and safeguards applied when necessary to eliminate or reduce them to an acceptable level. Examples of such safeguards include:

- An advance written agreement with the client as to the basis of remuneration.

- Disclosure to intended users of the work performed by the professional accountant in public practice and the basis of remuneration.
- Quality control policies and procedures.
- Review by an independent third party of the work performed by the professional accountant in public practice.

240.5 In certain circumstances, a professional accountant in public practice may receive a referral fee or commission relating to a client. For example, where the professional accountant in public practice does not provide the specific service required, a fee may be received for referring a continuing client to another professional accountant in public practice or other expert. A professional accountant in public practice may receive a commission from a third party (for example, a software vendor) in connection with the sale of goods or services to a client. Accepting such a referral fee or commission creates a self-interest threat to objectivity and professional competence and due care.

240.6 A professional accountant in public practice may also pay a referral fee to obtain a client, for example, where the client continues as a client of another professional accountant in public practice but requires specialist services not offered by the existing accountant. The payment of such a referral fee also creates a self-interest threat to objectivity and professional competence and due care.

240.7 The significance of the threat shall be evaluated and safeguards applied when necessary to eliminate the threat or reduce it to an acceptable level. Examples of such safeguards include:

- Disclosing to the client any arrangements to pay a referral fee to another professional accountant for the work referred.
- Disclosing to the client any arrangements to receive a referral fee for referring the client to another professional accountant in public practice.
- Obtaining advance agreement from the client for commission arrangements in connection with the sale by a third party of goods or services to the client.

240.8 A professional accountant in public practice may purchase all or part of another firm on the basis that payments will be made to individuals formerly owning the firm or to their heirs or estates. Such payments are not regarded as commissions or referral fees for the purpose of paragraphs 240.5–240.7 above.

SECTION 250

Marketing professional services

250.1 When a professional accountant in public practice solicits new work through advertising or other forms of marketing, there may be a threat to compliance with the fundamental principles. For example, a self-interest threat to compliance with the principle of professional behaviour is created if services, achievements, or products are marketed in a way that is inconsistent with that principle.

250.2 A professional accountant in public practice shall not bring the profession into disrepute when marketing professional services. The professional accountant in public practice shall be honest and truthful, and not:

(a) Make exaggerated claims for services offered, qualifications possessed, or experience gained; or

(b) Make disparaging references or unsubstantiated comparisons to the work of another.

If the professional accountant in public practice is in doubt about whether a proposed form of advertising or marketing is appropriate, the professional accountant in public practice shall consider consulting with the relevant professional body.

SECTION 260

Gifts and Hospitality

260.1 A professional accountant in public practice, or an immediate or close family member, may be offered gifts and hospitality from a client. Such an offer may create threats to compliance with the fundamental principles. For example, a self-interest or familiarity threat to objectivity may be created if a gift from a client is accepted; an intimidation threat to objectivity may result from the possibility of such offers being made public.

260.2 The existence and significance of any threat will depend on the nature, value, and intent of the offer. Where gifts or hospitality are offered that a reasonable and informed third party, weighing all the specific facts and circumstances, would consider trivial and inconsequential, a professional accountant in public practice may conclude that the offer is made in the normal course of business without the specific intent to influence decision making or to obtain information. In such cases, the professional accountant in public practice may generally conclude that any threat to compliance with the fundamental principles is at an acceptable level.

260.3 A professional accountant in public practice shall evaluate the significance of any threats and apply safeguards when necessary to eliminate the threats or reduce them to an acceptable level. When the threats cannot be eliminated or reduced to an acceptable level through the application of safeguards, a professional accountant in public practice shall not accept such an offer.

SECTION 270

Custody of client assets

270.1 A professional accountant in public practice shall not assume custody of client monies or other assets unless permitted to do so by law and, if so, in compliance with any additional legal duties imposed on a professional accountant in public practice holding such assets.

270.2 The holding of client assets creates threats to compliance with the fundamental principles; for example, there is a self-interest threat to professional behaviour and may be a self interest threat to objectivity arising from holding client assets. A professional accountant in public practice entrusted with money (or other assets) belonging to others shall therefore:

(a) Keep such assets separately from personal or firm assets

(b) Use such assets only for the purpose for which they are intended

(c) At all times be ready to account for those assets and any income, dividends, or gains generated, to any persons entitled to such accounting; and

(d) Comply with all relevant laws and regulations relevant to the holding of and accounting for such assets.

270.3 As part of client and engagement acceptance procedures for services that may involve the holding of client assets, a professional accountant in public practice shall make appropriate inquiries about the source of such assets and consider legal and regulatory obligations. For example, if the assets were derived from illegal activities, such as money laundering, a threat to compliance with the fundamental principles would be created. In such situations, the professional accountant may consider seeking legal advice.

SECTION 280

Objectivity – All services

280.1 A professional accountant in public practice shall determine when providing any professional service whether there are threats to compliance with the fundamental principle of objectivity resulting from having interests in, or relationships with, a client or its directors, officers or employees. For example, a familiarity threat to objectivity may be created from a family or close personal or business relationship.

280.2 A professional accountant in public practice who provides an assurance service shall be independent of the assurance client. Independence of mind and in appearance is necessary to enable the professional accountant in public practice to express a conclusion, and be seen to express a conclusion, without bias, conflict of interest, or undue influence of others. Sections 290 and 291 provide specific guidance on independence requirements for professional accountants in public practice when performing assurance engagements.

280.3 The existence of threats to objectivity when providing any professional service will depend upon the particular circumstances of the engagement and the nature of the work that the professional accountant in public practice is performing.

280.4 A professional accountant in public practice shall evaluate the significance of any threats and apply safeguards when necessary to eliminate them or reduce them to an acceptable level. Examples of such safeguards include:

- Withdrawing from the engagement team.
- Supervisory procedures.
- Terminating the financial or business relationship giving rise to the threat.
- Discussing the issue with higher levels of management within the firm.
- Discussing the issue with those charged with governance of the client.

If safeguards cannot eliminate or reduce the threat to an acceptable level, the professional accountant shall decline or terminate the relevant engagement.

Supplementary reading: Sections 300 to 370

PART C – PROFESSIONAL ACCOUNTANTS IN BUSINESS (INCLUDING CGMA DESIGNATION HOLDERS)

300 Introduction
310 Ethical conflicts
320 Conflicts of interest
330 Gifts, entertainment and other forms of inducements
340 Preparing and reporting information
350 Educational services
360 General standards/Professional competence and due care
370 Acts discreditable/Professional behaviour/Confidentiality

SECTION 300

Introduction

300.1 This Part of the Code applies to members in business (AICPA) who hold the CGMA credential and all professional accountants in business (CIMA) including those who hold the CGMA credential (or are entitled to do so).

Conceptual framework for members in business

300.2 Members may encounter various relationships or circumstances that create threats to the member's compliance with the rules and fundamental principles. The rules, fundamental principles and interpretations seek to address many situations; however, they cannot address all relationships or circumstances that may arise. Thus, in the absence of an interpretation that addresses a particular relationship or circumstance, a member should evaluate whether that relationship or circumstance would lead a reasonable and informed third party who is aware of the relevant information to conclude that there is a threat to the member's compliance with the rules and fundamental principles that is not at an acceptable level. When making that evaluation, the member should apply the conceptual framework approach as outlined in this interpretation.

300.3 The CGMA code specifies that in some circumstances, no safeguards can reduce a threat to an acceptable level. For example, the code specifies that a member may not subordinate the member's professional judgement to others without violating the Integrity and Objectivity Rule and Principles. A member may not use the conceptual framework to overcome this or any other prohibition or requirement in the code.

Conceptual framework approach

300.4 Under the conceptual framework approach, members should identify threats to compliance with the rules and fundamental principles and evaluate the significance of those threats. Members should evaluate identified threats both individually and in the aggregate because threats can have a cumulative effect on a member's compliance with the rules and fundamental principles. Members should perform three main steps in applying the conceptual framework approach:

(a) **Identify threats**. The relationships or circumstances that a member encounters in various engagements and work assignments or positions will often create different threats to complying with the rules. When a member encounters a relationship or circumstance that is not specifically addressed by a rule, fundamental principle or an interpretation, under this approach, the member should determine whether the relationship or circumstance creates one or more threats, such as those identified in paragraphs .07–.12 that follow. The existence of a threat does not mean that the member is not in compliance with the rules and fundamental principles; however, the member should evaluate the significance of the threat.

(b) **Evaluate the significance of a threat**. In evaluating the significance of an identified threat, the member should determine whether a threat is at an acceptable level. A threat is at an acceptable level when a reasonable and informed third party who is aware of the relevant information would be expected to conclude that the threat would not compromise the member's compliance with the rules and fundamental principles. Members should consider both qualitative and quantitative factors when evaluating the significance of a threat, including the extent to which existing safeguards already reduce the threat to an acceptable level. If the member evaluates the threat and concludes that a reasonable and informed third party who is aware of the relevant information would be expected to conclude that the threat does not compromise a member's compliance with the rules and fundamental principles, the threat is at an acceptable level and the member is not required to evaluate the threat any further under this conceptual framework approach.

(c) **Identify and apply safeguards**. If, in evaluating the significance of an identified threat, the member concludes that the threat is not at an acceptable level, the member should apply safeguards to eliminate the threat or reduce it to an acceptable level. The member should apply judgement in determining the nature of the safeguards to be applied because the effectiveness of safeguards will vary depending on the circumstances. When identifying appropriate safeguards to apply, one safeguard may eliminate or reduce multiple threats. In some cases, the member should apply multiple safeguards to eliminate or reduce one threat to an acceptable level. In other cases, an identified threat may be so significant that no safeguards will eliminate the threat or reduce it to an acceptable level, or the member will be unable to implement effective safeguards. Under such circumstances, providing the specific professional services would compromise the member's compliance with the rules, and the member should determine whether to decline or discontinue the professional services or resign from the employing organisation.

Threats

300.5 Many threats fall into one or more of the following six broad categories: adverse interest, advocacy, familiarity, self-interest, self-review, and undue influence (also referred to as "intimidation threat").

300.6 Examples of threats associated with a specific relationship or circumstance are identified in the interpretations of the code. Paragraphs .07–.12 of this section define and provide examples, which are not all inclusive, of each of these threat categories.

300.7 Adverse interest threat. The threat that a member will not act with objectivity, because the member's interests are opposed to the interests of the employing organisation. Examples of adverse interest threats include the following:

(a) A member has charged, or expressed an intention to charge, the employing organisation with violations of law.

(b) A member or the member's immediate family or close relative has a financial or another relationship with a vendor, customer, competitor, or potential acquisition of the employing organisation.

(c) A member has sued or expressed an intention to sue the employing organisation or its officers, directors, or employees.

300.8 Advocacy threat. The threat that a member will promote an organisation's interests or position to the point that his or her objectivity is compromised. Examples of advocacy threats include the following:

(a) Obtaining favourable financing or additional capital is dependent upon the information that the member includes in, or excludes from, a prospectus, an offering, a business plan, a financing application, or a regulatory filing.

(b) The member gives or fails to give information that the member knows will unduly influence the conclusions reached by an external service provider or other third party.

300.9 Familiarity threat. The threat that, due to a long or close relationship with a person or an employing organisation, a member will become too sympathetic to their interests or too accepting of the person's work or organisation's product or service. Examples of familiarity threats include the following:

(a) A member uses an immediate family's or a close relative's company as a supplier to the employing organisation.

(b) A member may accept an individual's work product with little or no review because the individual has been producing an acceptable work product for an extended period of time.

(c) A member's immediate family or close relative is employed as a member's subordinate.

(d) A member regularly accepts gifts or entertainment from a vendor or customer of the employing organisation.

300.10 Self-interest threat. The threat that a member could benefit, financially or otherwise, from an interest in, or relationship with, the employing organisation or persons associated with the employing organisation. Examples of self-interest threats include the following:

(a) A member's immediate family or close relative has a financial interest in the employing organisation.

(b) A member holds a financial interest (for example, shares or share options) in the employing organisation, and the value of that financial interest is directly affected by the member's decisions.

(c) A member is eligible for a profit or other performance-related bonus, and the value of that bonus is directly affected by the member's decisions.

300.11 Self-review threat. The threat that a member will not appropriately evaluate the results of a previous judgement made or service performed or supervised by the member, or an individual in the employing organisation, and that the member will rely on that service in forming a judgement as part of another service. Examples of self-review threats include the following:

(a) When performing an internal audit procedure, an internal auditor accepts work that he or she previously performed in a different position.

(b) The member accepts the work previously performed by the member, alone or with others, that will be the basis for providing another professional service.

300.12 Undue influence threat (also referred to as “intimidation threat”). The threat that a member will subordinate his or her judgement to that of an individual associated with the employing organisation or any relevant third party due to that individual’s position, reputation or expertise, aggressive or dominant personality, or attempts to coerce or exercise excessive influence over the member. Examples of undue influence threats include the following:

(a) A member is pressured to become associated with misleading information.

(b) A member is pressured to deviate from a company policy.

(c) A member is pressured to change a conclusion regarding an accounting or a tax position.

(d) A member is pressured to hire an unqualified individual.

Safeguards

300.13 Safeguards may partially or completely eliminate a threat or diminish the potential influence of a threat. The nature and extent of the safeguards applied will depend on many factors. To be effective, safeguards should eliminate the threat or reduce it to an acceptable level.

300.14 Safeguards that may eliminate a threat or reduce it to an acceptable level fall into two broad categories:

(a) Safeguards created by the profession, legislation, or regulation

(b) Safeguards implemented by the employing organisation.

300.15 The effectiveness of a safeguard depends on many factors, including those listed here:

(a) The facts and circumstances specific to a particular situation

(b) The proper identification of threats

(c) Whether the safeguard is suitably designed to meet its objectives

(d) The party(ies) who will be subject to the safeguard

(e) How the safeguard is applied

(f) The consistency with which the safeguard is applied

(g) Who applies the safeguard

(h) How the safeguard interacts with a safeguard from another category

(i) Whether the employing organisation is a public interest entity.

300.16 Examples of safeguards within each category are presented in the following paragraphs. Because these are only examples and are not intended to be all inclusive, it is possible that threats may be sufficiently mitigated through the application of other safeguards not specifically identified herein.

300.17 The following are examples of safeguards created by the profession, legislation, or regulation:

- Education and training requirements on ethics and professional responsibilities
- Continuing education requirements on ethics
- Professional standards and the threat of discipline
- Legislation establishing prohibitions and requirements for entities and employees
- Competency and experience requirements for professional licensure and credentials
- Professional resources, such as hotlines, for consultation on ethical issues.

300.18 Examples of safeguards implemented by the employing organisation are as follows:

- A tone at the top emphasising a commitment to fair financial reporting and compliance with applicable laws, rules, regulations, and corporate governance policies
- Policies and procedures addressing ethical conduct and compliance with laws, rules, and regulations

- Audit committee charter, including independent audit committee members
- Internal policies and procedures requiring disclosure of identified interests or relationships among the employing organisation, its directors or officers, and vendors, suppliers, or customers
- Internal policies and procedures related to purchasing controls
- Internal policies and procedures related to customer acceptance or credit limits
- Dissemination of corporate ethical compliance policies and procedures, including whistle-blower hotlines, the reporting structure, dispute resolution, or other similar policies, to promote compliance with laws, rules, regulations, and other professional requirements
- Human resource policies and procedures safeguarding against discrimination or harassment, such as those concerning a worker's religion, sexual orientation, gender, or disability
- Human resource policies and procedures stressing the hiring and retention of technically competent employees
- Policies and procedures for implementing and monitoring ethical policies
- Assigning sufficient staff with the necessary competencies to projects and other tasks
- Policies segregating personal assets from company assets
- Staff training on applicable laws, rules, and regulations
- Regular monitoring of internal policies and procedures
- A reporting structure whereby the internal auditor does not report to the financial reporting group
- Policies and procedures that do not allow an internal auditor to monitor areas where the internal auditor has operational or functional responsibilities
- Policies for promotion, rewards, and enforcement of a culture of high ethics and integrity
- Use of third-party resources for consultation as needed on significant matters of professional judgement.

SECTION 310

Ethical conflicts

310.1 An ethical conflict arises when a member encounters one or both of the following:

(a) Obstacles to following an appropriate course of action due to internal or external pressures
(b) Conflicts in applying relevant professional and legal standards.

For example, a member suspects a fraud may have occurred, but reporting the suspected fraud would violate the member's responsibility to maintain the confidentiality of his or her employer's confidential information.

310.2 Once an ethical conflict is encountered, a member may be required to take steps to best achieve compliance with the rules, fundamental principles and law. In weighing alternative courses of action, the member should consider factors such as the following:

(a) Relevant facts and circumstances, including applicable rules, laws, or regulations
(b) Ethical issues involved
(c) Established internal procedures.

310.3 The member should also be prepared to justify any departures that the member believes were appropriate in applying the relevant rules, fundamental principles and law. If the member was unable to resolve the conflict in a way that permitted compliance with the applicable rules, fundamental principles and law, the member may have to address the consequences of any violations.

310.4 Before pursuing a course of action, the member should consider consulting with appropriate persons within the organisation that employs the member.

310.5 If a member decides not to consult with appropriate persons within the organisation that employs the member, and the conflict remains unresolved after pursuing the selected course of action, the member should consider either consulting with other individuals for help in reaching a resolution or obtaining advice from an appropriate professional body or legal counsel. The member also should consider documenting the substance of the issue, the parties with whom the issue was discussed, details of any discussions held, and any decisions made concerning the issue.

310.6 If the ethical conflict remains unresolved, the member will in all likelihood be in violation of one or more rules or fundamental principles if he or she remains associated with the matter creating the conflict. Accordingly, the member should consider his or her continuing relationship with the specific assignment or employer.

Integrity and objectivity

310.7 Integrity and Objectivity Rule (AICPA): In the performance of any professional service, a member shall maintain objectivity and integrity, shall be free of conflicts of interest, and shall not knowingly misrepresent facts or subordinate his or her judgement to others.

310.8 Integrity Principle (CIMA): The principle of integrity imposes an obligation on all members to be straightforward and honest in all professional and business relationships.

Objectivity Principle (CIMA): The principle of objectivity imposes an obligation on all members not to compromise their professional or business judgement because of bias, conflict of interest or the undue influence of others.

Interpretations under the "Integrity and Objectivity Rule" and the "Integrity and Objectivity Principles"

Application of the conceptual framework for members in business and ethical conflicts

310.9 In the absence of an interpretation of the "Integrity and Objectivity Rule" and the Integrity and Objectivity principles that addresses a particular relationship or circumstance, a member should apply the "Conceptual Framework for Members in Business". (300.2–300.3).

310.10 A member will be considered in violation of the "Integrity and Objectivity Rule" and the Integrity and Objectivity principles if the member cannot demonstrate that safeguards were applied that eliminated or reduced significant threats to an acceptable level.

310.11 A member should consider the guidance in the "Ethical Conflicts" interpretation (310.1–310.6) when addressing ethical conflicts that may arise when the member encounters obstacles to following an appropriate course of action. Such obstacles may be due to internal or external pressures or to conflicts in applying relevant professional and legal standards, or both.

SECTION 320

Conflicts of interest

Conflicts of interest for members in business

320.1 A member in business may be faced with a conflict of interest when undertaking a professional service. In determining whether a professional service, relationship, or matter would result in a conflict of interest, a member should use professional judgement, taking into account whether a reasonable and informed third party who is aware of the relevant information would conclude that a conflict of interest exists.

320.2 A conflict of interest creates adverse interest and self-interest threats to the member's compliance with the "Integrity and Objectivity Rule" and the Integrity and Objectivity principles. For example, threats may be created when:

(a) a member undertakes a professional service related to a particular matter involving two or more parties whose interests with respect to that matter are in conflict

or

(b) the interests of a member with respect to a particular matter and the interests of a party for whom the member undertakes a professional service related to that matter are in conflict.

320.3 A party may include an employing organisation, a vendor, a customer, a lender, a shareholder, or another party.

320.4 The following are examples of situations in which conflicts of interest may arise:

- Serving in a management or governance position for two employing organisations and acquiring confidential information from one employing organisation that could be used by the member to the advantage or disadvantage of the other employing organisation.
- Undertaking a professional service for each of two parties in a partnership employing the member to assist in dissolving their partnership.
- Preparing financial information for certain members of management of the employing organisation who are seeking to undertake a management buy-out.

- Being responsible for selecting a vendor for the member's employing organisation when the member or his or her immediate family member could benefit financially from the transaction.
- Serving in a governance capacity or influencing an employing organisation that is approving certain investments for the company in which one of those specific investments will increase the value of the personal investment portfolio of the member or his or her immediate family member.

Identification of a conflict of interest

320.5 In identifying whether a conflict of interest exists or may be created, a member should take reasonable steps to determine:

(a) The nature of the relevant interests and relationships between the parties involved and

(b) the nature of the services and its implication for relevant parties.

320.6 The nature of the relevant interests and relationships and the services may change over time. The member should remain alert to such changes for the purposes of identifying circumstances that might create a conflict of interest.

Evaluation of a conflict of interest

320.7 When an actual conflict of interest has been identified, the member should evaluate the significance of the threat created by the conflict of interest to determine if the threat is at an acceptable level. Members should consider both qualitative and quantitative factors when evaluating the significance of the threat, including the extent to which existing safeguards already reduce the threat to an acceptable level.

320.8 In evaluating the significance of an identified threat, members should consider the following:

(a) The significance of relevant interests or relationships.

(b) The significance of the threats created by undertaking the professional service or services. In general, the more direct the connection between the member and the matter on which the parties' interests are in conflict, the more significant the threat to compliance with the rule will be.

320.9 If the member concludes that the threat is not at an acceptable level, the member should apply safeguards to eliminate the threat or reduce it to an acceptable level. Examples of safeguards include the following:

(a) Restructuring or segregating certain responsibilities and duties

(b) Obtaining appropriate oversight

(c) Withdrawing from the decision making process related to the matter giving rise to the conflict of interest

(d) Consulting with third parties, such as a professional body, legal counsel, or another professional accountant.

320.10 In cases where an identified threat may be so significant that no safeguards will eliminate the threat or reduce it to an acceptable level, or the member is unable to implement effective safeguards, the member should:

(a) decline to perform or discontinue the professional services that would result in the conflict of interest; or

(b) terminate the relevant relationships or dispose of the relevant interests to eliminate the threat or reduce it to an acceptable level.

Disclosure of a conflict of interest and consent

320.11 When a conflict of interest exists, the member should disclose the nature of the conflict to the relevant parties, including to the appropriate levels within the employing organisation and obtain their consent to undertake the professional service. The member should disclose the conflict of interest and obtain consent even if the member concludes that threats are at an acceptable level.

320.12 The member is encouraged to document the nature of the circumstances giving rise to the conflict of interest, the safeguards applied to eliminate or reduce the threats to an acceptable level, and the consent obtained.

320.13 When addressing a conflict of interest, a member is encouraged to seek guidance from within the employing organisation or from others, such as a professional body, legal counsel, or another professional accountant. When making disclosures and seeking guidance of third parties, the member should remain alert to the requirements of the "Confidential Information Obtained From Employment or Volunteer Activities", interpretation of the "Acts Discreditable Rule" and the Integrity and Objectivity principles (370.1 and 310.8). In addition, federal, state, or local statutes, or regulations concerning confidentiality of employer information may be more restrictive than the requirements contained in the CGMA code.

320.14 A member may encounter other threats to compliance with the "Integrity and Objectivity Rule" and the Integrity and Objectivity principles. This may occur, for example, when preparing or reporting financial information as a result of undue pressure from others within the employing organisation or financial, business or personal relationships that close relatives or immediate family members of the member have with the employing organisation. Guidance on managing such threats is covered by the "Knowing Misrepresentations in the Preparation of Financial Statements or Records", interpretation (340.1–340.2) and the "Subordination of Judgement by a Member", interpretation (340.3–340.13).

SECTION 330

Gifts, entertainment and other forms of inducements

Offering or accepting gifts or entertainment

330.1 For purposes of this interpretation, a customer or vendor of the member's employer includes a representative of the customer or vendor.

330.2 When a member offers to, or accepts gifts or entertainment from, a customer or vendor of the member's employer, self-interest, familiarity, or undue influence threats to the member's compliance with the "Integrity and Objectivity Rule" and the Integrity and Objectivity principles may exist.

330.3 Threats to compliance with the "Integrity and Objectivity Rule" and the "Integrity Principle" would not be at an acceptable level and could not be reduced to an acceptable level by the application of safeguards and the member would be presumed to lack integrity in violation of the "Integrity and Objectivity Rule" and the "Integrity Principle" in the following circumstances:

(a) The member offers to, or accepts gifts or entertainment from, a customer or vendor of the member's employer that violate applicable laws, rules, or regulations or the policies of the member's employer or the customer or vendor.

(b) The member knows of the violation or demonstrates recklessness in not knowing.

330.4 A member should evaluate the significance of any threats to determine if they are at an acceptable level. Threats are at an acceptable level when gifts or entertainment are reasonable in the circumstances. The member should exercise judgement in determining whether gifts or entertainment would be considered reasonable in the circumstances. The following are examples of relevant facts and circumstances:

- The nature of the gift or entertainment
- The occasion giving rise to the gift or entertainment
- The cost or value of the gift or entertainment
- The nature, frequency, and value of other gifts and entertainment offered or accepted
- Whether the entertainment was associated with the active conduct of business directly before, during, or after the entertainment
- Whether other customers or vendors also participated in the entertainment
- The individuals from the customer or vendor and a member's employer who participated in the entertainment.

330.5 Threats to compliance with the "Integrity and Objectivity Rule" and the "Objectivity Principle" would not be at an acceptable level and could not be reduced to an acceptable level through the application of safeguards if a member offers to, or accepts gifts or entertainment from, a customer or vendor of the member's employer that is not reasonable in the circumstances. The member would be considered to lack objectivity in violation of the "Integrity and Objectivity Rule" and the "Objectivity Principle" under these circumstances.

Offering or accepting other forms of inducements

330.6 Threats to compliance with the "Integrity and Objectivity Rule" and the Integrity and Objectivity principles may also exist when a member or his or her immediate family or close relative offer to, or accept from, a third party other forms of inducements such as, preferential treatment or inappropriate appeals to friendship or loyalty.

330.7 For example, self-interest threats are created when an inducement is made in an attempt to unduly influence actions or decisions, encourage illegal or unethical behaviour, or obtain confidential information, and undue influence threats are created if such an inducement is offered or accepted and it is followed by threats to make that offer public and damage the reputation of either the member or an immediate family member or close relative.

330.8 A member should evaluate the significance of any threats to determine if they are at an acceptable level. Threats are at an acceptable level when the inducement is reasonable in the circumstances [see 330.4] and not intended to encourage unethical behaviour.

330.9 Threats to compliance with the "Integrity and Objectivity Rule" and the Integrity and Objectivity principles would not be at an acceptable level and could not be reduced to an acceptable level through the application of safeguards if a member offers to, or accepts inducements from, a third party that are not reasonable in the circumstances or are intended to encourage unethical behaviour. The member would be considered to lack integrity and objectivity in violation of the "Integrity and Objectivity Rule" and the Integrity and Objectivity principles under these circumstances.

SECTION 340

Preparing and reporting information

Knowing misrepresentations in the preparation of financial statements or records

340.1 Members in business are often involved in the preparation and reporting of information that may either be made public or used by others inside or outside the employing organisation. Such information may include financial or management information, for example, forecasts and budgets, financial statements, management's discussion and analysis, and the management letter of representation provided to the auditors during the audit of the entity's financial statements.

340.2 Threats to compliance with the "Integrity and Objectivity Rule" and the Integrity and Objectivity principles would not be at an acceptable level and could not be reduced to an acceptable level by the application of safeguards, and the member would be considered to have knowingly misrepresented facts in violation of the "Integrity and Objectivity Rule" and the Integrity and Objectivity principles if the member:

(a) makes, or permits or directs another to make, materially false and misleading entries in an entity's financial statements or records

(b) fails to correct an entity's financial statements or records that are materially false and misleading when the member has the authority to record the entries; or

(c) signs, or permits or directs another to sign, a document containing materially false and misleading information.

Subordination of judgement

340.3 The "Integrity and Objectivity Rule" and the Integrity and Objectivity principles prohibit a member from knowingly misrepresenting facts or subordinating his or her judgement when performing professional services for an employer or on a volunteer basis. This interpretation addresses differences of opinion between a member and his or her supervisor or any other person within the member's organisation.

340.4 Self-interest, familiarity, and undue influence threats to the member's compliance with the "Integrity and Objectivity Rule" and the Integrity and Objectivity principles may exist when a member and his or her supervisor or any other person within the member's organisation have a difference of opinion relating to the application of accounting principles; auditing standards; or other relevant professional standards, including standards applicable to tax and consulting services or applicable laws or regulations.

340.5 A member should evaluate the significance of any threats to determine if they are at an acceptable level. Threats are at an acceptable level if the member concludes that the position taken does not result in a material misrepresentation of fact or a violation of applicable laws or regulations. If threats are not at an acceptable level, the member should apply the safeguards in paragraphs .06–.08 to eliminate or reduce the threat(s) to an acceptable level so that the member does not subordinate his or her judgement.

340.6 In evaluating the significance of any identified threats, the member should determine, after appropriate research or consultation, whether the result of the position taken by the supervisor or other person

(a) fails to comply with professional standards, when applicable

(b) creates a material misrepresentation of fact; or

(c) may violate applicable laws or regulations.

340.7 If the member concludes that threats are at an acceptable level the member should discuss his or her conclusions with the person taking the position. No further action would be needed under this interpretation.

340.8 If the member concludes that the position results in a material misrepresentation of fact or a violation of applicable laws or regulations, then threats would not be at an acceptable level. In such circumstances, the member should discuss his or her concerns with the supervisor.

340.9 If the difference of opinion is not resolved after discussing the concerns with the supervisor, the member should discuss his or her concerns with the appropriate higher level(s) of management within the member's organisation (for example, the supervisor's immediate superior, senior management, and those charged with governance).

340.10 If after discussing the concerns with the supervisor and appropriate higher level(s) of management within the member's organisation, the member concludes that appropriate action was not taken, then the member should consider, in no specific order, the following safeguards to ensure that threats to the member's compliance with the "Integrity and Objectivity Rule" and the Integrity and Objectivity principles are eliminated or reduced to an acceptable level:

- Determine whether the organisation's internal policies and procedures have any additional requirements for reporting differences of opinion.
- Determine whether he or she is responsible for communicating to third parties, such as regulatory authorities or the organisation's (former organisation's) external accountant. In considering such communications, the member should be cognizant of his or her obligations under the "Confidential Information Obtained from Employment or Volunteer Activities" interpretation (370.5-370.23) and the "Obligation of a Member to His or Her Employer's External Accountant" interpretation (340.14).
- Consult with his or her legal counsel regarding his or her responsibilities.
- Document his or her understanding of the facts, the accounting principles, auditing standards, or other relevant professional standards involved or applicable laws or regulations and the conversations and parties with whom these matters were discussed.

340.11 If the member concludes that no safeguards can eliminate or reduce the threats to an acceptable level or if the member concludes that appropriate action was not taken, then he or she should consider the continuing relationship with the member's organisation and take appropriate steps to eliminate his or her exposure to subordination of judgement.

340.12 Nothing in this interpretation precludes a member from resigning from the organisation at any time. However, resignation may not relieve the member of responsibilities in the situation, including any responsibility to disclose concerns to third parties, such as regulatory authorities or the employer's (former employer's) external accountant.

340.13 A member should use professional judgement and apply similar safeguards, as appropriate, to other situations involving a difference of opinion as described in this interpretation so that the member does not subordinate his or her judgement.

Obligation of a member to his or her employer's external accountant

340.14 The "Integrity and Objectivity Rule" and the Integrity and Objectivity principles require a member to maintain objectivity and integrity in the performance of a professional service. When dealing with an employer's external accountant, a member must be candid and not knowingly misrepresent facts or knowingly fail to disclose material facts. This would include, for example, responding to specific inquiries for which the employer's external accountant requests written representation.

SECTION 350

Educational services

350.1 Members who perform educational services, such as teaching full or part time at a university, teaching a continuing professional education course, or engaging in research and scholarship, are performing professional services and, therefore, are subject to the "Integrity and Objectivity Rule" and the Integrity and Objectivity principles.

SECTION 360

General standards/Professional competence and due care

General standards rule (AICPA)

360.1 A member shall comply with the following standards and with any interpretations thereof by bodies designated by Council.

(a) Professional Competence. Undertake only those professional services that the member or the member's firm can reasonably expect to be completed with professional competence.

(b) Due Professional Care. Exercise due professional care in the performance of professional services.

(c) Planning and Supervision. Adequately plan and supervise the performance of professional services.

(d) Sufficient Relevant Data. Obtain sufficient relevant data to afford a reasonable basis for conclusions or recommendations in relation to any professional services performed.

Professional competence and due care principle (CIMA)

360.2 The principle of Professional Competence and Due Care imposes the following obligations on all professional accountants:

(a) To maintain professional knowledge and skill at the level required to ensure that employers receive competent professional service

(b) To act diligently in accordance with applicable technical and professional standards when providing professional services.

Interpretations under the "General Standards Rule" and "Professional Competence and Due Care Principle"

Application of the conceptual framework for members in business and ethical conflicts

360.3 In the absence of an interpretation of the "General Standards Rule" and "Professional Competence and Due Care Principle" that addresses a particular relationship or circumstance, a member should apply the "Conceptual Framework for Members in Business" (300.2 – 300.3).

360.4 A member would be considered in violation of the "General Standards Rule" and "Professional Competence and Due Care Principle" if the member cannot demonstrate that safeguards were applied that eliminated or reduced significant threats to an acceptable level.

360.5 A member should consider the guidance in the "Ethical Conflicts" interpretation (310.1) when addressing ethical conflicts that may arise when the member encounters obstacles to following an appropriate course of action. Such obstacles may be due to internal or external pressures or to conflicts in applying relevant professional and legal standards, or both.

Professional competence and due care

360.6 Competence, in this context, means that the member or member's staff possesses the appropriate technical qualifications to perform professional services and, as required, supervises and evaluates the quality of work performed. Competence encompasses knowledge of the profession's standards, the techniques and technical subject matter involved, and the ability to exercise sound judgement in applying such knowledge in the performance of professional services.

360.7 A member's agreement to perform professional services implies that the member has the necessary competence to complete those services according to professional standards and to apply the member's knowledge and skill with reasonable care and diligence. However, the member does not assume a responsibility for infallibility of knowledge or judgement.

360.8 The member may have the knowledge required to complete the services in accordance with professional standards prior to performance. A normal part of providing professional services involves performing additional research or consulting with others to gain sufficient competence.

360.9 Threats to the member's compliance with the "General Standards Rule" and "Professional Competence and Due Care Principle" may exist if the member is performing professional services and the member has:

- insufficient time for properly performing or completing the relevant duties
- incomplete, restricted or otherwise inadequate information for performing the duties properly
- insufficient experience, training or education, or both; or
- inadequate resources for the proper performance of the duties.

360.10 The significance of the threats will depend on factors such as the extent to which the member is working with others, relative seniority in the business, and the level of supervision and review applied to the work. The member should evaluate the significance of any threats and apply safeguards, when necessary, to eliminate or reduce the threats to an acceptable level. Examples of such safeguards include:

- performing additional research or obtaining additional advice or training.
- ensuring that there is adequate time available for performing the relevant duties.
- obtaining assistance from someone with the necessary expertise.
- consulting, where appropriate, with
  - superiors within the employing organisation
  - independent experts; or
  - a relevant professional body.

360.11 If the member determines that the threats are so significant that no safeguards could eliminate or reduce the threats to an acceptable level, and therefore the member is unable to gain sufficient competence, the member should suggest the involvement of a competent person to perform the needed professional service, either independently or as an associate.

Submission of financial statements

360.12 When a member is a stockholder, a partner, a director, an officer, or an employee of an entity and, in this capacity, prepares or submits the entity's financial statements to third parties, the member should clearly communicate, preferably in writing, the member's relationship to the entity and should not imply that the member is independent of the entity. In addition, if the communication states affirmatively that the financial statements are presented in conformity with the applicable financial reporting framework, the member should comply with the "Accounting Principles Rule" and the "Professional Competence and Due Care Principle".

360.13 AICPA members should refer to the "Use of CPA Credential" interpretation (370.26) for additional guidance.

Compliance with standards/Professional competence and due care

Compliance with standards rule (AICPA)

360.14 A member who performs auditing, review, compilation, management consulting, tax, or other professional services shall comply with standards promulgated by bodies designated by Council.

Professional competence and due care principle (CIMA)

360.15 The principle of professional competence and due care imposes the following obligations on all professional accountants:

(a) To maintain professional knowledge and skill at the level required to ensure that employers receive competent professional service; and

(b) To act diligently in accordance with applicable technical and professional standards when providing professional services.

Interpretations under the "Compliance with Standards Rule" and the "Professional Competence and Due Care Principle"

Application of the conceptual framework for members in business and ethical conflicts

360.16 In the absence of an interpretation of the "Compliance with Standards Rule" and the "Professional Competence and Due Care Principle" that addresses a particular relationship or circumstance, a member should apply the "Conceptual Framework for Members in Business" (300.2–300.3).

360.17 A member would be considered in violation of the "Compliance with Standards Rule" and the "Professional Competence and Due Care Principle" if the member cannot demonstrate that safeguards were applied that eliminated or reduced significant threats to an acceptable level.

360.18 A member should consider the guidance in the "Ethical Conflicts" interpretation (310.1) when addressing ethical conflicts that may arise when the member encounters obstacles to following an appropriate course of action. Such obstacles may be due to internal or external pressures or to conflicts in applying relevant professional or legal standards, or both.

Accounting principles

Accounting principles rule (AICPA)

360.19 A member shall not (1) express an opinion or state affirmatively that the financial statements or other financial data of any entity are presented in conformity with generally accepted accounting principles or (2) state that he or she is not aware of any material modifications that should be made to such statements or data in order for them to be in conformity with generally accepted accounting principles, if such statements or data contain any departure from an accounting principle promulgated by bodies designated by Council to establish such principles that has a material effect on the statements or data taken as a whole. If, however, the statements or data contain such a departure and the member can demonstrate that due to unusual circumstances the financial statements or data would otherwise have been misleading, the member can comply with the rule by describing the departure, its approximate effects, if practicable, and the reasons why compliance with the principle would result in a misleading statement.

Professional competence and due care principle (CIMA)

360.20 The principle of professional competence and due care imposes the following obligations on all professional accountants:

(a) To maintain professional knowledge and skill at the level required to ensure that employers receive competent professional service

(b) To act diligently in accordance with applicable technical and professional standards when providing professional services.

Interpretations under the "Accounting Principles Rule" and the "Professional Competence and Due Care Principle"

Application of the Conceptual Framework for Members in Business and Ethical Conflicts

360.21 In the absence of an interpretation of the "Accounting Principles Rule" and the "Professional Competence and Due Care Principle" that addresses a particular relationship or circumstance, a member should apply the "Conceptual Framework for Members in Business" (30.2–300.3).

360.22 A member would be considered in violation of the "Accounting Principles Rule" and the "Professional Competence and Due Care Principle" if the member cannot demonstrate that safeguards were applied that eliminated or reduced significant threats to an acceptable level.

360.23 A member should consider the guidance in the "Ethical Conflicts" interpretation (310.1) when addressing ethical conflicts that may arise when the member encounters obstacles to following an appropriate course of action. Such obstacles may be due to internal or external pressures or to conflicts in applying relevant professional or legal standards, or both.

Responsibility for affirming that financial statements are in conformity with the applicable financial reporting framework (AICPA)

360.24 A member shall not state affirmatively that an entity's financial statements or other financial data are presented in conformity with generally accepted accounting principles (GAAP) if such statements or data contain any departure from an accounting principle promulgated by a body designated by Council to establish such principles. Members who affirm that financial statements or other financial data are presented in conformity with GAAP should comply with "Accounting Principles Rule". A member's representation in a letter or other communication that an entity's financial statements are in conformity with GAAP may be considered an affirmative statement within the meaning of this rule with respect to the member who signed the letter or other communication (for example, the member signed a report to a regulatory authority, a creditor, or an auditor).

Responsibility for affirming that financial statements are in conformity with the applicable financial reporting framework (CIMA)

360.25 A member of CIMA who has responsibility for the preparation or approval of the general purpose financial statements of an employing organisation shall be satisfied that those financial statements are presented in accordance with the applicable financial reporting standards.

Status of financial accounting standards board, Governmental accounting standards board, Federal accounting standards advisory board, and International accounting standards board interpretations (AICPA)

360.26 The "Accounting Principles Rule" authorizes Council to designate bodies to establish accounting principles. Council has designated the U.S. Financial Accounting Standards Board (FASB) as such a body and has resolved that FASB Accounting Standards Codification® (ASC) constitutes accounting principles as contemplated in the rule. Council designated the U.S. Governmental Accounting Standards Board (GASB), with respect to Statements of Governmental Accounting Standards issued in July 1984 and thereafter, as the body to establish financial accounting principles for state and local governmental entities, pursuant to the "Accounting Principles Rule". Council designated the U.S. Federal Accounting Standards Advisory Board (FASAB), with respect to Statements of Federal Accounting Standards adopted and issued in March 1993 and subsequently, as the body to establish accounting principles for federal government entities, pursuant to the "Accounting Principles Rule". Council designated the International Accounting Standards Board (IASB) as an accounting body for purposes of establishing international financial accounting and reporting principles.

360.27 Reference to GAAP in the "Accounting Principles Rule" means those accounting principles promulgated by bodies designated by Council, which are listed in paragraph .01 "Council Resolution Designating Bodies to Promulgate Technical Standards".

360.28 The AICPA Professional Ethics Division will look to the codification or statements and any interpretations thereof issued by FASB, GASB, FASAB, or IASB in determining whether a member of the AICPA has departed from an accounting principle established by a designated accounting standard-setter in FASB ASC, a Statement of Governmental Accounting Standards, a Statement of Federal Accounting Standards, or International Financial Reporting Standards (IFRS).

Departures from generally accepted accounting principles (AICPA)

360.29 It is difficult to anticipate all the circumstances in which accounting principles may be applied. However, there is a strong presumption that adherence to GAAP would, in nearly all instances, result in financial statements that are not misleading. The "Accounting Principles Rule" recognizes that, upon occasion, there may be unusual circumstances when the literal application of GAAP would have the effect of rendering financial statements misleading. In such cases, the proper accounting treatment to apply is that which will not render the financial statements misleading.

360.30 The question of what constitutes unusual circumstances, as referred to in the "Accounting Principles Rule" is a matter of professional judgement involving the ability to support the position that adherence to a promulgated principle within GAAP would be regarded generally by reasonable persons as producing misleading financial statements.

360.31 Examples of circumstances that may justify a departure from GAAP include new legislation or evolution of a new form of business transaction. Examples of circumstances that would not justify departures from GAAP include an unusual degree of materiality or conflicting industry practices.

360.32 If the statements or data contain such departures, see the "Accounting Principles Rule" for further guidance.

Financial statements prepared pursuant to financial reporting frameworks other than GAAP (AICPA)

360.33 Reference to GAAP in the "Accounting Principles Rule" means those accounting principles promulgated by bodies designated by Council. The bodies designed by Council to promulgate accounting principles are

- FASAB
- FASB
- GASB, and
- IASB.

360.34 Financial statements prepared pursuant to other accounting principles would be considered financial reporting frameworks other than GAAP within the context of the "Accounting Principles Rule".

360.35 However, the "Accounting Principles Rule" does not preclude a member from preparing or reporting on financial statements that have been prepared pursuant to financial reporting frameworks other than GAAP, such as:

(a) financial reporting frameworks generally accepted in another country, including jurisdictional variations of IFRS such that the entity's financial statements do not meet the requirements for full compliance with IFRS, as promulgated by the IASB

(b) financial reporting frameworks prescribed by an agreement or a contract

or

(c) other special purpose frameworks, including statutory financial reporting provisions required by law or a U.S. or foreign governmental regulatory body to whose jurisdiction the entity is subject.

360.36 In such circumstances, however, the financial statements or member's reports thereon should not purport that the financial statements are in accordance with GAAP and the financial statements or reports on those financial statements, or both, should clarify the financial reporting framework(s) used.

SECTION 370

Acts discreditable/Professional behaviour/Confidentiality

Acts discreditable rule (AICPA)

370.1 A member shall not commit an act discreditable to the profession.

Professional behaviour principle (CIMA)

370.2 The principle of professional behaviour imposes an obligation on all members to comply with relevant laws and regulations and avoid any action that the member knows or should know may discredit the profession.

Confidentiality principle (CIMA)

370.3 The principle of confidentiality imposes an obligation on all members to respect the confidentiality of information acquired as a result of professional and business relationships and, therefore, not disclose any such information to third parties without proper and specific authority, unless there is a legal or professional right or duty to disclose, nor use the information for the personal advantage of the professional accountant or third parties.

Interpretations under the "Acts Discreditable Rule" and "Professional Behaviour and Confidentiality Principles"

Application of the conceptual framework for members in business and ethical conflicts

370.4 In the absence of an interpretation of the "Acts Discreditable Rule" and the Professional Behaviour and Confidentiality principles that addresses a particular relationship or circumstance, a member should apply the "Conceptual Framework for Members in Business" (300.2–300.3).

370.5 A member would be considered in violation of the "Acts Discreditable Rule" and the Professional Behaviour and Confidentiality principles if the member cannot demonstrate that safeguards were applied that eliminated or reduced significant threats to an acceptable level.

370.6 A member should consider the guidance in the "Ethical Conflicts" interpretation (310.1) when addressing ethical conflicts that may arise when the member encounters obstacles to follow an appropriate course of action. Such obstacles may be due to internal or external pressures or to conflicts in applying relevant professional standards or legal standards, or both.

Discrimination and harassment in employment practices

370.7 A member would be presumed to have committed an act discreditable to the profession, in violation of the "Acts Discreditable Rule" and the "Professional Behaviour Principle" if a final determination, no longer subject to appeal, is made by a court or an administrative agency of competent jurisdiction that a member has violated any antidiscrimination laws of the country, state, or municipality, including those related to sexual and other forms of harassment.

Solicitation or disclosure of CPA/CIMA examination questions and answers

370.8 A member who solicits or knowingly discloses the Uniform CPA Examination or the CIMA Examination question(s) or answer(s), or both, without the AICPA's or CIMA's respective written authorisation shall be considered to have committed an act discreditable to the profession, in violation of the "Acts Discreditable Rule" and the "Professional Behaviour Principle".

Failure to file a tax return or pay a tax liability

370.9 A member who fails to comply with applicable federal, state, or local laws or regulations regarding (a) the timely filing of the member's personal tax returns or tax returns for the member's employer that the member has the authority to timely file or (b) the timely remittance of all payroll and other taxes collected on behalf of others may be considered to have committed an act discreditable to the profession, in violation of the "Acts Discreditable Rule" and the "Professional Behaviour Principle".

Negligence in the Preparation of Financial Statements or Records

370.10 A member would be considered in violation of the "Acts Discreditable Rule" and the "Professional Behaviour Principle" if the member, by virtue of his or her negligence, does any of the following:

(a) Makes, or permits or directs another to make, materially false and misleading entries in the financial statements or records of an entity

(b) Fails to correct an entity's financial statements that are materially false and misleading when the member has the authority to record an entry

(c) Signs, or permits or directs another to sign, a document containing materially false and misleading information.

Governmental bodies, commissions or other regulatory agencies

370.11 Many governmental bodies, commissions, or other regulatory agencies have established requirements, such as standards, guides, rules, and regulations, that members are required to follow in the preparation of financial statements or related information.

370.12 If a member prepares financial statements or related information (for example, management's discussion and analysis) for purposes of reporting to such bodies, commissions, or regulatory agencies, the member should follow the requirements of such organisations in addition to the applicable financial reporting framework.

370.13 A member's material departure from such requirements would be considered a violation of the "Acts Discreditable Rule" and the "Professional Behaviour Principle" unless the member discloses in the financial statements or related information that such requirements were not followed and the applicable reasons.

Indemnification and limitation of liability provisions

370.14 Certain governmental bodies, commissions, or other regulatory agencies (collectively, regulators) have established requirements through laws, regulations, or published interpretations that

(a) prohibit entities subject to their regulation (regulated entity) from including certain types of indemnification and limitation of liability provisions in agreements for the performance of audit or other attest or assurance services on behalf of the employing organisation that are required by such regulators

or

(b) provide that the existence of such provisions disqualifies a member from rendering such services to these entities.

370.15 If a member enters into, or directs or knowingly permits another individual to enter into, a contract for the performance of audit or other attest or assurance services that are subject to the requirements of these regulators, the member should not include, or knowingly permit or direct another individual to include, an indemnification or limitation of liability provision that would cause the regulated entity or a member to be in violation of such requirements or disqualify a member from providing such services to the regulated entity. A member who enters into, or directs or knowingly permits another individual to enter into, such an agreement for the performance of audit or other attest services would be considered in violation of the "Acts Discreditable Rule" and the "Professional Behaviour Principle".

Confidential information obtained from employment or volunteer activities

370.16 A member should maintain the confidentiality of his or her employer's confidential information and should not use or disclose any confidential employer information obtained as a result of an employment relationship, such as discussions with the employer's vendors, customers, or lenders (for example, any confidential information pertaining to a current or previous employer, subsidiary, affiliate, or parent thereof, as well as any entities for which the member is working in a volunteer capacity).

370.17 For purposes of this interpretation, confidential employer information is any proprietary information pertaining to the employer or any organisation for whom the member may work in a volunteer capacity that is not known to be available to the public and is obtained as a result of such relationships.

370.18 A member should be alert to the possibility of inadvertent disclosure, particularly to a close business associate or close relative or immediate family member. The member should also take reasonable steps to ensure that staff under his or her control or others within the employing organisation and persons from whom advice and assistance are obtained are aware of the confidential nature of the information.

370.19 When a member changes employment, a member should not use confidential employer information acquired as a result of a prior employment relationship to his or her personal advantage or the advantage of a third party, such as a current or prospective employer. The requirement to maintain the confidentiality of an employer's confidential information continues even after the end of the relationship between a member and the employer. However, the member is entitled to use experience and expertise gained through prior employment relationships.

370.20 A member would be considered in violation of the "Acts Discreditable Rule" and "Confidentiality Principle" if the member discloses or uses any confidential employer information acquired as a result of employment or volunteer relationships without the proper authority or specific consent of the employer or organisation for whom the member may work in a volunteer capacity, unless there is a legal or professional responsibility to use or disclose such information.

370.21 The following are examples of situations in which members are permitted or may be required to disclose confidential employer information or when such disclosure may be appropriate:

(a) Disclosure is permitted by law and authorised by the employer.

(b) Disclosure is required by law, for example, to

- comply with a validly issued and enforceable subpoena or summons or
- inform the appropriate public authorities of violations of law that have been discovered.

(c) There is a professional responsibility or right to disclose information, when not prohibited by law, to

- initiate a complaint with, or respond to any inquiry made by, the AICPA Professional Ethics Division or trial board of the AICPA or a duly constituted investigative or disciplinary body of a state CPA society, board of accountancy, or other regulatory body (AICPA)

- initiate a complaint with, or respond to any inquiry made by, the CIMA Professional Conduct Department or a duly constituted investigative or disciplinary body of CIMA, or other regulatory body (CIMA)
- protect the member's professional interests in legal proceedings
- comply with professional standards (for example, technical standards) and other ethics requirements; or
- report potential concerns regarding questionable accounting, auditing, or other matters to the employer's confidential complaint hotline or those charged with governance.

(d) Disclosure is permitted on behalf of the employer to

- obtain financing with lenders
- communicate with vendors and customers; or
- communicate with the employer's external accountant, attorneys, regulators, and other business professionals.

370.22 In deciding whether to disclose confidential employer information relevant factors to consider include the following:

(a) Whether all the relevant information is known and substantiated to the extent that it is practicable. When the situation involves unsubstantiated facts, incomplete information, or unsubstantiated conclusions, the member should use professional judgement in determining the type of disclosure to be made, if any.

(b) Whether the parties to whom the communication may be addressed are appropriate recipients.

370.23 A member may wish to consult with legal counsel prior to disclosing, or determining whether to disclose, confidential employer information.

370.24 Refer to the "Subordination of Judgement" interpretation (340.3–340.13) for additional guidance.

False, misleading, or deceptive acts in promoting or marketing professional services

370.25 A member would be in violation of the "Acts Discreditable Rule" and the "Professional Behaviour Principle" if the member promotes or markets the member's abilities to provide professional services or makes claims about the member's experience or qualifications in a manner that is false, misleading, or deceptive.

370.26 Promotional efforts would be false, misleading, or deceptive if they contain any claim or representation that would likely cause a reasonable person to be misled or deceived. This includes any representation about CPA licensure, CGMA credential or any other professional certification or accreditation that is not in compliance with the requirements of the relevant licensing authority or designating body.

Use of the CPA credential (AICPA)

370.27 A member should refer to applicable state accountancy laws and board of accountancy rules and regulations for guidance regarding the use of the CPA credential. A member who fails to follow the accountancy laws, rules, and regulations on use of the CPA credential in any of the jurisdictions in which the CPA practices would be considered to have used the CPA credential in a manner that is false, misleading, or deceptive and in violation of the "Acts Discreditable Rule".

Supplementary reading: Definitions

DEFINITIONS (PARTS A AND B)

In the CIMA Code of Ethics for Professional Accountants, the following expressions have the following meanings assigned to them:

Acceptable level

A level at which a reasonable and informed third party would be likely to conclude, weighing all the specific facts and circumstances available to the professional accountant at that time, that compliance with the fundamental principles is not compromised.

Advertising

The communication to the public of information as to the services or skills provided by professional accountants in public practice with a view to procuring professional business.

Assurance client

The responsible party that is the person (or persons) who:

(a) In a direct reporting engagement, is responsible for the subject matter; or

(b) In an assertion-based engagement, is responsible for the subject matter information and may be responsible for the subject matter.

Assurance engagement

An engagement in which a professional accountant in public practice expresses a conclusion designed to enhance the degree of confidence of the intended users other than the responsible party about the outcome of the evaluation or measurement of a subject matter against criteria. (For guidance on assurance engagements see the International Framework for Assurance Engagements issued by the International Auditing and Assurance Standards Board which describes the elements and objectives of an assurance engagement and identifies engagements to which International Standards on Auditing (ISAs), International Standards on Review Engagements (ISREs) and International Standards on Assurance Engagements (ISAEs) apply.)

Assurance team

(a) All members of the engagement team for the assurance engagement

(b) All others within a firm who can directly influence the outcome of the assurance engagement, including:

   (i) those who recommend the compensation of, or who provide direct supervisory, management or other oversight of the assurance engagement partner in connection with the performance of the assurance engagement

   (ii) those who provide consultation regarding technical or industry specific issues, transactions or events for the assurance engagement; and

   (iii) those who provide quality control for the assurance engagement, including those who perform the engagement quality control review for the assurance engagement.

Audit client

An entity in respect of which a firm conducts an audit engagement. When the client is a listed entity, audit client will always include its related entities. When the audit client is not a listed entity, audit client includes those related entities over which the client has direct or indirect control.

Audit engagement

A reasonable assurance engagement in which a professional accountant in public practice expresses an opinion whether financial statements are prepared, in all material respects (or give a true and fair view or are presented fairly, in all material respects,), in accordance with an applicable financial reporting framework, such as an engagement conducted in accordance with International Standards on Auditing. This includes a Statutory Audit, which is an audit required by legislation or other regulation.

Audit team

(a) All members of the engagement team for the audit engagement

(b) All others within a firm who can directly influence the outcome of the audit engagement, including:

   (i) Those who recommend the compensation of, or who provide direct supervisory, management or other oversight of the engagement partner in connection with the performance of the audit engagement including those at all successively senior levels above the engagement partner through to the individual who is the firm's Senior or Managing Partner (Chief Executive or equivalent)

   (ii) Those who provide consultation regarding technical or industry-specific issues, transactions or events for the engagement; and

   (iii) Those who provide quality control for the engagement, including those who perform the engagement quality control review for the engagement; and

(c) All those within a network firm who can directly influence the outcome of the audit engagement.

Close family

A parent, child or sibling who is not an immediate family member.

Contingent fee

A fee calculated on a predetermined basis relating to the outcome of a transaction or the result of the services performed by the firm. A fee that is established by a court or other public authority is not a contingent fee.

Direct financial interest

A financial interest:

(a) Owned directly by and under the control of an individual or entity (including those managed on a discretionary basis by others); or

(b) Beneficially owned through a collective investment vehicle, estate, trust or other intermediary over which the individual or entity has control, or the ability to influence investment decisions.

Director or officer

Those charged with the governance of an entity, or acting in an equivalent capacity, regardless of their title, which may vary from jurisdiction to jurisdiction.

Engagement partner

The partner or other person in the firm who is responsible for the engagement and its performance, and for the report that is issued on behalf of the firm, and who, where required, has the appropriate authority from a professional, legal or regulatory body.

Engagement quality control review

A process designed to provide an objective evaluation, on or before the report is issued, of the significant judgements the engagement team made and the conclusions it reached in formulating the report.

Engagement team

All partners and staff performing the engagement, and any individuals engaged by the firm or a network firm who perform assurance procedures on the engagement. This excludes external experts engaged by the firm or a network firm.

The term 'engagement team' also excludes individuals within the client's internal audit function who provide direct assistance on an audit engagement when the external auditor complies with the requirements of ASA 610 (Revised 2013) Using the work of internal auditors.

Existing accountant

A professional accountant in public practice currently holding an audit appointment or carrying out accounting, taxation, consulting or similar professional services for a client.

External expert

An individual (who is not a partner or a member of the professional staff, including temporary staff, of the firm or a network firm) or organisation possessing skills, knowledge and experience in a field other than accounting or auditing, whose work in that field is used to assist the professional accountant in obtaining sufficient appropriate evidence.

Financial interest

An interest in an equity or other security, debenture, loan or other debt instrument of an entity, including rights and obligations to acquire such an interest and derivatives directly related to such interest.

Financial statements

A structured representation of historical financial information, including related notes, intended to communicate an entity's economic resources or obligations at a point in time or the changes therein for a period of time in accordance with a financial reporting framework. The related notes ordinarily comprise a summary of significant accounting policies and other explanatory information. The term can relate to a complete set of financial statements, but it can also refer to a single financial statement, for example, a balance sheet, or a statement of revenues and expenses, and related explanatory notes.

Financial statements on which the firm will express an opinion

In the case of a single entity, the financial statements of that entity. In the case of consolidated financial statements, also referred to as group financial statements, the consolidated financial statements.

Firm

(a) A sole practitioner, partnership or corporation of professional accountants

(b) An entity that controls such parties, through ownership, management or other means; and

(c) An entity controlled by such parties, through ownership, management or other means.

Historical financial information

Information expressed in financial terms in relation to a particular entity, derived primarily from that entity's accounting system, about economic events occurring in past time periods or about economic conditions or circumstances at points in time in the past.

Immediate family

A spouse (or equivalent) or dependent.

Independence

Independence is:

(a) Independence of mind – the state of mind that permits the expression of a conclusion without being affected by influences that compromise professional judgement, thereby allowing an individual to act with integrity, and exercise objectivity and professional scepticism.

(b) Independence in appearance – the avoidance of facts and circumstances that are so significant that a reasonable and informed third party would be likely to conclude, weighing all the specific facts and circumstances, that a firm's, or a member of the audit or assurance team's, integrity, objectivity or professional scepticism has been compromised.

Indirect financial interest

A financial interest beneficially owned through a collective investment vehicle, estate, trust or other intermediary over which the individual or entity has no control or ability to influence investment decisions.

Key audit partner

The engagement partner, the individual responsible for the engagement quality control review, and other audit partners, if any, on the engagement team who make key decisions or judgements on significant matters with respect to the audit of the financial statements on which the firm will express an opinion. Depending upon the circumstances and the role of the individuals on the audit, 'other audit partners' may include, for example, audit partners responsible for significant subsidiaries or divisions.

Listed entity

An entity whose shares, stock or debt are quoted or listed on a recognised stock exchange, or are marketed under the regulations of a recognised stock exchange or other equivalent body.

Network

A larger structure:

(a) That is aimed at co-operation; and

(b) That is clearly aimed at profit or cost sharing or shares common ownership, control or management, common quality control policies and procedures, common business strategy, the use of a common brand-name, or a significant part of professional resources.

Network firm

A firm or entity that belongs to a network.

Office

A distinct sub-group, whether organised on geographical or practice lines.

Professional accountant

An individual who is a member of an IFAC member body.

Professional accountant in business

A professional accountant employed or engaged in an executive or non-executive capacity in such areas as commerce, industry, service, the public sector, education, the not for profit sector, regulatory bodies or professional bodies, or a professional accountant contracted by such entities.

Professional accountant in public practice

A professional accountant, irrespective of functional classification (for example, audit, tax or consulting) in a firm that provides professional services. This term is also used to refer to a firm of professional accountants in public practice.

Professional activity

An activity requiring accountancy or related skills undertaken by a professional accountant, including accounting, auditing, taxation, management consulting, and financial management.

Professional services

Professional activities performed for clients.

Public interest entity

(a) A listed entity; and

(b) An entity:

  (i) Defined by regulation or legislation as a public interest entity; or

  (ii) For which the audit is required by regulation or legislation to be conducted in compliance with the same independence requirements that apply to the audit of listed entities. Such regulation may be promulgated by any relevant regulator, including an audit regulator.

Related entity

An entity that has any of the following relationships with the client:

(a) An entity that has direct or indirect control over the client if the client is material to such entity

(b) An entity with a direct financial interest in the client if that entity has significant influence over the client and the interest in the client is material to such entity

(c) An entity over which the client has direct or indirect control

(d) An entity in which the client, or an entity related to the client under (c) above, has a direct financial interest that gives it significant influence over such entity and the interest is material to the client and its related entity in (c); and

(e) An entity which is under common control with the client (a 'sister entity') if the sister entity and the client are both material to the entity that controls both the client and sister entity.

Review client

An entity in respect of which a firm conducts a review engagement.

Review engagement

An assurance engagement, conducted in accordance with International Standards on Review Engagements or equivalent, in which a professional accountant in public practice expresses a conclusion on whether, on the basis of the procedures which do not provide all the evidence that would be required in an audit, anything has come to the accountant's attention that causes the accountant to believe that the financial statements are not prepared, in all material respects, in accordance with an applicable financial reporting framework.

Review team

(a) All members of the engagement team for the review engagement; and

(b) All others within a firm who can directly influence the outcome of the review engagement, including:

    (i) Those who recommend the compensation of, or who provide direct supervisory, management or other oversight of the engagement partner in connection with the performance of the review engagement including those at all successively senior levels above the engagement partner through to the individual who is the firm's Senior or Managing Partner (Chief Executive or equivalent)

(ii) Those who provide consultation regarding technical or industry specific issues, transactions or events for the engagement; and

(iii) Those who provide quality control for the engagement, including those who perform the engagement quality control review for the engagement; and

(iv) All those within a network firm who can directly influence the outcome of the review engagement.

Special purpose financial statements

Financial statements prepared in accordance with a financial reporting framework designed to meet the financial information needs of specified users.

Those charged with governance

The person(s) or organisation(s) (for example, a corporate trustee) with responsibility for overseeing the strategic direction of the entity and obligations related to the accountability of the entity. This includes overseeing the financial reporting process.

For some entities in some jurisdictions, those charged with governance may include management personnel, for example, executive members of a governance board of a private or public sector entity, or an owner-manager.

DEFINITIONS (PART C)

In Part C of the CIMA Code of Ethics for Professional Accountants, the following expressions have the following meanings assigned to them:

Acceptable level

An acceptable level is a level at which a reasonable and informed third party who is aware of the relevant information would be expected to conclude that a member's compliance with the rules or fundamental principles is not compromised.

Client

Any person or entity, other than the member's employer, that engages a member or member's firm to perform professional services and, if different, the person or entity with respect to which professional services are performed. For purposes of this definition for AICPA members, the term employer does not include the following:

(a) Person or entity engaged in public practice.

(b) Federal, state, and local government or component unit thereof, provided that the member performing professional services with respect to the entity is

   (i) directly elected by voters of the government or component unit thereof with respect to which professional services are performed;

   (ii) an individual who is (1) appointed by a legislative body and (2) subject to removal by a legislative body; or

   (iii) appointed by someone other than the legislative body, so long as the appointment is confirmed by the legislative body and removal is subject to oversight or approval by the legislative body.

Close relative

A parent, sibling, or nondependent child.

Council

The AICPA Council.

Employing organisation

Any entity that employs the member or engages the member on a contractual or volunteer basis in an executive, a staff, a governance, an advisory, or an administrative capacity to provide professional services.

Financial interest

An ownership interest in an equity or a debt security issued by an entity, including rights and obligations to acquire such an interest and derivatives directly related to such interest.

Financial statements

A presentation of financial data, including accompanying disclosures, if any, intended to communicate an entity's economic resources or obligations, or both, at a point in time or the changes therein for a period of time, in accordance with the applicable financial reporting framework. Tax returns and supporting schedules do not, for this purpose, constitute financial statements. The statement, affidavit, or signature of preparers required on tax returns neither constitutes an opinion on financial statements nor requires a disclaimer of such opinion.

Immediate family

A spouse, spousal equivalent, or dependent (regardless of whether the dependent is related).

Institute

The AICPA or CIMA.

Interpretation

Pronouncements issued by the AICPA and CIMA to provide guidelines concerning the scope and application of the rules of conduct and fundamental principles.

Member

A member of the AICPA is a member, an associate or affiliate member or international associate of the AICPA. A member of CIMA is a Fellow or Associate of the Institute, and includes, for the purposes of the disciplinary powers and procedures of the Institute, a person who ceased to be a member on or after June 14, 2003. When used in this code, the term member means a member in business or professional accountant in business and who is a CGMA (or entitled to use the designation CGMA).

Member(s) in business or professional accountant(s) in business

A member who is employed or engaged on a contractual or volunteer basis in a(n) executive, staff, governance, advisory, or administrative capacity in such areas as industry, the public sector, education, the not-for-profit sector, and regulatory or professional bodies. This does not include a member engaged in public practice.

Professional services

Include all services requiring accountancy or related skills that are performed by a member for an employer, or on a volunteer basis. These services include, but are not limited to accounting, tax, bookkeeping, management consulting, financial management, corporate governance, business valuation and educational services. For AICPA members, it also includes those services for which standards are promulgated by bodies designated by AICPA Council.

Public interest entity(ies)

Public interest entities are (a) all listed entities, including entities whose shares, stock, or debt are quoted or listed on a recognised stock exchange or marketed under the regulations of a recognised stock exchange or other equivalent body, and (b) any entity for which an audit is required by regulation or legislation to be conducted in compliance with the same independence requirements that apply to an audit of listed entities. Members may wish to consider whether additional entities should also be treated as public interest entities because they have a large number and wide range of stakeholders. Factors to be considered may include (a) the nature of the business, such as the holding of assets in a fiduciary capacity for a large number of stakeholders; (b) size; and (c) number of employees.

Public practice

Consists of the performance of professional services for a client by a member or member's firm.

Safeguards

Actions or other measures that may eliminate a threat or reduce a threat to an acceptable level.

Those charged with governance

The person(s) or organisation(s) (for example, a corporate trustee) with responsibility for overseeing the strategic direction of the entity and the obligations related to the accountability of the entity. This includes overseeing the financial reporting process. Those charged with governance may include management personnel (for example, executive members of a governance board or an owner-manager).

When an interpretation requires communicating with those charged with governance, the member should determine, considering the nature and importance of the particular circumstances and matter to be communicated, the appropriate person(s) within the entity's governance structure with whom to communicate. If the member communicates with a subgroup of those charged with governance (for example, an audit committee or an individual), the member should determine whether communication with all of those charged with governance is also necessary, so that they are adequately informed.

Threat(s)

Relationships or circumstances that could compromise a member's compliance with the rules or fundamental principles.

Supplementary reading: Annex 1 Preface and Contents

CIMA CODE OF ETHICS for professional accountants – Annex 1 (Sections 290 and 291)

CIMA PREFACE

Annex 1 comprises section 290 and 291 of the CIMA Code of Ethics which address the independence requirement for audit, review and other assurance engagements and apply a conceptual framework approach.

Also included is commentary on the independence requirements and the effective date and transitional provisions for public interest entities, partner rotation, non-assurance services, fees and compensation and evaluation policies.

For CIMA members providing non-audit assurance services, the Code contains new modified independence requirements relating to certain audit and review reports that include a restriction on use and distribution (290.500–290.514). Similar provisions are included in 291.21–291.27

Section 290: Independence – Audit and Review engagements

Section 291: Independence – Other assurance engagements

SECTION 290

INDEPENDENCE – AUDIT AND REVIEW ENGAGEMENTS

CONTENTS

Supplementary reading: Annex 1 290.1 to 290.39

Structure of section

290.1 This section addresses the independence requirements for audit engagements and review engagements, which are assurance engagements in which a professional accountant in public practice expresses a conclusion on financial statements. Such engagements comprise audit and review engagements to report on a complete set of financial statements and a single financial statement.

Independence requirements for assurance engagements that are not audit or review engagements are addressed in Section 291.

290.2 In certain circumstances involving audit engagements where the audit report includes a restriction on use and distribution and provided certain conditions are met, the independence requirements in this section may be modified as provided in paragraphs 290.500 to 290.514. The modifications are not permitted in the case of an audit of financial statements required by law or regulation.

290.3 In this section, the term(s):

(a) 'Audit,' 'audit team,' 'audit engagement,' 'audit client' and 'audit report' includes review, review team, review engagement, review client and review report; and

(b) 'Firm' includes network firm, except where otherwise stated.

A conceptual framework approach to independence

290.4 In the case of audit engagements, it is in the public interest and, therefore, required by this Code, that members of audit teams, firms and network firms shall be independent of audit clients.

290.5 The objective of this section is to assist firms and members of audit teams in applying the conceptual framework approach described below to achieving and maintaining independence.

290.6 Independence comprises:

(a) Independence of mind

The state of mind that permits the expression of a conclusion without being affected by influences that compromise professional judgement, thereby allowing an individual to act with integrity and exercise objectivity and professional scepticism.

(b) Independence in appearance

The avoidance of facts and circumstances that are so significant that a reasonable and informed third party would be likely to conclude, weighing all the specific facts and circumstances, that a firm's, or a member of the audit team's, integrity, objectivity or professional scepticism has been compromised.

290.7 The conceptual framework approach shall be applied by professional accountants to:

(a) Identify threats to independence

(b) Evaluate the significance of the threats identified; and

(c) Apply safeguards, when necessary, to eliminate the threats or reduce them to an acceptable level.

When the professional accountant determines that appropriate safeguards are not available or cannot be applied to eliminate the threats or reduce them to an acceptable level, the professional accountant shall eliminate the circumstance or relationship creating the threats or decline or terminate the audit engagement.

A professional accountant shall use professional judgement in applying this conceptual framework.

290.8 Many different circumstances, or combinations of circumstances, may be relevant in assessing threats to independence. It is impossible to define every situation that creates threats to independence and to specify the appropriate action. Therefore, this Code establishes a conceptual framework that requires firms and members of audit teams to identify, evaluate, and address threats to independence.

The conceptual framework approach assists professional accountants in practice in complying with the ethical requirements in this Code. It accommodates many variations in circumstances that create threats to independence and can deter a professional accountant from concluding that a situation is permitted if it is not specifically prohibited.

290.9 Paragraphs 290.100 and onwards describe how the conceptual framework approach to independence is to be applied. These paragraphs do not address all the circumstances and relationships that create or may create threats to independence.

290.10 In deciding whether to accept or continue an engagement, or whether a particular individual may be a member of the audit team, a firm shall identify and evaluate threats to independence. If the threats are not at an acceptable level, and the decision is whether to accept an engagement or include a particular individual on the audit team, the firm shall determine whether safeguards are available to eliminate the threats or reduce them to an acceptable level. If the decision is whether to continue an engagement, the firm shall determine whether any existing safeguards will continue to be effective to eliminate the threats or reduce them to an acceptable level or whether other safeguards will need to be applied or whether the engagement needs to be terminated. Whenever new information about a threat to independence comes to the attention of the firm during the engagement, the firm shall evaluate the significance of the threat in accordance with the conceptual framework approach.

290.11 Throughout this section, reference is made to the significance of threats to independence. In evaluating the significance of a threat, qualitative as well as quantitative factors shall be taken into account.

290.12 This section does not, in most cases, prescribe the specific responsibility of individuals within the firm for actions related to independence because responsibility may differ depending on the size, structure and organisation of a firm. The firm is required by International Standards on Quality Control (ISQCs) to establish policies and procedures designed to provide it with reasonable assurance that independence is maintained when required by relevant ethical requirements. In addition, International Standards on Auditing (ISAs) require the engagement partner to form a conclusion on compliance with the independence requirements that apply to the engagement.

Networks and Network firms

290.13 If a firm is deemed to be a network firm, the firm shall be independent of the audit clients of the other firms within the network (unless otherwise stated in this Code). The independence requirements in this section that apply to a network firm apply to any entity, such as a consulting practice or professional law practice, that meets the definition of a network firm irrespective of whether the entity itself meets the definition of a firm.

290.14 To enhance their ability to provide professional services, firms frequently form larger structures with other firms and entities. Whether these larger structures create a network depends on the particular facts and circumstances and does not depend on whether the firms and entities are legally separate and distinct. For example, a larger structure may be aimed only at facilitating the referral of work, which in itself does not meet the criteria necessary to constitute a network. Alternatively, a larger structure might be such that it is aimed at co-operation and the firms share a common brand name, a common system of quality control, or significant professional resources and consequently is deemed to be a network.

290.15 The judgement as to whether the larger structure is a network shall be made in light of whether a reasonable and informed third party would be likely to conclude, weighing all the specific facts and circumstances, that the entities are associated in such a way that a network exists. This judgement shall be applied consistently throughout the network.

290.16 Where the larger structure is aimed at co-operation and it is clearly aimed at profit or cost sharing among the entities within the structure, it is deemed to be a network. However, the sharing of immaterial costs does not in itself create a network. In addition, if the sharing of costs is limited only to those costs related to the development of audit methodologies, manuals, or training courses, this would not in itself create a network. Further, an association between a firm and an otherwise unrelated entity to jointly provide a service or develop a product does not in itself create a network.

290.17 Where the larger structure is aimed at cooperation and the entities within the structure share common ownership, control or management, it is deemed to be a network. This could be achieved by contract or other means.

290.18 Where the larger structure is aimed at co-operation and the entities within the structure share common quality control policies and procedures, it is deemed to be a network. For this purpose, common quality control policies and procedures are those designed, implemented and monitored across the larger structure.

290.19 Where the larger structure is aimed at co-operation and the entities within the structure share a common business strategy, it is deemed to be a network. Sharing a common business strategy involves an agreement by the entities to achieve common strategic objectives. An entity is not deemed to be a network firm merely because it co-operates with another entity solely to respond jointly to a request for a proposal for the provision of a professional service.

290.20 Where the larger structure is aimed at co-operation and the entities within the structure share the use of a common brand name, it is deemed to be a network. A common brand name includes common initials or a common name. A firm is deemed to be using a common brand name if it includes, for example, the common brand name as part of, or along with, its firm name, when a partner of the firm signs an audit report.

290.21 Even though a firm does not belong to a network and does not use a common brand name as part of its firm name, it may give the appearance that it belongs to a network if it makes reference in its stationery or promotional materials to being a member of an association of firms. Accordingly, if care is not taken in how a firm describes such memberships, a perception may be created that the firm belongs to a network.

290.22 If a firm sells a component of its practice, the sales agreement sometimes provides that, for a limited period of time, the component may continue to use the name of the firm, or an element of the name, even though it is no longer connected to the firm. In such circumstances, while the two entities may be practicing under a common name, the facts are such that they do not belong to a larger structure aimed at co-operation and are, therefore, not network firms. Those entities shall determine how to disclose that they are not network firms when presenting themselves to outside parties.

290.23 Where the larger structure is aimed at co-operation and the entities within the structure share a significant part of professional resources, it is deemed to be a network. Professional resources include:

- Common systems that enable firms to exchange information such as client data, billing and time records
- Partners and staff
- Technical departments that consult on technical or industry specific issues, transactions or events for assurance engagements
- Audit methodology or audit manuals; and
- Training courses and facilities.

290.24 The determination of whether the professional resources shared are significant, and therefore the firms are network firms, shall be made based on the relevant facts and circumstances. Where the shared resources are limited to common audit methodology or audit manuals, with no exchange of personnel or client or market information, it is unlikely that the shared resources would be significant. The same applies to a common training endeavour. Where, however, the shared resources involve the exchange of people or information, such as where staff are drawn from a shared pool, or a common technical department is created within the larger structure to provide participating firms with technical advice that the firms are required to follow, a reasonable and informed third party is more likely to conclude that the shared resources are significant.

Public interest entities

290.25 Section 290 contains additional provisions that reflect the extent of public interest in certain entities. For the purpose of this section, public interest entities are:

(a) All listed entities; and

(b) Any entity:

- (i) Defined by regulation or legislation as a public interest entity; or
- (ii) For which the audit is required by regulation or legislation to be conducted in compliance with the same independence requirements that apply to the audit of listed entities. Such regulation may be promulgated by any relevant regulator, including an audit regulator.

290.26 Firms and member bodies are encouraged to determine whether to treat additional entities, or certain categories of entities, as public interest entities because they have a large number and wide range of stakeholders. Factors to be considered include:

- The nature of the business, such as the holding of assets in a fiduciary capacity for a large number of stakeholders. Examples may include financial institutions, such as banks and insurance companies, and pension funds
- Size; and
- Number of employees.

Related entities

290.27 In the case of an audit client that is a listed entity, references to an audit client in this section include related entities of the client (unless otherwise stated). For all other audit clients, references to an audit client in this section include related entities over which the client has direct or indirect control.

When the audit team knows or has reason to believe that a relationship or circumstance involving another related entity of the client is relevant to the evaluation of the firm's independence from the client, the audit team shall include that related entity when identifying and evaluating threats to independence and applying appropriate safeguards.

Those charged with governance

290.28 Even when not required by the Code, applicable auditing standards, law or regulation, regular communication is encouraged between the firm and those charged with governance of the audit client regarding relationships and other matters that might, in the firm's opinion, reasonably bear on independence. Such communication enables those charged with governance to:

(a) Consider the firm's judgements in identifying and evaluating threats to independence

(b) Consider the appropriateness of safeguards applied to eliminate them or reduce them to an acceptable level, and

(c) Take appropriate action. Such an approach can be particularly helpful with respect to intimidation and familiarity threats.

Documentation

290.29 Documentation provides evidence of the professional accountant's judgements in forming conclusions regarding compliance with independence requirements. The absence of documentation is not a determinant of whether a firm considered a particular matter nor whether it is independent. The professional accountant shall document conclusions regarding compliance with independence requirements, and the substance of any relevant discussions that support those conclusions.

Accordingly:

(a) When safeguards are required to reduce a threat to an acceptable level, the professional accountant shall document the nature of the threat and the safeguards in place or applied that reduce the threat to an acceptable level; and

(b) When a threat required significant analysis to determine whether safeguards were necessary and the professional accountant concluded that they were not because the threat was already at an acceptable level, the professional accountant shall document the nature of the threat and the rationale for the conclusion.

Engagement period

290.30 Independence from the audit client is required both during the engagement period and the period covered by the financial statements. The engagement period starts when the audit team begins to perform audit services. The engagement period ends when the audit report is issued. When the engagement is of a recurring nature, it ends at the later of the notification by either party that the professional relationship has terminated or the issuance of the final audit report.

290.31 When an entity becomes an audit client during or after the period covered by the financial statements on which the firm will express an opinion, the firm shall determine whether any threats to independence are created by:

(a) Financial or business relationships with the audit client during or after the period covered by the financial statements but before accepting the audit engagement; or

(b) Previous services provided to the audit client.

290.32 If a non-assurance service was provided to the audit client during or after the period covered by the financial statements but before the audit team begins to perform audit services and the service would not be permitted during the period of the audit engagement, the firm shall evaluate any threat to independence created by the service. If a threat is not at an acceptable level, the audit engagement shall only be accepted if safeguards are applied to eliminate any threats or reduce them to an acceptable level. Examples of such safeguards include:

- Not including personnel who provided the non-assurance service as members of the audit team
- Having a professional accountant review the audit and non-assurance work as appropriate; or
- Engaging another firm to evaluate the results of the non-assurance service or having another firm re-perform the non-assurance service to the extent necessary to enable it to take responsibility for the service.

Mergers and Acquisitions

290.33 When, as a result of a merger or acquisition, an entity becomes a related entity of an audit client, the firm shall identify and evaluate previous and current interests and relationships with the related entity that, taking into account available safeguards, could affect its independence and therefore its ability to continue the audit engagement after the effective date of the merger or acquisition.

290.34 The firm shall take steps necessary to terminate, by the effective date of the merger or acquisition, any current interests or relationships that are not permitted under this Code. However, if such a current interest or relationship cannot reasonably be terminated by the effective date of the merger or acquisition, for example, because the related entity is unable by the effective date to effect an orderly transition to another service provider of a non-assurance service provided by the firm, the firm shall evaluate the threat that is created by such interest or relationship. The more significant the threat, the more likely the firm's objectivity will be compromised and it will be unable to continue as auditor.

The significance of the threat will depend upon factors such as:

- The nature and significance of the interest or relationship
- The nature and significance of the related entity relationship (for example, whether the related entity is a subsidiary or parent); and
- The length of time until the interest or relationship can reasonably be terminated.

The firm shall discuss with those charged with governance the reasons why the interest or relationship cannot reasonably be terminated by the effective date of the merger or acquisition and the evaluation of the significance of the threat.

290.35 If those charged with governance request the firm to continue as auditor, the firm shall do so only if:

(a) The interest or relationship will be terminated as soon as reasonably possible and in all cases within six months of the effective date of the merger or acquisition

(b) Any individual who has such an interest or relationship, including one that has arisen through performing a non-assurance service that would not be permitted under this section, will not be a member of the engagement team for the audit or the individual responsible for the engagement quality control review; and

(c) Appropriate transitional measures will be applied, as necessary, and discussed with those charged with governance. Examples of transitional measures include:
   - Having a professional accountant review the audit or non-assurance work as appropriate
   - Having a professional accountant, who is not a member of the firm expressing the opinion on the financial statements, perform a review that is equivalent to an engagement quality control review; or
   - Engaging another firm to evaluate the results of the non-assurance service or having another firm re-perform the non-assurance service to the extent necessary to enable it to take responsibility for the service.

290.36 The firm may have completed a significant amount of work on the audit prior to the effective date of the merger or acquisition and may be able to complete the remaining audit procedures within a short period of time. In such circumstances, if those charged with governance request the firm to complete the audit while continuing with an interest or relationship identified in paragraph 290.33, the firm shall do so only if it:

(a) Has evaluated the significance of the threat created by such interest or relationship and discussed the evaluation with those charged with governance

(b) Complies with the requirements of paragraph 290.35(b)–(c); and

(c) Ceases to be the auditor no later than the issuance of the audit report.

290.37 When addressing previous and current interests and relationships covered by paragraphs 290.33 to 290.36, the firm shall determine whether, even if all the requirements could be met, the interests and relationships create threats that would remain so significant that objectivity would be compromised and, if so, the firm shall cease to be the auditor.

290.38 The professional accountant shall document any interests or relationships covered by paragraphs 290.34 and 36 that will not be terminated by the effective date of the merger or acquisition and the reasons why they will not be terminated, the transitional measures applied, the results of the discussion with those charged with governance, and the rationale as to why the previous and current interests and relationships do not create threats that would remain so significant that objectivity would be compromised.

Other considerations

290.39 There may be occasions when there is an inadvertent violation of this section. If such an inadvertent violation occurs, it generally will be deemed not to compromise independence provided the firm has appropriate quality control policies and procedures in place, equivalent to those required by ISQCs, to maintain independence and, once discovered, the violation is corrected promptly and any necessary safeguards are applied to eliminate any threat or reduce it to an acceptable level. The firm shall determine whether to discuss the matter with those charged with governance.

Paragraphs 290.40 to 290.99 are intentionally left blank.

Supplementary reading: Annex 1 290.100 to 290.133

Application of the conceptual framework approach to independence

290.100 Paragraphs 290.102 to 290.231 describe specific circumstances and relationships that create or may create threats to independence. The paragraphs describe the potential threats and the types of safeguards that may be appropriate to eliminate the threats or reduce them to an acceptable level and identify certain situations where no safeguards could reduce the threats to an acceptable level. The paragraphs do not describe all of the circumstances and relationships that create or may create a threat to independence. The firm and the members of the audit team shall evaluate the implications of similar, but different, circumstances and relationships and determine whether safeguards, including the safeguards in paragraphs 200.12 to 200.15, can be applied when necessary to eliminate the threats to independence or reduce them to an acceptable level.

290.101 Paragraphs 290.102 to 290.126 contain references to the materiality of a financial interest, loan, or guarantee, or the significance of a business relationship. For the purpose of determining whether such an interest is material to an individual, the combined net worth of the individual and the individual's immediate family members may be taken into account.

Financial interests

290.102 Holding a financial interest in an audit client may create a self-interest threat. The existence and significance of any threat created depends on:

(a) The role of the person holding the financial interest

(b) Whether the financial interest is direct or indirect, and

(c) The materiality of the financial interest.

290.103 Financial interests may be held through an intermediary (for example, a collective investment vehicle, estate or trust). The determination of whether such financial interests are direct or indirect will depend upon whether the beneficial owner has control over the investment vehicle or the ability to influence its investment decisions. When control over the investment vehicle or the ability to influence investment decisions exists, this Code defines that financial interest to be a direct financial interest.

Conversely, when the beneficial owner of the financial interest has no control over the investment vehicle or ability to influence its investment decisions, this Code defines that financial interest to be an indirect financial interest.

290.104 If a member of the audit team, a member of that individual's immediate family, or a firm has a direct financial interest or a material indirect financial interest in the audit client, the self-interest threat created would be so significant that no safeguards could reduce the threat to an acceptable level. Therefore, none of the following shall have a direct financial interest or a material indirect financial interest in the client: a member of the audit team; a member of that individual's immediate family; or the firm.

290.105 When a member of the audit team has a close family member who the audit team member knows has a direct financial interest or a material indirect financial interest in the audit client, a self-interest threat is created. The significance of the threat will depend on factors such as:

- The nature of the relationship between the member of the audit team and the close family member; and
- The materiality of the financial interest to the close family member.

The significance of the threat shall be evaluated and safeguards applied when necessary to eliminate the threat or reduce it to an acceptable level. Examples of such safeguards include:

- The close family member disposing, as soon as practicable, of all of the financial interest or disposing of a sufficient portion of an indirect financial interest so that the remaining interest is no longer material
- Having a professional accountant review the work of the member of the audit team; or
- Removing the individual from the audit team.

290.106 If a member of the audit team, a member of that individual's immediate family, or a firm has a direct or material indirect financial interest in an entity that has a controlling interest in the audit client, and the client is material to the entity, the self-interest threat created would be so significant that no safeguards could reduce the threat to an acceptable level. Therefore, none of the following shall have such a financial interest: a member of the audit team; a member of that individual's immediate family; and the firm.

290.107 The holding by a firm's retirement benefit plan of a direct or material indirect financial interest in an audit client creates a self-interest threat. The significance of the threat shall be evaluated and safeguards applied when necessary to eliminate the threat or reduce it to an acceptable level.

290.108 If other partners in the office in which the engagement partner practices in connection with the audit engagement, or their immediate family members, hold a direct financial interest or a material indirect financial interest in that audit client, the self-interest threat created would be so significant that no safeguards could reduce the threat to an acceptable level. Therefore, neither such partners nor their immediate family members shall hold any such financial interests in such an audit client.

290.109 The office in which the engagement partner practices in connection with the audit engagement is not necessarily the office to which that partner is assigned. Accordingly, when the engagement partner is located in a different office from that of the other members of the audit team, professional judgement shall be used to determine in which office the partner practices in connection with that engagement.

290.110 If other partners and managerial employees who provide non-audit services to the audit client, except those whose involvement is minimal, or their immediate family members, hold a direct financial interest or a material indirect financial interest in the audit client, the self-interest threat created would be so significant that no safeguards could reduce the threat to an acceptable level. Accordingly, neither such personnel nor their immediate family members shall hold any such financial interests in such an audit client.

290.111 Despite paragraphs 290.108 and 290.110, the holding of a financial interest in an audit client by an immediate family member of:

(a) A partner located in the office in which the engagement partner practices in connection with the audit engagement, or

(b) A partner or managerial employee who provides non-audit services to the audit client, is deemed not to compromise independence if the financial interest is received as a result of the immediate family member's employment rights (for example, through pension or share option plans) and, when necessary, safeguards are applied to eliminate any threat to independence or reduce it to an acceptable level. However, when the immediate family member has or obtains the right to dispose of the financial interest or, in the case of a stock option, the right to exercise the option, the financial interest shall be disposed of or forfeited as soon as practicable.

290.112 A self-interest threat may be created if the firm or a member of the audit team, or a member of that individual's immediate family, has a financial interest in an entity and an audit client also has a financial interest in that entity. However, independence is deemed not to be compromised if these interests are immaterial and the audit client cannot exercise significant influence over the entity. If such interest is material to any party, and the audit client can exercise significant influence over the other entity, no safeguards could reduce the threat to an acceptable level. Accordingly, the firm shall not have such an interest and any individual with such an interest shall, before becoming a member of the audit team, either:

(a) Dispose of the interest; or

(b) Dispose of a sufficient amount of the interest so that the remaining interest is no longer material.

290.113 A self-interest, familiarity or intimidation threat may be created if a member of the audit team, or a member of that individual's immediate family, or the firm, has a financial interest in an entity when a director, officer or controlling owner of the audit client is also known to have a financial interest in that entity. The existence and significance of any threat will depend upon factors such as:

- The role of the professional on the audit team
- Whether ownership of the entity is closely or widely held
- Whether the interest gives the investor the ability to control or significantly influence the entity; and
- The materiality of the financial interest.

The significance of any threat shall be evaluated and safeguards applied when necessary to eliminate the threat or reduce it to an acceptable level. Examples of such safeguards include:

- Removing the member of the audit team with the financial interest from the audit team; or
- Having a professional accountant review the work of the member of the audit team.

290.114 The holding by a firm, or a member of the audit team, or a member of that individual's immediate family, of a direct financial interest or a material indirect financial interest in the audit client as a trustee creates a self-interest threat. Similarly, a self-interest threat is created when:

(a) A partner in the office in which the engagement partner practices in connection with the audit

(b) Other partners and managerial employees who provide non-assurance services to the audit client, except those whose involvement is minimal; or

(c) Their immediate family members, hold a direct financial interest or a material indirect financial interest in the audit client as trustee. Such an interest shall not be held unless:

– Neither the trustee, nor an immediate family member of the trustee, nor the firm are beneficiaries of the trust

- The interest in the audit client held by the trust is not material to the trust
- The trust is not able to exercise significant influence over the audit client; and
- The trustee, an immediate family member of the trustee, or the firm cannot significantly influence any investment decision involving a financial interest in the audit client.

290.115 Members of the audit team shall determine whether a self-interest threat is created by any known financial interests in the audit client held by other individuals including:

(a) Partners and professional employees of the firm, other than those referred to above, or their immediate family members; and

(b) Individuals with a close personal relationship with a member of the audit team.

Whether these interests create a self-interest threat will depend on factors such as:

- The firm's organisational, operating and reporting structure; and
- The nature of the relationship between the individual and the member of the audit team.

The significance of any threat shall be evaluated and safeguards applied when necessary to eliminate the threat or reduce it to an acceptable level. Examples of such safeguards include:

- Removing the member of the audit team with the personal relationship from the audit team
- Excluding the member of the audit team from any significant decision-making concerning the audit engagement; or
- Having a professional accountant review the work of the member of the audit team.

290.116 If a firm or a partner or employee of the firm, or a member of that individual's immediate family, receives a direct financial interest or a material indirect financial interest in an audit client, for example, by way of an inheritance, gift or as a result of a merger and such interest would not be permitted to be held under this section, then:

(a) If the interest is received by the firm, the financial interest shall be disposed of immediately, or a sufficient amount of an indirect financial interest shall be disposed of so that the remaining interest is no longer material

(b) If the interest is received by a member of the audit team, or a member of that individual's immediate family, the individual who received the financial interest shall immediately dispose of the financial interest, or dispose of a sufficient amount of an indirect financial interest so that the remaining interest is no longer material; or

(c) If the interest is received by an individual who is not a member of the audit team, or by an immediate family member of the individual, the financial interest shall be disposed of as soon as possible, or a sufficient amount of an indirect financial interest shall be disposed of so that the remaining interest is no longer material. Pending the disposal of the financial interest, a determination shall be made as to whether any safeguards are necessary.

290.117 When an inadvertent violation of this section as it relates to a financial interest in an audit client occurs, it is deemed not to compromise independence if:

(a) The firm has established policies and procedures that require prompt notification to the firm of any breaches resulting from the purchase, inheritance or other acquisition of a financial interest in the audit client

(b) The actions in paragraph 290.116 (a)–(c) are taken as applicable; and

(c) The firm applies other safeguards when necessary to reduce any remaining threat to an acceptable level. Examples of such safeguards include:

- Having a professional accountant review the work of the member of the audit team; or
- Excluding the individual from any significant decision-making concerning the audit engagement.

The firm shall determine whether to discuss the matter with those charged with governance.

Loans and Guarantees

290.118 A loan, or a guarantee of a loan, to a member of the audit team, or a member of that individual's immediate family, or the firm from an audit client that is a bank or a similar institution may create a threat to independence. If the loan or guarantee is not made under normal lending procedures, terms and conditions, a self-interest threat would be created that would be so significant that no safeguards could reduce the threat to an acceptable level. Accordingly, neither a member of the audit team, a member of that individual's immediate family, nor a firm shall accept such a loan or guarantee.

290.119 If a loan to a firm from an audit client that is a bank or similar institution is made under normal lending procedures, terms and conditions and it is material to the audit client or firm receiving the loan, it may be possible to apply safeguards to reduce the self-interest threat to an acceptable level. An example of such a safeguard is having the work reviewed by a professional accountant from a network firm that is neither involved with the audit nor received the loan.

290.120 A loan, or a guarantee of a loan, from an audit client that is a bank or a similar institution to a member of the audit team, or a member of that individual's immediate family, does not create a threat to independence if the loan or guarantee is made under normal lending procedures, terms and conditions. Examples of such loans include home mortgages, bank overdrafts, car loans and credit card balances.

290.121 If the firm or a member of the audit team, or a member of that individual's immediate family, accepts a loan from, or has a borrowing guaranteed by, an audit client that is not a bank or similar institution, the self-interest threat created would be so significant that no safeguards could reduce the threat to an acceptable level, unless the loan or guarantee is immaterial to both (a) the firm or the member of the audit team and the immediate family member, and (b) the client.

290.122 Similarly, if the firm or a member of the audit team, or a member of that individual's immediate family, makes or guarantees a loan to an audit client, the self-interest threat created would be so significant that no safeguards could reduce the threat to an acceptable level, unless the loan or guarantee is immaterial to both (a) the firm or the member of the audit team and the immediate family member, and (b) the client.

290.123 If a firm or a member of the audit team, or a member of that individual's immediate family, has deposits or a brokerage account with an audit client that is a bank, broker or similar institution, a threat to independence is not created if the deposit or account is held under normal commercial terms.

Business relationships

290.124 A close business relationship between a firm, or a member of the audit team, or a member of that individual's immediate family, and the audit client or its management, arises from a commercial relationship or common financial interest and may create self-interest or intimidation threats. Examples of such relationships include:

(a) Having a financial interest in a joint venture with either the client or a controlling owner, director, officer or other individual who performs senior managerial activities for that client.

(b) Arrangements to combine one or more services or products of the firm with one or more services or products of the client and to market the package with reference to both parties.

(c) Distribution or marketing arrangements under which the firm distributes or markets the client's products or services, or the client distributes or markets the firm's products or services.

Unless any financial interest is immaterial and the business relationship is insignificant to the firm and the client or its management, the threat created would be so significant that no safeguards could reduce the threat to an acceptable level. Therefore, unless the financial interest is immaterial and the business relationship is insignificant, the business relationship shall not be entered into, or it shall be reduced to an insignificant level or terminated.

In the case of a member of the audit team, unless any such financial interest is immaterial and the relationship is insignificant to that member, the individual shall be removed from the audit team. If the business relationship is between an immediate family member of a member of the audit team and the audit client or its management, the significance of any threat shall be evaluated and safeguards applied when necessary to eliminate the threat or reduce it to an acceptable level.

290.125 A business relationship involving the holding of an interest by the firm, or a member of the audit team, or a member of that individual's immediate family, in a closely-held entity when the audit client or a director or officer of the client, or any group thereof, also holds an interest in that entity does not create threats to independence if:

(a) The business relationship is insignificant to the firm, the member of the audit team and the immediate family member, and the client

(b) The financial interest is immaterial to the investor or group of investors; and

(c) The financial interest does not give the investor, or group of investors, the ability to control the closely-held entity.

290.126 The purchase of goods and services from an audit client by the firm, or a member of the audit team, or a member of that individual's immediate family, does not generally create a threat to independence if the transaction is in the normal course of business and at arm's length. However, such transactions may be of such a nature or magnitude that they create a self-interest threat. The significance of any threat shall be evaluated and safeguards applied when necessary to eliminate the threat or reduce it to an acceptable level. Examples of such safeguards include:

(a) Eliminating or reducing the magnitude of the transaction; or

(b) Removing the individual from the audit team.

Family and personal relationships

290.127 Family and personal relationships between a member of the audit team and a director or officer or certain employees (depending on their role) of the audit client may create self-interest, familiarity or intimidation threats. The existence and significance of any threats will depend on a number of factors, including the individual's responsibilities on the audit team, the role of the family member or other individual within the client and the closeness of the relationship.

290.128 When an immediate family member of a member of the audit team is:

(a) a director or officer of the audit client; or

(b) an employee in a position to exert significant influence over the preparation of the client's accounting records or the financial statements on which the firm will express an opinion, or was in such a position during any period covered by the engagement or the financial statements, the threats to independence can only be reduced to an acceptable level by removing the individual from the audit team. The closeness of the relationship is such that no other safeguards could reduce the threat to an acceptable level. Accordingly, no individual who has such a relationship shall be a member of the audit team.

290.129 Threats to independence are created when an immediate family member of a member of the audit team is an employee in a position to exert significant influence over the client's financial position, financial performance or cash flows. The significance of the threats will depend on factors such as:

- The position held by the immediate family member; and
- The role of the professional on the audit team.

The significance of the threat shall be evaluated and safeguards applied when necessary to eliminate the threat or reduce it to an acceptable level. Examples of such safeguards include:

- Removing the individual from the audit team; or
- Structuring the responsibilities of the audit team so that the professional does not deal with matters that are within the responsibility of the immediate family member.

290.130 Threats to independence are created when a close family member of a member of the audit team is:

(a) A director or officer of the audit client; or

(b) An employee in a position to exert significant influence over the preparation of the client's accounting records or the financial statements on which the firm will express an opinion.

The significance of the threats will depend on factors such as:

- The nature of the relationship between the member of the audit team and the close family member
- The position held by the close family member; and
- The role of the professional on the audit team.

The significance of the threat shall be evaluated and safeguards applied when necessary to eliminate the threat or reduce it to an acceptable level. Examples of such safeguards include:

- Removing the individual from the audit team; or
- Structuring the responsibilities of the audit team so that the professional does not deal with matters that are within the responsibility of the close family member.

290.131 Threats to independence are created when a member of the audit team has a close relationship with a person who is not an immediate or close family member, but who is a director or officer or an employee in a position to exert significant influence over the preparation of the client's accounting records or the financial statements on which the firm will express an opinion. A member of the audit team who has such a relationship shall consult in accordance with firm policies and procedures. The significance of the threats will depend on factors such as:

- The nature of the relationship between the individual and the member of the audit team
- The position the individual holds with the client; and
- The role of the professional on the audit team.

The significance of the threats shall be evaluated and safeguards applied when necessary to eliminate the threats or reduce them to an acceptable level. Examples of such safeguards include:

- Removing the professional from the audit team; or
- Structuring the responsibilities of the audit team so that the professional does not deal with matters that are within the responsibility of the individual with whom the professional has a close relationship.

290.132 Self-interest, familiarity or intimidation threats may be created by a personal or family relationship between (a) a partner or employee of the firm who is not a member of the audit team and (b) a director or officer of the audit client or an employee in a position to exert significant influence over the preparation of the client's accounting records or the financial statements on which the firm will express an opinion. Partners and employees of the firm who are aware of such relationships shall consult in accordance with firm policies and procedures. The existence and significance of any threat will depend on factors such as:

- The nature of the relationship between the partner or employee of the firm and the director or officer or employee of the client
- The interaction of the partner or employee of the firm with the audit team
- The position of the partner or employee within the firm; and
- The position the individual holds with the client.

The significance of any threat shall be evaluated and safeguards applied when necessary to eliminate the threat or reduce it to an acceptable level. Examples of such safeguards include:

- Structuring the partner's or employee's responsibilities to reduce any potential influence over the audit engagement; or
- Having a professional accountant review the relevant audit work performed.

290.133 When an inadvertent violation of this section as it relates to family and personal relationships occurs, it is deemed not to compromise independence if:

(a) The firm has established policies and procedures that require prompt notification to the firm of any breaches resulting from changes in the employment status of their immediate or close family members or other personal relationships that create threats to independence

(b) The inadvertent violation relates to an immediate family member of a member of the audit team becoming a director or officer of the audit client or being in a position to exert significant influence over the preparation of the client's accounting records or the financial statements on which the firm will express an opinion, and the relevant professional is removed from the audit team; and

(c) The firm applies other safeguards when necessary to reduce any remaining threat to an acceptable level. Examples of such safeguards include:
   (i) Having a professional accountant review the work of the member of the audit team; or
   (ii) Excluding the relevant professional from any significant decision-making concerning the engagement. The firm shall determine whether to discuss the matter with those charged with governance.

Supplementary reading: Annex 1 290.134 to 290.194

Employment with an audit client

290.134 Familiarity or intimidation threats may be created if a director or officer of the audit client, or an employee in a position to exert significant influence over the preparation of the client's accounting records or the financial statements on which the firm will express an opinion, has been a member of the audit team or partner of the firm.

290.135 If a former member of the audit team or partner of the firm has joined the audit client in such a position and a significant connection remains between the firm and the individual, the threat would be so significant that no safeguards could reduce the threat to an acceptable level. Therefore, independence would be deemed to be compromised if a former member of the audit team or partner joins the audit client as a director or officer, or as an employee in a position to exert significant influence over the preparation of the client's accounting records or the financial statements on which the firm will express an opinion, unless:

(a) The individual is not entitled to any benefits or payments from the firm, unless made in accordance with fixed pre-determined arrangements, and any amount owed to the individual is not material to the firm; and

(b) The individual does not continue to participate or appear to participate in the firm's business or professional activities.

290.136 If a former member of the audit team or partner of the firm has joined the audit client in such a position, and no significant connection remains between the firm and the individual, the existence and significance of any familiarity or intimidation threats will depend on factors such as:

- The position the individual has taken at the client
- Any involvement the individual will have with the audit team
- The length of time since the individual was a member of the audit team or partner of the firm; and
- The former position of the individual within the audit team or firm, for example, whether the individual was responsible for maintaining regular contact with the client's management or those charged with governance.

The significance of any threats created shall be evaluated and safeguards applied when necessary to eliminate the threats or reduce them to an acceptable level. Examples of such safeguards include:

- Modifying the audit plan
- Assigning individuals to the audit team who have sufficient experience in relation to the individual who has joined the client; or
- Having a professional accountant review the work of the former member of the audit team.

290.137 If a former partner of the firm has previously joined an entity in such a position and the entity subsequently becomes an audit client of the firm, the significance of any threat to independence shall be evaluated and safeguards applied when necessary to eliminate the threat or reduce it to an acceptable level.

290.138 A self-interest threat is created when a member of the audit team participates in the audit engagement while knowing that the member of the audit team will, or may, join the client sometime in the future. Firm policies and procedures shall require members of an audit team to notify the firm when entering employment negotiations with the client. On receiving such notification, the significance of the threat shall be evaluated and safeguards applied when necessary to eliminate the threat or reduce it to an acceptable level. Examples of such safeguards include:

- Removing the individual from the audit team; or
- A review of any significant judgements made by that individual while on the team.

Audit clients that are public interest entities

290.139 Familiarity or intimidation threats are created when a key audit partner joins the audit client that is a public interest entity as:

(a) A director or officer of the entity; or

(b) An employee in a position to exert significant influence over the preparation of the client's accounting records or the financial statements on which the firm will express an opinion.

Independence would be deemed to be compromised unless, subsequent to the partner ceasing to be a key audit partner, the public interest entity had issued audited financial statements covering a period of not less than twelve months and the partner was not a member of the audit team with respect to the audit of those financial statements.

290.140 An intimidation threat is created when the individual who was the firm's Senior or Managing Partner (Chief Executive or equivalent) joins an audit client that is a public interest entity as:

(a) An employee in a position to exert significant influence over the preparation of the entity's accounting records or its financial statements; or

(b) A director or officer of the entity. Independence would be deemed to be compromised unless twelve months have passed since the individual was the Senior or Managing Partner (Chief Executive or equivalent) of the firm.

290.141 Independence is deemed not to be compromised if, as a result of a business combination, a former key audit partner or the individual who was the firm's former Senior or Managing Partner is in a position as described in paragraphs 290.139 and 290.140, and:

(a) The position was not taken in contemplation of the business combination

(b) Any benefits or payments due to the former partner from the firm have been settled in full, unless made in accordance with fixed pre-determined arrangements and any amount owed to the partner is not material to the firm

(c) The former partner does not continue to participate or appear to participate in the firm's business or professional activities; and

(d) The position held by the former partner with the audit client is discussed with those charged with governance.

Temporary staff assignments

290.142 The lending of staff by a firm to an audit client may create a self-review threat. Such assistance may be given, but only for a short period of time and the firm's personnel shall not be involved in:

(a) Providing non-assurance services that would not be permitted under this section; or

(b) Assuming management responsibilities.

In all circumstances, the audit client shall be responsible for directing and supervising the activities of the loaned staff. The significance of any threat shall be evaluated and safeguards applied when necessary to eliminate the threat or reduce it to an acceptable level. Examples of such safeguards include:

- Conducting an additional review of the work performed by the loaned staff
- Not giving the loaned staff audit responsibility for any function or activity that the staff performed during the temporary staff assignment; or
- Not including the loaned staff as a member of the audit team.

Recent service with an audit client

290.143 Self-interest, self-review or familiarity threats may be created if a member of the audit team has recently served as a director, officer, or employee of the audit client. This would be the case when, for example, a member of the audit team has to evaluate elements of the financial statements for which the member of the audit team had prepared the accounting records while with the client.

290.144 If, during the period covered by the audit report, a member of the audit team had served as a director or officer of the audit client, or was an employee in a position to exert significant influence over the preparation of the client's accounting records or the financial statements on which the firm will express an opinion, the threat created would be so significant that no safeguards could reduce the threat to an acceptable level. Consequently, such individuals shall not be assigned to the audit team.

290.145 Self-interest, self-review or familiarity threats may be created if, before the period covered by the audit report, a member of the audit team had served as a director or officer of the audit client, or was an employee in a position to exert significant influence over the preparation of the client's accounting records or financial statements on which the firm will express an opinion. For example, such threats would be created if a decision made or work performed by the individual in the prior period, while employed by the client, is to be evaluated in the current period as part of the current audit engagement. The existence and significance of any threats will depend on factors such as:

- The position the individual held with the client
- The length of time since the individual left the client; and
- The role of the professional on the audit team.

The significance of any threat shall be evaluated and safeguards applied when necessary to reduce the threat to an acceptable level. An example of such a safeguard is conducting a review of the work performed by the individual as a member of the audit team.

Serving as a Director or Officer of an audit client

290.146 If a partner or employee of the firm serves as a director or officer of an audit client, the self-review and self-interest threats created would be so significant that no safeguards could reduce the threats to an acceptable level. Accordingly, no partner or employee shall serve as a director or officer of an audit client.

290.147 The position of Company Secretary has different implications in different jurisdictions. Duties may range from administrative duties, such as personnel management and the maintenance of company records and registers, to duties as diverse as ensuring that the company complies with regulations or providing advice on corporate governance matters. Generally, this position is seen to imply a close association with the entity.

290.148 If a partner or employee of the firm serves as Company Secretary for an audit client, self-review and advocacy threats are created that would generally be so significant that no safeguards could reduce the threats to an acceptable level. Despite paragraph 290.146, when this practice is specifically permitted under local law, professional rules or practice, and provided management makes all relevant decisions, the duties and activities shall be limited to those of a routine and administrative nature, such as preparing minutes and maintaining statutory returns. In those circumstances, the significance of any threats shall be evaluated and safeguards applied when necessary to eliminate the threats or reduce them to an acceptable level.

290.149 Performing routine administrative services to support a company secretarial function or providing advice in relation to company secretarial administration matters does not generally create threats to independence, as long as client management makes all relevant decisions.

Long association of senior personnel (including partner rotation) with an audit client

General provisions

290.150 Familiarity and self-interest threats are created by using the same senior personnel on an audit engagement over a long period of time. The significance of the threats will depend on factors such as:

- How long the individual has been a member of the audit team
- The role of the individual on the audit team
- The structure of the firm
- The nature of the audit engagement
- Whether the client's management team has changed; and
- Whether the nature or complexity of the client's accounting and reporting issues has changed.

The significance of the threats shall be evaluated and safeguards applied when necessary to eliminate the threats or reduce them to an acceptable level. Examples of such safeguards include:

- Rotating the senior personnel off the audit team
- Having a professional accountant who was not a member of the audit team review the work of the senior personnel; or
- Regular independent internal or external quality reviews of the engagement.

Audit clients that are public interest entities

290.151 In respect of an audit of a public interest entity, an individual shall not be a key audit partner for more than seven years. After such time, the individual shall not be a member of the engagement team or be a key audit partner for the client for two years. During that period, the individual shall not participate in the audit of the entity, provide quality control for the engagement, consult with the engagement team or the client regarding technical or industry-specific issues, transactions or events or otherwise directly influence the outcome of the engagement.

290.152 Despite paragraph 290.151, key audit partners whose continuity is especially important to audit quality may, in rare cases due to unforeseen circumstances outside the firm's control, be permitted an additional year on the audit team as long as the threat to independence can be eliminated or reduced to an acceptable level by applying safeguards. For example, a key audit partner may remain on the audit team for up to one additional year in circumstances where, due to unforeseen events, a required rotation was not possible, as might be the case due to serious illness of the intended engagement partner.

290.153 The long association of other partners with an audit client that is a public interest entity creates familiarity and self-interest threats. The significance of the threats will depend on factors such as:

- How long any such partner has been associated with the audit client
- The role, if any, of the individual on the audit team; and
- The nature, frequency and extent of the individual's interactions with the client's management or those charged with governance.

The significance of the threats shall be evaluated and safeguards applied when necessary to eliminate the threats or reduce them to an acceptable level. Examples of such safeguards include:

- Rotating the partner off the audit team or otherwise ending the partner's association with the audit client; or
- Regular independent internal or external quality reviews of the engagement.

290.154 When an audit client becomes a public interest entity, the length of time the individual has served the audit client as a key audit partner before the client becomes a public interest entity shall be taken into account in determining the timing of the rotation. If the individual has served the audit client as a key audit partner for five years or less when the client becomes a public interest entity, the number of years the individual may continue to serve the client in that capacity before rotating off the engagement is seven years less the number of years already served. If the individual has served the audit client as a key audit partner for six or more years when the client becomes a public interest entity, the partner may continue to serve in that capacity for a maximum of two additional years before rotating off the engagement.

290.155 When a firm has only a few people with the necessary knowledge and experience to serve as a key audit partner on the audit of a public interest entity, rotation of key audit partners may not be an available safeguard. If an independent regulator in the relevant jurisdiction has provided an exemption from partner rotation in such circumstances, an individual may remain a key audit partner for more than seven years, in accordance with such regulation, provided that the independent regulator has specified alternative safeguards which are applied, such as a regular independent external review.

Provision of non-assurance services to audit clients

290.156 Firms have traditionally provided to their audit clients a range of non-assurance services that are consistent with their skills and expertise. Providing non-assurance services may, however, create threats to the independence of the firm or members of the audit team. The threats created are most often self-review, self-interest and advocacy threats.

290.157 New developments in business, the evolution of financial markets and changes in information technology make it impossible to draw up an all-inclusive list of non-assurance services that might be provided to an audit client. When specific guidance on a particular non-assurance service is not included in this section, the conceptual framework shall be applied when evaluating the particular circumstances.

290.158 Before the firm accepts an engagement to provide a non-assurance service to an audit client, a determination shall be made as to whether providing such a service would create a threat to independence. In evaluating the significance of any threat created by a particular non-assurance service, consideration shall be given to any threat that the audit team has reason to believe is created by providing other related non-assurance services. If a threat is created that cannot be reduced to an acceptable level by the application of safeguards, the non-assurance service shall not be provided.

290.159 Providing certain non-assurance services to an audit client may create a threat to independence so significant that no safeguards could reduce the threat to an acceptable level. However, the inadvertent provision of such a service to a related entity, division or in respect of a discrete financial statement item of such a client will be deemed not to compromise independence if any threats have been reduced to an acceptable level by arrangements for that related entity, division or discrete financial statement item to be audited by another firm or when another firm re-performs the non-assurance service to the extent necessary to enable it to take responsibility for that service.

290.160 A firm may provide non-assurance services that would otherwise be restricted under this section to the following related entities of the audit client:

(a) An entity, which is not an audit client, that has direct or indirect control over the audit client

(b) An entity, which is not an audit client, with a direct financial interest in the client if that entity has significant influence over the client and the interest in the client is material to such entity; or

(c) An entity, which is not an audit client, that is under common control with the audit client, if it is reasonable to conclude that (a) the services do not create a self-review threat because the results of the services will not be subject to audit procedures and (b) any threats that are created by the provision of such services are eliminated or reduced to an acceptable level by the application of safeguards.

290.161 A non-assurance service provided to an audit client does not compromise the firm's independence when the client becomes a public interest entity if:

(a) The previous non-assurance service complies with the provisions of this section that relate to audit clients that are not public interest entities

(b) Services that are not permitted under this section for audit clients that are public interest entities are terminated before or as soon as practicable after the client becomes a public interest entity; and

(c) The firm applies safeguards when necessary to eliminate or reduce to an acceptable level any threats to independence arising from the service.

Management responsibilities

290.162 Management of an entity performs many activities in managing the entity in the best interests of stakeholders of the entity. It is not possible to specify every activity that is a management responsibility. However, management responsibilities involve leading and directing an entity, including making significant decisions regarding the acquisition, deployment and control of human, financial, physical and intangible resources.

290.163 Whether an activity is a management responsibility depends on the circumstances and requires the exercise of judgement. Examples of activities that would generally be considered a management responsibility include:

- Setting policies and strategic direction
- Directing and taking responsibility for the actions of the entity's employees
- Authorising transactions
- Deciding which recommendations of the firm or other third parties to implement
- Taking responsibility for the preparation and fair presentation of the financial statements in accordance with the applicable financial reporting framework; and
- Taking responsibility for designing, implementing and maintaining internal control.

290.164 Activities that are routine and administrative, or involve matters that are insignificant, generally are deemed not to be a management responsibility. For example, executing an insignificant transaction that has been authorised by management or monitoring the dates for filing statutory returns and advising an audit client of those dates is deemed not to be a management responsibility. Further, providing advice and recommendations to assist management in discharging its responsibilities is not assuming a management responsibility.

290.165 If a firm were to assume a management responsibility for an audit client, the threats created would be so significant that no safeguards could reduce the threats to an acceptable level. For example, deciding which recommendations of the firm to implement will create self-review and self-interest threats. Further, assuming a management responsibility creates a familiarity threat because the firm becomes too closely aligned with the views and interests of management. Therefore, the firm shall not assume a management responsibility for an audit client.

290.166 To avoid the risk of assuming a management responsibility when providing non-assurance services to an audit client, the firm shall be satisfied that a member of management is responsible for making the significant judgements and decisions that are the proper responsibility of management, evaluating the results of the service and accepting responsibility for the actions to be taken arising from the results of the service. This reduces the risk of the firm inadvertently making any significant judgements or decisions on behalf of management. The risk is further reduced when the firm gives the client the opportunity to make judgements and decisions based on an objective and transparent analysis and presentation of the issues.

Preparing accounting records and financial statements

General provisions

290.167 Management is responsible for the preparation and fair presentation of the financial statements in accordance with the applicable financial reporting framework. These responsibilities include:

- Originating or changing journal entries, or determining the account classifications of transactions; and
- Preparing or changing source documents or originating data, in electronic or other form, evidencing the occurrence of a transaction (for example, purchase orders, payroll time records, and customer orders).

290.168 Providing an audit client with accounting and bookkeeping services, such as preparing accounting records or financial statements, creates a self-review threat when the firm subsequently audits the financial statements.

290.169 The audit process, however, necessitates dialogue between the firm and management of the audit client, which may involve:

- The application of accounting standards or policies and financial statement disclosure requirements
- The appropriateness of financial and accounting control and the methods used in determining the stated amounts of assets and liabilities; or
- Proposing adjusting journal entries. These activities are considered to be a normal part of the audit process and do not, generally, create threats to independence.

290.170 Similarly, the client may request technical assistance from the firm on matters such as resolving account reconciliation problems or analysing and accumulating information for regulatory reporting. In addition, the client may request technical advice on accounting issues such as the conversion of existing financial statements from one financial reporting framework to another (for example, to comply with group accounting policies or to transition to a different financial reporting framework such as International Financial Reporting Standards). Such services do not, generally, create threats to independence provided the firm does not assume a management responsibility for the client.

Audit clients that are not public interest entities

290.171 The firm may provide services related to the preparation of accounting records and financial statements to an audit client that is not a public interest entity where the services are of a routine or mechanical nature, so long as any self-review threat created is reduced to an acceptable level. Examples of such services include:

- Providing payroll services based on client-originated data
- Recording transactions for which the client has determined or approved the appropriate account classification
- Posting transactions coded by the client to the general ledger
- Posting client-approved entries to the trial balance; and
- Preparing financial statements based on information in the trial balance.

In all cases, the significance of any threat created shall be evaluated and safeguards applied when necessary to eliminate the threat or reduce it to an acceptable level. Examples of such safeguards include:

- Arranging for such services to be performed by an individual who is not a member of the audit team; or
- If such services are performed by a member of the audit team, using a partner or senior staff member with appropriate expertise who is not a member of the audit team to review the work performed.

Audit clients that are public interest entities

290.172 Except in emergency situations, a firm shall not provide to an audit client that is a public interest entity accounting and bookkeeping services, including payroll services, or prepare financial statements on which the firm will express an opinion or financial information which forms the basis of the financial statements.

290.173 Despite paragraph 290.172, a firm may provide accounting and bookkeeping services, including payroll services and the preparation of financial statements or other financial information, of a routine or mechanical nature for divisions or related entities of an audit client that is a public interest entity if the personnel providing the services are not members of the audit team and:

(a) The divisions or related entities for which the service is provided are collectively immaterial to the financial statements on which the firm will express an opinion; or

(b) The services relate to matters that are collectively immaterial to the financial statements of the division or related entity.

Emergency situations

290.174 Accounting and bookkeeping services, which would otherwise not be permitted under this section, may be provided to audit clients in emergency or other unusual situations when it is impractical for the audit client to make other arrangements. This may be the case when (a) only the firm has the resources and necessary knowledge of the client's systems and procedures to assist the client in the timely preparation of its accounting records and financial statements, and (b) a restriction on the firm's ability to provide the services would result in significant difficulties for the client (for example, as might result from a failure to meet regulatory reporting requirements). In such situations, the following conditions shall be met:

(a) Those who provide the services are not members of the audit team

(b) The services are provided for only a short period of time and are not expected to recur; and

(c) The situation is discussed with those charged with governance.

Valuation services

General provisions

290.175 A valuation comprises the making of assumptions with regard to future developments, the application of appropriate methodologies and techniques, and the combination of both to compute a certain value, or range of values, for an asset, a liability or for a business as a whole.

290.176 Performing valuation services for an audit client may create a self-review threat. The existence and significance of any threat will depend on factors such as:

- Whether the valuation will have a material effect on the financial statements.
- The extent of the client's involvement in determining and approving the valuation methodology and other significant matters of judgement.
- The availability of established methodologies and professional guidelines.
- For valuations involving standard or established methodologies, the degree of subjectivity inherent in the item.
- The reliability and extent of the underlying data.
- The degree of dependence on future events of a nature that could create significant volatility inherent in the amounts involved.
- The extent and clarity of the disclosures in the financial statements.

The significance of any threat created shall be evaluated and safeguards applied when necessary to eliminate the threat or reduce it to an acceptable level. Examples of such safeguards include:

- Having a professional who was not involved in providing the valuation service review the audit or valuation work performed; or
- Making arrangements so that personnel providing such services do not participate in the audit engagement.

290.177 Certain valuations do not involve a significant degree of subjectivity. This is likely the case where the underlying assumptions are either established by law or regulation, or are widely accepted and when the techniques and methodologies to be used are based on generally accepted standards or prescribed by law or regulation. In such circumstances, the results of a valuation performed by two or more parties are not likely to be materially different.

290.178 If a firm is requested to perform a valuation to assist an audit client with its tax reporting obligations or for tax planning purposes and the results of the valuation will not have a direct effect on the financial statements, the provisions included in paragraph 290.191 apply. Audit clients that are not public interest entities.

290.179 In the case of an audit client that is not a public interest entity, if the valuation service has a material effect on the financial statements on which the firm will express an opinion and the valuation involves a significant degree of subjectivity, no safeguards could reduce the self-review threat to an acceptable level. Accordingly a firm shall not provide such a valuation service to an audit client.

Audit clients that are public interest entities

290.180 A firm shall not provide valuation services to an audit client that is a public interest entity if the valuations would have a material effect, separately or in the aggregate, on the financial statements on which the firm will express an opinion.

Taxation services

290.181 Taxation services comprise a broad range of services, including:

- Tax return preparation
- Tax calculations for the purpose of preparing the accounting entries
- Tax planning and other tax advisory services; and
- Assistance in the resolution of tax disputes.

While taxation services provided by a firm to an audit client are addressed separately under each of these broad headings; in practice, these activities are often interrelated.

290.182 Performing certain tax services creates self-review and advocacy threats. The existence and significance of any threats will depend on factors such as:

- The system by which the tax authorities assess and administer the tax in question and the role of the firm in that process
- The complexity of the relevant tax regime and the degree of judgement necessary in applying it
- The particular characteristics of the engagement; and
- The level of tax expertise of the client's employees.

Tax return preparation

290.183 Tax return preparation services involve assisting clients with their tax reporting obligations by drafting and completing information, including the amount of tax due (usually on standardised forms) required to be submitted to the applicable tax authorities. Such services also include advising on the tax return treatment of past transactions and responding on behalf of the audit client to the tax authorities' requests for additional information and analysis (including providing explanations of and technical support for the approach being taken). Tax return preparation services are generally based on historical information and principally involve analysis and presentation of such historical information under existing tax law, including precedents and established practice. Further, the tax returns are subject to whatever review or approval process the tax authority deems appropriate. Accordingly, providing such services does not generally create a threat to independence if management takes responsibility for the returns including any significant judgements made.

Tax calculations for the purpose of preparing accounting entries

Audit clients that are not public interest entities

290.184 Preparing calculations of current and deferred tax liabilities (or assets) for an audit client for the purpose of preparing accounting entries that will be subsequently audited by the firm creates a self-review threat. The significance of the threat will depend on:

(a) The complexity of the relevant tax law and regulation and the degree of judgement necessary in applying them

(b) The level of tax expertise of the client's personnel; and

(c) The materiality of the amounts to the financial statements.

Safeguards shall be applied when necessary to eliminate the threat or reduce it to an acceptable level.

Examples of such safeguards include:

- Using professionals who are not members of the audit team to perform the service
- If the service is performed by a member of the audit team, using a partner or senior staff member with appropriate expertise who is not a member of the audit team to review the tax calculations; or
- Obtaining advice on the service from an external tax professional.

Audit clients that are public interest entities

290.185 Except in emergency situations, in the case of an audit client that is a public interest entity, a firm shall not prepare tax calculations of current and deferred tax liabilities (or assets) for the purpose of preparing accounting entries that are material to the financial statements on which the firm will express an opinion.

290.186 The preparation of calculations of current and deferred tax liabilities (or assets) for an audit client for the purpose of the preparation of accounting entries, which would otherwise not be permitted under this section, may be provided to audit clients in emergency or other unusual situations when it is impractical for the audit client to make other arrangements. This may be the case when (a) only the firm has the resources and necessary knowledge of the client's business to assist the client in the timely preparation of its calculations of current and deferred tax liabilities (or assets), and (b) a restriction on the firm's ability to provide the services would result in significant difficulties for the client (for example, as might result from a failure to meet regulatory reporting requirements). In such situations, the following conditions shall be met:

(a) Those who provide the services are not members of the audit team

(b) The services are provided for only a short period of time and are not expected to recur; and

(c) The situation is discussed with those charged with governance.

Tax planning and other tax advisory services

290.187 Tax planning or other tax advisory services comprise a broad range of services, such as advising the client how to structure its affairs in a tax efficient manner or advising on the application of a new tax law or regulation.

290.188 A self-review threat may be created where the advice will affect matters to be reflected in the financial statements. The existence and significance of any threat will depend on factors such as:

- The degree of subjectivity involved in determining the appropriate treatment for the tax advice in the financial statements
- The extent to which the outcome of the tax advice will have a material effect on the financial statements
- Whether the effectiveness of the tax advice depends on the accounting treatment or presentation in the financial statements and there is doubt as to the appropriateness of the accounting treatment or presentation under the relevant financial reporting framework
- The level of tax expertise of the client's employees
- The extent to which the advice is supported by tax law or regulation, other precedent or established practice; and
- Whether the tax treatment is supported by a private ruling or has otherwise been cleared by the tax authority before the preparation of the financial statements.

For example, providing tax planning and other tax advisory services where the advice is clearly supported by tax authority or other precedent, by established practice or has a basis in tax law that is likely to prevail does not generally create a threat to independence.

290.189 The significance of any threat shall be evaluated and safeguards applied when necessary to eliminate the threat or reduce it to an acceptable level. Examples of such safeguards include:

- Using professionals who are not members of the audit team to perform the service
- Having a tax professional, who was not involved in providing the tax service, advise the audit team on the service and review the financial statement treatment
- Obtaining advice on the service from an external tax professional; or
- Obtaining pre-clearance or advice from the tax authorities.

290.190 Where the effectiveness of the tax advice depends on a particular accounting treatment or presentation in the financial statements and:

- The audit team has reasonable doubt as to the appropriateness of the related accounting treatment or presentation under the relevant financial reporting framework; and
- The outcome or consequences of the tax advice will have a material effect on the financial statements on which the firm will express an opinion.

The self-review threat would be so significant that no safeguards could reduce the threat to an acceptable level. Accordingly, a firm shall not provide such tax advice to an audit client.

290.191 In providing tax services to an audit client, a firm may be requested to perform a valuation to assist the client with its tax reporting obligations or for tax planning purposes. Where the result of the valuation will have a direct effect on the financial statements, the provisions included in paragraphs 290.175 to 290.180 relating to valuation services are applicable.

Where the valuation is performed for tax purposes only and the result of the valuation will not have a direct effect on the financial statements (that is, the financial statements are only affected through accounting entries related to tax), this would not generally create threats to independence if such effect on the financial statements is immaterial or if the valuation is subject to external review by a tax authority or similar regulatory authority. If the valuation is not subject to such an external review and the effect is material to the financial statements, the existence and significance of any threat created will depend upon factors such as:

- The extent to which the valuation methodology is supported by tax law or regulation, other precedent or established practice and the degree of subjectivity inherent in the valuation.
- The reliability and extent of the underlying data.

The significance of any threat created shall be evaluated and safeguards applied when necessary to eliminate the threat or reduce it to an acceptable level. Examples of such safeguards include:

- Using professionals who are not members of the audit team to perform the service
- Having a professional review the audit work or the result of the tax service; or
- Obtaining pre-clearance or advice from the tax authorities.

Assistance in the resolution of tax disputes

290.192 An advocacy or self-review threat may be created when the firm represents an audit client in the resolution of a tax dispute once the tax authorities have notified the client that they have rejected the client's arguments on a particular issue and either the tax authority or the client is referring the matter for determination in a formal proceeding, for example before a tribunal or court. The existence and significance of any threat will depend on factors such as:

- Whether the firm has provided the advice which is the subject of the tax dispute
- The extent to which the outcome of the dispute will have a material effect on the financial statements on which the firm will express an opinion
- The extent to which the matter is supported by tax law or regulation, other precedent, or established practice
- Whether the proceedings are conducted in public; and
- The role management plays in the resolution of the dispute.

The significance of any threat created shall be evaluated and safeguards applied when necessary to eliminate the threat or reduce it to an acceptable level. Examples of such safeguards include:

- Using professionals who are not members of the audit team to perform the service
- Having a tax professional, who was not involved in providing the tax service, advise the audit team on the services and review the financial statement treatment; or
- Obtaining advice on the service from an external tax professional.

290.193 Where the taxation services involve acting as an advocate for an audit client before a public tribunal or court in the resolution of a tax matter and the amounts involved are material to the financial statements on which the firm will express an opinion, the advocacy threat created would be so significant that no safeguards could eliminate or reduce the threat to an acceptable level. Therefore, the firm shall not perform this type of service for an audit client. What constitutes a 'public tribunal or court' shall be determined according to how tax proceedings are heard in the particular jurisdiction.

290.194 The firm is not, however, precluded from having a continuing advisory role (for example, responding to specific requests for information, providing factual accounts or testimony about the work performed or assisting the client in analysing the tax issues) for the audit client in relation to the matter that is being heard before a public tribunal or court.

Supplementary reading: Annex 1 290.195 to 290.222

Internal audit services

General provisions

290.195 The scope and objectives of internal audit activities vary widely and depend on the size and structure of the entity and the requirements of management and those charged with governance. Internal audit activities may include:

- Monitoring of internal control – reviewing controls, monitoring their operation and recommending improvements thereto
- Examination of financial and operating information – reviewing the means used to identify, measure, classify and report financial and operating information, and specific inquiry into individual items including detailed testing of transactions, balances and procedures
- Review of the economy, efficiency and effectiveness of operating activities including non-financial activities of an entity; and
- Review of compliance with laws, regulations and other external requirements, and with management policies and directives and other internal requirements.

290.196 Internal audit services involve assisting the audit client in the performance of its internal audit activities. The provision of internal audit services to an audit client creates a self-review threat to independence if the firm uses the internal audit work in the course of a subsequent external audit. Performing a significant part of the client's internal audit activities increases the possibility that firm personnel providing internal audit services will assume a management responsibility. If the firm's personnel assume a management responsibility when providing internal audit services to an audit client, the threat created would be so significant that no safeguards could reduce the threat to an acceptable level. Accordingly, a firm's personnel shall not assume a management responsibility when providing internal audit services to an audit client.

290.197 Examples of internal audit services that involve assuming management responsibilities include:

- Setting internal audit policies or the strategic direction of internal audit activities
- Directing and taking responsibility for the actions of the entity's internal audit employees
- Deciding which recommendations resulting from internal audit activities shall be implemented
- Reporting the results of the internal audit activities to those charged with governance on behalf of management
- Performing procedures that form part of the internal control, such as reviewing and approving changes to employee data access privileges
- Taking responsibility for designing, implementing and maintaining internal control; and
- Performing outsourced internal audit services, comprising all or a substantial portion of the internal audit function, where the firm is responsible for determining the scope of the internal audit work and may have responsibility for one or more of the matters noted in (a)–(f).

290.198 To avoid assuming a management responsibility, the firm shall only provide internal audit services to an audit client if it is satisfied that:

(a) The client designates an appropriate and competent resource, preferably within senior management, to be responsible at all times for internal audit activities and to acknowledge responsibility for designing, implementing, and maintaining internal control

(b) The client's management or those charged with governance reviews, assesses and approves the scope, risk and frequency of the internal audit services

(c) The client's management evaluates the adequacy of the internal audit services and the findings resulting from their performance

(d) The client's management evaluates and determines which recommendations resulting from internal audit services to implement and manages the implementation process; and

(e) The client's management reports to those charged with governance the significant findings and recommendations resulting from the internal audit services.

290.199 When a firm uses the work of an internal audit function, ISAs require the performance of procedures to evaluate the adequacy of that work. When a firm accepts an engagement to provide internal audit services to an audit client, and the results of those services will be used in conducting the external audit, a self-review threat is created because of the possibility that the audit team will use the results of the internal audit service without appropriately evaluating those results or exercising the same level of professional scepticism as would be exercised when the internal audit work is performed by individuals who are not members of the firm. The significance of the threat will depend on factors such as:

- The materiality of the related financial statement amounts
- The risk of misstatement of the assertions related to those financial statement amounts; and
- The degree of reliance that will be placed on the internal audit service.

The significance of the threat shall be evaluated and safeguards applied when necessary to eliminate the threat or reduce it to an acceptable level. An example of such a safeguard is using professionals who are not members of the audit team to perform the internal audit service.

Audit clients that are public interest entities

290.200 In the case of an audit client that is a public interest entity, a firm shall not provide internal audit services that relate to:

(a) A significant part of the internal controls over financial reporting

(b) Financial accounting systems that generate information that is, separately or in the aggregate, significant to the client's accounting records or financial statements on which the firm will express an opinion; or

(c) Amounts or disclosures that are, separately or in the aggregate, material to the financial statements on which the firm will express an opinion.

IT systems services

General provisions

290.201 Services related to information technology (IT) systems include the design or implementation of hardware or software systems. The systems may aggregate source data, form part of the internal control over financial reporting or generate information that affects the accounting records or financial statements, or the systems may be unrelated to the audit client's accounting records, the internal control over financial reporting or financial statements. Providing systems services may create a self-review threat depending on the nature of the services and the IT systems.

290.202 The following IT systems services are deemed not to create a threat to independence as long as the firm's personnel do not assume a management responsibility:

(a) Design or implementation of IT systems that are unrelated to internal control over financial reporting

(b) Design or implementation of IT systems that do not generate information forming a significant part of the accounting records or financial statements

(c) Implementation of 'off-the-shelf' accounting or financial information reporting software that was not developed by the firm if the customisation required to meet the client's needs is not significant; and

(d) Evaluating and making recommendations with respect to a system designed, implemented or operated by another service provider or the client.

Audit clients that are not public interest entities

290.203 Providing services to an audit client that is not a public interest entity involving the design or implementation of IT systems that (a) form a significant part of the internal control over financial reporting or (b) generate information that is significant to the client's accounting records or financial statements on which the firm will express an opinion creates a self-review threat.

290.204 The self-review threat is too significant to permit such services unless appropriate safeguards are put in place ensuring that:

(a) The client acknowledges its responsibility for establishing and monitoring a system of internal controls

(b) The client assigns the responsibility to make all management decisions with respect to the design and implementation of the hardware or software system to a competent employee, preferably within senior management

(c) The client makes all management decisions with respect to the design and implementation process

(d) The client evaluates the adequacy and results of the design and implementation of the system; and

(e) The client is responsible for operating the system (hardware or software) and for the data it uses or generates.

290.205 Depending on the degree of reliance that will be placed on the particular IT systems as part of the audit, a determination shall be made as to whether to provide such non-assurance services only with personnel who are not members of the audit team and who have different reporting lines within the firm. The significance of any remaining threat shall be evaluated and safeguards applied when necessary to eliminate the threat or reduce it to an acceptable level. An example of such a safeguard is having a professional accountant review the audit or non-assurance work.

Audit clients that are public interest entities

290.206 In the case of an audit client that is a public interest entity, a firm shall not provide services involving the design or implementation of IT systems that (a) form a significant part of the internal control over financial reporting or (b) generate information that is significant to the client's accounting records or financial statements on which the firm will express an opinion.

Litigation support services

290.207 Litigation support services may include activities such as acting as an expert witness, calculating estimated damages or other amounts that might become receivable or payable as the result of litigation or other legal dispute, and assistance with document management and retrieval. These services may create a self-review or advocacy threat.

290.208 If the firm provides a litigation support service to an audit client and the service involves estimating damages or other amounts that affect the financial statements on which the firm will express an opinion, the valuation service provisions included in paragraphs 290.175 to 290.180 shall be followed. In the case of other litigation support services, the significance of any threat created shall be evaluated and safeguards applied when necessary to eliminate the threat or reduce it to an acceptable level.

Legal services

290.209 For the purpose of this section, legal services are defined as any services for which the person providing the services must either be admitted to practice law before the courts of the jurisdiction in which such services are to be provided or have the required legal training to practice law. Such legal services may include, depending on the jurisdiction, a wide and diversified range of areas including both corporate and commercial services to clients, such as contract support, litigation, mergers and acquisition legal advice and support and assistance to clients' internal legal departments. Providing legal services to an entity that is an audit client may create both self-review and advocacy threats.

290.210 Legal services that support an audit client in executing a transaction (for example, contract support, legal advice, legal due diligence and restructuring) may create self-review threats. The existence and significance of any threat will depend on factors such as:

- The nature of the service
- Whether the service is provided by a member of the audit team; and
- The materiality of any matter in relation to the client's financial statements.

The significance of any threat created shall be evaluated and safeguards applied when necessary to eliminate the threat or reduce it to an acceptable level. Examples of such safeguards include:

- Using professionals who are not members of the audit team to perform the service; or
- Having a professional who was not involved in providing the legal services provide advice to the audit team on the service and review any financial statement treatment.

290.211 Acting in an advocacy role for an audit client in resolving a dispute or litigation when the amounts involved are material to the financial statements on which the firm will express an opinion would create advocacy and self-review threats so significant that no safeguards could reduce the threat to an acceptable level. Therefore, the firm shall not perform this type of service for an audit client.

290.212 When a firm is asked to act in an advocacy role for an audit client in resolving a dispute or litigation when the amounts involved are not material to the financial statements on which the firm will express an opinion, the firm shall evaluate the significance of any advocacy and self-review threats created and apply safeguards when necessary to eliminate the threat or reduce it to an acceptable level. Examples of such safeguards include:

- Using professionals who are not members of the audit team to perform the service; or
- Having a professional who was not involved in providing the legal services advise the audit team on the service and review any financial statement treatment.

290.213 The appointment of a partner or an employee of the firm as General Counsel for legal affairs of an audit client would create self-review and advocacy threats that are so significant that no safeguards could reduce the threats to an acceptable level. The position of General Counsel is generally a senior management position with broad responsibility for the legal affairs of a company, and consequently, no member of the firm shall accept such an appointment for an audit client.

Recruiting services

General provisions

290.214 Providing recruiting services to an audit client may create self-interest, familiarity or intimidation threats. The existence and significance of any threat will depend on factors such as:

- The nature of the requested assistance; and
- The role of the person to be recruited.

The significance of any threat created shall be evaluated and safeguards applied when necessary to eliminate the threat or reduce it to an acceptable level. In all cases, the firm shall not assume management responsibilities, including acting as a negotiator on the client's behalf, and the hiring decision shall be left to the client.

The firm may generally provide such services as reviewing the professional qualifications of a number of applicants and providing advice on their suitability for the post. In addition, the firm may interview candidates and advise on a candidate's competence for financial accounting, administrative or control positions.

Audit clients that are public interest entities

290.215 A firm shall not provide the following recruiting services to an audit client that is a public interest entity with respect to a director or officer of the entity or senior management in a position to exert significant influence over the preparation of the client's accounting records or the financial statements on which the firm will express an opinion:

- Searching for or seeking out candidates for such positions; and
- Undertaking reference checks of prospective candidates for such positions.

Corporate finance services

290.216 Providing corporate finance services such as:

- assisting an audit client in developing corporate strategies
- identifying possible targets for the audit client to acquire
- advising on disposal transactions
- assisting finance raising transactions; and
- providing structuring advice
- may create advocacy and self-review threats. The significance of any threat shall be evaluated and safeguards applied when necessary to eliminate the threat or reduce it to an acceptable level. Examples of such safeguards include:
- Using professionals who are not members of the audit team to provide the services; or
- Having a professional who was not involved in providing the corporate finance service advise the audit team on the service and review the accounting treatment and any financial statement treatment.

290.217 Providing a corporate finance service, for example advice on the structuring of a corporate finance transaction or on financing arrangements that will directly affect amounts that will be reported in the financial statements on which the firm will provide an opinion may create a self-review threat. The existence and significance of any threat will depend on factors such as:

- The degree of subjectivity involved in determining the appropriate treatment for the outcome or consequences of the corporate finance advice in the financial statements
- The extent to which the outcome of the corporate finance advice will directly affect amounts recorded in the financial statements and the extent to which the amounts are material to the financial statements; and
- Whether the effectiveness of the corporate finance advice depends on a particular accounting treatment or presentation in the financial statements and there is doubt as to the appropriateness of the related accounting treatment or presentation under the relevant financial reporting framework.

The significance of any threat shall be evaluated and safeguards applied when necessary to eliminate the threat or reduce it to an acceptable level. Examples of such safeguards include:

- Using professionals who are not members of the audit team to perform the service; or
- Having a professional who was not involved in providing the corporate finance service to the client advise the audit team on the service and review the accounting treatment and any financial statement treatment.

290.218 Where the effectiveness of corporate finance advice depends on a particular accounting treatment or presentation in the financial statements and:

(a) The audit team has reasonable doubt as to the appropriateness of the related accounting treatment or presentation under the relevant financial reporting framework; and

(b) The outcome or consequences of the corporate finance advice will have a material effect on the financial statements on which the firm will express an opinion.

The self-review threat would be so significant that no safeguards could reduce the threat to an acceptable level, in which case the corporate finance advice shall not be provided.

290.219 Providing corporate finance services involving promoting, dealing in, or underwriting an audit client's shares would create an advocacy or self-review threat that is so significant that no safeguards could reduce the threat to an acceptable level. Accordingly, a firm shall not provide such services to an audit client.

Fees

Fees – Relative size

290.220 When the total fees from an audit client represent a large proportion of the total fees of the firm expressing the audit opinion, the dependence on that client and concern about losing the client creates a self-interest or intimidation threat. The significance of the threat will depend on factors such as:

- The operating structure of the firm
- Whether the firm is well established or new; and
- The significance of the client qualitatively and/or quantitatively to the firm.

The significance of the threat shall be evaluated and safeguards applied when necessary to eliminate the threat or reduce it to an acceptable level. Examples of such safeguards include:

- Reducing the dependency on the client
- External quality control reviews; or
- Consulting a third party, such as a professional regulatory body or a professional accountant, on key audit judgements.

290.221 A self-interest or intimidation threat is also created when the fees generated from an audit client represent a large proportion of the revenue from an individual partner's clients or a large proportion of the revenue of an individual office of the firm. The significance of the threat will depend upon factors such as:

- The significance of the client qualitatively and/or quantitatively to the partner or office; and
- The extent to which the remuneration of the partner, or the partners in the office, is dependent upon the fees generated from the client.

The significance of the threat shall be evaluated and safeguards applied when necessary to eliminate the threat or reduce it to an acceptable level. Examples of such safeguards include:

- Reducing the dependency on the audit client
- Having a professional accountant review the work or otherwise advise as necessary; or
- Regular independent internal or external quality reviews of the engagement.

Audit clients that are public interest entities

290.222 Where an audit client is a public interest entity and, for two consecutive years, the total fees from the client and its related entities (subject to the considerations in paragraph 290.27) represent more than 15% of the total fees received by the firm expressing the opinion on the financial statements of the client, the firm shall disclose to those charged with governance of the audit client the fact that the total of such fees represents more than 15% of the total fees received by the firm, and discuss which of the safeguards below it will apply to reduce the threat to an acceptable level, and apply the selected safeguard:

- Prior to the issuance of the audit opinion on the second year's financial statements, a professional accountant, who is not a member of the firm expressing the opinion on the financial statements, performs an engagement quality control review of that engagement or a professional regulatory body performs a review of that engagement that is equivalent to an engagement quality control review ('a pre-issuance review'); or
- After the audit opinion on the second year's financial statements has been issued, and before the issuance of the audit opinion on the third year's financial statements, a professional accountant, who is not a member of the firm expressing the opinion on the financial statements, or a professional regulatory body performs a review of the second year's audit that is equivalent to an engagement quality control review ('a post-issuance review').

When the total fees significantly exceed 15%, the firm shall determine whether the significance of the threat is such that a post-issuance review would not reduce the threat to an acceptable level and, therefore, a pre-issuance review is required. In such circumstances a pre-issuance review shall be performed.

Thereafter, when the fees continue to exceed 15% each year, the disclosure to and discussion with those charged with governance shall occur and one of the above safeguards shall be applied. If the fees significantly exceed 15%, the firm shall determine whether the significance of the threat is such that a post-issuance review would not reduce the threat to an acceptable level and, therefore, a pre-issuance review is required. In such circumstances a pre-issuance review shall be performed.

Supplementary reading: Annex 1 290.223 to 290.514

Fees – Overdue

290.223 A self-interest threat may be created if fees due from an audit client remain unpaid for a long time, especially if a significant part is not paid before the issue of the audit report for the following year.

Generally the firm is expected to require payment of such fees before such audit report is issued. If fees remain unpaid after the report has been issued, the existence and significance of any threat shall be evaluated and safeguards applied when necessary to eliminate the threat or reduce it to an acceptable level. An example of such a safeguard is having an additional professional accountant who did not take part in the audit engagement provide advice or review the work performed. The firm shall determine whether the overdue fees might be regarded as being equivalent to a loan to the client and whether, because of the significance of the overdue fees, it is appropriate for the firm to be re-appointed or continue the audit engagement.

Contingent fees

290.224 Contingent fees are fees calculated on a predetermined basis relating to the outcome of a transaction or the result of the services performed by the firm. For the purposes of this section, a fee is not regarded as being contingent if established by a court or other public authority.

290.225 A contingent fee charged directly or indirectly, for example through an intermediary, by a firm in respect of an audit engagement creates a self-interest threat that is so significant that no safeguards could reduce the threat to an acceptable level. Accordingly, a firm shall not enter into any such fee arrangement.

290.226 A contingent fee charged directly or indirectly, for example through an intermediary, by a firm in respect of a non-assurance service provided to an audit client may also create a self-interest threat. The threat created would be so significant that no safeguards could reduce the threat to an acceptable level if:

(a) The fee is charged by the firm expressing the opinion on the financial statements and the fee is material or expected to be material to that firm

(b) The fee is charged by a network firm that participates in a significant part of the audit and the fee is material or expected to be material to that firm; or

(c) The outcome of the non-assurance service, and therefore the amount of the fee, is dependent on a future or contemporary judgement related to the audit of a material amount in the financial statements.

Accordingly, such arrangements shall not be accepted.

290.227 For other contingent fee arrangements charged by a firm for a non-assurance service to an audit client, the existence and significance of any threats will depend on factors such as:

- The range of possible fee amounts
- Whether an appropriate authority determines the outcome of the matter upon which the contingent fee will be determined
- The nature of the service; and
- The effect of the event or transaction on the financial statements.

The significance of any threats shall be evaluated and safeguards applied when necessary to eliminate the threats or reduce them to an acceptable level. Examples of such safeguards include:

- Having a professional accountant review the relevant audit work or otherwise advise as necessary; or
- Using professionals who are not members of the audit team to perform the non-assurance service.

Compensation and Evaluation policies

290.228 A self-interest threat is created when a member of the audit team is evaluated on or compensated for selling non-assurance services to that audit client. The significance of the threat will depend on:

- The proportion of the individual's compensation or performance evaluation that is based on the sale of such services
- The role of the individual on the audit team; and
- Whether promotion decisions are influenced by the sale of such services.

The significance of the threat shall be evaluated and, if the threat is not at an acceptable level, the firm shall either revise the compensation plan or evaluation process for that individual or apply safeguards to eliminate the threat or reduce it to an acceptable level. Examples of such safeguards include:

- Removing such members from the audit team; or
- Having a professional accountant review the work of the member of the audit team.

290.229 A key audit partner shall not be evaluated on or compensated based on that partner's success in selling non-assurance services to the partner's audit client. This is not intended to prohibit normal profit-sharing arrangements between partners of a firm.

Gifts and Hospitality

290.230 Accepting gifts or hospitality from an audit client may create self-interest and familiarity threats. If a firm or a member of the audit team accepts gifts or hospitality, unless the value is trivial and inconsequential, the threats created would be so significant that no safeguards could reduce the threats to an acceptable level. Consequently, a firm or a member of the audit team shall not accept such gifts or hospitality.

Actual or threatened litigation

290.231 When litigation takes place, or appears likely, between the firm or a member of the audit team and the audit client, self-interest and intimidation threats are created. The relationship between client management and the members of the audit team must be characterised by complete candour and full disclosure regarding all aspects of a client's business operations. When the firm and the client's management are placed in adversarial positions by actual or threatened litigation, affecting management's willingness to make complete disclosures, self-interest and intimidation threats are created. The significance of the threats created will depend on such factors as:

- The materiality of the litigation; and
- Whether the litigation relates to a prior audit engagement.

The significance of the threats shall be evaluated and safeguards applied when necessary to eliminate the threats or reduce them to an acceptable level. Examples of such safeguards include:

- If the litigation involves a member of the audit team, removing that individual from the audit team; or
- Having a professional review the work performed.

If such safeguards do not reduce the threats to an acceptable level, the only appropriate action is to withdraw from, or decline, the audit engagement.

Paragraphs 290.232 to 290.499 are intentionally left blank.

Reports that include a restriction on use and distribution

Introduction

290.500 The independence requirements in Section 290 apply to all audit engagements. However, in certain circumstances involving audit engagements where the report includes a restriction on use and distribution, and provided the conditions described in paragraphs 290.501 to 290.502 are met, the independence requirements in this section may be modified as provided in paragraphs 290.505 to 290.514.

These paragraphs are only applicable to an audit engagement on special purpose financial statements (a) that is intended to provide a conclusion in positive or negative form that the financial statements are prepared in all material respects, in accordance with the applicable financial reporting framework, including, in the case of a fair presentation framework, that the financial statements give a true and fair view or are presented fairly, in all material respects, in accordance with the applicable financial reporting framework, and (b) where the audit report includes a restriction on use and distribution. The modifications are not permitted in the case of an audit of financial statements required by law or regulation.

290.501 The modifications to the requirements of Section 290 are permitted if the intended users of the report (a) are knowledgeable as to the purpose and limitations of the report, and (b) explicitly agree to the application of the modified independence requirements. Knowledge as to the purpose and limitations of the report may be obtained by the intended users through their participation, either directly or indirectly through their representative who has the authority to act for the intended users, in establishing the nature and scope of the engagement. Such participation enhances the ability of the firm to communicate with intended users about independence matters, including the circumstances that are relevant to the evaluation of the threats to independence and the applicable safeguards necessary to eliminate the threats or reduce them to an acceptable level, and to obtain their agreement to the modified independence requirements that are to be applied.

290.502 The firm shall communicate (for example, in an engagement letter) with the intended users regarding the independence requirements that are to be applied with respect to the provision of the audit engagement.

Where the intended users are a class of users (for example, lenders in a syndicated loan arrangement) who are not specifically identifiable by name at the time the engagement terms are established, such users shall subsequently be made aware of the independence requirements agreed to by the representative (for example, by the representative making the firm's engagement letter available to all users).

290.503 If the firm also issues an audit report that does not include a restriction on use and distribution for the same client, the provisions of paragraphs 290.500 to 290.514 do not change the requirement to apply the provisions of paragraphs 290.1 to 290.232 to that audit engagement.

290.504 The modifications to the requirements of Section 290 that are permitted in the circumstances set out above are described in paragraphs 290.505 to 290.514. Compliance in all other respects with the provisions of Section 290 is required.

Public interest entities

290.505 When the conditions set out in paragraphs 290.500 to 290.502 are met, it is not necessary to apply the additional requirements in paragraphs 290.100 to 290.232 that apply to audit engagements for public interest entities.

Related entities

290.506 When the conditions set out in paragraphs 290.500 to 290.502 are met, references to audit client do not include its related entities. However, when the audit team knows or has reason to believe that a relationship or circumstance involving a related entity of the client is relevant to the evaluation of the firm's independence of the client, the audit team shall include that related entity when identifying and evaluating threats to independence and applying appropriate safeguards.

Networks and Network firms

290.507 When the conditions set out in paragraphs 290.500 to 290.502 are met, reference to the firm does not include network firms. However, when the firm knows or has reason to believe that threats are created by any interests and relationships of a network firm, they shall be included in the evaluation of threats to independence.

Financial interests, loans and guarantees, close business relationships and family and personal relationships

290.508 When the conditions set out in paragraphs 290.500 to 290.502 are met, the relevant provisions set out in paragraphs 290.102 to 290.145 apply only to the members of the engagement team, their immediate family members and close family members.

290.509 In addition, a determination shall be made as to whether threats to independence are created by interests and relationships, as described in paragraphs 290.102 to 290.145, between the audit client and the following members of the audit team:

(a) Those who provide consultation regarding technical or industry specific issues, transactions or events; and

(b) Those who provide quality control for the engagement, including those who perform the engagement quality control review.

An evaluation shall be made of the significance of any threats that the engagement team has reason to believe are created by interests and relationships between the audit client and others within the firm who can directly influence the outcome of the audit engagement, including those who recommend the compensation of, or who provide direct supervisory, management or other oversight of the audit engagement partner in connection with the performance of the audit engagement (including those at all successively senior levels above the engagement partner through to the individual who is the firm's Senior or Managing Partner (Chief Executive or equivalent)).

290.510 An evaluation shall also be made of the significance of any threats that the engagement team has reason to believe are created by financial interests in the audit client held by individuals, as described in paragraphs 290.108 to 290.111 and paragraphs 290.113 to 290.115.

290.511 Where a threat to independence is not at an acceptable level, safeguards shall be applied to eliminate the threat or reduce it to an acceptable level.

290.512 In applying the provisions set out in paragraphs 290.106 and 290.115 to interests of the firm, if the firm has a material financial interest, whether direct or indirect, in the audit client, the self-interest threat created would be so significant that no safeguards could reduce the threat to an acceptable level. Accordingly, the firm shall not have such a financial interest.

Employment with an audit client

290.513 An evaluation shall be made of the significance of any threats from any employment relationships as described in paragraphs 290.134 to 290.138. Where a threat exists that is not at an acceptable level, safeguards shall be applied to eliminate the threat or reduce it to an acceptable level.

Examples of safeguards that might be appropriate include those set out in paragraph 290.136.

Provision of non-assurance services

290.514 If the firm conducts an engagement to issue a restricted use and distribution report for an audit client and provides a non-assurance service to the audit client, the provisions of paragraphs 290.156 to 290.232 shall be complied with, subject to paragraphs 290.504 to 290.507.

Supplementary reading: Annex 1 291.1 to 291.138

Section 291

INDEPENDENCE – OTHER ASSURANCE ENGAGEMENTS

CONTENTS

Structure of section

291.1 This section addresses independence requirements for assurance engagements that are not audit or review engagements. Independence requirements for audit and review engagements are addressed in Section 290. If the assurance client is also an audit or review client, the requirements in Section 290 also apply to the firm, network firms and members of the audit or review team. In certain circumstances involving assurance engagements where the assurance report includes a restriction on use and distribution and provided certain conditions are met, the independence requirements in this section may be modified as provided in paragraphs 291.21 to 291.27.

291.2 Assurance engagements are designed to enhance intended users' degree of confidence about the outcome of the evaluation or measurement of a subject matter against criteria. The International Framework for Assurance Engagements (the Assurance Framework) issued by the International Auditing and Assurance Standards Board describes the elements and objectives of an assurance engagement and identifies engagements to which International Standards on Assurance Engagements (ISAEs) apply. For a description of the elements and objectives of an assurance engagement, refer to the Assurance Framework.

291.3 Compliance with the fundamental principle of objectivity requires being independent of assurance clients. In the case of assurance engagements, it is in the public interest and, therefore, required by this Code of Ethics, that members of assurance teams and firms be independent of assurance clients and that any threats that the firm has reason to believe are created by a network firm's interests and relationships be evaluated. In addition, when the assurance team knows or has reason to believe that a relationship or circumstance involving a related entity of the assurance client is relevant to the evaluation of the firm's independence from the client, the assurance team shall include that related entity when identifying and evaluating threats to independence and applying appropriate safeguards.

A conceptual framework approach to independence

291.4 The objective of this section is to assist firms and members of assurance teams in applying the conceptual framework approach described below to achieving and maintaining independence.

291.5 Independence comprises:

(a) Independence of mind

The state of mind that permits the expression of a conclusion without being affected by influences that compromise professional judgement, thereby allowing an individual to act with integrity and exercise objectivity and professional scepticism.

(b) Independence in appearance

The avoidance of facts and circumstances that are so significant that a reasonable and informed third party would be likely to conclude, weighing all the specific facts and circumstances, that a firm's, or a member of the assurance team's, integrity, objectivity or professional scepticism has been compromised.

291.6 The conceptual framework approach shall be applied by professional accountants to:

(c) Identify threats to independence

(d) Evaluate the significance of the threats identified; and

(e) Apply safeguards when necessary to eliminate the threats or reduce them to an acceptable level.

When the professional accountant determines that appropriate safeguards are not available or cannot be applied to eliminate the threats or reduce them to an acceptable level, the professional accountant shall eliminate the circumstance or relationship creating the threats or decline or terminate the assurance engagement.

A professional accountant shall use professional judgement in applying this conceptual framework.

291.7 Many different circumstances, or combinations of circumstances, may be relevant in assessing threats to independence. It is impossible to define every situation that creates threats to independence and to specify the appropriate action. Therefore, this Code establishes a conceptual framework that requires firms and members of assurance teams to identify, evaluate, and address threats to independence. The conceptual framework approach assists professional accountants in public practice in complying with the ethical requirements in this Code. It accommodates many variations in circumstances that create threats to independence and can deter a professional accountant from concluding that a situation is permitted if it is not specifically prohibited.

291.8 Paragraphs 291.100 and onwards describe how the conceptual framework approach to independence is to be applied. These paragraphs do not address all the circumstances and relationships that create or may create threats to independence.

291.9 In deciding whether to accept or continue an engagement, or whether a particular individual may be a member of the assurance team, a firm shall identify and evaluate any threats to independence. If the threats are not at an acceptable level, and the decision is whether to accept an engagement or include a particular individual on the assurance team, the firm shall determine whether safeguards are available to eliminate the threats or reduce them to an acceptable level. If the decision is whether to continue an engagement, the firm shall determine whether any existing safeguards will continue to be effective to eliminate the threats or reduce them to an acceptable level or whether other safeguards will need to be applied or whether the engagement needs to be terminated. Whenever new information about a threat comes to the attention of the firm during the engagement, the firm shall evaluate the significance of the threat in accordance with the conceptual framework approach.

291.10 Throughout this section, reference is made to the significance of threats to independence. In evaluating the significance of a threat, qualitative as well as quantitative factors shall be taken into account.

291.11 This section does not, in most cases, prescribe the specific responsibility of individuals within the firm for actions related to independence because responsibility may differ depending on the size, structure and organisation of a firm. The firm is required by ISQCs to establish policies and procedures designed to provide it with reasonable assurance that independence is maintained when required by relevant ethical standards.

Assurance engagements

291.12 As further explained in the Assurance Framework, in an assurance engagement the professional accountant in public practice expresses a conclusion designed to enhance the degree of confidence of the intended users (other than the responsible party) about the outcome of the evaluation or measurement of a subject matter against criteria.

291.13 The outcome of the evaluation or measurement of a subject matter is the information that results from applying the criteria to the subject matter. The term 'subject matter information' is used to mean the outcome of the evaluation or measurement of a subject matter. For example, the Framework states that an assertion about the effectiveness of internal control (subject matter information) results from applying a framework for evaluating the effectiveness of internal control, such as COSO1 or CoCo2 (criteria), to internal control, a process (subject matter).

291.14 Assurance engagements may be assertion-based or direct reporting. In either case, they involve three separate parties: a professional accountant in public practice, a responsible party and intended users.

291.15 In an assertion-based assurance engagement, the evaluation or measurement of the subject matter is performed by the responsible party, and the subject matter information is in the form of an assertion by the responsible party that is made available to the intended users.

291.16 In a direct reporting assurance engagement, the professional accountant in public practice either directly performs the evaluation or measurement of the subject matter, or obtains a representation from the responsible party that has performed the evaluation or measurement that is not available to the intended users. The subject matter information is provided to the intended users in the assurance report.

(1) 'Internal Control-Integrated Framework' The Committee of Sponsoring Organisations of the Treadway Commission.

(2) 'Guidance on Assessing Control – The CoCo Principles' Criteria of Control Board, The Canadian Institute of Chartered Accountants.

Assertion-based assurance engagements

291.17 In an assertion-based assurance engagement, the members of the assurance team and the firm shall be independent of the assurance client (the party responsible for the subject matter information, and which may be responsible for the subject matter). Such independence requirements prohibit certain relationships between members of the assurance team and (a) directors or officers, and (b) individuals at the client in a position to exert significant influence over the subject matter information.

Also, a determination shall be made as to whether threats to independence are created by relationships with individuals at the client in a position to exert significant influence over the subject matter of the engagement. An evaluation shall be made of the significance of any threats that the firm has reason to believe are created by network firm3 interests and relationships.

291.18 In the majority of assertion-based assurance engagements, the responsible party is responsible for both the subject matter information and the subject matter. However, in some engagements, the responsible party may not be responsible for the subject matter. For example, when a professional accountant in public practice is engaged to perform an assurance engagement regarding a report that an environmental consultant has prepared about a company's sustainability practices for distribution to intended users, the environmental consultant is the responsible party for the subject matter information but the company is responsible for the subject matter (the sustainability practices).

291.19 In assertion-based assurance engagements where the responsible party is responsible for the subject matter information but not the subject matter, the members of the assurance team and the firm shall be independent of the party responsible for the subject matter information (the assurance client). In addition, an evaluation shall be made of any threats the firm has reason to believe are created by interests and relationships between a member of the assurance team, the firm, a network firm and the party responsible for the subject matter.

Direct reporting assurance engagements

291.20 In a direct reporting assurance engagement, the members of the assurance team and the firm shall be independent of the assurance client (the party responsible for the subject matter). An evaluation shall also be made of any threats the firm has reason to believe are created by network firm interests and relationships.

Reports that include a restriction on use and distribution

291.21 In certain circumstances where the assurance report includes a restriction on use and distribution, and provided the conditions in this paragraph and in paragraph 291.22 are met, the independence requirements in this section may be modified. The modifications to the requirements of Section 291 are permitted if the intended users of the report (a) are knowledgeable as to the purpose, subject matter information and limitations of the report and (b) explicitly agree to the application of the modified independence requirements. Knowledge as to the purpose, subject matter information, and limitations of the report may be obtained by the intended users through their participation, either directly or indirectly through their representative who has the authority to act for the intended users, in establishing the nature and scope of the engagement. Such participation enhances the ability of the firm to communicate with intended users about independence matters, including the circumstances that are relevant to the evaluation of the threats to independence and the applicable safeguards necessary to eliminate the threats or reduce them to an acceptable level, and to obtain their agreement to the modified independence requirements that are to be applied.

291.22 The firm shall communicate (for example, in an engagement letter) with the intended users regarding the independence requirements that are to be applied with respect to the provision of the assurance engagement. Where the intended users are a class of users (for example, lenders in a syndicated loan arrangement) who are not specifically identifiable by name at the time the engagement terms are established, such users shall subsequently be made aware of the independence requirements agreed to by the representative (for example, by the representative making the firm's engagement letter available to all users).

See paragraphs 290.13 to 290.24 for guidance on what constitutes a network firm.

291.23 If the firm also issues an assurance report that does not include a restriction on use and distribution for the same client, the provisions of paragraphs 291.25 to 291.27 do not change the requirement to apply the provisions of paragraphs 291.1 to 291.159 to that assurance engagement. If the firm also issues an audit report, whether or not it includes a restriction on use and distribution, for the same client, the provisions of Section 290 shall apply to that audit engagement.

291.24 The modifications to the requirements of Section 291 that are permitted in the circumstances set out above are described in paragraphs 291.25 to 291.27. Compliance in all other respects with the provisions of Section 291 is required.

291.25 When the conditions set out in paragraphs 291.21 and 291.22 are met, the relevant provisions set out in paragraphs 291.104 to 291.134 apply to all members of the engagement team, and their immediate and close family members. In addition, a determination shall be made as to whether threats to independence are created by interests and relationships between the assurance client and the following other members of the assurance team:

(a) Those who provide consultation regarding technical or industry specific issues, transactions or events; and

(b) Those who provide quality control for the engagement, including those who perform the engagement quality control review.

An evaluation shall also be made, by reference to the provisions set out in paragraphs 291.104 to 291.134, of any threats that the engagement team has reason to believe are created by interests and relationships between the assurance client and others within the firm who can directly influence the outcome of the assurance engagement, including those who recommend the compensation, or who provide direct supervisory, management or other oversight, of the assurance engagement partner in connection with the performance of the assurance engagement.

291.26 Even though the conditions set out in paragraphs 291.21 to 291.22 are met, if the firm had a material financial interest, whether direct or indirect, in the assurance client, the self-interest threat created would be so significant that no safeguards could reduce the threat to an acceptable level.

Accordingly, the firm shall not have such a financial interest. In addition, the firm shall comply with the other applicable provisions of this section described in paragraphs 291.113 to 291.159.

291.27 An evaluation shall also be made of any threats that the firm has reason to believe are created by network firm interests and relationships.

Multiple responsible parties

291.28 In some assurance engagements, whether assertion-based or direct reporting, there might be several responsible parties. In determining whether it is necessary to apply the provisions in this section to each responsible party in such engagements, the firm may take into account whether an interest or relationship between the firm, or a member of the assurance team, and a particular responsible party would create a threat to independence that is not trivial and inconsequential in the context of the subject matter information.

This will take into account factors such as:

- The materiality of the subject matter information (or of the subject matter) for which the particular responsible party is responsible; and
- The degree of public interest associated with the engagement.

If the firm determines that the threat to independence created by any such interest or relationship with a particular responsible party would be trivial and inconsequential, it may not be necessary to apply all of the provisions of this section to that responsible party.

Documentation

291.29 Documentation provides evidence of the professional accountant's judgements in forming conclusions regarding compliance with independence requirements. The absence of documentation is not a determinant of whether a firm considered a particular matter nor whether it is independent.

The professional accountant shall document conclusions regarding compliance with independence requirements, and the substance of any relevant discussions that support those conclusions. Accordingly:

(a) When safeguards are required to reduce a threat to an acceptable level, the professional accountant shall document the nature of the threat and the safeguards in place or applied that reduce the threat to an acceptable level; and

(b) When a threat required significant analysis to determine whether safeguards were necessary and the professional accountant concluded that they were not because the threat was already at an acceptable level, the professional accountant shall document the nature of the threat and the rationale for the conclusion.

Engagement period

291.30 Independence from the assurance client is required both during the engagement period and the period covered by the subject matter information. The engagement period starts when the assurance team begins to perform assurance services with respect to the particular engagement. The engagement period ends when the assurance report is issued. When the engagement is of a recurring nature, it ends at the later of the notification by either party that the professional relationship has terminated or the issuance of the final assurance report.

291.31 When an entity becomes an assurance client during or after the period covered by the subject information on which the firm will express a conclusion, the firm shall determine whether any to independence are created by:

(a) Financial or business relationships with the assurance client during or after the period covered by the subject matter information but before accepting the assurance engagement; or

(b) Previous services provided to the assurance client.

291.32 If a non-assurance service was provided to the assurance client during or after the period covered by the subject matter information but before the assurance team begins to perform assurance services and the service would not be permitted during the period of the assurance engagement, the firm shall evaluate any threat to independence created by the service. If any threat is not at an acceptable level, the assurance engagement shall only be accepted if safeguards are applied to eliminate any threats or reduce them to an acceptable level. Examples of such safeguards include:

- Not including personnel who provided the non-assurance service as members of the assurance team
- Having a professional accountant review the assurance and non-assurance work as appropriate; or
- Engaging another firm to evaluate the results of the non-assurance service or having another firm re-perform the non-assurance service to the extent necessary to enable it to take responsibility for the service.

However, if the non-assurance service has not been completed and it is not practical to complete or terminate the service before the commencement of professional services in connection with the assurance engagement, the firm shall only accept the assurance engagement if it is satisfied:

(a) The non-assurance service will be completed within a short period of time; or

(b) The client has arrangements in place to transition the service to another provider within a short period of time.

During the service period, safeguards shall be applied when necessary. In addition, the matter shall be discussed with those charged with governance.

Other considerations

291.33 There may be occasions when there is an inadvertent violation of this section. If such an inadvertent violation occurs, it generally will be deemed not to compromise independence provided the firm has appropriate quality control policies and procedures in place equivalent to those required by ISQCs to maintain independence and, once discovered, the violation is corrected promptly and any necessary safeguards are applied to eliminate any threat or reduce it to an acceptable level. The firm shall determine whether to discuss the matter with those charged with governance.

Paragraphs 291.34 to 291.99 are intentionally left blank.

Application of the conceptual framework approach to independence

291.100 Paragraphs 291.104 to 291.159 describe specific circumstances and relationships that create or may create threats to independence. The paragraphs describe the potential threats and the types of safeguards that may be appropriate to eliminate the threats or reduce them to an acceptable level and identify certain situations where no safeguards could reduce the threats to an acceptable level. The paragraphs do not describe all of the circumstances and relationships that create or may create a threat to independence. The firm and the members of the assurance team shall evaluate the implications of similar, but different, circumstances and relationships and determine whether safeguards, including the safeguards in paragraphs 200.11 to 200.14 can be applied when necessary to eliminate the threats to independence or reduce them to an acceptable level.

291.101 The paragraphs demonstrate how the conceptual framework approach applies to assurance engagements and are to be read in conjunction with paragraph 291.28 which explains that, in the majority of assurance engagements, there is one responsible party and that responsible party is the assurance client. However, in some assurance engagements there are two or more responsible parties. In such circumstances, an evaluation shall be made of any threats the firm has reason to believe are created by interests and relationships between a member of the assurance team, the firm, a network firm and the party responsible for the subject matter. For assurance reports that include a restriction on use and distribution, the paragraphs are to be read in the context of paragraphs 291.21 to 291.27.

291.102 Interpretation 2005–01 provides further guidance on applying the independence requirements contained in this section to assurance engagements.

291.103 Paragraphs 291.104 to 291.120 contain references to the materiality of a financial interest, loan, or guarantee, or the significance of a business relationship. For the purpose of determining whether such an interest is material to an individual, the combined net worth of the individual and the individual's immediate family members may be taken into account.

Financial interests

291.104 Holding a financial interest in an assurance client may create a self-interest threat. The existence and significance of any threat created depends on:

(a) The role of the person holding the financial interest

(b) Whether the financial interest is direct or indirect, and

(c) The materiality of the financial interest.

291.105 Financial interests may be held through an intermediary (for example, a collective investment vehicle, estate or trust). The determination of whether such financial interests are direct or indirect will depend upon whether the beneficial owner has control over the investment vehicle or the ability to influence its investment decisions. When control over the investment vehicle or the ability to influence investment decisions exists, this Code defines that financial interest to be a direct financial interest.

Conversely, when the beneficial owner of the financial interest has no control over the investment vehicle or ability to influence its investment decisions, this Code defines that financial interest to be an indirect financial interest.

291.106 If a member of the assurance team, a member of that individual's immediate family, or a firm has a direct financial interest or a material indirect financial interest in the assurance client, the self-interest threat created would be so significant that no safeguards could reduce the threat to an acceptable level. Therefore, none of the following shall have a direct financial interest or a material indirect financial interest in the client: a member of the assurance team; a member of that individual's immediate family member; or the firm.

291.107 When a member of the assurance team has a close family member who the assurance team member knows has a direct financial interest or a material indirect financial interest in the assurance client, a self-interest threat is created. The significance of the threat will depend on factors such as:

- The nature of the relationship between the member of the assurance team and the close family member; and
- The materiality of the financial interest to the close family member.

The significance of the threat shall be evaluated and safeguards applied when necessary to eliminate the threat or reduce it to an acceptable level. Examples of such safeguards include:

- The close family member disposing, as soon as practicable, of all of the financial interest or disposing of a sufficient portion of an indirect financial interest so that the remaining interest is no longer material
- Having a professional accountant review the work of the member of the assurance team; or
- Removing the individual from the assurance team.

291.108 If a member of the assurance team, a member of that individual's immediate family, or a firm has a direct or material indirect financial interest in an entity that has a controlling interest in the assurance client, and the client is material to the entity, the self-interest threat created would be so significant that no safeguards could reduce the threat to an acceptable level. Therefore, none of the following shall have such a financial interest: a member of the assurance team; a member of that individual's immediate family; and the firm.

291.109 The holding by a firm or a member of the assurance team, or a member of that individual's immediate family, of a direct financial interest or a material indirect financial interest in the assurance client as a trustee creates a self-interest threat. Such an interest shall not be held unless:

(a) Neither the trustee, nor an immediate family member of the trustee, nor the firm are beneficiaries of the trust

(b) The interest in the assurance client held by the trust is not material to the trust

(c) The trust is not able to exercise significant influence over the assurance client; and

(d) The trustee, an immediate family member of the trustee, or the firm cannot significantly influence any investment decision involving a financial interest in the assurance client.

291.110 Members of the assurance team shall determine whether a self-interest threat is created by any known financial interests in the assurance client held by other individuals including:

- Partners and professional employees of the firm, other than those referred to above, or their immediate family members; and
- Individuals with a close personal relationship with a member of the assurance team.

Whether these interests create a self-interest threat will depend on factors such as:

- The firm's organisational, operating and reporting structure; and
- The nature of the relationship between the individual and the member of the assurance team.

The significance of any threat shall be evaluated and safeguards applied when necessary to eliminate the threat or reduce it to an acceptable level. Examples of such safeguards include:

- Removing the member of the assurance team with the personal relationship from the assurance team
- Excluding the member of the assurance team from any significant decision-making concerning the assurance engagement; or
- Having a professional accountant review the work of the member of the assurance team.

291.111 If a firm, a member of the assurance team, or an immediate family member of the individual, receives a direct financial interest or a material indirect financial interest in an assurance client, for example, by way of an inheritance, gift or as a result of a merger, and such interest would not be permitted to be held under this section, then:

(a) If the interest is received by the firm, the financial interest shall be disposed of immediately, or a sufficient amount of an indirect financial interest shall be disposed of so that the remaining interest is no longer material, or

(b) If the interest is received by a member of the assurance team, or a member of that individual's immediate family, the individual who received the financial interest shall immediately dispose of the financial interest, or dispose of a sufficient amount of an indirect financial interest so that the remaining interest is no longer material.

291.112 When an inadvertent violation of this section as it relates to a financial interest in an assurance client occurs, it is deemed not to compromise independence if:

(a) The firm has established policies and procedures that require prompt notification to the firm of any breaches resulting from the purchase, inheritance or other acquisition of a financial interest in the assurance client

(b) The actions taken in paragraph 291.111(a)–(b) are taken as applicable; and

(c) The firm applies other safeguards when necessary to reduce any remaining threat to an acceptable level. Examples of such safeguards include:

– Having a professional accountant review the work of the member of the assurance team; or

– Excluding the individual from any significant decision-making concerning the assurance engagement.

The firm shall determine whether to discuss the matter with those charged with governance.

Loans and Guarantees

291.113 A loan, or a guarantee of a loan, to a member of the assurance team, or a member of that individual's immediate family, or the firm from an assurance client that is a bank or a similar institution, may create a threat to independence. If the loan or guarantee is not made under normal lending procedures, terms and conditions, a self-interest threat would be created that would be so significant that no safeguards could reduce the threat to an acceptable level. Accordingly, neither a member of the assurance team, a member of that individual's immediate family, nor a firm shall accept such a loan or guarantee.

291.114 If a loan to a firm from an assurance client that is a bank or similar institution is made under normal lending procedures, terms and conditions and it is material to the assurance client or firm receiving the loan, it may be possible to apply safeguards to reduce the self-interest threat to an acceptable level. An example of such a safeguard is having the work reviewed by a professional accountant from a network firm that is neither involved with the assurance engagement nor received the loan.

291.115 A loan, or a guarantee of a loan, from an assurance client that is a bank or a similar institution to a member of the assurance team, or a member of that individual's immediate family, does not create a threat to independence if the loan or guarantee is made under normal lending procedures, terms and conditions. Examples of such loans include home mortgages, bank overdrafts, car loans and credit card balances.

291.116 If the firm or a member of the assurance team, or a member of that individual's immediate family, accepts a loan from, or has a borrowing guaranteed by, an assurance client that is not a bank or similar institution, the self-interest threat created would be so significant that no safeguards could reduce the threat to an acceptable level, unless the loan or guarantee is immaterial to both the firm, or the member of the assurance team and the immediate family member, and the client.

291.117 Similarly, if the firm, or a member of the assurance team, or a member of that individual's immediate family, makes or guarantees a loan to an assurance client, the self-interest threat created would be so significant that no safeguards could reduce the threat to an acceptable level, unless the loan or guarantee is immaterial to both the firm, or the member of the assurance team and the immediate family member, and the client.

291.118 If a firm or a member of the assurance team, or a member of that individual's immediate family, has deposits or a brokerage account with an assurance client that is a bank, broker, or similar institution, a threat to independence is not created if the deposit or account is held under normal commercial terms.

Business relationships

291.119 A close business relationship between a firm, or a member of the assurance team, or a member of that individual's immediate family, and the assurance client or its management arises from a commercial relationship or common financial interest and may create self-interest or intimidation threats.

Examples of such relationships include:

- Having a financial interest in a joint venture with either the client or a controlling owner, director or officer or other individual who performs senior managerial activities for that client.
- Arrangements to combine one or more services or products of the firm with one or more services or products of the client and to market the package with reference to both parties.
- Distribution or marketing arrangements under which the firm distributes or markets the client's products or services, or the client distributes or markets the firm's products or services.

Unless any financial interest is immaterial and the business relationship is insignificant to the firm and the client or its management, the threat created would be so significant that no safeguards could reduce the threat to an acceptable level. Therefore, unless the financial interest is immaterial and the business relationship is insignificant, the business relationship shall not be entered into, or shall be reduced to an insignificant level or terminated.

In the case of a member of the assurance team, unless any such financial interest is immaterial and the relationship is insignificant to that member, the individual shall be removed from the assurance team.

If the business relationship is between an immediate family member of a member of the assurance team and the assurance client or its management, the significance of any threat shall be evaluated and safeguards applied when necessary to eliminate the threat or reduce it to an acceptable level.

291.120 The purchase of goods and services from an assurance client by the firm, or a member of the assurance team, or a member of that individual's immediate family, does not generally create a threat to independence if the transaction is in the normal course of business and at arm's length. However, such transactions may be of such a nature or magnitude that they create a self-interest threat. The significance of any threat shall be evaluated and safeguards applied when necessary to eliminate the threat or reduce it to an acceptable level. Examples of such safeguards include:

- Eliminating or reducing the magnitude of the transaction; or
- Removing the individual from the assurance team.

Family and personal relationships

291.121 Family and personal relationships between a member of the assurance team and a director or officer or certain employees (depending on their role) of the assurance client, may create self-interest, familiarity or intimidation threats. The existence and significance of any threats will depend on a number of factors, including the individual's responsibilities on the assurance team, the role of the family member or other individual within the client, and the closeness of the relationship.

291.122 When an immediate family member of a member of the assurance team is:

(a) A director or officer of the assurance client, or

(b) An employee in a position to exert significant influence over the subject matter information of the assurance engagement, or was in such a position during any period covered by the engagement or the subject matter information, the threats to independence can only be reduced to an acceptable level by removing the individual from the assurance team. The closeness of the relationship is such that no other safeguards could reduce the threat to an acceptable level. Accordingly, no individual who has such a relationship shall be a member of the assurance team.

291.123 Threats to independence are created when an immediate family member of a member of the assurance team is an employee in a position to exert significant influence over the subject matter of the engagement. The significance of the threats will depend on factors such as:

- The position held by the immediate family member; and
- The role of the professional on the assurance team.

The significance of the threat shall be evaluated and safeguards applied when necessary to eliminate the threat or reduce it to an acceptable level. Examples of such safeguards include:

- Removing the individual from the assurance team; or
- Structuring the responsibilities of the assurance team so that the professional does not deal with matters that are within the responsibility of the immediate family member.

291.124 Threats to independence are created when a close family member of a member of the assurance team is:

- A director or officer of the assurance client; or
- An employee in a position to exert significant influence over the subject matter information of the assurance engagement.

The significance of the threats will depend on factors such as:

- The nature of the relationship between the member of the assurance team and the close family member
- The position held by the close family member; and
- The role of the professional on the assurance team.

The significance of the threat shall be evaluated and safeguards applied when necessary to eliminate the threat or reduce it to an acceptable level. Examples of such safeguards include:

- Removing the individual from the assurance team; or
- Structuring the responsibilities of the assurance team so that the professional does not deal with matters that are within the responsibility of the close family member.

291.125 Threats to independence are created when a member of the assurance team has a close relationship with a person who is not an immediate or close family member, but who is a director or officer or an employee in a position to exert significant influence over the subject matter information of the assurance engagement. A member of the assurance team who has such a relationship shall consult in accordance with firm policies and procedures. The significance of the threats will depend on factors such as:

- The nature of the relationship between the individual and the member of the assurance team
- The position the individual holds with the client; and
- The role of the professional on the assurance team.

The significance of the threats shall be evaluated and safeguards applied when necessary to eliminate the threats or reduce them to an acceptable level. Examples of such safeguards include:

- Removing the professional from the assurance team; or
- Structuring the responsibilities of the assurance team so that the professional does not deal with matters that are within the responsibility of the individual with whom the professional has a close relationship.

291.126 Self-interest, familiarity or intimidation threats may be created by a personal or family relationship between (a) a partner or employee of the firm who is not a member of the assurance team and (b) a director or officer of the assurance client or an employee in a position to exert significant influence over the subject matter information of the assurance engagement. The existence and significance of any threat will depend on factors such as:

- The nature of the relationship between the partner or employee of the firm and the director or officer or employee of the client
- The interaction of the partner or employee of the firm with the assurance team
- The position of the partner or employee within the firm; and
- The role of the individual within the client.

The significance of any threat shall be evaluated and safeguards applied when necessary to eliminate the threat or reduce it to an acceptable level. Examples of such safeguards include:

- Structuring the partner's or employee's responsibilities to reduce any potential influence over the assurance engagement; or
- Having a professional accountant review the relevant assurance work performed.

291.127 When an inadvertent violation of this section as it relates to family and personal relationships occurs, it is deemed not to compromise independence if:

(a) The firm has established policies and procedures that require prompt notification to the firm of any breaches resulting from changes in the employment status of their immediate or close family members or other personal relationships that create threats to independence

(b) The inadvertent violation relates to an immediate family member of a member of the assurance team becoming a director or officer of the assurance client or being in a position to exert significant influence over the subject matter information of the assurance engagement, and the relevant professional is removed from the assurance team; and

(c) The firm applies other safeguards when necessary to reduce any remaining threat to an acceptable level. Examples of such safeguards include:

  – Having a professional accountant review the work of the member of the assurance team; or
  – Excluding the relevant professional from any significant decision-making concerning the engagement.

The firm shall determine whether to discuss the matter with those charged with governance.

Employment with assurance clients

291.128 Familiarity or intimidation threats may be created if a director or officer of the assurance client, or an employee who is in a position to exert significant influence over the subject matter information of the assurance engagement, has been a member of the assurance team or partner of the firm.

291.129 If a former member of the assurance team or partner of the firm has joined the assurance client in such a position, the existence and significance of any familiarity or intimidation threats will depend on factors such as:

- The position the individual has taken at the client
- Any involvement the individual will have with the assurance team
- The length of time since the individual was a member of the assurance team or partner of the firm; and
- The former position of the individual within the assurance team or firm, for example, whether the individual was responsible for maintaining regular contact with the client's management or those charged with governance.

In all cases the individual shall not continue to participate in the firm's business or professional activities. The significance of any threats created shall be evaluated and safeguards applied when necessary to eliminate the threats or reduce them to an acceptable level. Examples of such safeguards include:

- Making arrangements such that the individual is not entitled to any benefits or payments from the firm, unless made in accordance with fixed pre-determined arrangements
- Making arrangements such that any amount owed to the individual is not material to the firm
- Modifying the plan for the assurance engagement
- Assigning individuals to the assurance team who have sufficient experience in relation to the individual who has joined the client; or
- Having a professional accountant review the work of the former member of the assurance team.

291.130 If a former partner of the firm has previously joined an entity in such a position and the entity subsequently becomes an assurance client of the firm, the significance of any threats to independence shall be evaluated and safeguards applied when necessary, to eliminate the threat or reduce it to an acceptable level.

291.131 A self-interest threat is created when a member of the assurance team participates in the assurance engagement while knowing that the member of the assurance team will, or may, join the client sometime in the future. Firm policies and procedures shall require members of an assurance team to notify the firm when entering employment negotiations with the client. On receiving such notification, the significance of the threat shall be evaluated and safeguards applied when necessary to eliminate the threat or reduce it to an acceptable level. Examples of such safeguards include:

- Removing the individual from the assurance team; or
- A review of any significant judgements made by that individual while on the team.

Recent service with an assurance client

291.132 Self-interest, self-review or familiarity threats may be created if a member of the assurance team has recently served as a director, officer, or employee of the assurance client. This would be the case when, for example, a member of the assurance team has to evaluate elements of the subject matter information the member of the assurance team had prepared while with the client.

291.133 If, during the period covered by the assurance report, a member of the assurance team had served as director or officer of the assurance client, or was an employee in a position to exert significant influence over the subject matter information of the assurance engagement, the threat created would be so significant that no safeguards could reduce the threat to an acceptable level. Consequently, such individuals shall not be assigned to the assurance team.

291.134 Self-interest, self-review or familiarity threats may be created if, before the period covered by the assurance report, a member of the assurance team had served as director or officer of the assurance client, or was an employee in a position to exert significant influence over the subject matter information of the assurance engagement. For example, such threats would be created if a decision made or work performed by the individual in the prior period, while employed by the client, is to be evaluated in the current period as part of the current assurance engagement.

The existence and significance of any threats will depend on factors such as:

- The position the individual held with the client
- The length of time since the individual left the client; and
- The role of the professional on the assurance team.

The significance of any threat shall be evaluated and safeguards applied when necessary to reduce the threat to an acceptable level. An example of such a safeguard is conducting a review of the work performed by the individual as part of the assurance team.

Serving as a Director or Officer of an assurance client

291.135 If a partner or employee of the firm serves a director or officer of an assurance client, the self-review and self-interest threats would be so significant that no safeguards could reduce the threats to an acceptable level. Accordingly, no partner or employee shall serve as a director or officer of an assurance client.

291.136 The position of Company Secretary has different implications in different jurisdictions. Duties may range from administrative duties, such as personnel management and the maintenance of company records and registers, to duties as diverse as ensuring that the company complies with regulation or providing advice on corporate governance matters. Generally, this position is seen to imply a close association with the entity.

291.137 If a partner or employee of the firm serves as Company Secretary for an assurance client, self-review and advocacy threats are created that would generally be so significant that no safeguards could reduce the threats to an acceptable level. Despite paragraph 291.135, when this practice is specifically permitted under local law, professional rules or practice, and provided management makes all relevant decisions, the duties and activities shall be limited to those of a routine and administrative nature, such as preparing minutes and maintaining statutory returns. In those circumstances, the significance of any threats shall be evaluated and safeguards applied when necessary to eliminate the threats or reduce them to an acceptable level.

291.138 Performing routine administrative services to support a company secretarial function or providing advice in relation to company secretarial administration matters does not generally create threats to independence, as long as client management makes all relevant decisions.

Supplementary reading: Annex 1 291.139 to 291.159

Long association of senior personnel with assurance clients

291.139 Familiarity and self-interest threats are created by using the same senior personnel on an assurance engagement over a long period of time. The significance of the threats will depend on factors such as:

- How long the individual has been a member of the assurance team
- The role of the individual on the assurance team
- The structure of the firm
- The nature of the assurance engagement
- Whether the client's management team has changed; and
- Whether the nature or complexity of the subject matter information has changed.

The significance of the threats shall be evaluated and safeguards applied when necessary to eliminate the threats or reduce them to an acceptable level.

Examples of such safeguards include:

- Rotating the senior personnel off the assurance team
- Having a professional accountant who was not a member of the assurance team review the work of the senior personnel; or
- Regular independent internal or external quality reviews of the engagement.

Provision of non-assurance services to assurance clients

291.140 Firms have traditionally provided to their assurance clients a range of non-assurance services that are consistent with their skills and expertise. Providing non-assurance services may, however, create threats to the independence of the firm or members of the assurance team. The threats created are most often self-review, self-interest and advocacy threats.

291.141 When specific guidance on a particular non-assurance service is not included in this section, the conceptual framework shall be applied when evaluating the particular circumstances.

291.142 Before the firm accepts an engagement to provide a non-assurance service to an assurance client, a determination shall be made as to whether providing such a service would create a threat to independence. In evaluating the significance of any threat created by a particular non-assurance service, consideration shall be given to any threat that the assurance team has reason to believe is created by providing other related non-assurance services. If a threat is created that cannot be reduced to an acceptable level by the application of safeguards the non-assurance service shall not be provided.

Management responsibilities

291.143 Management of an entity performs many activities in managing the entity in the best interests of stakeholders of the entity. It is not possible to specify every activity that is a management responsibility. However, management responsibilities involve leading and directing an entity, including making significant decisions regarding the acquisition, deployment and control of human, financial, physical and intangible resources.

291.144 Whether an activity is a management responsibility depends on the circumstances and requires the exercise of judgement. Examples of activities that would generally be considered a management responsibility include:

- Setting policies and strategic direction
- Directing and taking responsibility for the actions of the entity's employees
- Authorising transactions
- Deciding which recommendations of the firm or other third parties to implement; and
- Taking responsibility for designing, implementing and maintaining internal control.

291.145 Activities that are routine and administrative, or involve matters that are insignificant, generally are deemed not to be a management responsibility. For example, executing an insignificant transaction that has been authorised by management or monitoring the dates for filing statutory returns and advising an assurance client of those dates is deemed not to be a management responsibility. Further, providing advice and recommendations to assist management in discharging its responsibilities is not assuming a management responsibility.

291.146 Assuming a management responsibility for an assurance client may create threats to independence. If a firm were to assume a management responsibility as part of the assurance service, the threats created would be so significant that no safeguards could reduce the threats to an acceptable level. Accordingly, in providing assurance services to an assurance client, a firm shall not assume a management responsibility as part of the assurance service. If the firm assumes a management responsibility as part of any other services provided to the assurance client, it shall ensure that the responsibility is not related to the subject matter and subject matter information of an assurance engagement provided by the firm.

291.147 To avoid the risk of assuming a management responsibility related to the subject matter or subject matter information of the assurance engagement, the firm shall be satisfied that a member of management is responsible for making the significant judgements and decisions that are the proper responsibility of management, evaluating the results of the service and accepting responsibility for the actions to be taken arising from the results of the service. This reduces the risk of the firm inadvertently making any significant judgements or decisions on behalf of management. This risk is further reduced when the firm gives the client the opportunity to make judgements and decisions based on an objective and transparent analysis and presentation of the issues.

Other considerations

291.148 Threats to independence may be created when a firm provides a non-assurance service related to the subject matter information of an assurance engagement. In such cases, an evaluation of the significance of the firm's involvement with the subject matter information of the engagement shall be made, and a determination shall be made of whether any self-review threats that are not at an acceptable level can be reduced to an acceptable level by the application of safeguards.

291.149 A self-review threat may be created if the firm is involved in the preparation of subject matter information which is subsequently the subject matter information of an assurance engagement. For example, a self-review threat would be created if the firm developed and prepared prospective financial information and subsequently provided assurance on this information. Consequently, the firm shall evaluate the significance of any self-review threat created by the provision of such services and apply safeguards when necessary to eliminate the threat or reduce it to an acceptable level.

291.150 When a firm performs a valuation that forms part of the subject matter information of an assurance engagement, the firm shall evaluate the significance of any self-review threat and apply safeguards when necessary to eliminate the threat or reduce it to an acceptable level.

Fees

Fees – Relative size

291.151 When the total fees from an assurance client represent a large proportion of the total fees of the firm expressing the conclusion, the dependence on that client and concern about losing the client creates a self-interest or intimidation threat. The significance of the threat will depend on factors such as:

- The operating structure of the firm
- Whether the firm is well established or new; and
- The significance of the client qualitatively and/or quantitatively to the firm.

The significance of the threat shall be evaluated and safeguards applied when necessary to eliminate the threat or reduce it to an acceptable level. Examples of such safeguards include:

- Reducing the dependency on the client
- External quality control reviews; or
- Consulting a third party, such as a professional regulatory body or a professional accountant, on key assurance judgements.

291.152 A self-interest or intimidation threat is also created when the fees generated from an assurance client represent a large proportion of the revenue from an individual partner's clients. The significance of the threat shall be evaluated and safeguards applied when necessary to eliminate the threat or reduce it to an acceptable level. An example of such a safeguard is having an additional professional accountant who was not a member of the assurance team review the work or otherwise advise as necessary.

Fees – Overdue

291.153 A self-interest threat may be created if fees due from an assurance client remain unpaid for a long time, especially if a significant part is not paid before the issue of the assurance report, if any, for the following period. Generally the firm is expected to require payment of such fees before any such report is issued. If fees remain unpaid after the report has been issued, the existence and significance of any threat shall be evaluated and safeguards applied when necessary to eliminate the threat or reduce it to an acceptable level. An example of such a safeguard is having another professional accountant who did not take part in the assurance engagement provide advice or review the work performed. The firm shall determine whether the overdue fees might be regarded as being equivalent to a loan to the client and whether, because of the significance of the overdue fees, it is appropriate for the firm to be re-appointed or continue the assurance engagement.

Contingent fees

291.154 Contingent fees are fees calculated on a predetermined basis relating to the outcome of a transaction or the result of the services performed by the firm. For the purposes of this section, fees are not regarded as being contingent if established by a court or other public authority.

291.155 A contingent fee charged directly or indirectly, for example through an intermediary, by a firm in respect of an assurance engagement creates a self-interest threat that is so significant that no safeguards could reduce the threat to an acceptable level. Accordingly, a firm shall not enter into any such fee arrangement.

291.156 A contingent fee charged directly or indirectly, for example through an intermediary, by a firm in respect of a non-assurance service provided to an assurance client may also create a self-interest threat. If the outcome of the non-assurance service, and therefore, the amount of the fee, is dependent on a future or contemporary judgement related to a matter that is material to the subject matter information of the assurance engagement, no safeguards could reduce the threat to an acceptable level. Accordingly, such arrangements shall not be accepted.

291.157 For other contingent fee arrangements charged by a firm for a non-assurance service to an assurance client, the existence and significance of any threats will depend on factors such as:

- The range of possible fee amounts
- Whether an appropriate authority determines the outcome of the matter upon which the contingent fee will be determined
- The nature of the service; and
- The effect of the event or transaction on the subject matter information.

The significance of any threats shall be evaluated and safeguards applied when necessary to eliminate the threats or reduce them to an acceptable level. Examples of such safeguards include:

- Having a professional accountant review the relevant assurance work or otherwise advise as necessary; or
- Using professionals who are not members of the assurance team to perform the non-assurance service.

Gifts and Hospitality

291.158 Accepting gifts or hospitality from an assurance client may create self-interest and familiarity threats. If a firm or a member of the assurance team accepts gifts or hospitality, unless the value is trivial and inconsequential, the threats created would be so significant that no safeguards could reduce the threats to an acceptable level. Consequently, a firm or a member of the assurance team shall not accept such gifts or hospitality.

Actual or threatened litigation

291.159 When litigation takes place, or appears likely, between the firm or a member of the assurance team and the assurance client, self-interest and intimidation threats are created. The relationship between client management and the members of the assurance team must be characterised by complete candour and full disclosure regarding all aspects of a client's business operations. When the firm and the client's management are placed in adversarial positions by actual or threatened litigation, affecting management's willingness to make complete disclosures self-interest and intimidation threats are created. The significance of the threats created will depend on such factors as:

- The materiality of the litigation; and
- Whether the litigation relates to a prior assurance engagement.

The significance of the threats shall be evaluated and safeguards applied when necessary to eliminate the threats or reduce them to an acceptable level. Examples of such safeguards include:

- If the litigation involves a member of the assurance team, removing that individual from the assurance team; or
- Having a professional review the work performed.

If such safeguards do not reduce the threats to an acceptable level, the only appropriate action is to withdraw from, or decline, the assurance engagement.

Interpretation 2005–01 (Revised July 2009 to conform to changes resulting from the IESBA's project to improve the clarity of the Code)

Application of Section 291 to Assurance Engagements that are Not Financial Statement Audit

Engagements

This interpretation provides guidance on the application of the independence requirements contained in Section 291 to assurance engagements that are not financial statement audit engagements. This interpretation focuses on the application issues that are particular to assurance engagements that are not financial statement audit engagements. There are other matters noted in Section 291 that are relevant in the consideration of independence requirements for all assurance engagements. For example, paragraph 291.3 states that an evaluation shall be made of any threats the firm has reason to believe are created by a network firm's interests and relationships. It also states that when the assurance team has reason to believe that a related entity of such an assurance client is relevant to the evaluation of the firm's independence of the client, the assurance team shall include the related entity when evaluating threats to independence and when necessary applying safeguards. These matters are not specifically addressed in this interpretation.

As explained in the International Framework for Assurance Engagements issued by the International Auditing and Assurance Standards Board, in an assurance engagement, the professional accountant in public practice expresses a conclusion designed to enhance the degree of confidence of the intended users other than the responsible party about the outcome of the evaluation or measurement of a subject matter against criteria.

Assertion-based assurance engagements

In an assertion-based assurance engagement, the evaluation or measurement of the subject matter is performed by the responsible party, and the subject matter information is in the form of an assertion by the responsible party that is made available to the intended users. In an assertion-based assurance engagement independence is required from the responsible party, which is responsible for the subject matter information and may be responsible for the subject matter.

In those assertion-based assurance engagements where the responsible party is responsible for the subject matter information but not the subject matter, independence is required from the responsible party. In addition, an evaluation shall be made of any threats the firm has reason to believe are created by interests and relationships between a member of the assurance team, the firm, a network firm and the party responsible for the subject matter.

Direct reporting assurance engagements

In a direct reporting assurance engagement, the professional accountant in public practice either directly performs the evaluation or measurement of the subject matter, or obtains a representation from the responsible party that has performed the evaluation or measurement that is not available to the intended users. The subject matter information is provided to the intended users in the assurance report. In a direct reporting assurance engagement independence is required from the responsible party, which is responsible for the subject matter.

Multiple responsible parties

In both assertion-based assurance engagements and direct reporting assurance engagements there may be several responsible parties. For example, a public accountant in public practice may be asked to provide assurance on the monthly circulation statistics of a number of independently owned newspapers.

The assignment could be an assertion based assurance engagement where each newspaper measures its circulation and the statistics are presented in an assertion that is available to the intended users. Alternatively, the assignment could be a direct reporting assurance engagement, where there is no assertion and there may or may not be a written representation from the newspapers.

In such engagements, when determining whether it is necessary to apply the provisions in Section 291 to each responsible party, the firm may take into account whether an interest or relationship between the firm, or a member of the assurance team, and a particular responsible party would create a threat to independence that is not trivial and inconsequential in the context of the subject matter information.

This will take into account:

(a) The materiality of the subject matter information (or the subject matter) for which the particular responsible party is responsible; and

(b) The degree of public interest that is associated with the engagement.

If the firm determines that the threat to independence created by any such relationships with a particular responsible party would be trivial and inconsequential it may not be necessary to apply all of the provisions of this section to that responsible party.

Example

The following example has been developed to demonstrate the application of Section 291. It is assumed that the client is not also a financial statement audit client of the firm, or a network firm.

A firm is engaged to provide assurance on the total proven oil reserves of 10 independent companies. Each company has conducted geographical and engineering surveys to determine their reserves (subject matter). There are established criteria to determine when a reserve may be considered to be proven which the professional accountant in public practice determines to be suitable criteria for the engagement.

The proven reserves (in thousands of barrels) for each company as at December 31, 20X0 were as follows:

- Company 1 – 5,200
- Company 2 – 725
- Company 3 – 3,260
- Company 4 – 15,000
- Company 5 – 6,700

- Company 6 – 39,126
- Company 7 – 345
- Company 8 – 175
- Company 9 – 24,135
- Company 10 – 9,635
- **Total** – **104,301**

The engagement could be structured in differing ways:

Assertion-based engagements

A1 Each company measures its reserves and provides an assertion to the firm and to intended users.

A2 An entity other than the companies measures the reserves and provides an assertion to the firm and to intended users.

Direct reporting engagements

D1 Each company measures the reserves and provides the firm with a written representation that measures its reserves against the established criteria for measuring proven reserves. The representation is not available to the intended users.

D2 The firm directly measures the reserves of some of the companies.

Application of approach

A1 Each company measures its reserves and provides an assertion to the firm and to intended users. There are several responsible parties in this engagement (Companies 1–10). When determining whether it is necessary to apply the independence provisions to all of the companies, the firm may take into account whether an interest or relationship with a particular company would create a threat to independence that is not at an acceptable level. This will take into account factors such as:

- The materiality of the company's proven reserves in relation to the total reserves to be reported on; and
- The degree of public interest associated with the engagement (paragraph 291.28).

For example Company 8 accounts for 0.17% of the total reserves, therefore a business relationship or interest with Company 8 would create less of a threat than a similar relationship with Company 6, which accounts for approximately 37.5% of the reserves.

Having determined those companies to which the independence requirements apply, the assurance team and the firm are required to be independent of those responsible parties that would be considered to be the assurance client (paragraph 291.28).

A2 An entity other than the companies measures the reserves and provides an assertion to the firm and to intended users.

The firm shall be independent of the entity that measures the reserves and provides an assertion to the firm and to intended users (paragraph 291.19). That entity is not responsible for the subject matter and so an evaluation shall be made of any threats the firm has reason to believe are created by interests/relationships with the party responsible for the subject matter (paragraph 291.19). There are several parties responsible for the subject matter in this engagement (Companies 1–10). As discussed in example A1 above, the firm may take into account whether an interest or relationship with a particular company would create a threat to independence that is not at an acceptable level.

D1 Each company provides the firm with a representation that measures its reserves against the established criteria for measuring proven reserves. The representation is not available to the intended users.

There are several responsible parties in this engagement (Companies 1–10). When determining whether it is necessary to apply the independence provisions to all of the companies, the firm may take into account whether an interest or relationship with a particular company would create a threat to independence that is not at an acceptable level. This will take into account factors such as:

- The materiality of the company's proven reserves in relation to the total reserves to be reported on; and
- The degree of public interest associated with the engagement (paragraph 291.28).

For example, Company 8 accounts for 0.17% of the reserves, therefore a business relationship or interest with Company 8 would create less of a threat than a similar relationship with Company 6 that accounts for approximately 37.5% of the reserves.

Having determined those companies to which the independence requirements apply, the assurance team and the firm shall be independent of those responsible parties that would be considered to be the assurance client (paragraph 291.28).

D2 The firm directly measures the reserves of some of the companies. The application is the same as in example D1.

Effective date

This code is effective on January 1, 2011. Early adoption is permitted. The Code is subject to the following transitional provisions:

Public interest entities

(1) Section 290 of the Code contains additional independence provisions when the audit or review client is a public interest entity. The additional provisions that are applicable because of the new definition of a public interest entity or the guidance in paragraph 290.26 are effective on January 1, 2012. For partner rotation requirements, the transitional provisions contained in paragraphs 2 and 3 below apply.

Partner rotation

(2) For a partner who is subject to the rotation provisions in paragraph 290.151 because the partner meets the definition of the new term 'key audit partner,' and the partner is neither the engagement partner nor the individual responsible for the engagement quality control review, the rotation provisions are effective for the audits or reviews of financial statements for years beginning on or after December 15, 2011. For example, in the case of an audit client with a calendar year-end, a key audit partner, who is neither the engagement partner nor the individual responsible for the engagement quality control review, who had served as a key audit partner for seven or more years (that is, the audits of 2003–2010), would be required to rotate after serving for one more year as a key audit partner (that is, after completing the 2011 audit).

(3) For an engagement partner or an individual responsible for the engagement quality control review who immediately prior to assuming either of these roles served in another key audit partner role for the client, and who, at the beginning of the first fiscal year beginning on or after December 15, 2010, had served as the engagement partner or individual responsible for the engagement quality control review for six or fewer years, the rotation provisions are effective for the audits or reviews of financial statements for years beginning on or after December 15, 2011. For example, in the case of an audit client with a calendar year-end, a partner who had served the client in another key audit partner role for four years (that is, the audits of 2002–2005) and subsequently as the engagement partner for five years (that is, the audits of 2006–2010) would be required to rotate after serving for one more year as the engagement partner (that is, after completing the 2011 audit).

Non-assurance services

(4) Paragraphs 290.156–290.219 address the provision of non-assurance services to an audit or review client. If, at the effective date of the Code, services are being provided to an audit or review client and the services were permissible under the June 2005 Code (revised July 2006) but are either prohibited or subject to restrictions under the revised Code, the firm may continue providing such services only if they were contracted for and commenced prior to January 1, 2011, and are completed before July 1, 2011.

Fees – Relative size

(5) Paragraph 290.222 provides that, in respect of an audit or review client that is a public interest entity, when the total fees from that client and its related entities (subject to the considerations in paragraph 290.27) for two consecutive years represent more than 15% of the total fees of the firm expressing the opinion on the financial statements, a pre- or post-issuance review (as described in paragraph 290.222) of the second year's audit shall be performed. This requirement is effective for audits or reviews of financial statements covering years that begin on or after December 15, 2010. For example, in the case of an audit client with a calendar year end, if the total fees from the client exceeded the 15% threshold for 2011 and 2012, the pre- or post-issuance review would be applied with respect to the audit of the 2012 financial statements.

Compensation and evaluation policies

(6) Paragraph 290.229 provides that a key audit partner shall not be evaluated or compensated based on that partner's success in selling non-assurance services to the partner's audit client. This requirement is effective on January 1, 2012. A key audit partner may, however, receive compensation after January 1, 2012 based on an evaluation made prior to January 1, 2012 of that partner's success in selling non-assurance services to the audit client.

chapter

10

Preparing for the Assessment

Chapter learning objectives

This section is intended for use when you are ready to start revising for your CBA. It contains:

- a summary of useful revision techniques
- details of the format of the CBA
- two mock CBAs.

These should be attempted when you consider yourself to be ready for the CBA.

1 Revision technique

The first thing to say about revision is that it is an addition to your initial studies, not a substitute for them. In other words, do not coast along early in your course in the hope of catching up during the revision phase. On the contrary, you should be studying and revising concurrently from the outset. At the end of each week, and at the end of each month, get into the habit of summarising the material you have covered to refresh your memory of it.

As with your initial studies, planning is important to maximise the value of your revision work. You need to balance the demands for study, professional work, family life and other commitments. To make this work, you will need to think carefully about how to make best use of your time.

Begin as before by comparing the estimated hours you will need to devote to revision with the hours available to you in the weeks leading up to the examination. Prepare a written schedule setting out the areas you intend to cover during particular weeks, and break that down further into topics for each day's revision. To help focus on the key areas try to establish:

- which areas you are weakest on, so that you can concentrate on the topics where effort is particularly needed
- which areas are especially significant for the assessment – the topics that are tested frequently.

Do not forget the need for relaxation, and for family commitments. Sustained intellectual effort is only possible for limited periods, and must be broken up at intervals by lighter activities. And do not continue your revision timetable right up to the moment when you enter the assessment centre: you should aim to stop work a day or even 2 days before the exam. Beyond this point, the most you should attempt is an occasional brief look at your notes to refresh your memory.

By the time you begin your revision you should already have settled into a fixed work pattern: a regular time of day for doing the work, a particular location where you sit, particular equipment that you assemble before you begin and so on. If this is not already a matter of routine for you, think carefully about it now in the last vital weeks before the assessment.

You should have notes summarising the main points of each topic you have covered. Begin each session by reading through the relevant notes and trying to commit the important points to memory.

Usually, this will be just your starting point. Unless the area is one where you already feel very confident, you will need to track back from your notes to the relevant chapter(s) in the Study Text. This will refresh your memory on points not covered by your notes and fill in the detail that inevitably gets lost in the process of summarisation.

When you think you have understood and memorised the main principles and techniques, attempt an exam-standard question. At this stage of your studies, you should normally be expecting to complete such questions in something close to the actual time allocation allowed in the exam. After completing your effort, check the solution provided and add to your notes any extra points it reveals.

As the assessment approaches, consider the following list of techniques and make use of those that work for you:

(i) Summarise your notes into a more concise form, perhaps on index cards that you can carry with you for revision on the way into work.

(ii) Go through your notes with a highlighter pen, marking key concepts and definitions.

(iii) Summarise the main points in a key area by producing a wordlist, mind map or other mnemonic device.

(iv) For topics which you have found difficult, rework questions that you have already attempted, and compare your answers in detail with those provided in the Study Text.

(v) Rework questions you attempted earlier in your studies with a view to producing more 'polished' answers and to completing them within the time limits.

2 Format of the assessment

Structure of the assessment

Fundamentals of Ethics, Governance and Business Law is a Certificate Level subject and examination is by computer-based assessment ('CBA') only. Candidates are required to answer 75 objective test questions within 2 hours.

Objective test questions are used. The most common type is 'multiple choice', which requires you to select the correct answer from a number of possible alternatives. Other types of objective questions may be used and examples of possible questions are included in this chapter.

Assessment by CBA enables CIMA to access the whole syllabus, and the number of questions on each topic is selected according to 'study weightings' (see below).

Allocation of time

Many of the candidates who have failed CIMA Certificate level assessments in the past have done so because of poor assessment technique. It follows that it is crucial for candidates to adhere strictly to the time available for answering each question. Once that time has expired, the candidates should proceed to the next question, and return to any unfinished questions, if time allows after completion of the paper as a whole.

Each topic within the syllabus is given a weighting, so that students are aware of the percentage of time that they should spend studying individual topics. In general, the assessment will attempt to reflect those study weightings as closely as possible in the selection of questions.

The current syllabus weightings are as follows:

- Ethics and Business (15%)
- Ethical Conflict (10%)
- Corporate Governance (10%)
- Comparison of English Law with Alternative Legal Systems (10%)
- The Law of Contract (20%)
- The Law of Employment (10%)
- Company Administration and Finance (25%)

chapter

11

Mock Assessment 1

Chapter learning objectives

This section is intended for use when you have completed your study and initial revision. It contains a complete mock assessment.

This should be attempted as an exam conditions, timed mock. This will give you valuable experience that will assist you with your time management and examination strategy.

Certificate Level

Fundamentals of Ethics, Corporate Governance and Business Law

Instructions: attempt all 75 questions.

Time allowed 2 hours.

Do not turn the page until you are ready to attempt the examination under timed conditions.

Test your understanding questions

Test your understanding 1

Which one of the following is correct?

A The Supreme Court has a discretion in applying English Law or European Law

B The Supreme Court must apply European Law where it contradicts English Law

C The Supreme Court can apply English Law even if it contradicts European Law

D The Supreme Court must obtain approval to apply European Law where it contradicts English Law

Test your understanding 2

Which one of the following courts has no criminal jurisdiction?

A Divisional court of the Queen's Bench Division

B County Court

C Magistrates Court

D Crown Court

Test your understanding 3

With judicial precedent, subject to the hierarchy of the courts, previous court decisions should be followed. However, it can be possible to avoid following precedent.

Which *one* of the following is incorrect in relation to avoidance of precedent?

A A higher court can overrule a lower court decision

B Any court can distinguish the facts from those of an earlier decision

C Any court can reverse the decision of a previous court

D Any court need not apply an obiter dicta statement of an earlier court

Test your understanding 4

In relation to establishing a claim of negligence, which one of the following is incorrect?

A There must be sufficient proximity between the wrongdoer and the injured party

B The standard of care required is that expected by the reasonable person

C The same level of care is owed both to adults and children

D The level of care to be shown varies with the level of seriousness of the likely consequences of breach of duty

Test your understanding 5

Which one of the following is correct?

A A professional adviser can be liable to both the client who employs them and any other parties who they know will rely on information provided

B A professional adviser can be liable to anyone who relies on information they provide

C A professional adviser will be liable in negligence but not contract for any negligent advice provided

D A professional adviser cannot be liable where the only form of damage resulting from negligent advice given is financial loss

Test your understanding 6

The standard of proof to be satisfied in

(i) criminal actions and

(ii) civil actions is

A Beyond reasonable doubt for (i) and (ii)

B On a balance of probabilities for (i) and (ii)

C Beyond reasonable doubt for (i) and on a balance of probabilities for (ii)

D On a balance of probabilities for (i) and beyond reasonable doubt for (ii)

Test your understanding 7

Common Law developed from which one of the following?

A Equity

B Custom

C Decisions of the Court of Chancery

D Judicial precedent

Test your understanding 8

Where a dispute involves issues of European Law which are unclear, the matter must be referred to the European Court of Justice by which of the following English courts?

A All

B All the courts below the Supreme Court

C Only the Supreme Court

D Only the Court of Appeal and the Supreme Court

Test your understanding 9

Which one of the following contracts would not be presumed to be legally binding?

A One or both contracting parties were a business or company

B The contract was a collective agreement between employers and trade unions relating to terms of employment

C The contract is of a clearly commercial nature

D The contract involved money and this was a factor of significance

Test your understanding 10

In which one of the following instances will misrepresentation generally not be recognised?

A The contract contains half-truths

B In a contract of the utmost good faith, full disclosure is not made

C Information ceases to be accurate because of changed circumstances

D A party fails to disclose material facts

Test your understanding 11

In which one of the following instances will a term not be incorporated into a contract?

A Where a party signs the contract containing the term, whether they have read it or not

B Where the term is an exclusion clause invalidated by the Unfair Contract Terms Act 1977

C Where there is a course of dealing between the parties

D Where reasonable notice of the term is given but a contracting party remains unaware of its existence

Test your understanding 12

Liability in contract made by a business can never be excluded for which one of the following?

A Death or physical injury

B The implied conditions under the Sale of Goods Act 1979

C Financial loss

D Guarantees of goods given by manufacturers

Test your understanding 13

The following advertisement appeared in a farming magazine.

'Plough for sale. Little used, very good condition £1,000.'

How would this statement be defined at law?

A Advertising puff

B Offer to sell

C Invitation to treat

D Invitation to buy

Test your understanding 14

An offer was made by A to sell goods on the 1st April for £2,000. B the offeree telephoned A on the 5th April offering to pay £1,800 for the goods. On the 8th April, A offered to sell the goods to C for £1,900, and C accepted this offer on the same day. On the 7th April, B sent a letter to A which was received on the 10th April agreeing to pay the £2,000, the asked price for the goods.

A There is a contract between A and B created on the 7th April

B There is a contract between A and B created on the 10th April

C There is a contract between A and C

D There is no contract created

Test your understanding 15

A coat was displayed in a shop window with a price tag attached which read £10. The price tag should have read £100. X who saw this went into the shop and demanded the coat for £10.

Which one of the following is correct?

A As the window display is an offer, X can demand the coat at £10

B The window display is merely an invitation to treat and the shopkeeper does not have to sell the coat to X

C The shopkeeper can refuse to sell the coat for £10, but cannot refuse to sell the coat to X for £100 if X was prepared to pay this sum

D The shopkeeper would be bound to sell the coat to any customer prepared to pay this £100

Test your understanding 16

Which one of the following is incorrect?

A A contract term can be implied by a court on the ground of business efficacy

B A contract term can be implied by statute

C A contract term can be implied by a court on the basis of fairness between the parties

D A contract term can be implied by a court on the basis of trade custom

Test your understanding 17

Which one of the following statements is incorrect?

A Statute provides an implied term in sale of goods contracts that the goods are of satisfactory quality

B Statute provides an implied term in sale of goods contracts that the goods supplied must correspond with description

C Statute provides that failure to supply goods of satisfactory quality in a sale of goods contract constitutes breach of condition

D Statute provides that failure to provide goods in a sale of goods contract that correspond with description amounts to a breach of warranty

Test your understanding 18

Which one of the following statements is correct?

A In a contract, a breach of a condition will result in the contract being terminated

B In a contract, a breach of a condition is a breach of a term of fundamental importance to the contract

C In a contract, a breach of warranty entitles the injured party to terminate the contract

D In a contract, a breach of warranty can terminate a contract, but only on the basis of equity

Test your understanding 19

Which one of the following is incorrect?

A Exclusion clauses attempting to exclude liability for death or injury are void

B Statutory implied conditions giving consumers protection in sale of goods contracts can be excluded so long as the exclusion clause is reasonable

C Where the wording of an exclusion clause is ambiguous it will be interpreted against the party seeking to rely on it

D An unfair term does not bind a consumer but the contract may continue

Test your understanding 20

A contract will be discharged as a result of a frustrating event occurring.

Which one of the following will not bring about discharge of a contract?

A Performance becomes radically different from that anticipated

B Performance becomes more expensive and difficult than anticipated

C Physical impossibility of performance due to accidental destruction of subject matter

D If the contract is dependent on a future event which does not occur

Test your understanding 21

Which one of the following statements is incorrect?

A The remedy of damages for breach of contract is available as of right

B The remedy of specific performance for breach of contract is available as of right

C An order of injunction is given at the discretion of the court

D An order of rescission is given at the discretion of the court

Test your understanding 22

Which of the following statements is incorrect in relation to the determining of damages payable on breach of contract?

A The purpose of providing damages is to compensate the injured party

B Quantifying damages is determining the actual amount of the award to be made to the injured party

C The remoteness of damage issue is determined by considering the amount of damages the injured party reasonably expects on the basis of the contract breach and damages suffered

D An injured party has a duty to mitigate their loss

Test your understanding 23

An employer must provide a written statement of particulars to an employee within what period from the commencement of the employment?

A Within 1 week

B Within 1 month

C Within 2 months

D Within 6 weeks

Test your understanding 24

In order to determine whether or not a party is an employee or an independent contractor a number of tests have been devised.

Which one of the following is not a recognised test?

A Organisation test

B Control test

C Multiple test

D Supply and demand test

Test your understanding 25

Which one of the following statements is incorrect?

A An employer is normally liable for wrongs committed by employees

B An independent contractor has no statutory protection in respect of sick pay

C An independent contractor has no preferential rights over other creditors on the insolvency of the employer

D Employees and independent contractors are prohibited from delegating work to others

Test your understanding 26

Which one of the following is incorrect?

A A limited liability partnership has legal personality

B A minimum of two parties are required to form a limited liability partnership

C Partners in a limited liability partnership cannot be corporate bodies

D Individual members of a limited liability partnership will have no contractual liability to creditors of the partnership

Test your understanding 27

In relation to a private limited company, which one of the following is correct?

A Annual General Meetings must be held

B Articles of Association must be filed with a Registrar when seeking registration of the company

C The company will have perpetual succession

D Directors of the company would never be liable to company creditors

Test your understanding 28

Which one of the following statements is incorrect in relation to a public limited company?

A A company must have a minimum issued share capital of £50,000

B The company cannot issue only redeemable shares

C The company must have a certificate of incorporation and a trading certificate before it can validly commence business

D The company must have at least two members

Test your understanding 29

Which one of the following is not a general duty of directors?

A Duty to exercise independent judgement

B Duty not to accept benefits from third parties

C Duty to keep and notify registrar of charges

D Duty to exercise reasonable care, skill and diligence

Test your understanding 30

Which one of the following is correct in relation to an alteration of articles of association.

A Class rights can be altered

B Shareholder liability can be increased

C Members must pass an ordinary resolution

D The alteration must be *bona fide* and in the best interests of every member

Test your understanding 31

Which one of the following can be achieved by a public company only with court approval, in addition to a resolution of the members being passed?

A Change of company name

B Increase of share capital

C Reduction of share capital

D Change of the situation of the company registered office

Test your understanding 32

Which one of the following is correct?

A A private company can issue only redeemable shares

B A private and a public company can issue only redeemable shares

C A public company can issue redeemable preference shares

D A private company cannot issue redeemable preference shares

Test your understanding 33

Which of the following is not correct in relation to a reduction of capital by a public company?

A The company must have authority to reduce capital in its Articles of Association

B A special resolution must be passed

C A court order approving the reduction must be obtained

D The company may be ordered to add the words 'and reduced' after its name

Test your understanding 34

Which one of the following is incorrect?

A A private company can accept non-cash consideration in the return for shares without the need to have the consideration valued

B A public company can accept consideration in a contract of allotment of shares of less than market value so long as it is at least the same as the nominal value of the shares

C A public company can only accept money as consideration on an allotment of shares

D A private company can reduce share capital without reference to the court

Test your understanding 35

Which of the following is incorrect in relation to share capital?

A A company's shares may no longer be converted into stock

B A limited company must not acquire its own shares under any circumstances

C In the case of a public company, where shares are forfeited for failure to pay any sum, they must be cancelled

D When a public company issues further shares a statement of capital must be sent to the Registrar

Test your understanding 36

In relation to a company purchasing its own shares, which one of the following is correct?

A Capital can be used by both private and public companies

B Capital cannot be used by either private or public companies

C Public companies only can use capital to satisfy some of the debt

D Private companies only can use capital to satisfy some of the debt

Test your understanding 37

In relation to a company providing financial assistance for the acquisition of its own shares which one of the following is correct?

A A private company may provide financial assistance for the purchase of its own shares so long as it follows the correct procedure

B A bank cannot provide financial assistance for an acquisition of shares in the bank itself

C A private company is not subject to restrictions when providing financial assistance

D A public company cannot provide assistance to employees by providing loans which are used to purchase shares in the company

Test your understanding 38

Following the enactment of the Companies Act 2006, which one of the following statements is incorrect?

A A private company must have a secretary but he/she does not need to be qualified

B A private company can have only one member who is also the only director

C A sole member is distinct from the company at law

D A public company must have at least two directors

Test your understanding 39

A minority of members can give written, signed notice to the directors requiring them to hold a General Meeting. Which one of the following is the correct minimum shareholding this minority must have?

A 5%

B 10%

C 15%

D 25%

Test your understanding 40

Which one of the following is incorrect in relation to the use of an ordinary resolution with special notice?

A It must be used for the removal of a director

B It must be used for the removal of the company secretary

C It must be used for the removal of a director aged over 70 years

D It must be used for the removal of a director over the age of 16 years

Test your understanding 41

In relation to directors, which *one* of the following statements is incorrect?

A A director is an agent of the company

B A director is an officer of the company

C A company has a duty to have executive directors

D A shadow director is the main type of de facto director

Test your understanding 42

Directors do not owe a duty to which *one* of the following?

A Debenture holders

B Members as a body

C The Public at large

D Employees

Test your understanding 43

Where a director is party to wrongful trading which *one* of the following is a possible consequence for the individual?

A Being required to contribute to the assets of the company in liquidation

B A possible fine

C Imprisonment

D Being subject to an equitable remedy

Test your understanding 44

Which one of the following is incorrect where a director is in breach of statutory duty?

A The members cannot pass a resolution ratifying what has been done

B If the director in breach is also a member, he cannot vote in support of the ratification

C Articles cannot exempt directors from liability for breach of duty

D A director in breach can be liable to account for any secret profit obtained

Test your understanding 45

Alan, Barbara and Clive are the only members of Beeceedee Ltd with equal shareholdings. They are also the only directors of the company. Relations between the three parties have in the past been good. However, now, Alan and Barbara always vote against Clive at board meetings and are not prepared to listen to Clive's views. Further, on numerous occasions Alan and Barbara have refused to attend meetings. The quorum for board meetings and members meetings is two. Clive is unhappy generally with the way in which the company is now being run and wishes to petition for a winding up order.

Which one of the following is the appropriate action to obtain a winding up order?

A A derivative action

B An action on the basis of unfairly prejudicial conduct

C An action on the just and equitable ground

D A representative action

Test your understanding 46

Secs 994–996 of the Companies Act 2006 identifies a number of remedies which can be introduced by a court where an action for unfairly prejudicial conduct is brought.

Which one of the following is not a remedy identified in this section?

A An order regulating company affairs in the future

B Authorising criminal proceedings to be brought in the name of and on behalf of the company

C Authorising civil proceedings to be brought in the name of and on behalf of the company

D Requiring the company to buy the petitioner's shares at fair value

Test your understanding 47

Which one of the following is incorrect in relation to the company secretary?

A They can never contract on behalf of the company

B Qualification requirements attach to a company secretary of a public company but not a private company

C Details of the company secretary are entered in the same register as that used to register director details

D Some statutory provisions can render the company secretary criminally liable

Test your understanding 48

Corporate governance measures are primarily for the benefit of 'stakeholders'. Who are stakeholders in this context?

A All those directly or indirectly affected by the company's activities

B All those directly affected by the company's activities

C The shareholders

D All those indirectly affected by the company's activities

Test your understanding 49

To which type of company is the UK Corporate Governance Code primarily directed?

A All companies

B All public companies

C All private and public companies

D All listed public companies

Test your understanding 50

Which of the following is not a recommendation of the UK Corporate Governance Code?

A A board audit committee should be established

B The roles of Chairman and Managing Director should be combined

C At least one-half of the board should be made up of independent non-executive directors

D All directors should attend the AGM

Test your understanding 51

The two-tier board structure comprises a Supervisory Board and what other organ?

A A board representing the employees

B A board majority of non-executive directors

C An all-executive board

D A management board

Test your understanding 52

What is the most commonly used procedure adopted by the European Union for the creation of law?

A Consultation

B Codecision

C Assent

D Accord

Test your understanding 53

The European Union is at present made up of how many states?

A 18

B 22

C 27

D 28

Test your understanding 54

In which one of the following countries are individuals appointed judges at the beginning of their legal careers?

A Germany

B France

C Denmark

D Italy

Test your understanding 55

In the United States of America, all states with one exception have a common law system with court decisions establishing precedent. Which state is the exception?

A Ohio

B Missouri

C Louisiana

D Texas

Test your understanding 56

Hong Kong and Macau on transferring sovereignty to China did not change their legal systems. They continue to adopt the legal systems of England and which other country?

A Australia

B France

C Spain

D Portugal

Test your understanding 57

Which of the following is not an accurate description of what a company's code of ethics is likely to achieve?

A It tells employees what is expected of them in terms of behaviour

B It explains the approach and outlook of the organisation

C It encourages employees to take a consistent approach to ethical issues

D It eliminates the need for legislation

Test your understanding 58

In which country does legislation legally require professional accountants to speak up if they find themselves in a situation where they might not be able to comply with relevant legal, regulatory or standards frameworks?

A Italy

B The United States

C Germany

D Japan

Test your understanding 59

Which of the following actions by a company would not encourage employees to speak up if they encounter potentially serious cases of unprofessional or unethical behaviour?

A Introduce an employee helpline for ethics-related queries

B State in the company's code of ethics that employees have a duty to speak up

C Stress the importance of employees working together to meet ambitious sales targets

D Develop a culture where it is safe and acceptable for employees to raise concerns

Test your understanding 60

Which of the following is not an ethical value?

A Tolerance

B Truthfulness

C Training

D Transparency

Test your understanding 61

Which of the following does not specifically relate to business ethics?

A The financial viability of a business

B The behaviour of the business and its employees

C How a business conducts its relationships with its stakeholders

D How a company does business, rather than what it does

Test your understanding 62

Which of the following is not one of the five personal qualities that CIMA expects of its members?

A Reliability

B Respect

C Responsibility

D Reflection

Test your understanding 63

While reviewing the work of one of your colleagues, you discover that he has made some extremely serious mistakes. When you discuss this with him, it becomes clear that he does not have the understanding of financial matters that he requires to be a competent accountant. This violates CIMA's fundamental principle of:

A Integrity

B Objectivity

C Professional competence and due care

D Confidentiality

Test your understanding 64

You are working abroad and find yourself in a situation where a particular element of the country's legislation is in conflict with the IFAC Code of Ethics. In this situation, you should:

A Obey the law because it is mandatory to comply with legislation

B Obey the ethics code because it is internationally binding

C Obey the law because you have a public duty to uphold the law, but not to uphold ethics

D Obey the ethics code because it is a requirement of your profession

Test your understanding 65

Which of the following relates specifically to accountability?

A Taking responsibility for one's work and conclusions

B Maintaining clear records that provide evidence to back up conclusions

C Being answerable to queries in relation to one's work

D All of the above

Test your understanding 66

Which of the following relates to an ethical issue?

A Moving into a larger office as part of a plan to expand your business

B Introducing a new monthly reporting process to maximise efficiency

C Introducing a new IT system to ensure confidentiality of customer information

D Recruiting a new finance director

Test your understanding 67

Which of the following would be of the least help in developing an effective corporate ethics programme?

A Having a chairman and chief executive who champion ethics at every opportunity

B Providing copies of the company's code of ethics to trusted personnel only to avoid the document falling into the hands of competitors

C Incorporating ethical issues into new employee induction programmes

D Talking to the company's key stakeholders about the social and environmental issues they believe to be important

Test your understanding 68

In tackling ethical dilemmas, which of the following would not help you to find a solution?

A Establishing the facts and the ethical issues involved

B Referring to the CIMA and/or your company's code of ethics

C Following an established internal procedure

D Choosing to postpone tackling the issue due to pressure of deadlines

Test your understanding 69

One of your colleagues has just been passed over for promotion for the third time. She shows you evidence that only a small number of women have ever been promoted to positions of seniority within your company. This, she says, is an issue of:

A Harassment

B Discrimination

C Conflict of interest

D Bribery and corruption

Test your understanding 70

Which of the following is not an ethical issue for a bank?

A Providing accurate information about terms and conditions when advertising interest rates for customer loans

B Launching a premium account service for customers who are willing to pay a monthly charge for improved service

C Money laundering

D Disabled access to bank branches

Test your understanding 71

Which of the following ethical issues is most likely to be affected by new developments in information technology?

A Data protection

B Gifts and hospitality

C Harassment

D Health and safety

Test your understanding 72

Parliament has delegated wide powers to government ministers within their own departments. These ministers and their civil service departments are given the task of making rules and regulations within the guidelines of the enabling Acts. What is the usual form of these rules and regulations?

A Bye-laws

B Legislative Instruments

C Orders in Council

D Statutory Instruments

Test your understanding 73

There are several sources of European Union Law. Which of the following are directly applicable and automatically become law in member states?

A Treaties only

B Treaties and Regulations only

C Treaties, Regulations and Directives only

D Treaties, Regulations, Directives and Decisions

Test your understanding 74

In contract law, a misrepresentation is which *one* of the following?

A An untrue statement of fact or opinion which induces another to contract

B An untrue statement of fact, opinion or intention which induces another to contract

C An untrue statement of fact which induces another to contract

D An untrue statement of fact or intention which induces another to contract

Test your understanding 75

When deciding on whether a solution to an ethical dilemma is appropriate, which of the following questions is irrelevant?

A Do I feel comfortable about others knowing about my decision?

B Have I considered all parties who may be affected by my decision?

C Would a reasonable third party consider my decision fair?

D Is this the most appropriate decision considering my career aspirations?

Test your understanding answers

Test your understanding 1

B

Test your understanding 2

B

Test your understanding 3

C

Test your understanding 4

C

Test your understanding 5

A

Test your understanding 6

C

Test your understanding 7

B

Test your understanding 8

C

Test your understanding 9

B

Test your understanding 10

D

Test your understanding 11

B

Test your understanding 12

A

Test your understanding 13

C

Test your understanding 14

C

Test your understanding 15

B

Test your understanding 16

C

Test your understanding 17

D

Test your understanding 18

B

Test your understanding 19

B

Test your understanding 20

B

Test your understanding 21

B

Test your understanding 22

C

Test your understanding 23

C

Test your understanding 24

D

Test your understanding 25

D

Test your understanding 26

C

Test your understanding 27

C

Test your understanding 28

D

Test your understanding 29

C

Test your understanding 30

A

Test your understanding 31

C

Test your understanding 32

C

Test your understanding 33

A

Test your understanding 34

C

Test your understanding 35

B

Test your understanding 36

D

Test your understanding 37

C

Test your understanding 38

A

Test your understanding 39

B

Test your understanding 40

B

Test your understanding 41

C

Test your understanding 42

C

Test your understanding 43

A

Test your understanding 44

A

Test your understanding 45

C

Test your understanding 46

B

Test your understanding 47

A

Test your understanding 48

A

Test your understanding 49

D

Test your understanding 50

B

Test your understanding 51

D

Test your understanding 52

B

Test your understanding 53

D

Test your understanding 54

B

Test your understanding 55

C

Test your understanding 56

D

Test your understanding 57

D

Test your understanding 58

B

Test your understanding 59

C

Test your understanding 60

C

Test your understanding 61

A

Test your understanding 62

D

Test your understanding 63

C

Test your understanding 64

A

Test your understanding 65

D

Test your understanding 66

C

Test your understanding 67

B

Test your understanding 68

D

Test your understanding 69

B

Test your understanding 70

B

Test your understanding 71

A

Test your understanding 72

D

Test your understanding 73

B

Test your understanding 74

C

Test your understanding 75

D

chapter

12

Mock Assessment 2

Chapter learning objectives

This section is intended for use when you have completed your study and initial revision. It contains a complete mock assessment.

This should be attempted as an exam conditions, timed mock. This will give you valuable experience that will assist you with your time management and examination strategy.

Certificate Level

Fundamentals of Ethics, Corporate Governance and Business Law

Instructions: attempt all 75 questions.

Time allowed 2 hours.

Do not turn the page until you are ready to attempt the examination under timed conditions.

Test your understanding questions

Test your understanding 1

Which division of the High Court hears disputes in contract and tort?

A The Chancery Division

B The Commercial Division

C The Queen's Bench Division

D The Family Division

Test your understanding 2

Pattie sued Dave Builders Ltd for damages for faulty workmanship relating to an extension to Pattie's house. The amount claimed was £10,000 and the judge in the County Court found for the defendant. Pattie wishes to appeal. What is the position?

A She cannot appeal – the judge's decision in such a case is final

B She may appeal to the Crown Court for a re-trial

C She may appeal to the Court of Appeal

D She may appeal to the High Court

Test your understanding 3

In negligence actions on exceptional occasions, the courts reverse the burden of proof and require the defendant to prove no breach of duty of care occurred. What are the requirements for this reversing of the burden of proof to occur?

(i) The harm would not happen if proper care were taken.

(ii) The defendant alleges contributory negligence on the part of the plaintiff.

(iii) The defendant was in control of the situation.

(iv) The only apparent explanation for what has occurred is breach of duty by the defendant.

A (i), (ii) and (iv)

B (i), (iii) and (iv)

C (i), (ii) and (iii)

D (ii), (iii) and (iv)

Test your understanding 4

Which one of the following is a frequently used method of creating law used by the European Union?

A Codecision

B Assent

C Accord

D Confirmation

Test your understanding 5

Today, law in France is mainly created by the legislative body and so is codified. Which one of the following areas is not codified in France?

A Contract

B Company Law

C Family Law

D Tort

Test your understanding 6

Which one of the following is an influence that has contributed to the development of the legal system of Denmark?

A Roman Law

B The Code *Civile* from France

C German jurisprudence

D English constitutional theory

Test your understanding 7

In China, more than 800,000 mediation committees function in rural and urban areas. Which one of the following correctly identifies by percentage the extent to which these committees deal with civil disputes?

A Over 60%

B Over 70%

C Over 80%

D Over 90%

Test your understanding 8

Which one of the following correctly identifies the Institution(s) of the European Union that pass new laws?

A The European Parliament and the Council of the European Union

B The Council of the European Union and the European Commission

C The European Parliament and the European Commission

D The European Commission alone

Test your understanding 9

Equity as a source of English Law was developed by which court?

A The Exchequer Court

B The House of Lords

C The Court of Chancery

D The Kings Bench Court

Test your understanding 10

Which one of the following is not a form of delegated legislation?

A Bye-laws

B Requisitional orders

C Statutory Instruments

D Orders on Council

Test your understanding 11

A promise in isolation cannot be sued upon, however a promise will be respected at law on the basis of promissory estoppel. Which *one* of the following is not a requirement for promissory estoppel to apply?

A The promise must be based on an already existing contract

B The promise is the basis upon which the court action is commenced

C The promissor intends the promise to be acted upon

D The promisee does act in reliance on the promise

Test your understanding 12

A specific performance order will rarely be granted in relation to which one of the following?

A A commercial transaction

B To a minor

C An employment contract

D A building contract

Test your understanding 13

Which one of the following is incorrect?

A A promise to provide consideration in return for consideration already provided by another is not good consideration

B A promise to perform an existing obligation to the promise is not good consideration

C A promise to perform an existing obligation to a third party is not good consideration

D A promise to perform an existing public duty is not good consideration

Test your understanding 14

Ria writes to Sarah offering to buy Sarah's boat for £500. In her letter, she writes 'If I don't hear from you, I shall consider it mine and pick it up on Friday'. Which of the following best describes the legal position as to whether or not a contract exists?

A There is a contract because Ria waived the need for acceptance

B There is a contract because Sarah complied with Ria's terms exactly

C There is a contract because acceptance can be inferred from Sarah's conduct

D There is no contract because there is no positive act to indicate acceptance

Test your understanding 15

Misrepresentation is defined as a false statement of fact or law which induces another party to contract. Misrepresentation can however be found not in that communicated, but in that which is not communicated. Which one of the following does not as a general rule constitute misrepresentation?

A Failure to disclose full material facts in a contract of the utmost good faith

B Failure to communicate changed circumstances

C Failure to communicate fully relevant information, although that which is communicated is accurate

D Failure to disclose facts where it is known by the silent party that the other is deceiving himself

Test your understanding 16

Rescission is an equitable remedy, and so will not be granted if the court believes that to do so would be unfair. Which one of the following is correct in relation to the granting of rescission as a remedy?

A Rescission becomes effective once the court order is made

B Rescission must be exercised reasonably promptly

C Rescission can be awarded under s2(1) Misrepresentation Act 1967

D Rescission can be awarded under s2(2) Misrepresentation Act 1967 in addition to the remedy of damages

Test your understanding 17

Express terms can be incorporated into a contract in a number of ways. Which one of the following is not an acceptable method of such incorporation?

A Actual notice

B Reasonable notice

C Signature

D Policy

Test your understanding 18

Which one of the following is incorrect?

A A condition is a term that the parties intended to be of fundamental importance

B A warranty is a term that the parties did not intend to be of fundamental importance

C If a condition is breached, the contract is automatically terminated

D If a warranty is breached, the innocent party cannot treat the contract as discharged

Test your understanding 19

An exemption clause in a contract will be interpreted contra proferentem. On this basis, which one of the following statements is incorrect?

A An exemption clause, where it is clear, will not be upheld if the contract breach is of a serious nature

B An exemption clause stating that warranties are excluded will not be interpreted as including conditions also

C A clause providing that 'nothing in this agreement' shall make the contracting party liable would be restricted to contract law and so not include a tortuous claim

D A clause which is ambiguous will be interpreted against the party seeking to rely on the clause

Test your understanding 20

A breach of condition is a serious breach of contract that gives the innocent party the right to end the contract. However, this right is subject to certain rights and obligations. Which *one* of the following is an applicable right/obligation?

A The right must be exercised reasonably promptly

B If the innocent party 'affirms' the contract, the right to terminate is then lost

C If the innocent party 'affirms' where a breach of condition has occurred, this reduces the contractual obligations that need to be satisfied by the innocent party

D If the right to terminate the contract is exercised, the innocent party need perform no further contractual obligations

Test your understanding 21

The Unfair Contract Terms Act 1977 provides that an attempt by any person to exclude or restrict their liability for death or personal injury resulting from negligence in any contract is:

A Void unless reasonable

B Effective only in a non-consumer transaction

C Void

D Valid if the other party to the contract knows of the exclusion clause or has been given reasonable notice of it

Test your understanding 22

When deciding upon damages payable on breach of contract, the courts consider the remoteness of the damage. In determining whether or not the loss or damage is too remote, which *one* of the following is not accurate?

A Loss recognised is that which may reasonably have been in the contemplation of both parties at the time of contracting

B Where the type of loss suffered is foreseeable, the loss is recoverable irrespective of its extent

C Damages will be awarded for loss that is considered as fairly and reasonably arising naturally

D Damages will be awarded for loss arising in the usual course of things from the breach

Test your understanding 23

When deciding upon the measure of damages payable in contract, which one of the following is accurate?

A Damages will never be awarded for speculative profits which might have accrued

B Damages will never be awarded in relation to the possible loss of future profits

C Damages will always be awarded for loss of profits suffered when the contract ends

D Damages will always be awarded where some loss has definitely been suffered but it is difficult to assess the extent of the loss

Test your understanding 24

Which one of the following statements relating to contract claims and the relevance of contributory negligence is inaccurate?

A A party buying goods from a dealer cannot be guilty of contributory negligence for not checking the goods

B A claimant in a contract action cannot be liable for contributory negligence

C A party cannot be liable for contributory negligence in a fraud action

D A party will not be liable for contributory negligence where the action is based on a failure to satisfy an obligation that is strict

Test your understanding 25

For a deed to be valid, certain requirements must be satisfied. Which one of the following is not a requirement for a valid deed to be prepared?

A It must be signed

B It must be witnessed

C It must be sealed

D It must be delivered

Test your understanding 26

Employers owe certain implied duties to employees. In which *one* of the following instances, does a duty to provide work not exist?

A Where the employee's remuneration depends upon the work done

B Where the employee needs work to maintain reputation

C Where the employee needs work to maintain familiarity with technical change

D Where the employee is participating in an ongoing staff training programme

Test your understanding 27

Some grounds for unfair dismissal are deemed to be automatically unfair whilst other reasons may be presumed unfair, but the employer has the opportunity of successfully opposing the claim. In which one of the following instances will it not always be deemed a basis for recognised automatic unfair dismissal?

A Where an employee brings a court action against the employer in good faith to enforce a statutory right, where no right in fact exists

B Where an employee is selected for redundancy contrary to an agreed arrangement or custom, without good reason

C Where an employee fails to comply with orders on the basis of valid health and safety grounds

D Where an employee is pregnant

Test your understanding 28

Where a dismissed employee claims wrongful dismissal, which one of the following is incorrect?

A The claim can be based on dismissal without proper notice

B The claim will be brought to court, not tribunal

C The claim will essentially be for breach of contract

D The claimant has a duty to mitigate loss by seeking other employment

Test your understanding 29

Which *one* of the following is incorrect in relation to a Limited Liability Partnership ('LLP')?

A Partners of an LLP are agents of the LLP

B Most LLPs are professional firms

C An LLP must have at least two designated members

D The Limited Liability Partnerships Act 2000 imposes a formal management structure on all LLPs

Test your understanding 30

Which one of the following is incorrect in relation to a private company limited by shares?

A A private company limited by shares is fully liable for its debts and obligations

B In the case of a single member company, the shareholder cannot also act as the sole director

C A private company is a separate legal person distinct from its shareholders

D The board is the agent of the company

Test your understanding 31

Which one of the following is correct in relation to a public company limited by shares?

A The company must have at least one director

B All public limited companies are listed on a stock exchange

C The company must have a qualified company secretary

D The company can commence trading as soon as it receives a certificate of incorporation

Test your understanding 32

Which one of the following statement is correct in relation to company contracts?

A A third party who has acted in good faith can enforce ultra vires contracts against the company

B A company may enter into any contract irrespective of its constitution

C A company may not amend its ability to contract by placing restrictions in its Articles of Association

D Shareholders cannot prevent a company from entering into an ultra vires contract

Test your understanding 33

Which one of the following statements is correct in relation to the articles of association?

A A company may change its articles by the directors passing a special resolution

B All provisions in the articles of association are contractual

C Articles of association are private documents

D In the event of any conflict between the memorandum and articles of association, the memorandum prevails

Test your understanding 34

Which one of the following is incorrect in relation to petitions for a winding up order?

A In the event of a petition by a shareholder on the 'just and equitable' ground, an order can be made against a solvent or insolvent company

B A company is deemed to be unable to pay its debts if the court is satisfied that that is the case

C The company may petition for a winding up order against itself by passing a special resolution

D Once a company is wound up, its name is deleted from the register at Companies House

Test your understanding 35

Which one of the following statements is correct in relation to the Articles of Association?

A The Memorandum of Association must be filed alongside the Articles of Association prior to incorporation

B A company must have Articles of Association prescribing regulations for the company

C A company may amend its Articles by written resolution

D Any amendments made need only be filed with the statutory books and records

Test your understanding 36

Which of the following are not required when incorporating a company?

A Statement of capital and initial shareholdings

B Statement of proposed officers

C Statement of compliance

D Completed annual return

Test your understanding 37

Who is able to register a company by submitting the required documents in electronic form?

A Persons who are the proposed directors of the company

B Persons who are promoting the company

C Persons who act as company registration agents

D Persons who are the proposed subscribers to the memorandum

Test your understanding 38

Which one of the following is not required to be stated on all websites, business letters and order forms by the Companies Act 2006?

A The nature of the company's business

B The name of the company

C The company's registered number

D The address of the company's registered office

Test your understanding 39

Which of the following must be carried out to take advantage of the provisions in the Companies Act 2006 which facilitate electronic communications with shareholders as a matter of course?

A A board resolution authorising electronic communication

B An amendment to the articles of association authorising electronic communication

C An amendment to the Memorandum of Association authorising electronic communication

D An announcement on the company's website stating that future communications with shareholders will be in electronic form

Test your understanding 40

ABC plc has issued shares on terms that they will be bought back by the company five years after the date of issue. What are the shares called?

A Ordinary shares

B Preference shares

C Redeemable shares

D Deferred shares

Test your understanding 41

Which of the following resolutions may be passed by a private company in place of other resolutions?

A An ordinary resolution with special notice

B A written resolution

C A ordinary resolution passed at an AGM

D A special resolution

Test your understanding 42

An auditor may be removed by ordinary resolution with special notice. What is special notice?

A 28 days notice to the shareholders

B 28 days notice to the directors

C 28 days notice to the company

D 28 days notice to the auditor

Test your understanding 43

Which one of the following statements regarding the Rule in Foss v Harbottle (1843) is incorrect?

A The case sets down a rule of procedure

B Where there has been a wrong to the company, it is for the company to decide on the appropriate action

C Where the act complained of can be ratified by the members, the minority cannot maintain an action

D Minority shareholders are entitled to sue in the company's name if the act complained of was carried out by the directors

Test your understanding 44

The liquidator of FGH Ltd has successfully brought proceedings against Freda, one of the directors, for fraudulent trading under section 213 of the Insolvency Act 1986. Which of the following may the court do?

(i) Order Freda to make a contribution to the company's assets.

(ii) Impose a fine on Freda.

(iii) Disqualify Freda from being a director for up to 15 years.

A (i) and (iii) only

B (ii) and (iii) only

C (i) only

D (i), (ii) and (iii)

Test your understanding 45

Which *one* of the following is a business name?

A Jack Wilson Ltd

B High Street Computers

C Enterprise plc

D Morrisey LLP

Test your understanding 46

A, B and C are about to set up in business as a general partnership. In the absence of agreement to the contrary, how will the law presume that they are to share profits?

A One third each

B According to the proportion in which they have invested capital

C According to the hours that each of them will work in the business

D According to age and expertise

Test your understanding 47

What is meant by the expression 'lifting the veil of incorporation'?

A The company is treated as if it were fully liable for all its debts

B The shareholders are treated as though they were carrying on business in partnership

C The directors are treated as partners and are fully liable for the company's debts

D The company is treated as if it were not a separate person at law

Test your understanding 48

Which one of the following statements is incorrect regarding a company's registered office?

A The registered office is the postal address of the company

B The registered office is the place where the company maintains its statutory registers

C The registered office must be a place where the company carries on business

D The address of the registered office may be changed by ordinary resolution of the shareholders

Test your understanding 49

Which one of the following statements is correct in relation to contracts entered into on behalf of a private company limited by shares before it has been registered?

A The contract is enforceable against the company after registration

B The contract is void against the company

C The contract may be ratified by the directors after registration

D The contract cannot be enforced against anyone if it was entered into in the name of the unregistered company

Test your understanding 50

Which of the following is paid first when a company is in liquidation?

A Debenture holders secured by fixed charge

B Preference shareholders

C Employees who are owed wages of £800

D Debenture holders secured by floating charge

Test your understanding 51

How does the framework-based approach to ethics differ from the rules-based approach?

A The framework-based approach uses legal language

B The framework-based approach requires a detailed rule book

C The framework-based approach sets out rules covering all eventualities

D The framework-based approach sets out general guidelines

Test your understanding 52

Which of the following statements most accurately expresses different approaches to ethical regulations?

A Breaches of ethics have less serious consequences than breaches of the criminal law

B Ethical frameworks let the individual decide about how they should act in particular situations

C Regulations provide a 'thou shallt not' approach to behaviour, whereas framework approaches encourage positive behaviour in support of ethical conduct

D The framework approach is best suited to practical problem-solving in ethics

Test your understanding 53

Which statement is the most accurate of the statements?

A Laws can never be broken, even if they breach ethics

B Ethical breaches always have to be justified, even if they result from the breach of a law

C Legal breaches often result in ethical breaches

D Ethical breaches often result in legal breaches

Test your understanding 54

Why do we need codes of professional ethics?

A To resolve disputes

B To punish bad accountants

C To protect the reputation of the profession

D To improve the quality of service to the public

Test your understanding 55

Which is a correct statement?

A The IFAC Codes of conduct deal with accountants working internationally, while CIMA only applies to business done in Britain

B The CIMA Code is inferior to IFAC's Code

C The IFAC Code reflects the standards laid down by CIMA

D The IFAC Code is reflected in the CIMA Code

Test your understanding 56

An accountant who answers accusations that their work has failed to meet professional standards demonstrates which concept?

A Accountability

B Reliability

C Social responsibility

D Independence

Test your understanding 57

Which is the best explanation of social responsibility?

A Social responsibility means the accountant is responsible to all of society equally

B Social responsibility means that the accountant should do additional things to support social initiatives

C Social responsibility means that the accountant has to be squeaky clean in his or her social as well as professional life

D Social responsibility means that the accountant should always be aware of the broader social consequences of his actions

Test your understanding 58

Which of these is a good indicator of accountability:

A Having regular reviews with your line manager to explain how you are working

B Keeping accurate records in an orderly way

C Always explaining your decisions when you make them

D Being an able accountant

Test your understanding 59

You believe that one of your colleagues has knowingly provided misleading information. If your belief is true, which of CIMA's fundamental principles has your colleague breached?

A Professional competence and due care

B Integrity

C Objectivity

D Confidentiality

Test your understanding 60

Why should an accountant continually develop?

A Because management accounting changes so fast that you need to keep up with it to stay marketable for employment

B Because continual development means that the client always gets a better service every time he or she uses your services

C Because professional competence rests on checking what you do know, adding to knowledge and skills and challenging habitual working practices

D Because management accounting needs to reflect the evolving climate in business and finance

Test your understanding 61

Which of the following is not one of the Seven Principles of Public Life issued by the Committee on Standards in Public Life?

A Courtesy

B Openness

C Integrity

D Leadership

Test your understanding 62

Your employer is having liquidity problems and has reached its overdraft limit. The finance director has asked you to review the company's accounting policies to see if a change could improve the presentation of the financial accounts, which are supplied on a monthly basis to the bank. From an ethical perspective, what is the most appropriate action for you to take?

A Seek advice from your professional body

B Do as requested and seek advice afterwards

C Do as requested

D Go off sick

Test your understanding 63

Which of the following is **not** one of the personal qualities and virtues specifically sought by CIMA?

A Courtesy

B Timeliness

C Respect

D Selflessness

Test your understanding 64

A project that your manager is keen on looks set to have problems showing a profit in the first year. Thereafter, it is projected to make a healthy margin. You are aware of the way in which the system has gaps, which could hide the weak performance in the first year and could be disguised, and your manager asks you what they are and whether you can implement them. Do you:

A Tell him that the company systems do not permit any variance from the accounting method that would show up the weakness?

B Say that you know how to help him, but you can't because you don't think it's right to give false information?

C Prepare the financial reports in the way he requests, but get him to send you an e-mail confirming he asked you for this unrepresentative report?

D Do what he says, because he's the client?

Test your understanding 65

Which of these is correct? The importance of the ethical rule is to be judged by the:

A cost of breach to the individual bound by that rule

B social consequences for breach of the rule

C impact on the profession of the rule

D the context within which it is applied

Test your understanding 66

Which is a correct statement about CIMA's Code of ethics:

A It covers all ethical eventualities

B It covers unusual situations in practice which are unlikely to give rise to ethical problems

C It gives the general principles to guide behaviour, rather than any specific guidance on how to act in particular circumstances

D It can only be understood if read in conjunction with the IFAC Code

Test your understanding 67

What is ethical conduct for a CIMA accountant?

A Doing what you think is right for society

B Thinking that what you are doing is socially right

C Thinking about the social consequences of what you do before you do it

D Doing things that you believe comply with the CIMA Code

Test your understanding 68

Which one of the following statements is incorrect in relation to corporate governance?

A Corporate governance is primarily concerned with the effective control business efficacy and accountability of the management of public listed companies

B Corporate governance does not affect private companies

C Corporate governance is intended to benefit stakeholders

D The term 'stakeholders' is wider than shareholders and employees

Test your understanding 69

Which one of the following statements is incorrect in relation to the interaction of corporate governance with business ethics and company law?

A Corporate governance is primarily concerned with the effective control business efficacy and accountability of the management of public listed companies

B Corporate governance does not affect private companies

C Corporate governance business ethics and company law are made up of entirely separate principles

D The term 'stakeholders' is wider than shareholders and employees

Test your understanding 70

The UK Corporate Governance Code is referred to as 'soft law.' What does this expression mean?

A The Code contains principles which, if broken, may give rise to civil liability only

B The Code contains principles which, if broken, are punishable by relatively small fines

C The Code contains principles which, if broken, only oblige the board to disclose the reasons for the breach

D The Code contains principles which, if broken, have no consequences whatsoever

Test your understanding 71

In the event of any breach of the UK Corporate Governance Code, who will decide whether any further action is taken against the directors?

A The Financial Services Authority

B The Stock Exchange

C The Department of Trade and Industry

D The shareholders

Test your understanding 72

In the United States, the Sarbanes-Oxley Act was passed in 2002 following the major scandal after the collapse of the giant American corporation, Enron. Which of the following is incorrect in relation to the Sarbanes-Oxley Act ('the Act')?

A The Act created the Public Company Accounting Oversight Board ('PCAOB')

B The Act requires all auditors of public companies to be registered with the PCAOB

C The Act requires the separate disclosure of the fees received by auditors for audit and all other fees

D The Act requires directors to be professionally qualified to act as directors of public companies

Test your understanding 73

The two-tier board structure comprises a Management Board and what other organ?

A An Employee Representation Board

B A Government Representation Board

C A Non-Executive Board

D A Supervisory Board

Test your understanding 74

Which of the following is not a recommendation of the UK Corporate Governance Code?

A Only persons who have industrial experience should be recruited as non-executive directors

B The board should be subject to formal annual evaluation of performance

C All directors should receive induction

D The board should use the AGM to communicate with investors and encourage their participation

Test your understanding 75

Which of the following is not part of the regulatory framework for companies?

A The Companies Act 2006

B The Sarbanes-Oxley Act 2002

C The UK Corporate Governance Code 2012

D The Stock Exchange Listing Regulations 1984

Test your understanding answers

Test your understanding 1

C

Test your understanding 2

C

Test your understanding 3

B

Test your understanding 4

A

Test your understanding 5

D

Test your understanding 6

C

Test your understanding 7

D

Test your understanding 8

A

Test your understanding 9

C

Test your understanding 10

B

Test your understanding 11

B

Test your understanding 12

A

Test your understanding 13

C

Test your understanding 14

D

Test your understanding 15

D

Test your understanding 16

B

Test your understanding 17

D

Test your understanding 18

C

Test your understanding 19

A

Test your understanding 20

B

Test your understanding 21

C

Test your understanding 22

B

Test your understanding 23

A

Test your understanding 24

B

Test your understanding 25

C

Test your understanding 26

D

Test your understanding 27

D

Test your understanding 28

B

Test your understanding 29

D

Test your understanding 30

B

Test your understanding 31

C

Test your understanding 32

A

Test your understanding 33

D

Test your understanding 34

A

Test your understanding 35

B

Test your understanding 36

D

Test your understanding 37

C

Test your understanding 38

A

Test your understanding 39

B

Test your understanding 40

C

Test your understanding 41

B

Test your understanding 42

C

Test your understanding 43

D

Test your understanding 44

D

Test your understanding 45

B

Test your understanding 46

A

Test your understanding 47

D

Test your understanding 48

C

Test your understanding 49

B

Test your understanding 50

A

Test your understanding 51

D

Test your understanding 52

D

Test your understanding 53

A

Test your understanding 54

D

Test your understanding 55

D

Test your understanding 56

A

Test your understanding 57

D

Test your understanding 58

C

Test your understanding 59

B

Test your understanding 60

C

Test your understanding 61

A

Test your understanding 62

A

Test your understanding 63

D

Test your understanding 64

B

Test your understanding 65

D

Test your understanding 66

A

Test your understanding 67

D

Test your understanding 68

B

Test your understanding 69

C

Test your understanding 70

C

Test your understanding 71

D

Test your understanding 72

D

Test your understanding 73

D

Test your understanding 74

A

Test your understanding 75

C

Index

Index

Index

Index

Index

W

Index